MARA VORHEES

ST PETERSBURG
CITY GUIDE

INTRODUCING ST PETERSBURG

The candy stripes of Chesme Church (p146)

It seemed like a lark. When Peter the Great built this city on a swamp, his subjects humoured the Emperor. When he declared it the new capital, they were less amused.

But history has shown that the forward-thinking, Westward-looking tsar was inspired. Gradually, St Petersburg evolved from a swampy backwater into a modern European city, Russia's 'window to the West'. Unlike Moscow's red bricks and onion domes, St Petersburg's network of canals and baroque and neoclassical architecture give the city a European flavour, no doubt because it was built by Italian architects. Even the residents of St Petersburg fancy themselves 'European' and somehow slightly more sophisticated than their more easterly compatriots.

St Petersburg has always been a city of ideas. Petersburgers incited the Russian Revolution, ushering in 70 years of communist rule. And it was St Petersburg that encouraged democracy when the tide began to change.

Nowadays, this city's citizens are breaking down the barriers of generations past and exploring new ideas, investigating the possibilities of consumerism, creativity and career. It's not only Rastrelli's architecture and Tchaikovsky's operas that entice visitors, but also beatnik bands, edgy art galleries, underground clubs and delectable dining. St Pete's bohemian side gives a glimpse into the 21st century; and (to borrow a communist slogan) the future is bright!

St Petersburg is legendary for its White Nights: those long summer days when the sun barely dips below the horizon. Revels start in May, when the city finally succumbs to spring and the parks are filled with flowering trees. But even when the skies are grey and the ground is covered in snow, the rich culture of St Petersburg dazzles and delights.

ST PETERSBURG LIFE

Despite the city's history of radicalism, residents of St Petersburg eschew innovation when it comes to changing the face of their beloved Piter.

Controversy surrounds the city's spurt of development. Residents are galvanised by the construction of a modern Mariinsky Theatre. Plans to build a super-tall skyscraper have provoked massive protests. Even the refurbishment of a long-deserted island on the edge of the centre is raising eyebrows. 'That old Petersburg, with its empty squares...full of picturesque ruins, it's being torn down,' complained one activist. 'Everything will spin and shine according to European standards.'

This lament captures the concern of many residents – not only that their cherished city will lose its aesthetic appeal, but also that hidden places will be uncovered, that everything old will be new again.

Nobody can deny that St Petersburg looks spectacular. Hundreds of theatres, palaces and historic buildings have been overhauled. Luxury hotels, shopping malls and entertainment complexes are bringing the city into the 21st century. Residents undoubtedly appreciate this investment into their hometown. But there is a fear that amid all the upgrades, something special – something uniquely St Petersburg – will be lost.

The city's counterculture has deep roots, as deep as the basement galleries hanging avant-garde paintings, as deep as the bomb shelters housing hip music clubs. The same anti-establishment strain that fuelled revolutions and inspired artistic movements today is expressed as conservatism: a reticence to accept the flashy consumerism and nonstop newness that pervades Russian culture. Or maybe, that *is* radicalism.

Stepping out to enjoy St Petersburg's ballet and opera scene

HIGHLIGHTS

NEVSKY PROSPEKT

'There is nothing more beautiful than Nevsky Prospekt,' wrote Nikolai Gogol, 'at least not in St Petersburg.' The city's most prominent address is also its main retail centre and thoroughfare, home to the swankiest shops and hottest nightlife.

❶ Gostiny Dvor
Shop till you drop at this 18th-century neoclassical trading arcade (p153)

❷ Strolling the street
Pedestrian zone on Nevsky pr

❸ Eliseevsky
Get your gourmet groceries at this Style Moderne masterpiece (p152)

❹ Singer Building
Sip coffee and browse through the books in this whimsical landmark (p74)

❺ Anichkov Most
Rearing horses occupy each corner of the striking Anichkov bridge (p76)

SENSUAL ST PETERSBURG

The Russian penchant for the sensual side of life is notorious. Literature is filled with descriptions of lavish feasts and alcoholic binges. Every opera includes a steamy love affair, every ballet a romantic interlude. And no storyline is complete without a battle or brawl, usually fuelled by love or alcohol or both.

❶ Russian cuisine
Sample the steaming soups and delectable delicacies that exemplify Russian cuisine (p160)

❷ Banya
Cleanse body and soul by sweating it out at a bathhouse (p197)

❸ Mariinsky Theatre
Be moved by the music, inspired by the grace (p188)

❹ Yusupov Palace
Where the Mad Monk Grigory Rasputin met his sordid end (p102)

❺ Museum of Erotica
Get up close and personal with Rasputin's massive member (p87)

❻ Nightlife
Let loose during a night on the town (p178)

1

SPLASHY ST PETERSBURG

St Petersburg is defined by its geography, which is – in a word – wet. The city makes a splash with its wet weather and network of waterways.

2

3

1 Raising of the bridges on the Neva River
Watch the ships pass in the night (p236)

2 Peterhof fountains
Count more than 140 fountains sprinkled across the grounds (p217)

3 Church of the Saviour on Spilled Blood
Snap a photo of the multicoloured domes (p72)

4 Canal cruises
Cruise the canals, ride the rivers and behold the bridges (p246)

5 Admiralty
Look for the landmark golden spire of the original naval headquarters (p67)

5

A TSAR'S LIFE

The imperial capital for more than 200 years, St Petersburg is packed with palaces glittering with gilt moulding, crystal chandeliers, marble columns and parquet floors. Peek inside a tsar's life (and get an understanding of why the Russian Revolution occurred).

1

❶ Gatchina
Explore the overgrown grounds of this tsarist country estate (p223)

❷ Catherine Palace
All that glitters is...at the Great Hall (p220)

❸ Monplaisir
Visit Peter's favourite retreat by the sea (p218)

❹ Winter Palace of Peter I
Explore the restored remains of Peter's original palace on the Neva (p67)

2

3

4

ART SMART

St Petersburg was built by artists and visionaries so it should come as no surprise that the city overflows with artistry, even today. Creative types will be thrilled by the city's world-class museums and cutting-edge contemporary art scene.

1 Street artists
Survey the scenes at the Souvenir Market (p153) depicting spectacular St Petersburg

2 Museum of Decorative & Applied Arts
Admire an amazing collection of artistry housed in stunning surroundings (p86)

3 Russian Museum
Peruse the Russian masters from Rublev to Roerich (p76)

1 Nuptial photographs
Toast newlyweds in front of the Bronze Horseman (p101)

2 Alexander Nevsky Monastery
Say a prayer at the city's oldest monastery (p90)

3 Walrus Club
Engage in St Petersburg's wackiest winter tradition: a swim in the icy Neva (p116)

1

CEREMONIAL ST PETERSBURG

St Petersburg was the centre of the rituals and rigmarole – the inseparable ceremonies of the monarchy and the Orthodox Church – of tsarist Russia. But the lives of everyday Ivans and Olgas are marked by smaller-scale ceremonies that are no less significant.

2

3

CONTENTS

Continued from previous page

THE AUTHOR

Mara Vorhees

Mara's first visit to St Petersburg (then Leningrad) was in 1988, when she ditched her tour group for friendly black marketeers and thereafter dedicated herself to ending the Cold War.

She has returned to Russia many times, spending the first half of the 1990s learning Russian and the second half working on a foreign aid project in the Urals. She reappeared in St Petersburg to celebrate the city's tercentenary, where her favourite feature was the 'Ice Khaus', a frozen-solid ice-sculpture exhibit and vodka bar that was built on the Neva.

Mara has written extensively about Russia, her stories appearing in the *Boston Globe, LA Times* and *Executive Travel.* She is also the author of Lonely Planet's *Moscow City Guide* and co-author of *Russia & Belarus* and *Trans-Siberian Railway.* When she's not roaming around Russia, Mara lives in Somerville, Massachusetts with her husband and her cat.

MARA'S TOP ST PETERSBURG DAY

My top day in St Petersburg starts with a steaming cappuccino and a croissant from Baltic Bread (p169). Around the corner is Maltevsky Market (p154), where I stock my kitchen with pink salmon, fresh produce and aromatic spices. After that I amble over to Tauride Gardens (p85) to watch the children playing and lovers embracing amidst the spring blooms. Shopping and strolling has worked up my appetite, so I stop for a bowl of soup at the cosy subterranean Sunduk (p168).

I spend the afternoon at Pushkinskaya 10 (p91), a complex of galleries and studios, including the often wacky but always interesting Museum of Non-Conformist Art. Then I make my way through the crowds on Nevsky pr, stopping to browse at the charming art market in front of St Catherine Church and at the behemoth bookstore Dom Knigi (p151).

For the evening, I head to The Other Side (p184) to feast on eclectic eats and to hear live music from some tropical place. As the evening wears on, I duck around the corner to St Petersburg's hidden inner-city summer beach bar, Dunes (p180), where I dance away the rest of the night under the twilight sky.

LONELY PLANET AUTHORS

Why is our travel information the best in the world? It's simple: our authors are independent, dedicated travellers. They don't research using just the internet or phone, and they don't take freebies in exchange for positive coverage. They travel widely, to all the popular spots and off the beaten track. They personally visit thousands of hotels, restaurants, cafés, bars, galleries, palaces, museums and more – and they take pride in getting all the details right, and telling it how it is. Think you can do it? Find out how at **lonelyplanet.com**.

GETTING STARTED

So you are planning a trip to St Petersburg? You are in for a treat. Russia's 'second capital' is the number-one attraction for many visitors.

St Petersburg is a far easier place to visit than it was a decade ago. Thanks to the proliferation of privately owned 'mini-hotels' and Western-operated luxury hotels, there is no shortage of excellent places to stay at all price levels. You'll probably want to make reservations – if only because many places are hard to find – but you will have no difficulty booking a place to your liking.

Upon arrival, you may not think that things are geared to tourists: signs are not in English and transport from the airport is tricky. But let it be known that this is like Disneyworld compared to the 'olden days'. Appreciate the advances that have been made and accept the rest as part of the adventure.

One word of warning: the single most annoying thing you will have to do is take care of your visa. Apply early and apply often (see p249).

WHEN TO GO

Everybody wants to visit St Petersburg during White Nights (late June), when the sun never sets and the city celebrates all night long. It is indeed spectacular (see the boxed text, below). The downside, of course, is that because everyone wants to visit during White Nights, the crowds are bigger and prices are higher.

One way to avoid the pitfalls of the peak season is to come in May, when the days are already long and languorous. Temperatures may not be as warm, but the sky stays light late into the evening, and the summer crowds have not yet arrived. The city gets spruced up for the May holidays (p244) and for City Day (p18), both celebratory times in St Petersburg. However, many services, offices and museums have limited hours during the first half of May, due to the run of public holidays.

Early autumn is a standout season, when the city's parks are filled with colourful leaves and the cultural calendar recommences after the summer holidays. Winter is surprisingly festive, as St Petersburg has a long tradition of brightening up the dark nights with cultural events, winter festivals and other celebrations. The deepest, darkest part of winter is undeniably cold but, if you are prepared, it can be an adventure. Furs and vodka keep people warm, and snow-covered landscapes are picturesque. Sledders and skiers are in seventh heaven.

No matter when you come, it's bound to rain a bit (unless it snows), so pack an umbrella. St Petersburg gets as much as 65cm of precipitation a year.

FESTIVALS

June is the most celebratory month in St Petersburg. All of the institutions want to get in on the influx of tourists as the weather warms up, so the city's cultural calendar is packed. The last 10 days, especially, are marked by general merrymaking and staying out late (or early, depending on how you look at it). White Nights (see the boxed text, below) spills over into July. As temperatures rise, more

WHITE NIGHTS

The sun has barely set over the Gulf of Finland when the eastern sky begins to grow light again. Indeed, St Petersburg's northern latitude means that around the summer solstice – when the days are longest – the night sky takes on a silvery hue, but the darkness never comes.

If the Russians ever needed an excuse to stay out all night and celebrate, this is it. At the end of June and the beginning of July, St Petersburg is open around the clock.

Graduates drink to their successes on the banks of the Neva; lovers stroll along the quiet canals; crowds congregate to watch the raising and lowering of the drawbridges. The cultural calendar during this period is packed, as the Stars of White Nights Festival compiles a program of opera, ballet and symphony that represents the best of Russian music and dance. At all hours of the night, the city streets are filled with revellers singing, dancing and drinking in the twilight.

top picks

FESTIVALS

- Stars of White Nights Festival (p18)
- International Festival of Contemporary Art (p18)
- Early Music Festival (p19)
- Victory Day (p18)
- Sergei Kuryokhin International Festival (p18)
- Easter (Paskha) (right)
- Arts Square Winter Festival (p19)

and more visitors descend on the city and the cultural calendar is extended into the summer. During August, many Russians retreat to their *dachas* (country cottages) to escape summer in the city, and the cultural calendar is quiet. Though residents make themselves scarce, tourists abound.

January

ORTHODOX CHRISTMAS

Russia celebrates Orthodox Christmas (Rozhdestvo) on 6 January. Similar to the Epiphany in the Christian calendar, it commemorates the baptism of Jesus. Exclusively a religious holiday, it is not widely celebrated, although services are held at churches and cathedrals around the city. Many offices and services are closed for the first week of January.

February

MARIINSKY BALLET FESTIVAL

www.mariinsky.ru

The city's principal dance theatre hosts a week-long international festival, usually in mid- to late February, where the talents of the cream of Russian ballet dancers and many international stars are showcased.

DEFENDER OF THE MOTHERLAND DAY

Celebrated on 23 February, this unofficial holiday traditionally honours veterans and soldiers. It has become a sort of counterpart to International Women's Day and is now better known as 'Men's Day', although the extent of the celebration is limited.

MASLENITSA

Akin to Mardi Gras, this fête celebrates the end of winter and kicks off Orthodox Lent. 'Maslenitsa' comes from the Russian word for butter, which is a key ingredient in the festive treat, bliny. Besides bingeing on Russian pancakes, the week-long festival also features horse-drawn sledges, story-telling clowns and beer-drinking bears. It culminates in the burning of a scarecrow to welcome spring. Exact dates depend on the dates of Orthodox Easter, but it is usually in February or early March.

Look for a special program at the Mariinsky Theatre (p188), bonfires and other festivities at Yelagin Island (p120) and bliny on the menus at restaurants around town.

March

MONOCLE INTERNATIONAL MONO-PERFORMANCE FESTIVAL

www.baltichouse.spb.ru

This biannual festival usually takes place in March, hosted by the theatre Baltic House (see p191) during odd-numbered years. With both international and local participants, the event focuses on 'one-man shows', especially from northern and Eastern Europe.

INTERNATIONAL WOMEN'S DAY

Russia's favourite holiday – 8 March – was founded to honour the women's movement. These days, men buy champagne, flowers and chocolates for their better halves – and for all the women in their lives.

April

EASTER

The main holiday of the Orthodox Church's year is Easter (Paskha). The date varies, but it is often a different date from its Western counterpart, usually in April or early May. Forthcoming dates are 19 April 2009, 4 April 2010, 24 April 2011, 15 April 2012 and 5 May 2013.

Forty days of fasting, known as Veliky Post, lead up to the religious holiday. Easter Day kicks off with celebratory midnight services, after which people eat special dome-shaped cakes known as *kulichy* and curd-cakes called *paskha*, and may exchange painted wooden Easter eggs. Many banks, offices and museums are closed on Easter Monday.

A TOAST TO THE LADIES

Ask any Russian woman to name her favourite holiday, and she is sure to say International Women's Day, celebrated on 8 March. Some cynics say it is the one day of the year when Russian men are nice to their mates.

International Women's Day has been recognised in various countries since the late 19th century, but in Russia the festive day has revolutionary roots. On 8 March 1917 textile workers in St Petersburg protested against the food shortages, which were directly related to Russia's involvement in WWI. The women's strike 'for bread and peace' merged with riots that were spreading throughout the city. The uprising – which would become known as the February Revolution – forced the abdication of Tsar Nicholas II. Later, the celebrated Soviet feminist and communist Alexandra Kollontai convinced Lenin to make 8 March an official holiday.

These days most Russians have forgotten about the political implications of the day. But nobody misses the opportunity to drink champagne and toast the ladies.

SERGEI KURYOKHIN INTERNATIONAL FESTIVAL

SKIF; www.kuryokhin.ru

A three-day avant-garde festival in late April brings together an impressive array of international figures for alternative modern music and performance. The festival pays tribute to the eclectic Russian musician Sergei Kuryokhin, a key figure from the Leningrad rock and jazz underground who died in 1996.

May

VICTORY DAY

Celebrating the end of WWII, 9 May is a day of national and international importance. It holds a special spot on the calendar in St Petersburg, where residents remember the breaking of the Nazi blockade. Crowds assemble at Piskaryovskoe Cemetery (p121) to commemorate the victims. A victory parade along Nevsky pr culminates in fireworks over the Neva in the evening.

CITY DAY

Mass celebrations and merrymaking are held throughout the city centre on 27 May, the city's official birthday, known as *den goroda* (city day). Brass bands, folk-dancing and mass drunkenness are the salient features of this perennial favourite, which marks the day when Peter the Great made a cross on Zayachy Island and announced 'Here will be a city'.

June

MESSAGE TO MAN

www.message-to-man.spb.ru

A well-respected festival of short, animated and documentary films, Poslaniye k Cheloveku is held annually in mid-June in the neighbouring Dom Kino and Rodina cinemas.

FESTIVAL OF FESTIVALS

www.filmfest.ru

St Petersburg's annual international film festival is held during the White Nights in late June. Co-sponsored by Lenfilm and hosted at cinemas around the city, the festival is a non-competitive showcase of the best Russian and world cinema.

STARS OF WHITE NIGHTS FESTIVAL

www.mariinsky.ru

From late May until mid-July, this annual festival is a venue for world premieres, international stars and special tributes to the city's opera and ballet doyens. Performances are held around the city, especially at the Mariinsky Theatre (p188), the Hermitage Theatre (p188) and the Rimsky-Korsakov Conservatory (p189). Four weeks of festivities culminate in a fabulous ball at Tsarskoe Selo (p219), which draws the event to a close.

INTERNATIONAL FESTIVAL OF CONTEMPORARY ART

www.p10.nonmuseum.ru

While this event takes place at venues around the city, the big bash is at Pushkinskaya 10 (p91), as 30 June is the 'birthday' of this artistic institution. Exhibitions, performances, art auctions and general celebrations fill the once-abandoned apartment block.

July

KLEZFEST

☎ 713 3889; www.klezfest.ru

This music festival celebrates Klezmer music, the Jewish folk music from 18th- and

19th-century Eastern Europe. Hundreds of musicians from Russia, Europe and the USA come to perform in venues around St Petersburg. The city also hosts seminars and other cultural events for musicians and music-lovers.

September & October

EARLY MUSIC FESTIVAL

www.earlymusic.ru

This ground-breaking musical festival aims to revive forgotten masterpieces from the Middle Ages, the Renaissance and the baroque era. The festival always features the production of a baroque opera, as well as performances by the Catherine the Great Orchestra. Musicians come from around the world to perform at various venues from mid-September until early October. See p190 for an interview with the co-director of Early Music Russia.

DEFILE ON THE NEVA

Defile na Neve; www.defilenaneve.ru

One of the most important fashion events in St Petersburg is held in mid-October at the boutique Defile (p151). There is a week of fashion shows, parties and symposia which allows up-and-coming and established designers to showcase their latest lines. A second fashion show takes place in April.

ST PETERSBURG OPEN

www.spbopen.ru

Since 1995, St Petersburg has hosted this men's tennis tournament at the end of October. The event has been attracting players from around the world to compete at SCC Peterburgsky Stadium (p200). This is where Marat Safin first attracted attention when he took the trophy in consecutive years.

November

DAY OF RECONCILIATION & ACCORD

The former October Revolution day – 7 November – is still an official holiday, although it is hardly acknowledged. It still is, however, a big day for flag-waving and protesting by old-school Communist Party members, especially in front of Gostiny Dvor (p75) and pl Ostrovskogo (p75). Makes for a great photo-op.

December

ARTS SQUARE WINTER FESTIVAL

www.artsquarewinterfest.ru

Maestro Yury Temirknaov presides over this musical highlight, which takes place every year at the Shostakovich Philharmonia (p189) on pl Iskusstv (Arts Sq; p74). For 10 days at the end of December and the beginning of January, artists stage both classical and contemporary works, including symphonic music and opera, as well as less traditional musical forms, jazz and puppet theatre.

NEW YEAR

Petersburgers see in the New Year (Novy God) by trading gifts, drinking champagne and listening to the Kremlin chimes on the radio or TV. Although Novy God has not reached the degree of commercialism of Christmas in the West, it is a gift-giving holiday. Dedya Moroz (Grandfather Frost) and Snezhinka (Snow Girl) dole out treats to deserving youngsters.

COSTS & MONEY

Experts estimate that the average monthly salary in St Petersburg is about R15,000. Considering that the average for Russia as a whole is about R10,700 per month, it seems that Petersburgers are doing pretty well for themselves.

Unfortunately, these numbers do not convey how far these roubles go, which is not very far. St Petersburg is the second most expensive city in Russia and the twelfth most expensive city in the world, according to a 2007 report by Mercer Human Resource Consulting. The

HOW MUCH?

Litre of petrol: R18-22

Litre of bottled water: R15-30

Bottle of Baltika beer: R40

Souvenir T-shirt: R500

Bliny: R60

Admission to the Hermitage: R350

Business lunch: R200

Cappuccino: R60

Public toilet: R10

Matryoshka (nesting doll): R500

top picks

PASSING AS A RUSSIAN IN ST PETERSBURG *JM_Dreaming*

At a restaurant Embrace the culture and order a bottle of vodka. The look of sheer horror and infinite respect on the faces of fellow travellers – priceless! Especially when your bottle comes accompanied only by shot glasses and 'black' Russian rye.

At the shopping centre Pay cash. If you *must* pay by credit card, allow extra time. Think 30 minutes, three different counters and five perplexed sales assistants.

At the supermarket Take the shopping basket. Not worth blowing your cover by trying to explain to the hardened *grom-baba* (literal translation – thunder woman) that you only came for one item.

At the ballet Consider 'Foreigner' versus 'Russian' prices for Mariinsky Theatre. Camouflage by dressing up like a local (no jeans: theatre is taken seriously). Stern babushkas are tough to trick, but not impossible. When the third bell rings, slip in with the crowds.

At the Hermitage Don't bother! Babushkas holding rubber batons are all-knowing. Concede you are a 'Foreigner', pay X-times the 'Russian' price, leave your jacket at the cloakroom and immerse yourself in the atmosphere of one of the world's richest art collections.

ranking puts St Petersburg ahead of such famously pricey places as Paris, Singapore and New York.

Travellers will not find too many bargains in St Petersburg, although it is possible to live frugally by taking public transport, self-catering and sleeping in hostels. Anyone who is coming from Moscow will be pleasantly surprised to learn that St Petersburg is significantly cheaper than the capital, which ranked number one in the world on Mercer's list.

Expect to pay at least R600 per head for a meal in a nice restaurant. Many offer business lunch specials, which usually include three courses, for as little as R200. This is an excellent way to sample some restaurants where you would otherwise pay much higher prices. If you self-cater or dine exclusively at budget places you can probably get by on R400 for meals.

Lodging prices are also high, although the proliferation of privately owned 'mini-hotels' means that there is no shortage of excellent midrange accommodation options. The going rate for a bed in a hostel is about R600, but you will pay anywhere from R2200 for a private room, and from R3200 if you want private facilities. The good news is that most midrange options are nicely renovated and efficiently run, offering good service and even a touch of style. Prices for luxury hotels start at €150 and go all the way up.

Although dual pricing for hotels and transport no longer exits, as a foreigner in Russia you'll still often find yourself paying more than a local for museums and theatre tickets. The mark-up for foreigners is extreme – often as much as 10 times the price that Russians pay (although you may be able to avoid it if you have a student identification). Take heart that the extra money you shell out is desperately needed to protect the very works of art and artefacts you've come to see.

INTERNET RESOURCES

There is no shortage of information about St Petersburg on the web. See also the respective chapters for more suggestions.

www.bcam.spb.ru Peter Sobolev's excellent Wandering Camera includes some 400 albums and thousands of photos of the city.

www.encspb.ru The Encyclopaedia of St Petersburg is encyclopaedic in its coverage of art, architecture, geography, society, economy and more.

www.eng.gov.spb.ru Official portal of the St Petersburg city government.

www.hermitagemuseum.org Take an on-line tour of the fabulous art collection before you visit in person.

www.nevsky-prospekt.com This walk down Main Street St Pete includes architectural descriptions, history and other fun facts, as well as plenty of photos.

www.other.spb.ru Most visitors to St Petersburg miss 'the other side' of the city, but you won't want to after reading this strange and hilarious account. Alas, it may already be too late.

www.petersburgcity.com The official English-language portal offers local news and events, contemporary culture and city life, as well as the standard tourist fare.

www.saint-petersburg.com One of the best places to start your research. The site includes a virtual city tour, online hotel booking and descriptions of tourist sights.

www.sptimes.ru Website of the local English-language newspaper, the *St Petersburg Times*.

ADVANCE PLANNING

If you are the organised type, you'll want to take care of a few things before you arrive in St Petersburg:

- Apply for your visa! This is an absolute must for absolutely everybody. You can do it at the last minute, but it may cost you your first-born child. See p249 for details.
- Reserve a place to stay, especially if you are coming during the busy summer months. See p202.
- Book a taxi from the airport. Most hotels, mini-hotels, hostels and hire services will make these arrangements for you for a reasonable rate. Otherwise, you can book a taxi from a private company for about R500. You will pay approximately three times more if you jump in an unreserved cab upon arrival at the airport, so it's worth the price of the international phone call. See p238.
- Order your tickets to visit the Hermitage (p131; www.hermitagemuseum.org). You can buy them at the museum on the day you visit, but buying in advance over the internet allows you to skip the queue.
- Check the schedule at the Mariinsky Theatre (p188; www.mariinsky.ru) and order your tickets ahead of time to ensure great seats and avoid language difficulties.

HISTORY

On a warm August afternoon in 1782, a large crowd gathered along the Neva River's south embankment. On a balcony above, Empress Catherine appeared and dedicated to St Petersburg its newest monument: the Bronze Horseman, a soaring likeness of the city's founder, Peter the Great, commanding a half-wild steed. Immortalised in the words of Pushkin, 'Behold the image sit and ride, upon his brazen horse astride.'

CITY BY THE SEA

Precocious Prince

For three centuries, Moscow hosted Russia's ruler tsars. The onion-domed capital of the Ivans was shrouded in mystery and intrigue. The precocious Peter never fitted in.

Born in 1672, Peter was the son of Tsar Alexey I and his second wife Natalya Narishkina. He was one of 16 siblings. His spindly frame grew to be an imposing 2m tall and he suffered from a twitchy form of epilepsy. He loved ditching the claustrophobic Kremlin and traipsing through the countryside with his chums, staging mock military manoeuvres and sailing into make-believe naval battles. When his mother arranged a marriage for him to secure the family's aristocratic connections, the teenager reluctantly consented. But a few years later he sent his first wife to a nunnery and took up with a Lithuanian peasant girl, Catherine I, whom he adored and married.

Peter was also exceptional for his insatiable curiosity about the outside world. He spent long hours in the city quarter for foreign merchants, who regaled the young prince with tales of the wonders of the new modern age. Once on the throne, he became the first tsar to venture beyond the border. Travelling in disguise, Peter and a raucous Russian entourage crisscrossed the continent, meeting with monarchs, dining with dignitaries and carousing with commoners. He recruited admirals, academics and artisans to apply their skill in his service. Peter was more than ever convinced that Russians were still living in a dark age. He vowed to replace superstition with science, backwardness with progress, East with West.

Peter abruptly ended his European expedition when news came of a Kremlin coup. His claim to the throne was illegitimate, some whispered. After his father died, the families of the two tsarinas clashed over the royal legacy: the Miloslavsky clan claimed lineage back to Ivan and represented the best of old Muscovy, while the upstart Narishkins were of recent Tatar and distant Scottish bloodlines. When he was only 10 years old, Peter watched in horror as his uncle was murdered by a Moscow mob, stirred by family rivalry. Eventually, a joint settlement was reached by which the boy shared the throne with his dim-witted half-brother, while his ambitious older stepsister acted as regent. In 1689, at the age of 17, Peter was ready: he consigned his sister to a nunnery and declared himself as tsar. Old Muscovy's resentment of this act prompted the coup, which now brought Peter back from Europe.

Enough was enough. Peter began to impose his strong will on Russia. He vengefully punished the plotters, sending more than 1000 to their death and instilling fear in many thousands. He

1672

Peter Alexeyevich Romanov is born in Moscow to Alexey Mikhailovich and his second wife Natalya Narishkina. He grows up to be known as Peter the Great.

1703

On 27 May Peter the Great establishes the Peter & Paul Fortress on Zayachy Island, thus founding the new city of Sankt Pieter Burkh, Russia's 'window to the West'.

1712–14

At the behest of Peter I, government institutions begin to move from Moscow, and St Petersburg assumes the administrative and ceremonial role as the Russian capital.

ESSENTIAL READING

Here's your syllabus for St Petersburg History 101.

- *Sunlight at Midnight* (D Bruce Lincoln) Focusing on the colourful characters of the imperial period and the dramatic events leading up to the revolution, this definitive history is at once highly readable and academically rigorous.
- *Peter the Great: A Biography* (Lindsey Hughes) Never pulling punches in her detailed retelling of his less-than-laudable personal life and his often barbaric childishness, Hughes manages to present both the genius and failings of Peter I.
- *Pushkin's Buttons* (Serena Vitale) A fascinating account of the duel that killed the national bard.
- *Nicholas and Alexandra* (Robert Massey) Part love story and part political thriller, Massey's historical account gives the nitty-gritty on the royal family, Rasputin and the resulting revolution.
- *Ten Days That Shook the World* (John Reed) This classic eyewitness account of the Russian Revolution by American journalist John Reed makes for a fascinating read.
- *Hope Against Hope* (Nadezhda Mandelstam) The wife of poet Osip Mandelstam wrote this memoir about their lives as dissidents in Stalinist Russia. The title is a play on words, as *nadezhda* means 'hope' in Russian.
- *The 900 Days: The Siege of Leningrad* (Harrison Salisbury) This forensic reconstruction is not for those with a passing interest in the blockade, but for those who want to vicariously suffer through the darkest hours of St Petersburg.

humiliated and subdued the old elite, forcing aristocrat elders to shave their beards and wear Western clothes. He subordinated the Orthodox Church to earthly political authority, and banished Old Believers who cursed him as the Antichrist. He upended the established social order, forbidding arranged marriages and promoting the humble to high rank. He even changed the date of New Year's Day – from September to January. By now, the undisputed tsar had grown to despise the old capital, and was ready to start afresh.

Great Northern War

Peter was anxious to turn Russia Westward, and he saw the Baltic Sea as the channel for change. The problem was that Sweden already dominated the region. It had been more than 400 years since Russia's medieval hero prince, Alexander Nevsky, had defeated the Swedes near the site of Peter's expanding ambition. The territory, however, had long ago passed out of Russian influence. In 1700 Peter put his new army to the test against the powerful Swedish Empire, and the Great Northern War was on. For the next 20 years northern Europe's modernising autocrats, Charles II and Peter, fought for supremacy over the eastern Baltic.

To Peter's dismay, his troops were badly beaten in their first engagement at the Battle of Narva in Estonia, by a smaller, more adept Swedish force. But Russia found allies in Poland, Saxony and Denmark, who diverted Charles' attention. Peter used the opportunity to revamp his army and launch his navy. He established a small Baltic foothold on the tiny Isle of Hares (Zayachy Island) at the mouth of the Neva River, and used it as a base to rout a nearby Swedish garrison. This primitive outpost fort would become Peter's northern capital.

By the time Charles tried to retake the territory, Peter commanded a formidable fighting force. Russia's first naval victory came at the Battle of Hanko, where a galley fleet overwhelmed a Swedish squadron and secured Russian control over the Neva and access to the Gulf. His

1725

Thirteen years after St Petersburg was declared the new capital, its population has grown to 40,000 and as much as 90% of all foreign trade passes through its port.

1728

After the death of Peter I and two years of rule by his wife, his grandson Peter II returns the Russian capital back to Moscow.

1732

Empress Anna reverses the decision of Peter II and moves the capital to St Petersburg, presiding over the recommencement of the city's construction and development.

military chief and boyhood friend, Alexander Menshikov, ripped off a string of impressive battlefield victories, further extending Russian presence on the Baltic coast and causing his Scandinavian foe to flee. Like the last sardine at a smorgasbord, the Swedish empire expired. The Great Northern War shifted the balance of power in the Baltic to the advantage of Peter's Russia. Hostilities were officially concluded with the signing of the Treaty of Nystad, in 1721, which formally ceded Sweden's extensive eastern possessions to Russia, including its new capital city, St Petersburg.

Peter's Paradise

Peter did not wait for the war to end before he started building. The wooden palisade encampment on Hares' Isle became the red-brick Peter & Paul Fortress (p113). In June 1703 Peter gave the site a name – Sankt Pieter Burkh, in his favourite Dutch tongue and after his patron saint, who stands guard before the gates to paradise.

There was a reason why until now the area had only attracted a few Finnish fishermen for settlement. It was a swamp. The Neva River runs from nearby Lake Ladoga, Europe's largest, and flows into the Gulf of Finland through a low-lying delta of marshy flood-prone islands, more manageable for moose than man. Although it is close to the Arctic Circle, winds and waters from the Atlantic bring moderate and moist weather. This means that winter, during which the delta freezes up, is relatively short: a matter of no small significance to Peter.

Peter's vision for the new capital was grandiose; so was the task ahead. To find enough dry ground for building, swamps were drained out and wetlands were filled in. To protect the land from flooding, seawalls were built up and canals were laid down. A hands-on autocrat, Peter pitched in with the hammering, sawing and joining. Thousands of fortune-seeking foreigners were imported to lend expertise: architects and engineers who designed the city's intricate waterways and craftsmen and masons who chiselled its stone foundations. The hard labour of digging ditches and moving muck was performed by non-voluntary recruits. Peter pressed 30,000 peasant serfs per year into capital construction gangs. Their ranks were supplemented with Russian convict labourers and Swedish prisoners of war. The work regimen was strict and living conditions were stark: more than 100,000 died amid the mucous and mud. But those who survived could earn personal freedom and a small piece of marshland to call their own.

Russia's new city by the sea began to take shape, inspired by Peter's recollections of canal-lined Amsterdam. The locus of power was the military stronghold, the Peter & Paul Fortress. Next, he ordered the chief accompaniments of tsarist authority – a church and a prison. The first tavern was the German-owned Triumphant Osteria of the Four Frigates, where Peter would order his favourite drink – vodka with cayenne pepper. The first stone palace belonged to the former Dutch merchant captain and first commander of Russia's Baltic Fleet, Cornelius Cruys. A more impressive dwelling put up by the territory's first governor-general, Alexander Menshikov, soon adorned the Vasilevsky Island embankment (see p110).

Peter abandoned his wooden cabin for a modest Dutch-style townhouse across the river in the new Summer Garden (see p71). Nearby, on the future site of the Admiralty, a bustling shipyard was assembling his new navy. Impatient to develop a commercial port, Peter offered a generous reward to the first three ships to drop anchor at the new town docks. The presence of so many foreigners gave the crude swampy settlement a more cosmopolitan feel than the poshest parlours of pious Moscow.

1741–61

Empress Elizabeth fulfils her father's goal of a grand European capital, commissioning the construction of countless sumptuous buildings and creating a glittering court.

1757

Empress Elizabeth oversees the establishment of the Imperial Academy of Arts by Count Ivan Shuvalov, her Minister of Education and sometimes lover, who some called the 'Maecenas of the Russian Enlightenment'.

1754–62

Chief architect Bartolomeo Rastrelli constructs the rococo Winter Palace on the embankment of the Neva River as the primary residence of the royal family. Empress Elizabeth dies three months before the Winter Palace is completed.

In 1712 the tsar officially declared St Petersburg to be the capital. Inspired by the Vatican's crossed keys to paradise, he adopted a city coat of arms that presented crossed anchors topped with an imperial crown. Peter requested the rest of Russia's ruling elite join him, or else. He said Pieter Burkh was the place they ought to be, so they packed up their carriages and moved to the Baltic Sea. The tsar's royal court, the imperial senate and foreign embassies were relocated to damper digs. Fearing Peter's wrath, Moscow's old aristocratic families reluctantly began to arrive. Apprehension turned to appal. To them Peter's paradise was a peaty hell. They were ordered to bring their own stones to the party, with which to build elegant mansions and in which to start behaving like Westerners (see the boxed text, above). It all seemed surreal.

STONED IN ST PETE

Peter envisioned a splendid imperial capital, shimmering in polished marble and granite. Unfortunately, the site he chose to build on was more muddy than rocky. The dreamer tsar was undaunted. He ordered Russia's governors to start loading up wagons with bricks and stones, and send them immediately to St Petersburg. Building in stone outside the capital was forbidden. He decreed a stone tax, by which all new arrivals to the city were obliged to bring with them a fixed amount of stone before they could enter. Every ship that entered the port also was required to pay a stone tariff (not so unusual for a guy who previously issued a tax on beards). St Petersburg's rocky revenue laws remained in effect for six decades.

When Peter died of gangrene in 1725, at the age of 52, some thought they might get the chance to quit his quixotic quagmire, but they were wrong. The wilful spirit of Peter the Great continued to possess the city and bedevil its inhabitants. Within less than a hundred years of its improbable inception, a new magnificent capital would stand on the edge of Europe.

IMPERIAL CAPITAL

Peter's Heirs

By the end of the 18th century St Petersburg would take its place among Europe's grand cities. But in the years immediately following Peter's death, the fate of the Baltic bastion was still uncertain.

While Peter's plans for his imperial capital were clear, those for his personal legacy were murky. His eldest son and heir apparent, Alexey, was estranged from his father early on, suspected of plotting against him later, and tortured to death in the Peter & Paul Fortress finally. The evidence was flimsy. On his death bed, Peter tried to dictate a last will, but could not name an heir before his galloping ghost departed into the grey mist. His wife Catherine I assumed the throne for the next two years, with Peter's pal Menshikov acting as de-facto tsar. When she died, the reaction started.

The Petersburg-Moscow power struggle was on. The aristocracy's Old Muscovite faction seized the opportunity to influence the succession. Without his protector, the mighty Menshikov was stripped of all titles and property, and sent packing into Siberian exile. Peter's 11-year-old grandson, Peter II, was chosen as an unlikely heir. Delivering to his enabling patrons, the pliable Peter II returned the capital to Moscow. The city's population fell by a half; its public works came to rest. When Peter II eventually got up the nerve to order Petersburgers to go back, he was ignored by the disdainful nobles. But this reversal of urban fortune proved short-lived.

The Romanovs were a delicate dynasty and the teen tsar soon succumbed to smallpox. Moscow's princely power-brokers now entrusted the throne to another supposed weakling, Duchess

1762

Seventeen years after their marriage, a coup against Peter III brings to the throne his wife Catherine II (Catherine the Great), ushering in the era of Russian Enlightenment.

1764

Catherine the Great begins purchasing paintings from European collectors and putting them on display in her 'hermitage', thus forming the foundations for the collection that will later become the State Hermitage Museum.

1768–74

Victories in the Russo-Turkish War expand Russian control in southern Ukraine. To commemorate the decisive Battle of Chesme, Catherine commissions the Chesme Church in Southern St Petersburg and the Chesme Column at Tsarskoe Selo.

ICE QUEEN

In 1737 Empress Anna gave promising young Russian architect Peter Eropkin a cool commission. Anna was in a celebratory mood after a victorious conclusion to the Russo-Turkish War. It was a royal ritual to build something spectacular after military triumphs, but usually in stone and mortar. Anna wanted her victory palace to be carved in ice.

Eropkin stacked blocks of ice, cut from the river, to make the frosty mansion. The interior was 15m by 6m and the ornamental roof turrets topped 30m tall. The inside featured ice furniture and an ice throne, while outside was an ice garden with icicle trees and a life-size ice elephant sculpture. The entrance was guarded by ice cannons, which supposedly were capable of firing – you guessed it – ice balls.

Anna was delighted by Eropkin's creation. She could not resist using it to amuse her court and abuse a count. She demanded that Prince Golitsyn, who had incurred her displeasure, should marry a rather rotund Kalmyk girl at the ice palace. A carnival-like wedding followed, and the couple was forced to spend the night and consummate the marriage on an ice bed. Anna's frozen inspiration was a big hit with city residents that season, but eventually the fun melted away.

In recent years the city has revived the tradition of building ice palaces to wile away winter nights. Under Hermitage direction, a replica of Anna's ice palace was built in 2006 on Palace Sq.

Anna Ivanovna, Peter the Great's niece. But Anna was no pushover – she was the first in a line of tough women rulers. In 1732 Anna declared St Petersburg to be the capital once more, and bade everyone back to the Baltic. Making the offer more enticing, she recommenced glamorous capital construction projects. Wary of scheming Russian elites, she recruited talented German state administrators. Still, the city recovered slowly. A big fire in 1737 left entire neighbourhoods in charred ruins. Even Anna spent much time ruling from Moscow. St Petersburg remained only half built, its dynamism diminished.

Not until the reign of Peter's second-oldest daughter, the Empress Elizabeth (r 1741–62), did the city's imperial appetite return in full. Elizabeth created one of the most dazzling courts in Europe. She loved the pomp as much as the power. Her 20-year reign was a nonstop aristocratic cabaret. The Empress was a bit eccentric, enjoying a hedonistic lifestyle that revolved around hunting, drinking and dancing. She loved most to host elaborate masquerade balls, at which she performed countless costume changes, apparently preferring to end the night in drag. Bawdy though she was, Elizabeth also got the Russian elite hooked on high culture. The court was graced by poets, artists and philosophers. Journalism and theatre gained popularity, and an Academy of Arts was founded. While her resplendent splurges may have left imperial coffers empty, Elizabeth made her father's majestic dream a reality.

Aristocratic Soul

Peter's determined drive to build a modern state transformed the means and expression of power: military revolution replaced medieval mercenaries; secular law replaced ecclesiastical canon; bureaucratic order replaced personal impulse. St Petersburg now displayed all the features of a seriously imperial capital: stately façade, hierarchical heart and aristocratic soul.

The city's physical appearance reflected the transition. The centre of power moved across the river to the Neva's south bank. Empress Elizabeth's baroque beauty, the Winter Palace (p125), was meant to impress – and how could it not, with more than a quarter of a million exquisitely

1773

Emilian Pugachev, a Don Cossack, claims to be the overthrown Peter III and begins a peasant uprising, which must be quelled by brute force. The Pugachev Rebellion curbs the liberal tendencies of Catherine the Great.

1796

Upon the death of Catherine the Great, her son Paul I ascends the throne. One of his first acts as tsar is to decree that women can never again rule Russia.

1799

The birth of poet Alexander Pushkin ushers in the era of Russian Romanticism and the Golden Age of Russian literature. Revered as the national bard, Pushkin's legacy endures to this day.

embellished square feet. She forbade any new building to rise higher than her 1000-room, 2000-windowed, multicolumned mansion. The immense Palace Sq (Dvortsovaya pl; p66) could host as many as 50 parading infantry battalions at once. Across the square was an imposing semicircular structure housing the instruments of statecraft: General Staff, Treasury and Foreign Office. Its august archways led out to a beaming boulevard, the city's central artery, the Nevsky pr. The commanding Admiralty (p67) stretched along nearly 400m of the south embankment, adorned with ancient heroes like conqueror Alexander the Great and sea goddess Isis and topped with a gleaming gold spire. The city's monumental mélange reinforced its imperial pretension, with each ruler adding a personal stylistic touch: Peter's restrained baroque, Elizabeth's reckless rococo, Catherine's refined neoclassicism.

St Petersburg was a city of ranks, literally. The capital's social hierarchy reflected Peter's image of a well-ordered modern state. To minimise the personal influence of the old nobility, Peter created a Table of Ranks, which formally assigned social status on the basis of service to the emperor. The table included 14 stations in the military forces, civil administration and imperial court. In this system, inheritance was no longer an exclusive means to elite status, as resourceful newcomers were rewarded too. Living quarters and salary were determined by rank. Each service had its own colour-coded uniforms, with distinguishing pecking-order plumage. Social manners followed suit: a lowly titular counsellor in a shabby overcoat could easily get a collegiate assessor's nose out of joint by addressing him as 'Your Nobleness' instead of the appropriate 'Your High Nobleness'. Not surprisingly, the old aristocratic families still managed to be well represented in the upper echelon.

Despite Peter's meritocratic meddling, St Petersburg was in essence an aristocratic city. Capital life was infused by blue bloodlines. Although the tsar could upset the balance, for the most part power came by entitlement and property was passed down. Yes, it was possible for the capable and clever to climb the Table of Ranks, but they'd better have a noble patron to give them a boost. The aristocratic elite that once sneered at Peter's vision of a cosmopolitan capital eventually came to wallow in it. They imported tastes and manners from their slightly more sophisticated continental cousins. European fashion and philosophy were conspicuously consumed. So far did it go that St Petersburg's aristocrats preferred to speak French *l'un a l'autre*. Ancestral connections to kings and queens past became a coveted social commodity. Myths about family origin were eagerly propagated, with the ruling Romanovs taking the cup for uncovering their long-lost genetic link to Julius Caesar.

Enlightened Empress – Despotic Dame

In 1745, at the age of 16, Sophie Augusta of Prussia was betrothed to Duke Peter of Holstein: quite a score for her ambitious mother, as Peter was a Romanov and heir to the Imperial Russian throne. Sophie moved to St Petersburg, learned to speak Russian, delighted the court with her coy charm, and took the name Catherine when she converted to Orthodoxy. A nice start for sure, but who would figure that a French-tutored Fräulein from Stettin would one day reach Peter's lofty status and earn the moniker 'Great'.

More than just a court coquette, Catherine possessed keen political instincts and a strong appetite for power, attributes that had adverse effects on the men in her life. Her husband Tsar Peter III, as it turned out, was a bit of a flake and not terribly interested in ruling. In a plot hatched by aristocrat Prince Orlov, Catherine was complicit in a coup that landed her on the throne, lifted her

1800

St Petersburg has grown exponentially in its first century, and its population reaches 220,000. By this time, the city has gained all the glory of a cosmopolitan capital.

1801

Tsar Paul is murdered in his bedroom in the fortress-like Mikhailovsky Castle. The coup places on the throne Alexander I, who vows to continue the reformist policies of his grandmother.

1812–14

Alexander I oversees Russia's victory in the Napoleonic Wars. By war's end, Russian troops occupy Paris and Russia becomes Europe's greatest power. Monuments are strewn about St Petersburg, including the Alexander Column and Narva Gates.

conspiratorial consort to general-in-chief, and left her helpless husband face down at his country estate. She followed Peter I's example of paranoid parenting. Indeed, she made her successor son, Grand Duke Paul, so insecure that when he finally took the throne he built a fortified castle in the middle of the city and locked himself in (see Mikhailovsky Castle, p74). Of course, just because you are paranoid does not mean that people are not out to get you: Paul's reign was cut short when some disgruntled drunken officers strangled him to death with his bedroom curtains.

Catherine, by contrast, prospered. Despite the details of her unsavoury ascension, she reigned for a satisfying 34 years. Catherine presided over a golden age for St Petersburg. Relations between crown and aristocracy were never better. High society strolled through handsome parks, gabbed in smoky salons and waltzed across glittering ballrooms. The city benefited from her literary leanings, acquiring a splendid public library (p75) and the graceful Smolny Institute (p83), for fine-tuning fair maidens. The Russian Empire, meanwhile, expanded to ever greater distances.

Empress Catherine was a charter member of a club of 18th-century monarchs known as the 'enlightened despots' – dictators who could hum Haydn. On the 'enlightened' side, Catherine corresponded with French philosophers, patronised the arts and sciences, promoted public education and introduced the potato to national cuisine. On the 'despotic' side, Catherine connived with fellow enlightened friends to carve up Poland, censored bad news and imprisoned the messengers, tightened serfs' bonds of servitude to their lords, and introduced the potato to national cuisine.

And what of young Catherine's coquettish charms? They matured into full-blown avaricious desires. She may have been conversant in several tongues, but she did not know the word 'moderation' in any of them. When it comes to Russian rulers, Catherine tops the list for most voracious, salacious and bodacious. The Hermitage is one of the world's great art holdings because of her compulsion to collect and obsession to outbid. Her team of French chefs had Catherine looking like a subject in one of her prized Rubens. Nor was she shy about s-e-x. Her ladies-in-waiting were entreated to test the stamina of new palace guards to satisfy their mistress' curiosity. She doted on a succession of rising officers – promoting them to high rank, rewarding them with luxury villas, and banishing them to frontier outposts when her fickle flame burnt out. It was good to be the tsarina.

Contrary to popular myth, Catherine did not die while getting off her horse. She suffered a stroke in the bath, and at age 67 was carried off by the Bronze Horseman through the steamy haze to the other side.

GREAT POWER PETERSBURG

1812 Overture

The downside to becoming a great power in European politics is that you get drawn into European wars. Though, in fairness to the Hanovers and Hapsburgs, the Romanovs were pretty good at picking fights on their own. From the 19th century on, Russia was at war and St Petersburg was transformed.

It was Napoleon who coined the military maxim, 'first we engage, then we will see'. That was probably not the best tactic to take with Russia. Tsar Alexander first clashed with Napoleon after joining an ill-fated anti-French alliance with Austria and Prussia. The resulting Treaty of Tilsit was not so bad for Russia – as long as Alexander cooperated with Napoleon's designs against Britain. Alexander reneged; Napoleon avenged. The Little Corporal targeted Moscow, instead of the more heavily-armed Petersburg. His multinational, 600,000-strong force got there just in time for winter and had little to show for the effort, besides vandalising the Kremlin.

1824

St Petersburg experiences the worst flood in its history, when water levels rise more than 4m. At least 500 people are killed, thousands are injured and more than 300 buildings are destroyed.

1825

After the death of Alexander I, reformers assemble on Senate Sq to protest the succession of conservative Nicholas I. The new tsar brutally crushes the so-called Decembrist Revolt, killing hundreds in the process.

1849

Author Fyodor Dostoevsky is arrested and imprisoned for participating in discussions with a liberal intellectual group known as Petrashevsky Circle. He is exiled to Siberia for four years of hard labour.

Hungry, cold and dispirited, they retreated westward, harried by Marshal Kutuzov's troops. The Grande Armée was ground up: only 20,000 survived. Napoleon was booked for an island vacation, while Russia became the continent's most feared nation.

The War of 1812 was a defining event for Russia, stirring nationalist exaltation and orchestral inspiration. Catherine's favourite grandson, Alexander I, presided over a period of prosperity and self-assuredness in the capital. His army's exploits were immortalised in triumphal designs that recalled imperial Rome: Kazan Cathedral (p73), Alexander Column (p66) and Narva Gates (p147) – shining symbols for a new Russian empire that stretched across half the globe.

More wars and more monuments bedecked the city throughout the 19th century. St Petersburg was a military capital. When Peter I died, one in six residents was a member of the armed forces; a hundred years later the ratio was one in four. It was a city of immense parade grounds, swaggering elite regiments, and epaulette-clad nobility. St Petersburg came to exhibit a patriotic culture that saw the capital as more than just European, the epicentre of a transcendent Russia whose greatness came from within. The Bronze Horseman looked on approvingly.

God Preserve Thy People

War did more than confer Great Power status on Russia: it was also a stimulus for new ideas on political reform and social change. In the 19th century, the clash of ideas spilled out of salons and into its streets.

On a frosty December morning in 1825 more than a thousand soldiers amassed on Senate Sq (now Decembrists' Sq, p101), with the intention of upsetting the royal succession. When Alexander I died unexpectedly without a legitimate heir, the throne was supposed to pass to his liberal-minded brother Constantine, Viceroy of Poland, but he declined, preferring not to complicate his contented life. Instead, the new tsar would be Alexander's youngest brother, Nicholas I, a cranky conservative with a fastidious obsession for barracks-style discipline. The Decembrists revolt was staged by a small cabal of officers, veterans of the Napoleonic Wars, who saw first-hand how people in other countries enjoyed greater freedom and prosperity. They demanded Constantine and a constitution, but instead got exile and execution. The 'people', however, were now part of the discussion.

Russia's pathetic performance in another war prompted another reform attempt, this time initiated by the tsar. In the 1850s, better-equipped British and French armies really stuck it to Russia in a fight over the Crimean peninsula. The new emperor Alexander II concluded from the fiasco that Russia had to catch up with the West, or watch its empire unravel. A slew of reform decrees were issued, promoting public education, military reorganisation and economic modernisation. A sensitive sort, Alexander dropped the death penalty and curtailed corporal punishment. The Tsar Liberator abolished serfdom, kind of – his solution that serfs pay their masters redemptive fees in exchange for freedom pleased no one.

By now the 'people' were becoming less abstract. Political movements that claimed to better understand and represent them were sprouting up. On a Sunday morning in March 1881 several young student members of the Peoples' Will radical sect waited nervously by the Griboedov Canal as the tsar's procession passed. Their homemade bombs hardly dented the royal armoured coach, but badly wounded scores of spectators and fatally shredded the reforming monarch when he insisted on leaving his carriage to investigate. On the hallowed site, the magnificent and melancholy Church of the Saviour on Spilled Blood (p72) was constructed, its twisting onion domes trying to steady St Petersburg's uncertain present with Russia's enduring past.

1851

Upon completion of the construction of Nikolaevsky Station (now Moscow Station), the first trains linking Moscow and St Petersburg begin running, introducing rail travel to Russia.

1853–56

Britain and France side against Russia in the Crimean War, a war that's characterised by inept command and bloody stalemate, until it is finally ended by Alexander II.

1861

The emancipation of the serfs frees up labour to feed the Russian industrial revolution. Workers flood into the capital, leading to overcrowding, poor sanitation, disease epidemics and societal discontent.

THE MAD MONK

Russia's most legendary letch and holy man was Grigory Rasputin, mystic and healer. He was born in 1869 into poverty in a small village east of the Urals. After a dissolute boyhood and a short-lived marriage, he discovered religion. Rasputin preached (and practiced) that the way to divine grace was through sin and redemption: binge drinking and engaging in sexual orgies, and then praying for forgiveness.

St Petersburg's high society was receptive to Rasputin's teachings. Despite his heavy drinking and sexual scandals – or perhaps because of them – he earned the adoration of an army of aristocratic ladies. More notable, Rasputin endeared himself to Emperor Nicholas II and his wife Alexandra. The healer had the power to ease the pain of their son Alexey, who suffered from haemophilia.

The holy man's scandalous behaviour and his influence over the queen invoked the ire of the aristocracy. The powerful Prince Felix Yusupov and the tsar's cousin Grand Duke Dmitry decided that the Siberian peasant must be stopped. On a wintry night in 1916, they invited Rasputin to the sumptuous Yusupov Palace (p102) overlooking the Moyka. They plied the monk with wine and cakes that were laced with potassium cyanide, which seemed to have no effect. In a panic, the perpetrators then shot the priest at close range. Alarmingly, this didn't seem to get the job done either. Rasputin finally drowned when he was tied up in a sheet and dropped into the icy Neva River. He was buried in secret at Pushkin (p219).

Besides mystical powers and lecherous behaviour, Grigory Rasputin is famous for another exceptional attribute: his enormous penis (30cm, if you must know). Legend has it that Rasputin's foes did not stop at murder; apparently, they also castrated him. Yusupov's maid supposedly found Rasputin's oversized organ when cleaning the apartment after the murder.

Which explains the prize artefact at the so-called Museum of Erotica (p87): it is indeed Rasputin's preserved penis. Even in its detached state, the Mad Monk's massive member is still attracting attention.

Great Power competition compelled a state-directed campaign of economic development. St Petersburg was the centre of a robust military-industrial economy, to fight the wars of the modern age. A ring of ugly sooty smokestacks grew up around the still handsome city centre. Tough times in the rural villages and job opportunities in the new factories hastened a human flood into the capital. By the 1880s, the population climbed past a million, with hundreds of thousands cramped into slummy suburban squalor. Public health was befouled, public manner was debased. The gap between high society and the lower depths had long been manageable, but now they kept running into each other. The people had arrived.

God Save the Tsar

'We, workers and inhabitants of the city of St Petersburg, our wives, children, and helpless old parents, have come to you, Sovereign, to seek justice and protection.' So read the petition that a large group of workers intended to present to Tsar Nicholas II on a Sunday in January 1905.

Nicholas II ascended the throne in 1894, when his iron-fisted father, Alexander III, a real autocrat's autocrat, died suddenly. Nicholas was of less steely stuff. Most contemporary accounts agree: he was a good guy and a lousy leader; possessive of his power to decide, except that he could never make up his mind. In 1904 Nicholas followed the foolish advice of a cynical minister, who said that what Russia needed most was a 'small victorious war' to get peoples'

1870

After breaking from the Academy of Arts, a group of upstart artists known as the Peredvizhniki (Wanderers) starts organising travelling exhibitions to widen their audience.

1881

A bomb kills Alexander II as he travels home along the Griboedov Canal. His reactionary son, Alexander III, undoes many of his reforms, but oversees the construction of the Trans-Siberian Railway.

1890

Queen of Spades, Pyotr Tchaikovsky's opera based on the poem by Alexander Pushkin, premieres at the Mariinsky Theatre, drawing excited crowds and rave reviews.

minds off their troubles. Unfortunately, the Russo-Japanese War ended in humiliating defeat and the people were more agitated than ever.

By January 1905 the capital was a hotbed of political protest. As many as 100,000 workers were on strike, the city had no electricity and all public facilities were closed. Nicholas and the royals departed for their palace retreat at Tsarskoe Selo (p219). In this charged atmosphere, Father Georgy Gapon, an Orthodox priest who apparently lived a double life as holy man and police agent, organised a peaceful demonstration of workers and their families to protest the difficult conditions. Their petition called for eight-hour work days and better wages, an end to the war and universal suffrage.

Singing *God Save the Tsar,* the crowd solemnly approached the Winter Palace, hoping to present its requests to the tsar personally. Inside, the mood was jittery: panicky guardsmen fired on the demonstrators, at first as a warning and then directly into the crowd. More than 1000 people were killed by the gunshots or the trampling that followed. Although Nicholas was not even in the palace at the time, the events of Bloody Sunday shattered the myth of the Father Tsar. The Last Emperor was finally able to restore order by issuing the October Manifesto, which promised a constitutional monarchy and civil rights; in fact, not much really changed.

At the start of WWI, nationalist fervour led St Petersburg to change its name to the more Slavic, less German-sounding Petrograd. A hundred years earlier, war with France had made the Russian Empire a great power, but now yet another European war threatened its very survival. The empire was fraying at the seams as the old aristocratic order limped onward into battle. Only the strength of the Bronze Horseman could hold it all together. But Peter's legacy rested on the shoulders of an imperial inheritor who was both half-hearted reformer and irresolute reactionary: the combination proved revolutionary.

CRADLE OF COMMUNISM

Act One: Down with the Autocracy

In 1917, 23 February began like most days in Petrograd since the outbreak of the war. The men went off to the metalworks and arms factories. The women went out to receive the daily bread ration. And the radical set went out to demonstrate, as it happened to be International Women's Day. Although each left their abode an ordinary individual, by day's end they would meld into the most infamous 'mass' in modern history: the Bronze Horseman's heirs let go of the reigns; the Russian Revolution, a play in three acts, had begun.

After waiting long hours in the winter chill for a little food, the women were told that there would be none. This news coincided with the end of the day shift and a sweaty outpouring from the factory gates. Activist provocateurs joined the fray as the streets swelled with the tired, the hungry, and now the angry. The crowd assumed a political purpose. They marched to the river, intent on crossing to the palace side and expressing their discontent to somebody. But they were met at the bridge by gendarmes and guns.

Similar meetings had occurred already, in July and October, on which occasions the crowd retreated. But now it was February and one did not need a bridge to cross the frozen river. First a brave few, then emboldened small groups, finally a defiant horde of hundreds were traversing the ice-laden Neva toward the Winter Palace.

They congregated in the Palace Sq, demanding bread, peace and an end to autocracy. Inside, contemptuous counts stole glances at the unruly rabble, and waited for them to grow tired and disperse. But they did not go home. Instead, they went around the factories and spread the call

1896	1900	1902–04
At the coronation of Nicholas II, a stampede by the massive crowd ends with more than a thousand deaths and almost as many injuries.	By the turn of the 20th century, St Petersburg is Russia's cultural centre, producing masterpieces in music, literature and art. It is also at the centre of political unrest. The population is estimated at 1,440,000.	Clashes in the Far East lead to the Russo-Japanese War, with unexpectedly disastrous results for the Russians. The war diverts resources and stirs up dissent in the capital.

for a general strike. By the next day a quarter of a million people were rampaging through the city centre. Overwhelmed local police took cover.

When word reached the tsar, he ordered military troops to restore order. But his troops were no longer hardened veterans: they were long dead at the front. Rather, freshly conscripted peasant youths in uniform were sent to put down the uprising. When commanded to fire on the demonstration, they instead broke rank, dropped their guns and joined the mob. At that moment, the 300-year-old Romanov dynasty and 500-year-old tsarist autocracy came to an end.

Act Two: All Power to the Soviets

Perhaps the least likely political successor to the tsar in February 1917 was the radical socialist Bolshevik Party. The Bolsheviks were on the fringe of the fringe of Russia's political left. Party membership numbered a few thousand, at best. Yet, in less than eight months, the Bolsheviks occupied the Winter Palace, proclaiming Petrograd the capital of a worldwide socialist revolution.

In the days that followed Nicholas' abdication, a Provisional Government was established. It mainly comprised political liberals, representing reform-minded nobles, pragmatic civil servants, and professional and business interests. Simultaneously, a rival political force emerged, the Petrograd Soviet. The Soviet (the Russian word for council) was composed of more populist and radical elements, representing the interests of the workers, peasants, soldiers and sailors. Both political bodies were based at the Tauride Palace (p85).

The Provisional Government saw itself as a temporary instrument, whose main task was to create some form of constitutional democracy. It argued over the details of organising an election and convention, rather than deal with the issues that had caused the revolution – bread and peace. At first, the Soviet deferred to the Provisional Government, but this soon changed.

On 3 April, Bolshevik leader Vladimir Lenin arrived at the Finland Station (p122) from exile in Switzerland. Lenin's passage across enemy lines had been arranged by German generals, who hoped that he would stir things up at home, and thus distract Russia from their ongoing war. As expected, Lenin upset the political status quo as soon as he arrived. His rabid revolutionary rhetoric polarised Petrograd. In the Soviet, the Bolshevik faction went from cooperative to confrontational. But even his radical pals dismissed Lenin as a stinging gadfly, rather than a serious foe. By summer's end, Lenin had proved them wrong.

The Provisional Government not only refused to withdraw from the war but, at the instigation of the allies, launched a new offensive – prompting mass desertion at the front. Meanwhile, the economic situation continued to deteriorate. The same anarchic anger that fuelled the February Revolution was felt on the streets again. Lenin's Bolsheviks were the only political party in sync with the public mood. September elections in the Petrograd Soviet gave the Bolsheviks a majority.

Lenin had spent his entire adult life waiting for this moment. For 20 years he did little else than read about, write about, and rant about revolution. He enjoyed Beethoven, but avoided listening to his music from concern that the sentiment it evoked would make him lose his revolutionary edge. A successful revolution, Lenin observed, had two preconditions: first, the oppressed classes were politically mobilised and ready to act; and second, the ruling class was internally divided and questioned its will to continue. This politically explosive combination now existed. If the Bolsheviks waited any longer, he feared, the Provisional Government would get its act together and impose a new bourgeois political order, ending his dream of socialist revolution in Russia. On 25 October the Bolsheviks staged their coup. It was not exactly a secret, yet there was not

1905

Hundreds of people are killed when troops fire on peaceful protestors presenting a petition to the tsar. Nicholas II is held responsible for the tragedy, dubbed 'Bloody Sunday'.

1914

Russia enters WWI, simultaneously invading Austrian Galicia and German Prussia with minimal success. St Petersburg changes its name to the less Germanic sounding Petrograd.

1916

After invoking the ire of aristocrats, Grigory Rasputin the 'Mad Monk' is killed. A group of plotters invite him round to Yusupov Palace for cyanide-laced tea, and then drown him in the icy Moyka River.

CHECK YOUR CALENDAR

For hundreds of years, Russia was out of sync with the West. Until 1700 Russia dated its years from 'creation', which was determined to be approximately 5508 years before the birth of Christ. So at that time the year 1700 was considered the year 7208 in Russia. Peter – Westward-looking as he was – instituted a reform to date the years from the birth of Christ, as they did in Europe.

Things got complicated again in the 18th century, when most of Europe abandoned the Julian calendar in favour of the Gregorian calendar and Russia did not follow suit. By 1917 Russian dates were 13 days out of sync with European dates – which explains how the October Revolution could have taken place on 7 November.

Finally, the all-powerful Soviet regime made the necessary leap. The last day of January 1918 was followed by 14 February 1918, aligning dates from then on with those in the West.

In this book we use dates corresponding to the current Gregorian calendar that is used worldwide. However, even history is not always straightforward, as other accounts may employ the calendars that were the convention at that time. Tell *that* to your history professor.

much resistance. According to Lenin's chief accomplice and coup organiser, Leon Trotsky, 'power was lying in the streets, waiting for someone to pick it up.' Bolshevik Red Guards seized a few buildings and strategic points. The Provisional Government was holed up in the tsar's private dining room in the Winter Palace, protected by a few Cossacks, the Petrograd chapter of the Women's Battalion of Death, and a one-legged commander of a bicycle regiment. Before dessert could be served, their dodgy defences cracked. Mutinous mariners fired a window-shattering salvo from the cruiser *Aurora* (p117).

At the Tauride Palace the Soviet remained in emergency session late into the night, when Lenin finally announced that the Provisional Government had been arrested and the Soviet was now the supreme power in Russia. Half the deputies walked out in disgust. Never one to miss an opportunity, Lenin quickly called a vote to make it official. It passed. Incredibly, the Bolsheviks were now in charge.

Act Three: Up with Bolsheviks, Down with Communists

Nobody really believed the Bolsheviks would be around for long. Even Lenin said that, if they could hold on for just 100 days, their coup would be a success by providing future inspiration. It was one thing to occupy a few palaces in Petrograd, but across the empire's far-flung regions Bolshevik-brand radicalism was not so popular. From 1918 to 1921 civil war raged in Russia: between monarchists and socialists, imperialists and nationalists, aristocrats and commoners, believers and atheists. When it was over, somehow Soviet power was still standing. In the final act of the Russian Revolution, the scene shifted from the Petrograd stage. The imperial capital would never be the same.

In December 1917, an armistice was arranged and peace talks began with the Axis Powers. The Bolsheviks demanded a return to prewar imperial borders, but Germany insisted on the liberation of Poland, where its army was squatting. Trotsky defiantly walked out of negotiations, declaring 'neither war, nor peace'. The German high command was a bit confused and not at all amused – hostilities immediately resumed. Lenin had vowed never to abandon the capital, but that was before a German battle fleet cruised into the Gulf of Finland. Exit stage left. In 1918 the Bolsheviks vacated their new pastel digs in Petrograd and relocated behind the ancient red

1917

The February Revolution results in the abdication of Nicholas II, followed by the Bolshevik coup in October. Vladimir Ilych Lenin seizes power and civil war ensues.

1918

Lenin pulls Russia out of WWI and moves the capital to Moscow. Civil war continues throughout the country, and Petrograd enters a period of political and cultural decline.

1920

The ongoing civil war and the change of capital take their toll in St Petersburg. The population falls to 722,000, one-third of the prerevolutionary figure.

BONES OF CONTENTION

What happened to the last members of the royal family – even after their execution in 1918 – is a mixture of the macabre, the mysterious and the just plain messy.

The Romanov remains resurfaced back in 1976, when a group of local scientists discovered them near Yekaterinburg. So politically sensitive was this issue that the discovery was kept secret until the remains were finally fully excavated in 1991. The bones of nine people were tentatively identified as Tsar Nicholas II, his wife Alexandra, three of their four daughters, the royal doctor and three servants. Absent were any remains of daughter Maria or the royal couple's only son, the tsarevich Alexey.

According to a 1934 report filed by one of the assassin-soldiers, all five children died with their parents when they were shot by a firing squad in Yekaterinburg. The bodies were dumped in an abandoned mine, followed by several grenades intended to collapse the mine shaft. When the mine did not collapse, two of the children's bodies were set on fire, and the others were doused with acid and buried in a swamp. Even then, most of the acid soaked away into the ground – leaving the bones to be uncovered 73 years later.

In mid-1998 the royal remains were finally given a proper burial in the Romanov crypt at SS Peter & Paul Cathedral (p113), alongside their predecessors dating back to Peter the Great. A 19-gun salute bade them a final farewell. President Boris Yeltsin was present, together with many Romanov family members.

The Orthodox Church, however, never acknowledged that these were actually the Romanov remains, and church officials did not attend the burial. Instead, the church canonised the royal family in recognition of their martyrdom.

Despite the controversy, it seemed the story had finally come to an end (however unsatisfying for some). But in 2007 archaeologists in Yekaterinburg found the bodies of two more individuals – a male aged between 10 and 13 and a female aged 18 to 23. The location corresponds with the site described in the 1934 report; and the silver fillings in the teeth are similar to those in the other family members. Scientists are stating that it is 'highly likely' that these are the remains of the tsarevich Alexey and his sister Maria. The confirmation of their identities and the proper burial of the bones may at last provide closure to this 80-year-old tragedy.

bricks of Moscow. It was supposed to be temporary (Lenin personally preferred St Petersburg). But Russia was turning inward, and Peter's window to the West was closing.

Along with the loss of its capital political status, St Petersburg also lost its noble social status. The aristocratic soul gave up the proletarian body. The royal family had always set the standards for high society, but now the royals were on the run. No Romanov stepped forward to claim the once coveted throne. Nicholas II and his family meanwhile, were placed under house arrest in the Alexander Palace at Tsarskoe Selo (p219), before leaving on a one-way trip to Siberia. The breakdown of the old order made the old elite vulnerable. The tsar's favourite ballerina, Mathilda Kshesinskaya, pleaded in vain as her Style Moderne mansion was commandeered by the Bolsheviks as party headquarters (see p117). The more fortunate families fled with the few valuables they could carry; the less fortunate who stayed were harassed, dispossessed and disposed of eventually.

The revolution began in Petrograd and ended there, when in March 1921 Kronshtadt sailors staged a mutiny. These erstwhile Bolshevik boosters demanded the democracy they had been promised now that the civil war was won. But Lenin, who had since renamed his political party 'the Communists', was reluctant to relinquish political power. The sailors' revolt was brutally suppressed in a full-scale military assault across the frozen bay, confirming the historical adage that revolutions consume their young.

1921

Once strong supporters of the Bolshevik cause, sailors and soldiers at Kronshtadt rebel against the communists' increasingly dictatorial regime. The rebellion is brutally suppressed. It is the last revolt against Communist rule until the Soviet collapse.

1924

At the age of 53, Lenin dies without designating a successor. The city changes its name to Leningrad in his honour. Power is assumed by a 'triumvirate' but Stalin increasingly takes control.

1934

Leningrad party boss Sergei Kirov is murdered as he leaves his office at the Smolny Institute. The assassination kicks off the Great Purges, ushering in Stalin's reign of terror.

RED PITER

Soviet Second City

Moscow finally reclaimed its coveted ancient title with the caveat that it was now the world's first communist capital. Petrograd consoled itself as the Soviet second city.

In Russia, it has always been the case that status and wealth flow from political power. Thus, the redesignation of the capital prompted the departure of the bureaucracies: the government ministries, the military headquarters, the party apparatus, which took with them a host of loyal servants and servile lackeys. The population dropped by two-thirds from its prewar count. Economic exchange was reduced to begging and bartering. To make matters worse, the food shortages that first sparked the revolution during the war continued well after. Fuel was also in short supply, as homes went unheated, factory gates stayed shut and city services were stopped. Petrograd was left naked by the Neva.

The new regime needed a new identity. The old aristocratic labels would not do. The city underwent a name-changing mania – streets, squares and bridges were given more appropriate socialist sobriquets. Once known as Orlov Sq, the plaza fronting Smolny Institute was renamed after the Dictatorship of the Proletariat. Znamenskaya Sq, named after a nearby church, became Uprising Sq (pl Vosstaniya). The city itself was rechristened Leningrad in 1924, to honour the scourge of the old empire. The change ran much deeper: make no mistake, the old aristocratic world was gone. 'For centuries, our grandfathers and fathers have had to clean up their shit', railed Trotsky, 'now it is time they clean up ours.' Noble pedigree became a marker for discrimination and exploitation. Family mansions were expropriated; art treasures were seized; churches were closed.

SOVIETSKY ANEKDOT

A Soviet census-taker stops a man along Nevsky Pr:
Where were you born? St Petersburg.
Where did you go to school? Petrograd.
Where do you live now? Leningrad.
Where would you like to live? St Petersburg.

Leningrad was eventually revived with a proletarian transfusion. At the beginning of the 1930s the socialist state launched an intensive campaign of economic development, which reinvigorated the city's industrial sector. New scientific and military research institutes were fitted upon the city's strong higher-education foundations. On the eve of WWII, the population climbed to over three million. Public works projects for the people were undertaken – polished underground metro stations, colossal sports complexes and streamlined constructivist buildings muscled in next to the peeling pastels and cracked baroque of the misty past. Even the Bronze Horseman was seen around town in a commissar's cloak.

Who Murdered Sergei Kirov?

Though no longer the capital, Leningrad still figured prominently in Soviet politics. The Leningrad party machine, headquartered in the Smolny Institute (p83), was a plum post in the Communist Party. The First Secretary, head of the Leningrad organisation, was always accorded a seat on the Politburo, the executive board of Soviet power. In the early years Leningrad was a crucial battle front in the bloody intraparty competition to succeed Lenin.

Lenin died at the age of 53 from a stroke, without designating a successor. He was first replaced by a troika of veteran Old Bolsheviks, including Leningrad party head, Alexander Zinoviev. But

1940

Rapid industrialisation shows results: the population of the city has rebounded, reaching 3.1 million, and Leningrad is now responsible for 11% of Soviet industrial output.

1941

The Nazis invade the Soviet Union and Leningrad is surrounded, blocking residents from all sources of food and fuel, as the city comes under attack.

1942

On 9 August, the Leningrad Radio Orchestra performs the Seventh Symphony by Dmitry Shostakovich. Musicians are given special rations to ensure they can perform, and the music is broadcast throughout the city.

their stay on top was brief, outmanoeuvred by the most unlikely successor to Lenin's mantle, Josef Stalin, a crude disaffected bureaucrat of Georgian descent.

In 1926 Zinoviev was forced to relinquish his Leningrad seat to Sergei Kirov, a solid Stalin man. The transition reflected deeper changes in the Communist Party: Zinoviev was a haughty Jewish intellectual from the first generation of salon-frequenting socialist talkers, while Kirov was a humble Russian provincial from the second generation of socialist dirty-work doers. Stalin's rise to the top was testimony to his personal appeal to these second-generation Bolsheviks.

In high-profile Leningrad, Kirov soon became one of the most popular party bosses. He was a zealous supporter of Stalin's plans for rapid industrialisation, which meant heavy investment in the city. But the manic-paced economic campaign could not be sustained, causing famine and food shortages. Kirov emerged as a proponent of a more moderate course instead of the radical pace that Stalin still insisted on. The growing rift in the leadership was exposed at a 1934 Party congress, where a small cabal of regional governors secretly connived to remove Stalin in a bureaucratic coup and replace him with Kirov. It was an offer that Kirov flatly refused.

But it was hard to keep a secret from Stalin. Wary of Kirov's rising appeal, Stalin ordered that he be transferred to party work in Moscow, where he could be watched more closely. Kirov found reasons to delay the appointment. He remained in Leningrad – but not for long. On 1 December 1934 as he left a late-afternoon meeting, Kirov was shot from behind and killed, in the corridor outside his Smolny office.

Who murdered Sergei Kirov? The trigger was pulled by Leonid Nikolaev, also a party member – hence his access to the building – and reportedly a disgruntled devotee of the displaced Zinoviev. But circumstantial evidence pointed the finger at Stalin. Kirov's murder was the first act in a much larger drama. According to Stalin, it proved that the party was infiltrated by saboteurs and spies. The ensuing police campaign to uncover these hidden enemies became known as the Great Purges, which consumed nearly the entire postrevolutionary Soviet elite. Leningrad intellectuals were especially targeted. More than 50 Hermitage curators were imprisoned, including the Asian art specialist, accused of being an agent of Japanese imperialism, and the medieval armour specialist, accused of harbouring weapons. Successive waves of arrest, exile and execution effectively transformed the Leningrad elite, making it much younger, less assertive and more Soviet. When it was finally over, Stalin stood as personal dictator of unrivalled power – even by tsarist standards.

The Siege

On 22 June 1941 Leningraders were basking in the summer solstice when Foreign Minister Molotov interrupted state radio to announce an 'unprecedented betrayal in the history of civilized nations'. That day, German Nazi forces launched a full-scale military offensive across the Soviet Union's western borders. Stalin's refusal to believe that Hitler would break their nonaggression pact left Leningrad unprepared and vulnerable.

The German codename for its assault on Leningrad was Operation Nordlicht (Operation Northern Lights). Der Fuhrer ordered his generals to raze the city to the ground, rather than incur the cost of feeding and heating its residents in winter. By July German troops had reached the suburbs, inflicting a daily barrage of artillery bombardment and aerial attacks. All Leningraders were mobilised around the clock to dig trenches, erect barricades, board up buildings. The city's factories were dismantled brick by brick and shipped to the other side of the Urals. Hermitage staff crated up Catherine's collection for a safer interior location; what they did not

1944

The Germans retreat. Leningrad emerges from its darkest hour, but more than one million are dead from starvation and illness. The city's population has dropped to an estimated 600,000.

1956

After the death of Stalin, party leader Nikita Khrushchev makes a 'Secret Speech' denouncing Stalin, thus commencing a period of economic reform and cultural thaw.

1964

A coup against Khrushchev brings Leonid Brezhnev to power, ushering in the so-called 'Years of Stagnation'. Poet and future Nobel laureate Joseph Brodsky is labelled a 'social parasite' and sent into exile.

get out in time was buried on the grounds of the Summer Garden (see the boxed text, p130). The spires of the Admiralty and Peter & Paul Fortress were camouflaged in coloured netting, which was changed according to the weather and season. The youngest and oldest residents were evacuated; everybody else braced. The Bronze Horseman withdrew under a cover of sandbags.

At the end of August the Germans captured the east-bound railway: Leningrad was cut off. Instead of a bloody street fight, the Nazi command vowed to starve the city to death. Food stocks were low to begin with, but became almost nonexistent after napalm bombs burned down the warehouse district. Moscow dispatched tireless and resourceful Dmitry Pavlov to act as Chief of Food Supply. Pavlov's teams ransacked cellars, broke into box cars, and tore up floorboards in search of leftover cans and crumbs. The city's scientists were pressed to develop something edible out of yeast, glue and soap. As supplies dwindled, pets and pests disappeared. A strict ration system was imposed and violators were shot. Workers received 15 ounces (425g) of bread per day; everyone else got less. It was not enough. The hunger was relentless, causing delirium, disease and death. Hundreds of thousands succumbed to starvation, corpses were strewn atop snow-covered streets, mass graves were dug on the outskirts (see p121).

Relief finally arrived in January, when food supplies began to reach the city from across the frozen Lake Ladoga lifeline. Trucks made the perilous night-time trek on ice roads, fearing the *Luftwaffe* above and chilled water below. Soviet military advances enabled the supply route to stay open in the spring when the lake thawed. Leningrad survived the worst; still the siege continued. The city endured the enemy's pounding guns for two more years. At last, in January 1944, the Red Army arrived in force. They pulverised the German front with more rockets and shells than were used at Stalingrad. Within days, Leningrad was liberated.

Composer Dmitry Shostakovich premiered his Seventh Symphony for a small circle of friends in his Leningrad flat in 1941. His performance was interrupted by a night raid of German bombers. He stopped and sent his family into the basement, then played on in anguish and defiance as sirens sounded and fires flashed outside. In spring 1942 the symphony was performed in Moscow and broadcast by radio to Leningrad, to whom it was dedicated.

The 900 days marked history's longest military siege of a modern city. The city was badly battered – but not beaten. The Bronze Horseman arose from the rubble; the St Petersburg spirit was resilient.

THE RETURN OF PETER

From Dissent to Democracy

Throughout the Soviet period, Moscow kept suspicious eyes trained on Leningrad. After WWII, Stalin launched the 'Leningrad Affair', a sinister purge of the Hero City's youthful political and cultural elite, who were falsely accused of trying to create a rival capital. Several thousand were arrested, several hundred were executed. Kremlin commies were committed to forcing conformity onto the city's free-thinking intellectuals and keeping closed the window to the West. They ultimately failed.

Leningrad's culture club was irrepressible. Like in tsarist times, it teased, goaded, and defied its political masters. Stalin terrorised, Khrushchev cajoled and Brezhnev banished, yet the city still became a centre of dissent. As from Radishchev to Pushkin, so from Akhmatova to Brodsky. By the 1970s the city hosted a thriving independent underground of jazz and rock musicians, poets and painters, reformists and radicals. Like the Neva in spring, these cultural

1985

A little-known reformer named Mikhail Gorbachev defeats Leningrad boss Grigory Romanov and is elected General Secretary of the Communist Party. He institutes policies of perestroika (restructuring) and glasnost (openness).

1990

St Petersburg has recovered from the mid-century war and benefited from industrial and economic development. In the last decade of the 20th century, the city's population tops five million.

1991

On Christmas day, Mikhail Gorbachev announces the dissolution of the Soviet Union. His rival Boris Yeltsin becomes the first president of the newly independent Russian Federation.

currents overflowed when Mikhail Gorbachev finally came to power and declared a new policy of openness and honesty. The Leningrad democratic movement was unleashed.

Gorbachev forced long-time Leningrad party boss Grigory Romanov (no relation to the royals) and his communist cronies into retirement. He held elections for local office that brought to power the liberal-minded Anatoly Sobchak, the darling of the progressive intelligentsia and the first popularly elected mayor in the city's history. Leningrad was at the forefront of democratic change, as the old regime staggered toward the exit.

Where Gorbachev sought to breathe new life into Soviet socialism, his rival Boris Yeltsin was intent on killing it. Just two months after Sobchak's historic election, a last gasp of reactionary hardliners staged a coup. While Yeltsin mollified Moscow, a hundred thousand protestors filled Palace Sq in Leningrad. The ambivalent soldiers sent to arrest Sobchak disobeyed orders, and instead escorted him to the local TV station, where the mayor denounced the coup and encouraged residents to do the same. Anxiously waiting atop flimsy barricades, anticommunist demonstrators spent the evening in fear of approaching tanks. But the inebriated coup plotters lost their nerve, and as the fog lifted, only the Bronze Horseman appeared.

Local Cop Makes Good

When St Petersburg native Vladimir Putin was elected president in 2000, speculation was rife that he would transfer the Russian capital back to his home town. When Lenin relocated the capital to Moscow rather hastily in 1918, it was supposed to be a temporary move. Furthermore, the new millennium brought a new regime: what better way to make a significant break with the past? Most importantly, Putin's personal attachment to his home town was significant.

Born in 1952, Putin spent his childhood in the Smolny district. Little Vlad went to school in the neighbourhood and took a law degree at Leningrad State University, before working in Moscow and East Germany for the KGB. In 1990 he returned to his home town, where he was promptly promoted through the ranks of local politics. By 1994 he was deputy to St Petersburg mayor Anatoly Sobchak. In his office in the Smolny Institute, Putin famously replaced the portrait of Lenin with one of Peter the Great.

As the city economy slowly recovered from collapse and shock, Sobchak was voted out of office in 1996. Putin was then recruited by fellow Leningrader, Anatoly Chubais, to join him in the capital in the Kremlin administration. After another rapid rise through the ranks, he took over the FSB (the postcommunist KGB). In 1999, after Yeltsin sacked two prime ministers in quick succession, politically unknown Putin was offered the inauspicious post. On New Year's Eve, Yeltsin finally resigned and Putin was appointed acting president.

The rest is history. Since then he has won two presidential elections and enjoys immense popularity, despite his increasingly autocratic leanings. Putin will not go down in history as a liberal democrat, but will be seen as the leader that finally established a semblance of stability after more than a decade of political crisis. That, plus US$75 (€52) per barrel oil prices will get you 65% approval ratings. It looks like Putin and his police pals will be around for a few more years at least. Speculation has him serving as prime minister again or perhaps taking a different influential post after his presidential term expires in 2008.

Putin's fondness for his home town is undiminished. Unlike Peter I, he apparently did not care to expend the political capital required to move the political capital. However, he did extend a gesture to that effect by relocating the Constitutional Court from Moscow to the old Imperial

2000

Economic difficulty and political instability have caused a decline in the Russian population; the population of St Petersburg drops to 4,628,000. St Petersburg native Vladimir Putin is elected President of Russia.

2003

Despite accusations of power abuse and election manipulation, Putin's favoured candidate prevails in local elections. Winning 63% of the popular vote, Valentina Matvienko becomes the governor of St Petersburg.

2003

A year's worth of festivities are organised to commemorate the tercentenary of the founding of St Petersburg. Museums, theatres and palaces are refurbished and thousands of visitors descend on the city to celebrate.

Senate. Who needs a bunch of judges nearby scrutinising presidential decrees anyway? Putin also renovated the Konstantinovsky Palace in Strelna (p219) for his personal use as a presidential palace. Now he – in the best tradition of his tsarist forebears – can host his friends and foreign leaders in St Petersburg style.

Finding the Future in the Past

In 1991, by popular referendum, the citizens of Leningrad voted resoundingly to change their city's name once more. They chose to restore its original name, the name of its founder, St Petersburg.

As reviled as the communist regime may have been, it still provided a sufficient standard of living, a predictable day at the office and a common target for discontent. The familiar ways of life suddenly changed. The communist collapse caused enormous personal hardship; economic security and social status were put in doubt. Mafia gangs and bureaucratic fangs dug into the emerging market economy, creating contemptible crony capitalism. The democratic movement splintered into petty rivalries and political insignificance. One of its shining stars, Galina Starovoitova – social scientist turned human rights advocate – was brazenly shot dead in her apartment stairwell in 1998. Out on the street, meanwhile, prudish reserve gave wave to outlandish exhibitionism. Uncertainty and unfairness found expression in an angry and sometimes xenophobic reaction.

With the old order vanquished, the battle to define the new one was on. The symbols of the contending parties were on display throughout the city. The nouveaux riches quickly claimed Nevsky pr for their Milano designer get-ups and Bavarian driving machines. (In Russia cars still have the right of way over pedestrians – even on the sidewalk.) The disaffected youth used faded pink courtyard walls to spray-paint Zenith football insignias, swastikas and the two English words they all seem to know. Every major intersection was adorned with gigantic billboard faces of prima ballerinas and pop singers sipping their favourite cups of coffee. And, like all their St Petersburg predecessors, the new ruling elite wants to leave its own distinctive mark on the city: the proposed Gazprom skyscraper. Nothing says 'I own you' quite like a 300m tower of glass and steel (see the boxed text, p57).

Hazy may be the future, but St Petersburg has found a steadying source of unity in its past. Its legacy as Peter's grand imperial capital was never lost; it was just hidden under communist scaffolding. St Petersburg *is* a European city and it *is* Russia's window on the West. In 2003 residents finally felt sure enough about their future to embrace their past with a summer-long tercentennial celebration. Decades of proletarian indifference were scrubbed off the city's elegant Old World façade, restoring its dignified glow. Fireworks illuminated the city's famous golden spires, gleaming anew. A parade of tall sailing ships from around the world gracefully skimmed down the Neva, to the delight of the large crowds along the embankment. All had come to celebrate Russia's city by the sea, and pay homage to the Bronze Horseman, whose restless spirit still haunts its streets.

ARTS

It was Europe – France, Italy, Germany and the Netherlands – that inspired Peter to build this 'window to the West'. And much of the artistry that defines the city exhibits European influences. St Petersburg's most prominent architect was Bartolomeo Rastrelli, an Italian who engraved rococo ornamentation on every façade, including the Winter Palace. Today this baroque building, as part of the magnificent Hermitage, contains one of the world's finest collections of European art. Russian ballet grew out of the teachings of French and Italian masters.

Despite the evident European influences, the city's Russian roots are a more essential source of inspiration for its artistic genius. Musicians and writers have long looked to Russian history, folk culture and other nationalistic themes. One need only peruse the gravestones of the great artists at Tikhvin Cemetery to appreciate the uniquely Russian nature of their body of work.

That St Petersburg produced so many artistic, literary and musical masterpieces is in itself a source of wonder for the city's visitors and inhabitants today. Strolling from one art-filled room to another through the never-ending Winter Palace; grappling with Dostoevsky's existentialist questions while wandering around Sennaya pl; sitting in silent awe as a ballerina bends her body into impossible shapes…such are the sources of inspiration that St Petersburg holds in store for you.

LITERATURE

The love of literature is an integral part of Russian culture: most Ivans and Olgas will wax rhapsodic on the Russian classics without any hesitation. With the end of Soviet censorship, however, it seems that the literati are not sure what to do with their new-found freedom. Slowly but surely, new authors are emerging, exploring literary genres from historical fiction to science fiction.

Check out what the person next to you on the metro is reading: more than likely, it's a celebrity rag or a murder mystery. Action-packed thrillers and detective stories have become wildly popular in the 21st century, with Darya Dontsova, Alexandra Marinina and Boris Akunin ranking amongst the best-selling and most widely translated authors. Realist writers such as Tatyana Tolstaya and Ludmilla Petrushevskaya engage readers with their moving portraits of everyday people living their everyday lives. Meanwhile, social critics like Viktor Pelevin continue the Soviet literary tradition of using dark humour and fantastical storylines to provide scathing social commentary.

Surprisingly, however, St Petersburg is not a magnet for Russian writers in the 21st century (unlike artists and musicians). The contemporary literary scene is largely based in Moscow, and – to some degree – abroad, as émigré writers continue to be inspired and disheartened by their motherland.

top picks

LITERARY SIGHTS

- **Dostoevsky Museum** (p93)
- **Pushkin Flat-Museum** (p72)
- **Sennaya Pl** (p96)
- **Dostoevsky Houses** (p96)
- **Nabokov Museum** (p104)
- **Alexander Blok House-Museum** (p105)
- **Pushkin House** (p110)

Romanticism in the Golden Age

Among the many ways that Peter and Catherine the Great brought Westernisation and modernisation to Russia was the introduction of a modern alphabet. Prior to this time, written Russian was used almost exclusively in the Orthodox church, which employed an archaic and incomprehensible Church Slavonic. During the Petrine era, it became increasingly acceptable to use popular language in literature. This development paved the way for two centuries of Russian literary prolificacy, with St Petersburg at its centre.

Romanticism was a reaction against the strict social rules and scientific rationalisation of previous periods, exalting emotion and aesthetics. Nobody embraced Russian romanticism more than the national bard, Alexander Pushkin. Pushkin lived and died in St Petersburg. Most famously, his last address on the Moyka River is now a suitably hagiographic museum, its interior preserved exactly as it was at the moment of his death in 1837 (see p72). The duel that killed him is also remembered with a monument on the site (see p124).

Pushkin's epic poem *Yevgeny Onegin* (Eugene Onegin) is set – in part – in the imperial capital. He savagely ridicules its foppish aristocratic society, despite being a fairly consistent fixture of it himself for most of his adult life. The wonderful short story *The Queen of Spades* is set in the house of a countess on Nevsky pr and is the weird supernatural tale of a man who uncovers her Mephistophelean gambling trick. Published posthumously, *The Bronze Horseman* is named for the statue of Peter the Great that stands on pl Dekabristov (p101). The story takes place during the great flood of 1824. The main character is the lowly clerk Evgeny, who has lost his beloved in the flood. Representing the hopes of the common people, he takes on the empire-building spirit of Peter the Great, represented by the animation of the Bronze Horseman.

No other figure in world literature is more closely connected with St Petersburg than Fyodor Dostoevsky (1821–81). He was among the first writers to navigate the murky waters of the human subconscious, blending powerful prose with psychology, philosophy and spirituality. Born in Moscow, Dostoevsky moved to the imperial capital in 1838, aged 16, to begin his literary and journalistic career.

His career was halted – but ultimately shaped – by his casual involvement with a group of young free-thinkers called the Petrashevsky Circle. Nicholas I decided to make an example of some of these liberal thinkers, arresting them and sentencing them to death. After a few months in the Peter & Paul Fortress prison, Dostoevsky and his cohorts were assembled for execution. As the guns were aimed and ready to fire, the death sentence was suddenly called off – a joke! – and the group was committed instead to a sentence of hard labour in Siberia. After Dostoevsky was pardoned by Alexander II and returned to St Petersburg, he wrote *Notes from the House of the Dead* (1861), a vivid recounting of his prison sojourn.

The ultimate St Petersburg novel and literary classic is *Crime and Punishment* (1866). It is a tale of redemption, but also acknowledges the 'other side' of the regal capital: the gritty, dirty city that spawned unsavoury characters and unabashed poverty.

In his later works, *The Idiot, The Possessed* and *The Brothers Karamazov,* Dostoevsky was explicit in his criticism of the revolutionary movement as being morally bankrupt. A true believer, he asserted that only by following Christ's ideal could humanity be saved. An incorrigible Russophile, Dostoevsky eventually turned against St Petersburg and its European tendencies. His final home near Vladimirskaya pl now houses the Dostoevsky Museum (p93) and he is buried at Tikhvin Cemetery (p90).

Amidst the epic novels of Pushkin, Tolstoy and Dostoevsky, an absurdist short-story writer like Nikolai Gogol (1809–52) sometimes gets lost in the annals of Russian literature. But his troubled genius created some of Russian literature's most memorable characters, including Akaki Akakievich, tragicomic hero of *The Overcoat,* and the brilliant Major Kovalyev, who chases his errant nose around St Petersburg in *The Nose*. Gogol came to St Petersburg from his native Ukraine in 1829, and wrote and lived here for a decade before spending his final years abroad. He was not impressed by the legendary capital: in a letter to his mother he described it as a place where 'people seem more dead than alive' and complained endlessly about the air pressure, which he believed caused illness. He was nevertheless inspired to write a number of absurdist stories, collectively known as *The Petersburg Tales,* which are generally recognised as the zenith of his creativity.

Symbolism in the Silver Age

The late 19th century saw the rise of the symbolist movement, which emphasised individualism and creativity, purporting that artistic endeavours were exempt from the rules that bound other parts of society. The outstanding figures of this time were the novelists Vladimir Solovyov (1853–1900), Andrei Bely (1880–1934) and Alexander Blok (1880–1921) as well as the poets Sergei Yesenin, Lev Gumilev and Anna Akhmatova. The Stray Dog Café (p181), an underground bar on pl Iskusstv (Arts Sq), was a popular meeting place where Symbolist writers, musicians and artists exchanged ideas and shared their work.

Blok and Bely, who both lived in St Petersburg, were the most renowned writers of the Symbolist movement. While Bely was well known and respected for his essays and philosophical discourses, it is his mysterious novel *Petersburg* for which he is remembered. Its language is both literary and musical: it seems the author was paying as much attention to the sound of his words as to their meaning. The plot, however difficult to follow, revolves around a revolutionary who is hounded by the Bronze Horseman (the same statue that harasses Pushkin's character).

Blok took over where Dostoevsky left off, writing of prostitutes, drunks and other characters marginalised by society. Blok sympathised with the revolutions and he was praised by the Bolsheviks. His novel *The Twelve,* published in 1918, is pretty much a love letter to Lenin. However, he later became disenchanted with the revolution and consequently fell out of favour; he died a sad, lonely poet. In one of his last letters, he wrote, 'She did devour me, lousy, snuffling dear Mother Russia, like a sow devouring her piglet'. The flat where he spent the last eight years of his life is now a museum (see p105).

Revolutionary Literature

The immediate aftermath of 1917 saw a creative upswing in Russia. Inspired by social change, writers carried over these principles into their work, pushing revolutionary ideas and groundbreaking styles.

The trend was temporary, of course. The Bolsheviks were no connoisseurs of culture; and the new leadership did not appreciate literature unless it directly supported the goals of communism. Some writers managed to write within the system, penning some excellent poetry and plays in the 1920s; however, most found little inspiration in the prevailing climate of art

ST PETERSBURG LITERATURE

- *Anna Karenina* (Leo Tolstoy) Represents the pinnacle of Russian literature. Set partially in St Petersburg, Tolstoy's tragedy of a woman who violates the rigid sexual code of her time offers an alternative for readers who don't have time for *War and Peace.*
- *The Bronze Horseman* (Alexander Pushkin) Pushkin's poetic epic sees the sculpture of Peter the Great coming to life after a ruinous flood that all but wipes out the city.
- *Buddha's Little Finger* (Victor Pelevin) The story of a St Petersburg poet who fluctuates between two nightmares. Just when he gets comfortable in the schizophrenic ward of a hospital in the 1990s, he wakes up in the midst of the Russian civil war. This darkly comic author won the 1993 Russian Book Prize for his short stories.
- *The Cat and the Cook* (Ivan Krylov) Russia's favourite fabulist, who is buried in Tikhvin Cemetery, has been translated into English – to the delight of children and adults alike. Although Krylov wrote in verse, the translation is prose, accompanied by whimsical folkloric illustrations.
- *Crime and Punishment* (Fyodor Dostoevsky) Dostoevsky's quintessential St Petersburg novel: a poor, tortured student takes control of his destiny by killing a nasty old moneylender. If only it were all that simple…
- *The Idiot* (Fyodor Dostoevsky) If you can't get enough of Dostoevsky, why not tackle this tome, which takes place both in St Petersburg and in nearby Pavlovsk. The descriptions are not quite as evocative as those in *Crime and Punishment,* but the characters are equally complex and the debates no less esoteric.
- *Incidences* (Daniil Kharms) Kharms died in a Leningrad prison in the 1940s, long before his secret musings saw the light of day. Yet these absurdist vignettes are political only in the grim hopelessness of the society they depict.
- *The Madonnas of Leningrad* (Debra Dean) Tells of an old Russian émigré who, as she loses her mind to Alzheimer's, is swept back to her days working at the Hermitage during the Siege, when she was sustained by her love of the art that no longer hung on the walls.
- *The Master of Petersburg* (JM Coetzee) Coetzee imagines Dostoevsky's return to St Petersburg to investigate the death of his stepson. It is a powerfully written tale of grief, paying homage to Dostoevsky.
- *Nevsky Prospekt* (Nikolai Gogol) A superb evocation of the city's vast main avenue and the amusing characters that haunt it. This short story will entice any first-time readers to discover Gogol's other *St Petersburg Tales*.
- *Petersburg* (Andrei Bely) Bely's modernist novel is often compared to Joyce's *Ulysses.* At once baffling and thrilling, it weaves together snippets of personal stories, capturing the mysticism of the Symbolist movement and the strife of 1905 St Petersburg.
- *Poem Without a Hero* (Anna Akhmatova) This epic poem describes St Petersburg with both realism and monumentalism, somehow capturing the contradictory relationship Akhmatova had with her home town.
- *Pushkin House* (Andrei Bitov) This highly lauded novel revolves around the titular literary institute on Vasilevsky Island (see p110) and is crammed with references to the Russian writers who are remembered there. Eccentric characters, nonlinear plotlines and imagined dialogue add up to an insightful commentary on Soviet life.
- *Speak, Memory* (Vladimir Nabokov) As the title implies, the celebrated novelist Vladimir Nabokov lets his memory speak in this memoir of his childhood in St Petersburg. His characteristically evocative prose makes for a tale that is more impressionistic than factual, but nonetheless fascinating.
- *The Twelve* (Alexander Blok) Blok's long poem describes 12 Bolshevik soldiers marching through the streets of revolutionary Petrograd in the midst of a blizzard. Critics did not respond well to the obvious comparison between the soldiers and the 12 Apostles who followed Christ.
- *We* (Yevgeny Zamyatin) Although Zamyatin moved to Petrograd to join the Bolsheviks, his 'counter-revolutionary' writings were mostly banned by the Soviets. In the best Orwellian tradition, this dystopian novel is part fantastic science fiction, part scathing political critique.
- *We the Living* (Ayn Rand) While Rand always generates mixed reviews, this novel – based in part on her own youth in Leningrad – is unlike her other work. Three young dreamers struggle to establish their identities in postrevolutionary Russia; there are no happy endings.

'serving the people'. Stalin announced that writers were 'engineers of the human soul' and as such had a responsibility to write in a partisan direction.

The clampdown on diverse literary styles culminated in the late 1930s with the creation of socialist realism, a literary form created to promote the needs of the state, praise industrialisation and demonise social misfits. While Stalin's propaganda machine was churning out novels with titles such as *How the Steel Was Tempered* and *Cement,* St Petersburg's literary community was secretly writing about life under a tyranny. The long-established tradition of underground writing flourished.

Literature of Dissent

Throughout the 20th century, many talented writers were faced with silence, exile or death, as a result of the imposing standards of the Soviet system. Many accounts of Soviet life were *samizdat* publications, secretly circulated among the literary community. The Soviet Union's most celebrated writers – the likes of Boris Pasternak, Mikhail Bulgakov and Andrei Bitov – were silenced in their own country, while their works received international acclaim.

No literary figure is as inextricably linked to the fate of St Petersburg-Petrograd-Leningrad as Anna Akhmatova (1889–1966), the long-suffering poet whose work contains bittersweet depictions of the city she loved. Akhmatova's family was imprisoned and killed; her friends exiled, tortured and arrested; her colleagues constantly hounded – but she refused to leave her beloved city and died there in 1966. Her former residence in the Fountain House now contains the Anna Akhmatova Museum (p87).

In 1946 Akhmatova's work was denounced by Communist Party officials as 'the poetry of a crazed lady, chasing back and forth between boudoir and chapel'. As a reward for her cooperation in the war effort, Akhmatova was allowed to publish again after WWII. Nonetheless, she was cautious, and she worked in secret on masterpieces such as *Requiem*. Through all this, her love for her city was unconditional and unblinking. As she wrote in *Poem Without a Hero:* 'The capital on the Neva; Having forgotten its greatness; Like a drunken whore; Did not know who was taking her'.

When Nikita Khrushchev came to power in 1953, he relaxed the most oppressive restrictions on artists and writers. As this so-called 'thaw' slowly set in, a group of young poets known as 'Akhmatova's Orphans' started to meet at her apartment to read and discuss their work. The star of the group was the fiercely talented Joseph Brodsky. Brodsky seemed to have no fear of the consequences of writing his mind. In 1964 he was tried for 'social parasitism' and exiled to the north of Russia. His sentence was shortened after concerted international protests led by French philosopher Jean-Paul Sartre. He returned to Leningrad in 1965, only to immediately resume his thorn-in-the-side activities.

During Brodksy's absence, Khrushchev had been overthrown and replaced by a more conservative Brezhnev. It was Brezhnev who came up with the plan to silence troublemaker writers by sending them into foreign exile. Brodsky was put on a plane to Germany in 1972.

The postglasnost era of the 1980s and 1990s uncovered a huge library of work that had been suppressed during the Soviet period. Authors such as Yevgeny Zamyatin, Daniil Kharms, Anatoly Rybakov, Venedict Erofeev and Andrei Bitov – banned in the Soviet Union – are now recognised for their cutting-edge commentary and significant contributions to world literature.

BALLET

First introduced in the 17th century, ballet in Russia evolved as an offshoot of French dance combined with Russian folk and peasant dance techniques. In 1738, French dance master Jean Baptiste Lande established the Imperial Ballet School in St Petersburg – a precursor to the famed Vaganova School of Choreography (see p75).

The French dancer and choreographer Marius Petipa (1819–1910) is considered to be the father of Russian ballet, acting as principal dancer and Premier Ballet Master of the Imperial Theatres and Imperial Ballet. All told, he produced more than 60 full ballets, including the classics *Sleeping Beauty* and *Swan Lake*.

In 1907, Petipa wrote in his diary, 'I can state that I created a ballet company of which everyone said: St Petersburg has the greatest ballet in all Europe'. At the turn of the 20th century, the heyday of Russian ballet, St Petersburg's Imperial School of Ballet rose to world prominence, producing superstar after superstar. Names such as Vaslav Nijinsky, Anna Pavlova, Mathilda Kshesinskaya, George Balanchine, Michel Fokine and Olga Spessivtzeva turned the Mariinsky Theatre (p188) into the world's most dynamic display of the art of dance.

Sergei Diaghilev graduated from the St Petersburg Conservatory, but he abandoned his dream of becoming a composer when his professor, Nikolai Rimsky-Korsakov, told him he had no talent for music. Instead he turned his attention to dance, and his Ballets Russes took Europe by storm. The Petipa-inspired choreography was daring and dynamic, and the stage décor was painted by artists such as Alexander Benois, Mikhail Larionov, Natalya Goncharova and Leon Bakst. The overall effect was an artistic, awe-inducing display unlike anything that was taking place elsewhere in Europe.

A TALE OF TWO BALLERINAS

In the West, most people associate Russian ballet with the male stars whose well-documented flights from the Soviet Union made them household names: Nureyev, Nijinsky, Baryshnikov. But to Petersburgers, the magic of the dance is tied to two women – Anna Pavlova and Mathilda Kshesinskaya.

Pavlova, born just outside St Petersburg in 1881, first danced at the Mariinsky in 1899. Within a decade she and Nijinsky were dancing together in some of the most exciting productions the world had seen, mainly choreographed by Michel Fokine. In 1909, when the Ballets Russes in Paris produced Fokine's *Les Sylphides* (*Chopiana* in Russia), audiences were rapturous. Pavlova's light-as-air grace was an instant sensation. In 1912 she emigrated to form her own ballet company in the West. Her ambassadorial skills (representing ballet, that is) remain unmatched. She is largely credited for taking ballet to the US. Her most remembered role is in Fokine's *The Dying Swan,* written especially for her. Anna Pavlova died in 1931, while touring the Netherlands. She caught pneumonia after her train derailed and she went out in the cold to see what happened. Apparently, just before she died she asked to hold her costume and hear the music from *The Dying Swan*.

Mathilda Kshesinskaya, born in 1872 near Peterhof, graduated from the Imperial School of Ballet and instantly became its star. She was the first Russian dancer to master 32 consecutive *fouettés en tournant* (spins done in place on one leg), then considered the ultimate achievement in ballet. She was also the subject of curiosity and admiration for her private life, as she was the lover of Nicholas II before he became tsar. She hosted glamorous balls in her mansion that were attended by the elite of St Petersburg society. She emigrated to France in 1920, where she lived and taught ballet until she died in 1971. She is revered as a heroine of her times – for her outspokenness, her professional mastery and for the debonair way she controlled her own affairs. Her old mansion now houses the Museum of Political History (p117), but there's a wonderful exhibition about the ballerina inside.

Under the Soviets, ballet was treated as a natural resource. It enjoyed highly privileged status, which allowed schools like the Vaganova and companies like the Kirov to maintain a level of lavish production and no-expense-spared star-searches. Still, the story of 20th-century Russian ballet is connected with the West, to where so many of its brightest stars emigrated or defected. Anna Pavlova, Vaslav Nijinsky, Rudolf Nureyev, Mikhail Baryshnikov, George Balanchine, Natalya Makarova, Mathilda Kshesinskaya, to name a few, all found fame in Western Europe or America.

The Kirov, whose home is the Mariinsky Theatre (p188; the company is sometimes referred to as the Mariinsky Opera and Ballet), has been rejuvenated under the fervent directorship of Valery Gergiev. The Mariinsky's calling card has always been its flawless classical ballet, but in recent years, names like William Forsythe and John Neumeier have brought modern choreography to this establishment. The Mariinsky's credibility on the world stage is set to soar further in 2008 on completion of its controversial new theatre being built adjacent to the old one on the Kryukov Canal (see p56).

MUSIC

St Petersburg has a rich musical legacy, dating back to the days when the Group of Five and Peter Tchaikovsky composed here. Opera and classical music continue to draw crowds, and the Mariinsky and the Philharmonia regularly sell out their performances of home-grown classics. (Surprisingly, earlier music – such as baroque and medieval music – is not as well known or as well loved. But the directors of the Early Music Festival are out to change that – see the boxed text, p190).

Music-lovers come in all shapes and sizes, however. Even when rock-and-roll was illegal, it was being played in basements and garages. Now, 20 years after the weight of censorship has been lifted, St Petersburg is the centre of *russky rok,* a magnet for musicians and music-lovers, who are drawn to its atmosphere of innovation and creation.

Classical Music & Opera

As the cultural heart of Russia, St Petersburg was a natural draw for generations of composers, its rich cultural life acting as inspiration for talent from throughout Russia. Mikhail Glinka is often considered the father of Russian classical music. In 1836 he premiered *A Life for the Tsar* in St Petersburg. While European musical influences were evident, the story was based on

Russian history, recounting the dramatic tale of a peasant, Ivan Susanin, who sacrificed himself to save Mikhail Romanov.

In the second half of the 19th century, several influential schools – based in the capital – formed, from which emerged some of Russia's most famous composers and finest music. The so-called Group of Five – Modest Mussorgsky, Nikolai Rimsky-Korsakov, Alexander Borodin, César Cui and Mily Balakirev – looked to folk music for uniquely Russian themes. They tried to develop a distinct sound using unusual tonal and harmonic devices. Their main opponent was Anton Rubinstein's conservatively rooted Russian Musical Society, which became the St Petersburg Conservatory in 1861. The competition between the two schools was fierce. Rimsky-Korsakov wrote in his memoirs: 'Rubinstein had a reputation as a pianist, but was thought to have neither talent nor taste as a composer.'

Pyotr Tchaikovsky (1840–93) seemed to find the middle ground, embracing Russian folklore and music as well as the disciplines of the Western European composers. In 1890 Tchaikovsky's *Queen of Spades* premiered at the Mariinsky. His adaptation of the famous Pushkin tale surprised and invigorated the artistic community, especially as his deviations from the original text – infusing it with more cynicism and a brooding sense of doom – tied the piece to contemporary St Petersburg.

Tchaikovsky is widely regarded as the doyen of Russian national composers and his output, including the magnificent *1812 Overture,* his concertos and symphonies, the ballets *Swan Lake, Sleeping Beauty* and *The Nutcracker,* and his opera *Yevgeny Onegin* are among the world's most popular classical works. They are certainly the shows that are staged most often at the Mariinsky and other theatres around St Petersburg (see p188).

Following in Tchaikovsky's romantic footsteps was the innovative Igor Stravinsky (1882–1971). He fled Russia after the revolution, but his memoirs credit his childhood in St Petersburg as having a major effect on his music. *The Rite of Spring* (which created a furore at its first performance in Paris), *Petrouchka* and *The Firebird* were all influenced by Russian folk music. The official Soviet line was that Stravinsky was a 'political and ideological renegade'; but he was rehabilitated after he visited the USSR and was formally received by Khrushchev himself.

Similarly, the ideological beliefs and experimental style of Dmitry Shostakovich (1906–75) led to him being alternately praised and condemned by the Soviet government. As a student at the Petrograd conservatory, Shostakovich failed his exams in Marxist methodology, but still managed to write his First Symphony before he graduated in 1926. He wrote brooding, bizarrely dissonant works, as well as accessible traditional classical music. After official condemnation by Stalin, his Seventh Symphony (Leningrad Symphony) brought him honour and international standing when it was performed during WWII. The authorities changed their mind again and banned his anti-Soviet music in 1948, then 'rehabilitated' him after Stalin's death. These days he is held in high esteem as the namesake of the acclaimed Shostakovich Philharmonic Hall (p189), where the local symphony orchestra regularly performs.

top picks

ST PETERSBURG ALBUMS

- **Pictures at an Exhibition** Modest Mussorgsky
- **Seventh Symphony (Leningrad Symphony)** Dmitry Shostakovich
- **Ubiytsy sredi nas** Dva Samolyota (Two Airplanes)
- **Kollektsioner Oruzhiya or Granatoviy Album** Splean
- **Udelyvaem Ameriku** Nachalo Leningrad

Since 1988 Valery Gergiev has revitalised the Kirov Opera company, which continues to perform at the Mariinsky Theatre (p188). The Russian classics still top the list of performances (thanks, in part, to the demands of the tourists). But Gergiev is also willing to be a little adventurous, taking on operas that had not been performed in half a century or more. In 2003 he undertook an ambitious production of Shostakovich's opera *The Nose* (based on Gogol's surreal story, see p40).

Gergiev is also responsible for initiating the Stars of White Nights Festival (p18), an annual event which showcases the best and brightest dancers and musicians.

See p188 and p189 for details of St Petersburg venues for opera and classical music.

ST PETE'S LOCAL BEATS

Yury Vosskresensky is a photographer, journalist and co-owner of City Bar, one of St Petersburg's favourite expat bars (see p179). Yury books bands to play at City Bar on Friday and Saturday nights, so he stays on top of the local music scene, too. We spoke with Yury about contemporary music in St Pete.

St Petersburg is widely considered Russia's best music city – meaning the best place to hear great music, the best place to be a musician. Is this true?
It's definitely true. All of the classic Russky Rock groups are from Petersburg: Grebenshchikov (*Akvarium*), Kino, Televizor, NOM, Sekret. The city's favourite home-town band is Dva Samolyota. These guys have moved on to other projects, but they still play together once a year at Griboedov (p184).

Those are old-timers. What about new up-and-coming groups?
It's not only the old guys. Petersburg's legacy continues with younger groups like Splean. Billy's Band plays music that you won't hear anywhere else – romantic, jazzy, Tom Waits–type stuff. Of course, you can't talk about music in Petersburg without mentioning Shnurov (see the boxed text, opposite)...

Where is the best place in the city to hear great music?
It depends on the kind of music. JFC Jazz Club (p185) has talented, interesting musicians playing just about every single night.

For punk, there is usually something going at Fish Fabrique (p184) or Orlandina (p184). Tunnel Club (p183) is a very specialised place with a beautiful interior and the best techno music. It attracts a strange clientele but it is perfect for those people who like that kind of thing. For artsy, indie rock music, Red Club (p185) and Griboedov (p184) are great choices.

What is new in the St Petersburg club scene?
Maina (p184) is a brand new club, *[less than six months old at the time of research]*, which is trying something totally unique. It is located on the outskirts of town in a residential area – a so-called 'bedroom district'. There is nothing going on out there, but *everybody* lives there. Maina is an upscale place with a cool, industrial interior. It provides a high level of service and brings in great musicians – real stars. It is catering to the class of people that appreciates quality – beautiful surroundings, excellent entertainment – but providing it in a completely new, unusual location. For now, this place is very popular, but it will be interesting to see how Maina succeeds.

Another very interesting new concert space is called the Place (p185), near Baltiysky vokzal. Right now, this part of the city seems like it is out of the way, but it is developing very quickly and soon it will have its own cultural life.

What makes St Petersburg such an exciting music town?
Petersburg is a synthetic city. It has a bad climate; it has always been plagued by floods. We have a saying in Russia that a mad town attracts mad people. Mad people are often creative people.

Rock

Russian music is not all about classical composers. Ever since the 'bourgeois' Beatles filtered through in the 1960s, Russians both young and old have supported the rock revolution. Starved of decent equipment and the chance to record or perform to big audiences, Russian rock groups initially developed underground. By the 1970s – the Soviet hippy era – the music had developed a huge following among the disaffected, distrustful youth.

Although bands initially imitated their Western counterparts, a home-grown sound was emerging in Leningrad in the 1980s. Boris Grebenshchikov and his band Akvarium (Aquarium) caused sensations wherever they performed; his folk rock and introspective lyrics became the emotional cry of a generation. Yury Shevchuk and his band DDT emerged as the country's main rock band. The god of Russian rock was Viktor Tsoy and his group Kino. His early death in a 1990 car crash ensured his legend a long life. On the anniversary of Tsoy's death (15 August), fans still gather to play his tunes and remember the musician, especially at his grave at Bogoslovskogo Cemetery.

Many contemporary favourites in St Petersburg have been playing together since the early days. The most prominent (and perhaps most popular) local fixture is Dva Samolyota (Two Airplanes), a ska band exhibiting influences of Latin-jazz, reggae and afro-beat. These days the

MY NAME IS SHNUR

Leningrad, the punk ska band from St Petersburg, was banned from the radio and forbidden from performing in Moscow. But such controversy only fuelled its popularity. Lead singer Sergei Shnurov claims 'Our songs are just about the good sides of life – vodka and girls that is.'

But besides being rowdy and bawdy, the lyricist is known for his ironic insights on contemporary culture. 'Money' satirises society's pervasive consumerism, while 'WWW' is a commentary on the alienation caused by modern technology. Most famously, 'Menya Zovut Shnur' ('My Name is Shnur') and its accompanying animated video are a harsh critique of authority.

Nowadays, Leningrad is widely played on Russian radio, thanks in part to filler noise that covers up the most vulgar lyrics. The brassy 14-piece ensemble has toured Europe and America, and was featured on the soundtrack to the 2005 film *Everything is Illuminated*. But that doesn't mean the spunky, punky band is going mainstream. Leningrad continues to act in ways that are unexpected, uncouth and outrageous; and the fans wouldn't have it any other way.

group plays together only occasionally, but its members are still fixtures on the local scene, as drummer Sasha Sindalovsky is the owner of the town's top music club, Griboedov (p184), and bassist Anton Belyankin owns Datscha and Fidel (p182).

St Petersburg is responsible for producing several groups that are now world renowned. Ranking among Russia's most widely respected and admired musicians of the 21st century is Splean (not 'Spleen', as a sort of tribute to the Fab Four). These rockers' wide-ranging styles and straightforward, almost poetic lyrics have earned them fans around the world, but they got their start right here in St Pete. Bad behaviour, biting lyrics and punky ska sound combine to make Leningrad another enduring favourite (see the boxed text, above).

Perhaps metal rockers Amatory have always had the stuff of legends. Certainly fans of their rough guitar and growling vocals thought so. But when Gang, their lead guitarist, died from liver cancer in 2007, it sealed their place in St Petersburg rock history (if leaving the group's future in question).

Switch on Russian MTV and you'll see local versions of boy bands and disco divas all doing their sometimes desultory, sometimes foot-tapping stuff. Meanwhile, St Petersburg clubs (see p183) are filled with garage bands, new wave, punk, hard rock and more than a few Beatles cover bands.

VISUAL ARTS

It should come as no surprise that St Petersburg is an artistic place. The city was designed by artists, so it is certainly picturesque. In the early years, aristocrats and emperors filled their palaces with endless collections of paintings and applied arts, guaranteeing a steady stream of artistic production. These days, hundreds of thousands of visitors come here to see the masterpieces that hang in the Hermitage and in the Russian Museum.

But St Petersburg's artistic tradition is not only historical. The city's winding waterways, crumbling castles and colourful characters continue to inspire creative types. Artists assail passers-by as they stroll down Nevsky pr, inviting them to sit for a portrait or peruse their cityscapes. Smaller streets are lined with galleries displaying pretty pictures of gold-domed churches or grittier depictions of darker places (see p150). The souvenir market (p153) is filled with watercolours; nightclubs double as art galleries (see Art-Vokzal, p183, or Manhattan, p184). St Petersburg has always been a city of artists and poets, and that legacy endures.

Academy of Arts

Known both as the Imperial Academy of Arts and the St Petersburg Academy of Arts, this official state-run artistic institution was founded in 1757 by Count Ivan Shuvalov, a political advisor, education minister and longtime lover of Empress Elizabeth. It was Catherine the Great who moved the Academy out of Shuvalov's home, commissioning the present neoclassical building on Vasilevsky Island (see p110).

The Academy was responsible for the education and training of young artists. It focused heavily on French-influenced academic art, which incorporated neoclassicism and romanticism. Painters like Fyodor Alexeyev and Grigory Chernetsev came out of the Academy of Arts.

Peredvizhniki

In the 19th century, artist Ivan Kramskoy led the so-called 'revolt of 14' whereby a group of upstart artists broke away from the powerful but conservative Academy of Arts. The mutineers considered that art should be a force for national awareness and social change, and they depicted common people and real problems in their paintings. The Peredvizhniki (Wanderers), as they called themselves, travelled around the country in an attempt to widen their audience (thus inspiring their moniker).

The Peredvizhniki included Vasily Surikov, who painted vivid Russian historical scenes, and Nikolai Ghe, who favoured both historical and biblical landscapes. Perhaps the best loved of all Russian artists, Ilya Repin has works that range from social criticism *(Barge Haulers on the Volga)* to history *(Cossacks Writing a Letter to the Turkish Sultan)* to portraits.

Many Peredvizhniki masterpieces are on display at the Russian Museum (p76), as well as the Brodsky House-Museum (p74).

By the end of the 19th century, Russian culture was retreating from Western influences and looking instead to nationalistic themes and folk culture for inspiration. Artists at this time invented the *matryoshka,* the quintessential Russian nesting doll. One of the world's largest collections of *matryoshkas* is on display at the Toy Museum (p118).

Mikhail Vrubel was inspired by Byzantine mosaics and Russian fairytales. Painters like Nikolai Roerikh and Mikhail Nesterov incorporated mystical themes, influenced by Russian folklore and religious traditions. All of these masters are prominently featured at the Russian Museum.

top picks

CONTEMPORARY ART

- Russian Museum – Benois Wing (p77)
- Pushkinskaya 10 (p91)
- Museum of Anna Akhmatova (p87)
- Manege Central Exhibition Hall (p104)
- Marble Palace (p72)
- New Exhibition Hall (p91)

Avant-Garde

From about 1905 Russian art became a maelstrom of groups, styles and 'isms', as it absorbed decades of European change in a few years. It finally gave birth to its own avant-garde futurist movements.

Mikhail Larionov and Natalya Goncharova were the centre of a Cézanne-influenced group known as the Knave of Diamonds. This husband-wife team went on to develop neoprimitivism, based on popular arts and primitive icons. They worked closely with Sergei Diaghilev, the founder of Ballets Russes, designing costumes and sets for the ballet company that brought together some of the era's greatest dancers, composers and artists (see p43).

The most radical members of the Knave of Diamonds formed a group known as Donkey's Tail, which exhibited the influences of cubism and futurism. Larionov and Goncharova were key members of this group, as well as Marc Chagall and Kazmir Malevich.

In 1915 Malevich announced the arrival of Suprematism. His utterly abstract geometrical shapes (with the black square representing the ultimate 'zero form') finally freed art from having to depict the material world and made it a doorway to higher realities. See one of his four *Black Square* paintings – and other examples of Russian avant-garde – at the Hermitage (p143).

Works by all of these artists are on display at the Russian Museum, as well as the Brodsky House-Museum.

Soviet Art

Futurists turned to the needs of the revolution – education, posters, banners – with enthusiasm. They had a chance to act on their theories of how art shapes society. But at the end of the 1920s abstract art fell out of favour. The Communist Party wanted socialist realism. Images abounded of striving workers, heroic soldiers and inspiring leaders, some of which are on display at the Russian Museum. Two million sculptures of Lenin and Stalin dotted the country; Malevich ended up painting portraits and doing designs for Red Square parades.

After Stalin, an avant-garde 'Conceptualist' underground group was allowed to form. Ilya Kabakov painted or sometimes just arranged the debris of everyday life to show the gap between the promises and realities of Soviet existence. Erik Bulatov's 'Sotsart' pointed to the devaluation of language by ironically reproducing Soviet slogans or depicting words disappearing over the horizon. In 1962 artists set up a show of 'unofficial' art in Moscow: Khrushchev called it 'dogshit' and sent it back underground.

Neo-Academism & Non-Conformist Art

As the centre of the avant-garde movement in Russia at the turn of the last century, St Petersburg never gave up its ties to barrier-breaking, gut-wrenching, head-scratching art. And since the end of communism the city has rediscovered its seething artistic underbelly.

Much of St Petersburg's contemporary art scene revolves around Pushkinskaya 10, a centre where artists and musicians continue to congregate and create (see p91). This place was 'founded'

PAINTING PUSHKINSKAYA

Evgeny Tykotsky is an artist who has been living at Pushkinskaya 10 (p91) since its 'founding' in the late 1980s. His whimsical paintings have hung in the Russian Museum, the Anna Akhmatova Museum in the Fountain House and the Museum of Non-Conformist Art. We talked to Evgeny about the history of Pushkinskaya 10 .

Tell me how you came to live here.

In the late 1980s, these apartment blocks stood empty. No one lived here. The lifts were falling down; old grumpy cats ate the rubbish in the yard; there was no water or electricity. The houses were empty! One day, some artists, musicians and bandits wandered past and noticed that no one lived there and decided to move in. That was 1989. They moved in and took over. That was the squat.

I meant to move in there with the rest. But first I went to borrow some money from my grandmother. Then I found myself a bottle of port wine *[Do not confuse this with port! It's another beastie altogether.]* and after that I couldn't move very well. Someone carried me into a spare room to sleep for a while. When I woke up, I saw my friends – well, they weren't friends yet, but they are friends anyway... They were all asleep with the sleep of the dead (possibly from port wine). So I found some Living Water and sprinkled them with it. They all woke up and started to paint...

This house was first filled with dilettantes, and professionals, and amateurs...but mostly it was filled with poets. It was filled with children of the Moon!

It all sounds very magical. How does that time – the late 1980s – compare with Pushkinskaya 10 today?

Well, how can you compare your youth and your first love with adulthood? You are now an adult, you are no longer 17 years old, you have had many loves... You like some, you don't like others, and if you don't like this one, well, never mind, he is gone now anyway. But your first love you remember your entire life. And that's how you might compare this period with what used to be.

That was a wild period. It was love and life; we drank wine and vodka; we painted, we fell in love...

There was no light or water in the house. Bellonka – my neighbour above me – she had water and I had electricity. So in the evening I would borrow some water, then make supper on my little electric stove and invite her to sup with me... We would spend the evenings talking about family, about art, about all sorts of things. That's how our paintings were born. There were many marvellous times then.

Now we are a 'Society of Artists'. There is something official about it all. It's like any living being: it's born like some dandelion under the asphalt; then it grows and breaks through the asphalt. That's the first real life, that little growth! Then it grows up and it's a dandelion, and it loses its flower and fades...like us, we are all fading.

What do you have to say to artists today – young people who don't have the Living Water and the cats and the port wine to inspire them?

People – I say this to any person, not just an artist: love and be loved. That's all, you don't need anything else. The rest will come. If someone stops loving you, you will be horribly upset, suffer and think and all that. And from that tragedy will be born a painting, music, poetry. And if you are loved, that will also give birth to art and poetry that is not coloured by tragedy. That's all. What else can I possibly wish them?

But of course, if those young ones need something, let them come, let them visit me personally! We will sit and talk! Perhaps they will understand something of this life then!

in the late 1980s, when a bunch of artists, musicians and other plagues on society moved into an abandoned building near Pl Vosstaniya (see the boxed text, p49, for an insider's account of this history). The centre has since developed into an artistic and cultural institution that is unique in Russia, if not the world.

In the early 1990s Timur Novikov founded the neo-academic movement as an antidote to 'the barbarism of modernism'. This return to classicism (albeit with a street-level, junkshop feel) culminated in his foundation of the Museum of the New Academy of Fine Arts, which is housed at Pushkinskaya 10. Although he died in 2002, he continues to cast a long shadow on the city's artistic scene.

Over the years, the hodgepodge of artists, exhibits and studio space at Pushkinskaya 10 has grown. The centre is now officially known as the Free Culture Society, although it's still often referred to by its original address. In 1998 the Free Culture Society opened the Museum of Non-Conformist Art, with its own collection of 'unofficial' art from the 20th and 21st centuries. Most importantly, the various museums and galleries at Pushkinskaya 10 showcase the ever-growing oeuvre of its member artists, including not only paintings but also photographs, sculptures, collages, videos, set and graphic designs, and music.

CINEMA

The Lenfilm studio on the Petrograd Side was a centre of the Soviet film industry, producing many much-loved Russian comedies and dramas – most famously, Sergei Eisenstein's *October* (1928). Lenfilm has continued in the postcommunist era to work with some success as a commercial film studio. However, the removal of Soviet-era state funding for film-making has inevitably led to torpor in the local industry.

There are, of course, exceptions. Ever since the *Russian Ark* (2002), St Petersburg native Alexander Sokurov has been recognised as one of Russia's most talented contemporary directors. The world's first unedited feature film, the *Russian Ark* was shot in one unbroken 90-minute frame. Sokurov's films have tackled a wide range of subjects and he is in the midst of a tetralogy of films about world leaders, including Hitler *(Molokh)*, Lenin *(Taurus)* and Japanese Emperor Hirohito *(The Sun)*. Sokurov's most recent triumph was *Alexandra,* the moving tale of an elderly woman who visits her grandson at an army base in Grozny. The title role is played by Galina Vishnevskaya, opera doyenne and wife of composer/conductor Mstislav Rostropovich.

A rising star in St Petersburg's film industry is Alexey German, who gained attention with his 1998 film *Khrustalyov! My Car!* Based on a story by Joseph Brodsky (see p43), the film tells the tale of a well-loved military doctor who was arrested during Stalin's 'Doctor's Plot'. In more recent years, this prolific director has put out *Garpastum,* set in prerevolutionary Petrograd, and *Hard to be a God,* an adaptation of the popular science-fiction book.

Other Lenfilm successes include Alexey Balabanov's *Of Freaks and Men,* the joint project of Boris Frumin and Yury Lebedev *Undercover,* and Andrei Kravchuk's *The Italian,* all of which enjoyed some critical acclaim in the West.

St Petersburg hosts the Festival of Festivals (p18), an annual noncompetitive film event in June. Partly sponsored by Lenfilm, the festival is no doubt an attempt to draw film-makers to this fair city, as well as to draw attention to its films. A smaller but more innovative event is Message to Man (p18), a festival featuring documentary, short and animated film. For a list of local cinemas, see p192.

THEATRE

While it may not be completely accessible to most travellers due to language barriers, theatre plays a major role in St Petersburg performing arts. At least a dozen drama and comedy theatres dot the city streets, not to mention puppet theatres and musical theatres (see p190 for a list of venues). As in all areas of the performing arts, contemporary playwrights do not receive as much attention as well-known greats and adaptations of famous literature. Nonetheless, drama has a long history in Russia and St Petersburg, as the cultural capital, has always been at the forefront.

In the early days, theatre was an almost exclusive vehicle of the Orthodox Church, used to spread its message and convert believers. In the 19th century, however, vaudeville found its

ST PETERSBURG ON THE SCREEN

- *Brother* (*Brat;* Alexey Balabanov; 1997) This gangster drama portrays the harshness of post-Soviet Russia, as a geeky kid – played by superstar Sergei Brodov – returns from his army service and joins his brother working as a hit man in St Petersburg. It has become a cult movie for the postperestroika generation.
- *End of St Petersburg* (*Konets Sankt-Peterburga;* Vsevolod Pudovkin; 1927) Produced to commemorate the 10th anniversary of the October Revolution, this silent film was a landmark for Soviet realist cinema.
- *Errors of Youth* (*Oshibki Yunosti;* Boris Frumin; 1978) After dishonesty in the army, boredom in the countryside and failure in love, the superfluous Soviet man Dmitry Gurianov ends up as a black marketeer in Leningrad. A brave attempt at realism, the film was, of course, banned.
- *Garpastum* (Alexey German; 2005) The Russian *Field of Dreams.* Two brothers – passionate football fans – hatch a scheme to buy their own playing field. Unfortunately, a little thing called WWI interferes.
- *Golden Eye* (1995) The James Bond film features Pierce Brosnan as 007 driving along the Moyka river in a tank. Many scenes were shot – at least partially – at Lenfilm and in St Petersburg.
- *Irony of Fate* (*Ironiya Sudby;* Eldar Ryazanov; 1975) This national favourite is screened every New Year's Eve. After a mind-bending party in Moscow, the protagonist wakes up in Leningrad, unbeknownst to him. Lo and behold, his key fits into the lock of an identical building at the same address in a different town. Comedy ensues.
- *The Italian* (*Italienets;* Andrei Kravchuk; 2007) An orphan decides to give up on being adopted by an Italian couple to run away in search of his birth parents. The film does not skimp on gory details about the tough life of a runaway, but in the end it's a feel-good movie.
- *October* (*Oktyabr;* Sergei Eisenstein; 1928) Eisenstein's brilliant depiction of the Russian Revolution. The lighting needs of the production left the entire city without electricity during the shoot. The most famous scene – the storming of the Winter Palace – remains an almost unmatched piece of cinematography.
- *Of Freaks and Men* (*Pro Urodov i Lyudey;* Alexey Balabanov; 1998) A change of gear for Balabanov, this dark art-house film portrays the lives of pornographers in prerevolutionary Petrograd. Shot in sepia tones using the style of early Russian cinema, it has some astounding scenes.
- *Russian Ark* (*Russky Kovcheg;* Alexander Sokurov; 2002) Filmed in one single 96-minute tracking shot, Sokurov's masterpiece is an eccentric film that muses on the history and destiny of Russia through the metaphor of a stroll through the Hermitage.
- *Undercover* (*Ne Legal;* Boris Frumin & Yury Lebedev; 2005) A post-Soviet version of a Cold War thriller. A Soviet spy, who has long been working in Helsinki, must return to Leningrad as an undercover agent. The film was lauded for its comedic perspective and its minimal anti-Soviet sentiment.

way to Russia. More often than not, these biting, satirical one-act comedies poked fun at the rich and powerful. Playwrights like Alexander Pushkin and Mikhail Lermontov decried the use of their art as a tool of propaganda or evangelism. Other writers – Nikolai Gogol, Alexander Griboyedov and Alexander Ostrovsky – took it a step further, writing plays that attacked not just the aristocracy but the bourgeoisie as well. Anton Chekhov wrote for St Petersburg newspapers before writing one-act, vaudevillian works. Yet it is his full-length plays that are his legacy.

Towards the end of the 19th century Maxim Gorky represented an exception to this trend in anti-establishment theatre. His play *The Song of the Stormy Petrel* raised workers to a level superior to that of the intellectual. This production was the first of what would be many socialist realist performances, thus earning its author the esteem of the Soviet authorities.

The futurists had their day on the stage, mainly in the productions of the energetic and tirelessly inventive director Vsevolod Meyerhold, who was one of the most influential figures of modern theatre. His productions of Alexander Blok's *The Fair Show Booth* (1906) and Vladimir Mayakovsky's *Mystery-Bouffe* (1918) caused sensations at the time. Both Anna Akhmatova and Dmitry Shostakovich cited Meyerhold's 1935 production of *Queen of Spades* by Tchaikovsky as one of the era's most influential works.

During the Soviet period, drama was used primarily as a propaganda tool. When foreign plays were performed, it was for a reason – hence the popularity in Russia of *Death of a Salesman,* which showed the inevitable result of Western greed and decadence. However, just after the revolution, theatre artists were given great, if short-lived, freedom to experiment – anything to make theatre accessible to the masses. Avant-garde productions flourished for a while, notably under the mastery of poet and director Igor Terentyev. Artists such as Pavel Filonov and Malevich participated in production and stage design.

Even socialist theatre was strikingly experimental: the Theatre of Worker Youth, under the guidance of Mikhail Sokolovsky, used only amateur actors and encouraged improvisation, sudden plot alterations and interaction with audience members, striving to redefine the theatre-going experience. Free theatre tickets were given out at factories; halls that once echoed with the jangle of their upper-class audience's jewellery were now filled with sailors and workers. The tradition of sending army regiments and schoolchildren to the theatre continues to this day. See p190 for more information on theatres in St Petersburg.

ARCHITECTURE

Peter's intention was to build a city that rivalled Paris and Rome for architectural splendour. He envisioned grand avenues, weaving waterways and magnificent palaces. While he did not live to see this dream become a reality, he made a pretty good start. And his successors – especially Empresses Anna, Elizabeth and Catherine – carried out their own even more elaborate versions of their forebear's plan. Today, central St Petersburg is a veritable museum of 18th- and 19th-century architecture, with enough baroque, classical and empire-style extravagances to keep you ogling indefinitely.

PETRINE BAROQUE

The first major building in the city was the Peter & Paul Fortress (p113), completed in 1704 and still intact today. Peter recruited Domenico Trezzini from Switzerland to oversee early projects. It was Trezzini more than any other architect who created the style known as Petrine Baroque – heavily influenced by Dutch architecture, of which Peter was enamoured (like everything else from Holland). Trezzini's buildings included the Alexander Nevsky Monastery (p90), the SS Peter & Paul Cathedral (p113) within the fortress and Twelve Colleges (p110) on Vasilevsky Island.

Initially, most funding was diverted to the war against Sweden, meaning there simply wasn't enough money to create the European-style city that Peter dreamed of. Once Russia's victory was secured in 1709, the city began to see feverish development. In 1711 the Grand Perspective, later Nevsky Prospekt, was initially built as a road to transport building supplies from Russia's interior. Nevsky pr was supposed to be a perfectly straight avenue heading to Novgorod. The existing kink (at pl Vosstaniya) is attributed to a miscalculation by builders.

Stone construction was banned outside the new capital, in order to ensure that there would be a sufficient number of masons free to work on the city. Peter ordered Trezzini to create a unified city plan designed around Vasilevsky Island. He also recruited Frenchman Jean Baptiste Alexander LeBlond from Paris. The two architects focused their efforts on Vasilevsky Island, even though most people preferred to live across the river on the higher ground of Admiralty Island. The pink Menshikov Palace (p110) was the finest in the city, far grander than Peter's Winter Palace (p67).

THE AGE OF RASTRELLI

Empress Anna oversaw the completion of many of Peter's unfinished projects, including Kunstkamera (p107) and Twelve Colleges (p110). Most significantly, she hired Italian Bartolomeo Rastrelli as chief architect, a decision that more than any other has influenced the city's look today. His major projects under Anna's reign were the Manege Central Exhibition Hall (p104) and the Third Summer Palace, which has since been destroyed. Rastrelli's greatest work, however, was yet to come.

Anna left her mark on the face of St Petersburg in many ways. She ordered all nobles to pave the street in front of their properties, thus ensuring the reinforcement of the Neva Embankment and other major thoroughfares. A massive fire in 1737 wiped out the unsightly and run-down wooden housing that surrounded the Winter Palace, thus freeing the historic centre for the centralised city planning that would be implemented under Empress Elizabeth.

Elizabethan St Petersburg was almost entirely the work of Rastrelli, whose Russian baroque style became synonymous with the city. His crowning glory, of course, was the construction and remodelling of the Winter Palace (p66), which he completed in 1762, shortly after Elizabeth's death.

Rastrelli's second major landmark was Anichkov Palace (p76) on the Fontanka. After that creation, he became the city's most fashionable architect; commissions soon followed to build Stroganov Palace (p73), Vorontsov Palace (p75), Kamennoostrovsky Palace (p120), Catherine Palace at Tsarskoe Selo (p220) and the extension of LeBlond's Grand Palace at Peterhof (p217). The sumptuous Smolny Cathedral (p83) is another Rastrelli landmark. His original design included a massive bell tower that would have been the tallest structure in Russia. The death of Empress Elizabeth in 1761 prevented him from completing it.

Rastrelli's baroque style would go out of fashion quickly after Elizabeth's death. But his legacy would endure, as he created some of the most stunning façades in the city, thus contributing to the Italianate appearance of contemporary St Petersburg.

CATHERINE'S RETURN TO CLASSICISM

Despite her fondness for Elizabeth, Catherine the Great was not a fan of her predecessor's increasingly elaborate and sumptuous displays of wealth and power. Catherine's major philosophical interest was the Enlightenment, which had brought the neoclassical style to the fore in Western Europe. As a result, she began her long reign by departing from baroque architecture and introducing neoclassicism to Russia.

The first major neoclassical masterpiece in Catherine's St Petersburg was the Academy of Arts (p110) on Vasilevsky Island, designed by Jean-Baptiste-Michel Vallin de la Mothe. Catherine employed a wide range of architects, including foreigners such as Vallin de la Mothe, Scot Charles Cameron and Italians Antonio Rinaldi and Giacomo Quarenghi; she also commissioned many home-grown architects such as Ivan Starov and Vasily Bazhenov.

Catherine's plan was to make the palace embankment the centrepiece of the city. To this end, she commissioned the Little Hermitage by Vallin de la Mothe, followed by the Old Hermitage and the Hermitage Theatre (p188) on the other side of the Winter Canal. These buildings on Dvortsovaya pl (p66) were followed by Quarenghi's magnificent Marble Palace (p72). Catherine also developed the embankment west of the Winter Palace, now the English Embankment (Angliyskaya nab), creating a marvellous imperial vista for those arriving in the city by boat.

The single most meaningful addition was the Bronze Horseman (p101) by Etienne-Maurice Falconet, an equestrian statue dedicated to Peter the Great. It is perched atop an enormous 1500-tonne boulder from the Gulf of Finland, known as Thunder Stone, which is supposedly the largest stone ever moved by man. Falconet worked on the statue for a staggering 22 years and returned to Paris an angry, frustrated man. He never even saw the completed version of this most enduring of St Petersburg's monuments.

Other notable additions to the cityscape during Catherine's reign included the new Gostiny Dvor (Merchant Yard; p75), one of the world's oldest surviving shopping centres. Elizabeth had commissioned Rastrelli to rebuild an arcade that had burned down in 1736; but Catherine removed Rastrelli from the project and had it completed by Vallin de la Mothe, who created a more subtle and understated neoclassical façade. The purest classical construction in St Petersburg was perhaps Vasily Stasov's Tauride Palace (p85), built for Prince Potemkin and surrounded by William Gould's expansive English gardens.

RUSSIAN EMPIRE STYLE

Alexander I (r 1801–25) ushered in the new century with much hope that he would see through Catherine's reforms, becoming the most progressive tsar yet. His most enduring architectural legacy would be the new Alexandrian Empire style, a Russian counterpart to the style that had become popular in prewar Napoleonic France. This style was pioneered by a new generation of architects, most famously Carlo Rossi.

Before the Napoleonic Wars, the two most significant additions to the cityscape were the Strelka, the 'tongue of land' at the tip of Vasilevsky Island, and Kazan Cathedral, prominently placed on Nevsky pr by Andrei Voronikhin. The Strelka (p107) had long been the subject of designs and proposals as a centrepiece to St Petersburg. Thomas de Thomon finally rebuilt Quarenghi's Stock Exchange and added the much-loved Rostral Columns to the tip of the island. The end result created a stunning sight during summer festivities when the columns lit the sky with fire, a tradition that still continues today. The Kazan Cathedral (p73) is a fascinating anomaly in St

Petersburg's architectural history. It had been commissioned by Paul and reflected his tastes and desire to fuse Catholicism and Orthodoxy. As such it is strikingly un-Russian, borrowing many of its features from contemporaneous Italian architecture from Rome and Florence.

Following the Napoleonic wars, Carlo Rossi initiated several projects of true genius. This Italian architect defined the historic heart of St Petersburg with his imperial buildings – arguably even more than Rastrelli. On Palace Sq, he created the sumptuous General Staff Building (p66), which managed to complement Rastrelli's Winter Palace without outshining it. The building's vast length – punctuated by white columns – and the magnificent triumphal arch make Palace Sq one of the most awe-inspiring urban environments in the world. The final touch to Palace Sq was added by Auguste Montferrand, who designed the Alexander Column (p66), a monument to the 1812 trouncing of Napoleon. On the pedestal of the Alexander Column, a bas-relief depicts winged figures holding up a plaque which reads, 'To Alexander I from a grateful Russia'. Rossi also completed Mikhailovsky Palace (now the Russian Museum; p76) as well as the Gardens behind it and Mikhailovskaya Sq (now Arts Sq, p74) in front of it.

Rossi's genius continued to shine through the reactionary rule of Nicholas I. In fact, Nicholas was the last of the Romanovs to initiate mass municipal architecture; and so Rossi remained in favour, despite Nicholas' personal preference for Slavic-revival style that was very popular in Moscow.

Rossi's largest projects under Nicholas were the redesign of Senate Sq (now pl Dekabristov; p101) and Alexandrinskaya Sq (now pl Ostrovskogo; p75), including the Alexandrinsky Theatre (p190) and Theatre St (now ul Zodchego Rossi). The Theatre St ensemble is a masterpiece of proportions: its width (22m) is the same height as its buildings, and the entire street is exactly ten times the size (220m).

IMPERIAL ST PETERSBURG

Although Rossi continued to transform the city, the building that would redefine the city's skyline was St Isaac's Cathedral (p100). An Orthodox church built in a classical style, it is the fourth largest cathedral in Europe. Montferrand's unique masterpiece took over three decades to construct and remains the highest building in St Petersburg. Nicholas I denied Montferrand his dying wish to be buried inside St Isaac's Cathedral, as he considered it too high an honour for an artisan.

Nicholas' reign saw the construction of St Petersburg's first permanent bridge across the Neva (Annunciation Bridge, now Lieutenant Schmidt Bridge) and Russia's first railroad (linking the capital to Tsarskoe Selo). A more useful line to Moscow began service in 1851, and Nikolaevsky Station (now known as Moscow Station; Moskovsky vokzal) was built to accommodate it.

Other projects completed during Nicholas' reign had a military theme: Stasov's Trinity Cathedral (p98) was built for the barracks of the Izmailovsky Regiment; the Narva Gates (p147) was another monument to the 1812 defeat of Napoleon; and the Moscow Gates (p146) commemorated victory against the Ottoman Empire in 1828. One final masterpiece of the era was Shtakenschneider's fantasy on the Fontanka, the Beloselsky-Belozersky Palace (p94).

The reigns of Alexander II and III saw few changes to the overall building style in St Petersburg. Industrialisation under Alexander II meant filling in several canals, most significantly the Ligovsky Canal (now Ligovsky pr). A plan to fill in Griboedov Canal proved too expensive to execute and the canal remains one of the city's most charming.

The main contribution of Alexander III was the Church of the Resurrection of Christ, better known as the Church of the Saviour on Spilled Blood (p72), built on the site of his father's 1881 assassination. Alexander III insisted the church be in the Slavic revival style, which explains its uncanny similarity to St Basil's Cathedral on Red Sq in Moscow. Architects Malyshev and Parland designed its spectacular multicoloured tiling, the first hints of the Russian Style Moderne that would take the city by storm by the end of the 19th century. Painters such as Mikhail Nesterov and Mikhail Vrubel contributed to the interior design.

That the ineffective and conservative Nicholas II presided over one of the city's most exciting architectural periods was pure chance. As the city became richer and richer during the 19th century, the industrialist and merchant classes began building mansions in the fêted Art Nouveau style, known in Russia as Style Moderne. The Petrograd side was the most fashionable of the era, so that is where the majority of Style Moderne buildings were constructed. The back streets reveal many gems from the late 19th century and early 20th century, including the fabulous mansion of the ballet dancer Mathilda Kshesinskaya, which now houses the Museum of Political History (p117).

SOVIET LENINGRAD

As in all other spheres, the collapse of the tsarist regime in 1917 led to huge changes in architecture. In the beleaguered city, all major building projects stopped; the palaces of the aristocracy and the mansions of the nouveaux riches were turned over to the state or split up into communal apartments. As the Germans approached Petrograd in 1918, the title of capital returned to Moscow; the city went into a decline that was to last until the 1990s.

The architectural form that found favour under the Bolsheviks in the 1920s was constructivism. Combining utilitarianism and utopianism, this modern style sought to advance the socialist cause, using technological innovation and slick unembellished design. Pl Stachek is rich with such buildings, such as the Kirov Region Administrative Building on Kirovskaya pl and the incredibly odd Communication Workers' Palace of Culture on the Moyka Canal.

Stalin considered the opulence of the imperial centre of renamed Leningrad to be a potentially corrupting influence on the people. So, from 1927, he initiated a plan to relocate the centre to the south of the city's historic heart. His traditional neoclassical tastes prevailed. The prime example of Stalinist architecture is the vast House of Soviets (p145), which was meant to be the centrepiece of the new city centre. Noi Trotsky began this magnificent monstrosity in 1936, although it was not finished until after the war (by which time Trotsky had himself been purged). With its columns and bas-reliefs, it is a great example of Stalinist neoclassical design – similar in many ways to the imperial neoclassicism pioneered a century beforehand. The House of Soviets was never used as the Leningrad government building, as the plan was shelved after Stalin's death in 1953.

WWII and Stalin's old age saved many buildings of great importance: the Church of the Saviour on Spilled Blood, for example, was slated for destruction before the German invasion of the Soviet Union intervened. Many other churches and historical buildings, however, were destroyed.

During the eras of Khrushchev and Brezhnev, St Petersburg's imperial heritage was cautiously respected, as the communist leadership took a step back from Stalin's excesses. Between the 1950s and 1970s, a housing shortage led to the construction of high-rise Soviet apartment buildings, which would cover huge swathes of the city outside the historic centre. For many visitors, this is their first and last view of the city. Examples of archetypal post-Stalinist Soviet architecture include the massive Grand Concert Hall (p189) near pl Vosstaniya and the nondescript Finland Station (p122) on the Vyborg Side.

top picks

QUIRKY ARCHITECTURE

- **Chesme Church** (p146) Many consider this gothic masterpiece to be St Petersburg's single most impressive church. Despite its small size, its magnificent colour scheme and sense of movement are striking.
- **Church of St John the Baptist** (p87) Byzantine meets Muscovite revival. The wonderful façade of this unique church is completely atypical of its time and place.
- **Tower House** (p116) One of the many Style Moderne masterpieces on the Petrograd Side, Tower House rises majestically over Kamennoostrovsky pr with its balconies and unusual crenulations borrowed from English medieval castles.
- **Vitebsk Station** (p239) Built in 1904, Russia's oldest train station is graced with a gorgeous Style Moderne interior.
- **House of Soviets** (p145) The best representative of high Stalinism in the city, this magnificent monstrosity on Moskovsky pr is right out of *1984*. Don't miss the fantastic frieze depicting the working people's struggle.
- **Morskoy vokzal** (p235) Overlooking the Baltic, the quintessentially constructivist sea terminal is worth the trip out to the tip of Vasilevsky Island.

CONTEMPORARY ST PETERSBURG

Contemporary building efforts have been focused on the reconstruction of imperial-era buildings, many of which were derelict and literally falling down due to 70 years of neglect. Some success stories include the renovation of the Grand Hotel Europe (p205), Mikhailovsky Castle (p74) and Gostiny Dvor (p75), as well as most of the palaces and cathedrals around town. The renovation of Pochtamtskaya ul – including the main post office and the new Popov Communications Museum (p104) – is a stunning example of introducing new technology and design without altering the historic façade.

As so much energy has gone into preservation efforts in the historic centre, a modern St Petersburg architecture has not emerged. That said, some cutting-edge (and controversial) architectural projects are under way: see below.

ENVIRONMENT & PLANNING

Among its many nicknames, St Petersburg is the 'Northern Capital', the 'City of 101 Islands' and the 'City of 300 Bridges'. All are apt monikers for this northerly city, which today sits on 42 islands at the mouth of the Neva River, connected by some 340 bridges.

The low-lying, marshy environment means that St Petersburg is vulnerable to flooding. Plaques around the city mark the water levels from past floods, the most famous of which was the great flood of 1824, which killed some hundreds of people and inspired Pushkin's brooding masterpiece *The Bronze Horseman*. This marshy wetlands necessitated the many canals that now weave their way around the city.

GREEN ST PETERSBURG

The most significant environmental problem in St Petersburg is the pollution of the Neva River and the Baltic Sea, mainly from industrial sources. Air pollution is also a concern, especially due to the increase in automobile traffic and uncontrolled emissions by vehicles, but it is mitigated to some extent by the winds off the sea.

In 1998 experts estimated that some 40% of residential sewage was dumped – untreated – into the Neva and/or the Gulf of Finland. As many as 500 companies dumped industrial waste into the river system.

Greenpeace has operated an office in Russia since 1992. However, like most nonprofit organisations, it is subject to incessant police harassment and endures constant problems with its registration status. In 2007 Greenpeace commenced its Clean Neva campaign to monitor and publicise the pollution levels in the river and its tributaries. The initial results were shocking, showing that discharge far exceeded the allowable concentrations of oil products and other dangerous chemicals. (Follow the progress of the campaign at www.saveneva.ru.)

Environmentalists have become concerned about industrial projects all around the Gulf of Finland that threaten the coastline. The Leningrad Nuclear Power Station (LAES) at Sosnovy Bor, 80km west of St Petersburg, is one of the oldest Chernobyl-type reactors in the world. It has been the site of past leakages and at least one major accident in 1975. Activists claim that the plant is dangerous and should be shut down before another disaster occurs, citing the particular risk for workers who do not have the benefit of proper safety regulations. Meanwhile, LAES has commenced plans to construct a new treatment centre for nuclear waste on site.

In more positive developments, after some pressure from local activists, the city has taken steps to implement programmes for separate waste collection and recycling, including the purchase of necessary containers. Local housing authorities have promised that the necessary legislation would be passed to bring the system of waste collection to EU standards as early as 2007. However, it's not clear how useful such recycling bins and collection systems are, as the city lacks the waste-processing facilities to treat the refuse.

URBAN PLANNING & DEVELOPMENT

St Petersburg has had more than its fair share of urban planners. Starting with Peter the Great, every regime change was accompanied by a change in vision for the city and every new ruler sought some way to leave their mark on it. The current post-Soviet regime is no exception (although the parties leaving their mark are as much corporate as governmental).

The cityscape of St Petersburg is so architecturally rich that any movement for change or modernisation raises concern. There is a sense that the 'historic heart', at least, should remain 'historic'. As such, new construction generates some degree of controversy. Critics argue that even the Soviets didn't have the nerve to alter the imperial centre beyond the bare minimum.

GAZPROM CITY

No urban development project raises as many concerns as the notorious Gazprom City. At the suggestion of public relations consultants, no doubt, Russia's largest oil company changed the name of its project to Okhta Centre, named after a tributary of the Neva.

The name may have changed, but the beast has not. The Okhta Centre is supposed to be the city's first super-tall skyscraper, towering almost 400m over the Neva (that's three time higher than the spire of the SS Peter & Paul Cathedral). The only other structure that even comes close to that height is the 310m TV tower, which is well removed from the historic heart. The Okhta Centre is planned to occupy the site of an abandoned factory on the Vyborg Side, just opposite Smolny Cathedral (p83). The €1.6-billion bill will be shared evenly by Gazprom and St Petersburg city.

The design, product of another British firm RMJM, is for a rocketlike glass-and-steel structure that has been called the 'corn cob' and 'Gaz-zilla'. There is a small contingent of supporters that cites the project's economic benefits and architectural innovation, but most residents are against this intrusion on the historic city skyline. Even Unesco has raised objections, indicating that continuing with construction could lead to the inclusion of St Petersburg on its 'World Heritage in Danger' list.

In September 2007 – on the anniversary of the first day of the Siege of Leningrad – protesters took to the streets. Political opposition leaders teamed up with architecture buffs and historians, recruiting as many as 5000 residents to participate in the March of the Preservation of St Petersburg. 'Gazprom, go home!' residents chanted; however, it's not clear if anyone was listening.

The new Mariinsky II, under construction behind the present theatre on Teatralnaya pl at the time of research, is one example of a project that has generated some controversy (see p101). This remarkable building will totally break with St Petersburg's architectural tradition, and in doing so inevitably enrage many more traditional residents. Dominique Perrault's unique design is a black marble theatre wrapped in a vast irregular golden glass dome, the so-called 'golden envelope'. Without doubt the first major architectural addition to the city in the 21st century, Mariinsky II is due to open in 2009.

Another project is underway just around the corner at New Holland (Novaya Gollandiya; p105). Financed by a Moscow billionaire, the 18th-century island neighbourhood will be converted into a 21st-century urban space, combining retail, cultural and residential buildings. It is expected to be completed in 2010. The London architecture firm that won the bid, Foster & Partners, is responsible for the famous 'gherkin' in London and the new complex on the site of the old Rossiya Hotel in Moscow. The architects promise to restore the old timber warehouses and to maintain the low-rise norm of the neighbourhood; but sceptics are still suspicious. The most controversial construction project is undoubtedly the much maligned Okhta Centre (see Gazprom City, above).

GOVERNMENT & POLITICS

St Petersburg is extreme – not only geographically but also politically and ideologically. St Pete's radical ideas have more than once been at the forefront of political change in Russia. Most famously, this is where the revolutions occurred in 1905 and 1917. Years later, St Petersburg would play a leading role in the democratic movement, spawning reformers like Galina Starovoitova and Anatoly Chubais, as well as the less-than-democratic future president, Vladimir Putin.

In June 1991 Leningrad residents voted to restore the city's original name. When a group of hardline communists tried to overthrow the reformist Mikhail Gorbachev, hundreds of thousands of St Petersburg residents took to the streets in protest, filling Dvortsovaya pl in front of the Winter Palace. Mayor Anatoly Sobchak appeared on local TV to denounce the coup, encouraging others to do the same.

The city's enthusiasm for democracy did not ultimately spread to the rest of Russia. The economic collapse and political chaos of the 1990s resulted in a backlash against liberal reformers. Sobchak's rueful comment was that 'We have not achieved a democracy, but rather a police state over the past 10 years'.

One of Putin's first acts as president was to divide Russia into seven 'super-regions'. The city of St Petersburg makes up one part of the Northwest Region of Russia, which includes the autonomous republics of Karelia and Komi, much of Western Arctic Russia and the enclave of Kaliningrad. That means there are three separate strata of power: the local governor, the regional presidential envoy and the national government. As of 2005, both the local governor and the regional presidential envoy are proposed by the president and approved by the legislative assembly (not popularly elected).

The local governor works in tandem with the St Petersburg legislative assembly to run the city. The main seat of power in the city is the governor's office at Smolny Institute (p83), currently occupied by Valentina Matvienko, a Putin loyalist and former presidential envoy to the Northwest Region.

Matvienko's tenure in Smolny has been marked by economic growth and unprecedented development, which explains why the population is generally complacent. Throughout Russia, citizens are enjoying stability and prosperity, elements that have been absent for a quarter of a century or more. It's easy to understand how they can overlook the occasional diversion from the democratic path.

Although Matvienko enjoys broad support, she has come under fire for her support of Gazprom City (see the boxed text, p57), as well as for her close alliance with Putin. She certainly has not strayed far from the president's side. Matvienko publicly urged Putin to stay on for a third presidential term (in 2008), even though the constitutional limit is two. In 2006 – one year before her term would expire – she was reappointed for another term and approved by the legislature.

St Petersburg was one of several cities around Russia that hosted Dissenters' Marches in the lead-up to the 2008 presidential election. The protest rallies were organised by the Other Russia, a broad umbrella-group of opposition leaders, including former chess champion Gary Kasparov. On each occasion, thousands of people marched down Nevsky pr, calling for Matvienko's dismissal as well as for electoral and judicial reforms at a federal level. Local media hardly covered the Dissenters' March, while Governor Matvienko called the protesters 'youth of extremist persuasion'.

The first of such events was held almost exactly one year before the scheduled presidential election on 3 March 2008. Follow-up rallies took place in April, June and September, the latter targeting the construction of Gazprom City. As many as 5000 residents marched to protest the administration's acquiescence to big business (see p57).

Nobody can deny the apolitical attitude that is prevalent not only in St Petersburg but throughout Russia. While the Rose and Orange Revolutions have taken place just next door in Georgia and Ukraine, Russians stand quietly by and watch President Putin censor their press and handpick his successor. But nobody is indifferent to the fate of the stunning St Petersburg skyline: if anything can act as a political motivator in this town, it's the preservation of their cherished *Piter*.

MEDIA

While the days of *Pravda* are long gone, the mass media in recent years has been a battleground, where the Kremlin and big business fight for control of the so-called 'free' press. As a result of such battles, the Russian press now is largely self-censoring, rather than government-censored. Newspapers and TV stations that were critical of the Kremlin have been largely silenced; you are unlikely to read or see much criticism of the government anywhere in the Russian media.

NEWSPAPERS & MAGAZINES

Though a far cry from the one-note news days of the Soviet era, most of Russia's biggest papers are mouthpieces for the various powerful bodies that own them, be they political parties or rich businessmen. The public – long used to reading between the lines – know how to take a bit from here, a bit from there, and imagine a truth that's somewhere in between.

The most popular Russian dailies are *Izvestia* (www.izvestiya.ru in Russian), *Kommersant* (www.kommersant.com) and *Vedomosti* (www.vedomosti.com), which is affiliated with the *Financial Times* and the *Wall Street Journal*. The government's official newspaper is the *Rossiyskaya Gazeta* (www.rg.ru in Russian), while the tabloids are represented by *Komsomolskaya Pravda*.

Novaya Gazeta (www.novayagazeta.ru) is a well-known liberal rag that is published in Moscow. It was famous mainly for its column by investigative reporter, Anna Politkovskaya, who was tragically murdered in 2006. She gained notoriety after playing an active role in negotiations with Chechen rebels during hostage crises in 2002 and 2004, as well as for her fervent opposition to the Chechen War. Her controversial book, *Putin's Russia*, was published in the UK in 2004; *A Russian Diary: A Final Account* was published posthumously.

TELEVISION

He who controls the TV controls the country – and no one understands this better than President Putin. In 2000 his administration conducted a heavy-handed legal attack on the owners of NTV, which was then a relatively professional, independent national TV station. The multimillionaire owner, Vladimir Gusinsky, was hounded for tax evasion and corruption charges, until he finally fled to Spain.

Few commentators regarded Gusinsky as any more corrupt than any other oligarch (or high-level politician for that matter); that he was being singled out seemed a clear signal that Putin's new government wished to control voices of dissent and encourage progovernment reporting. In 2001 gas giant Gazprom conducted a surprise buy-out of a controlling portion of NTV shares. Dozens of reporters quit the station, and its programming and acerbic tone were changed overnight. Now, in terms of independent journalism, there's little to distinguish NTV from the state-owned channels.

Not that Russian TV is managed by some Soviet-styled spooks. In fact the heads of the main state channels – Channel 1 and Rossiya – were among those young journalists who gave Russian audiences a taste of editorial freedom in the 1990s. Many faces on the screen are still the same, but news and analysis are increasingly transforming into ideological brainwashing. Only RenTV, a private channel owned by the state power grid, has coverage that somewhat deviates from the party line. RenTV purportedly broadcast the most complete coverage of the Dissenters' March in 2007, showing violent clashes between protesters and police.

Despite the range of channels, most Russian TV is an appalling mix of South American soap operas which are dubbed in Russian, Soviet films, straight-to-video Hollywood pap and endless musical concerts.

RADIO

Most of St Petersburg's popular radio stations play a mix of trashy Euro pop and its even more over-the-top Russian variant. Still, their play lists are often unexpectedly eclectic. Some of the more popular FM stations include: Eldoradio (101.4 MHz); Radio Modern (104 MHz); the grating Europa Plus (100.5 MHz); and the more diversified Radio Nostalgie (105.3 MHz). More Russian content can be heard on Kanal Melodia (91.1 MHz), Russky Shanson (100.9 MHz) and Russkoe Radio (104.4 MHz). Two stations focus almost exclusively on local news and features: Eko Peterburga (91.5 MHz) and Severnaya Stolitsa (105.9 MHz).

FASHION

On first impressions, conspicuous consumption seems to be the theme of Russian fashionistas, as New Russia is awash in exclusive designer labels and exorbitant price tags. Connoisseurs argue, however, that *la mode* in St Petersburg is becoming more sophisticated, now creatively mixing well-known Western brands with up-and-coming local designers.

Russian models have certainly taken the fashion world by storm, with beauties such as Natalya Vodianova and Evgenia Volodina dominating the pages of *Vogue* and *Elle*. St Petersburg designers are also attracting increasing attention, both at home and abroad. Tatiana Parfionova is Russian fashion's most famous name. Ever since she took home the 'Golden Button' award from her premiere in 1995, her tsarina-inspired designs and hand-embroidered embellishments have attracted world-wide attention.

Local designer Lilia Kisselenko organises the biannual Defile on the Neva (p19). This *prêt-à-porter* (ready-to-wear) event takes place in April and October at venues around the city, showcasing designers' collections from around Russia.

Such high fashion is not so interesting to the average Sveta or Sergei on the street, though. These days, most Russians wear the same clothes as their counterparts in the West: blue jeans, business suits and anything in between. St Petersburg's many shopping centres are filled with the same stores that you might find anywhere in Europe.

Only winter differentiates Russian style, bringing out the best or the worst of it, depending on your perspective. Fur is still the most effective and most coveted way to stay warm. Some advice from a local fashion connoisseur: 'Your protests that fur is cruel are likely to be met by blank stares and an uncomfortable shifting of feet. Don't come in winter if that offends you.'

NEIGHBOURHOODS

top picks

- **Russian Museum** (p76)
- **Church of the Saviour on Spilled Blood** (p72)
- **Pushkinskaya 10** (p91)
- **Kunstkamera** (p107)
- **Peter & Paul Fortress** (p113)
- **Monument to the Heroic Defenders of Leningrad** (p145)
- **Museum of Political History** (p117)
- **Museum of Railway Technology** (p146)
- **Tikhvin Cemetery** (p90)

NEIGHBOURHOODS

Water-loving Peter the Great intended that the Neva River would be the centre of St Petersburg, with Vasilevsky Island as its glittering centrepiece. However, the lack of bridges between the islands hindered development, and most people wanted to build on the higher, less flood-prone land around the Admiralty. Even Peter's despotism couldn't change people's preference and the centre of the city is now solidly south of the Neva, focused on Nevsky pr between Dvortsovaya pl (Palace Sq) and Moscow Station (Moskovsky vokzal).

In this guide we have divided the city into nine digestible neighbourhoods, each with its own characteristic appeal. We begin with St Petersburg's Historic Heart, an area so dense with museums, palaces and churches that one might spend days in this district only (indeed, many tourists do!). The Historic Heart includes the main stretch of Nevsky pr between the Hermitage and the Fontanka River, as well as the area east of Isaakievskaya pl (St Isaac's Sq) to the Summer Garden.

'The Petrograd Side is actually where it all began: Peter's city grew out of the Peter & Paul Fortress, prominently placed on Zayachy Island'

East of the Historic Heart is Liteyny, surrounding the busy avenue of the same name, and Smolny, the quiet but historic government district around which the Neva curves on its final approach to the sea. Due south of here are Vladimirskaya and Vosstaniya, which form the area around the two busy commercial squares, Vladimirskaya pl (Vladimir Sq) and pl Vosstaniya (Uprising Sq). Vosstaniya contains the less dynamic, easterly half of Nevsky pr, home to Moscow Station and Alexander Nevsky Monastery.

West of Vladimirskaya and Vosstaniya is Sennaya, which takes its name from Sennaya pl (Haymarket Sq). The area around the haymarket, Dostoevsky's stomping ground, was overrun with poverty and squalor during the 19th century. Today it is still a gritty but lively place, full of colourful characters. West of the Historic Heart and Sennaya is the Mariinsky district, named after the world-famous Mariinsky Theatre. In these quiet historic streets, graceful canals wend their way to the sea past palaces and churches that are just off the beaten tourist trail.

Dividing the Neva River is Vasilevsky Island, the huge triangle of land that Peter the Great thought would be the centre of the city. Today, Vasilevsky functions as the intellectual heart, housing the university, the Academy of Arts and other august institutions.

North and east of Vasilevsky Island, the Petrograd Side is actually where it all began: Peter's city grew out of the Peter & Paul Fortress, prominently placed on Zayachy Island. The Petrograd Side is dominated by the fashionable, Style Moderne Petrogradsky Island, a busy residential neighbourhood with plenty of shops and restaurants and a handful of museums. This neighbourhood also includes the pleasant, green northern islands: Kamenny, Yelagin and Krestovsky.

The Vyborg Side is a huge swathe of land north of the Neva River. Largely industrial and residential, it contains some of the city's offbeat points of interest, including Kresty Prison, Piskaryovskoe Cemetery and Udelnaya Fair. Visitors arriving from or departing to Finland will pass through either Finland Station (Finlyandsky vokzal) or Ladoga Station (Ladozhsky vokzal).

Back over the Neva, a vast area stretches south, encompassing Stalin's communist city centre which is still more Leningrad than St Petersburg. The appropriately named Southern St Petersburg includes some wonderful historic oddities, Stalinist monoliths and parkland, as well as the bus station (Avtovokzal No 2), the train stations Baltic Station (Baltiysky vokzal) and Vitebsk Station (Vitebsky vokzal), and Pulkovo Airport.

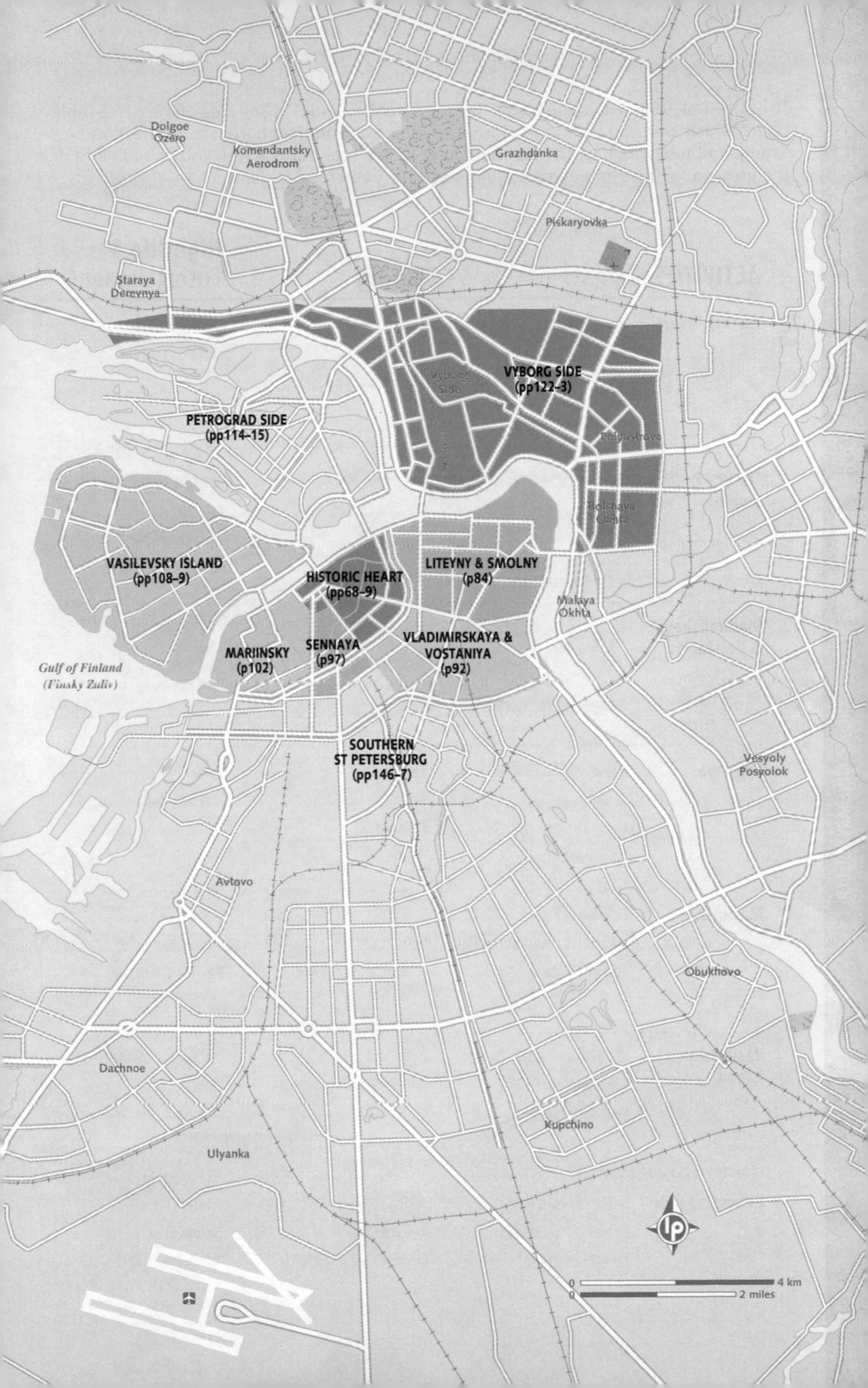

Dolgoe
Ozero
Komendantsky
Aerodrom
Grazhdanka
Piskaryovka
Staraya
Derevnya
VYBORG SIDE
(pp122–3)
Vyborg
Side
PETROGRAD SIDE
(pp114–15)
Polyustrovo
Bolshaya
Okhta
VASILEVSKY ISLAND
(pp108–9)
HISTORIC HEART
(pp68–9)
LITEYNY & SMOLNY
(p84)
Malaya
Okhta
MARIINSKY
(p102)
SENNAYA
(p97)
VLADIMIRSKAYA &
VOSTANIYA
(p92)
Gulf of Finland
(Finsky Zaliv)
SOUTHERN
ST PETERSBURG
(pp146–7)
Vesyoly
Posyolok
Avtovo
Obukhovo
Dachnoe
Kupchino
Ulyanka
0
4 km
0
2 miles

ITINERARY BUILDER

The table below allows you to plan a day's worth of activities in any area of the city. Simply select which area you wish to explore, and then mix and match from the corresponding listings to build your day. The first item in each cell represents a well-known highlight of the area, while the other items are more off-the-beaten-track gems.

AREA / ACTIVITIES	Sights	Eating	Nightlife & Entertainment
Historic Heart	**Russian Museum** (p76) **Church of the Saviour on Spilled Blood** (p72) **State Hermitage Museum** (p125)	**Pelmeny Bar** (p164) **Onegin** (p164) **The Other Side** (p165)	**Datscha** (p182) **Shostakovich Philharmonia** (p189) **Mod** (p183)
Liteyny & Smolny	**Smolny Cathedral** (p83) **Museum of Decorative & Applied Arts** (p86) **Anna Akhmatova Museum in the Fountain House** (p87)	**Black Cat, White Cat** (p168) **Sunduk** (p168) **Vox** (p168)	**JFC Jazz Club** (p185) **City Bar** (p179) **Probka** (p180)
Vladimirskaya & Vosstaniya	**Alexander Nevsky Monastery** (p90) **Dostoevsky Museum** (p93) **Pushkinskaya 10** (p91)	**Imbir** (p169) **Bistrot Garçon** (p170) **Cat Café** (p170)	**Che** (p184) **Griboedov** (p184) **Fish Fabrique** (p184)
Sennaya	**Railway Museum** (p97) **Sennaya pl** (p96) **Yusupov Gardens** (p98)	**Karavan** (p171) **Testo** (p171) **Fasol** (p171)	**Cynic** (p179) **Havana Club** (p182) **Manhattan** (p184)
Mariinsky	**St Isaac's Cathedral** (p100) **Nikolsky Cathedral** (p103) **Yusupov Palace** (p102)	**The Idiot** (p172) **Stolle** (p173) **Crocodile** (p172)	**Mariinsky Theatre** (p188) **Shamrock** (p180) **Rimsky-Korsakov Conservatory** (p189)
Vasilevsky Island	**Menshikov Palace** (p110) **Kunstkamera** (p107) **Geological Museum** (p111)	**Restoran** (p173) **Russky Kitsch** (p173) **Cheburechnaya** (p174)	**Die Kneipe** (p180) **Island** (p183) **Black & White** (p181)
Petrograd Side	**Cruiser Aurora** (p117) **Peter & Paul Fortress** (p113) **Yelagin Island** (p120)	**Tbilisi** (p175) **Aquarel** (p174) **Russian Fishing** (p174)	**Bridge Lounge** (p179) **Tunnel Club** (p183) **Orlandina** (p184)

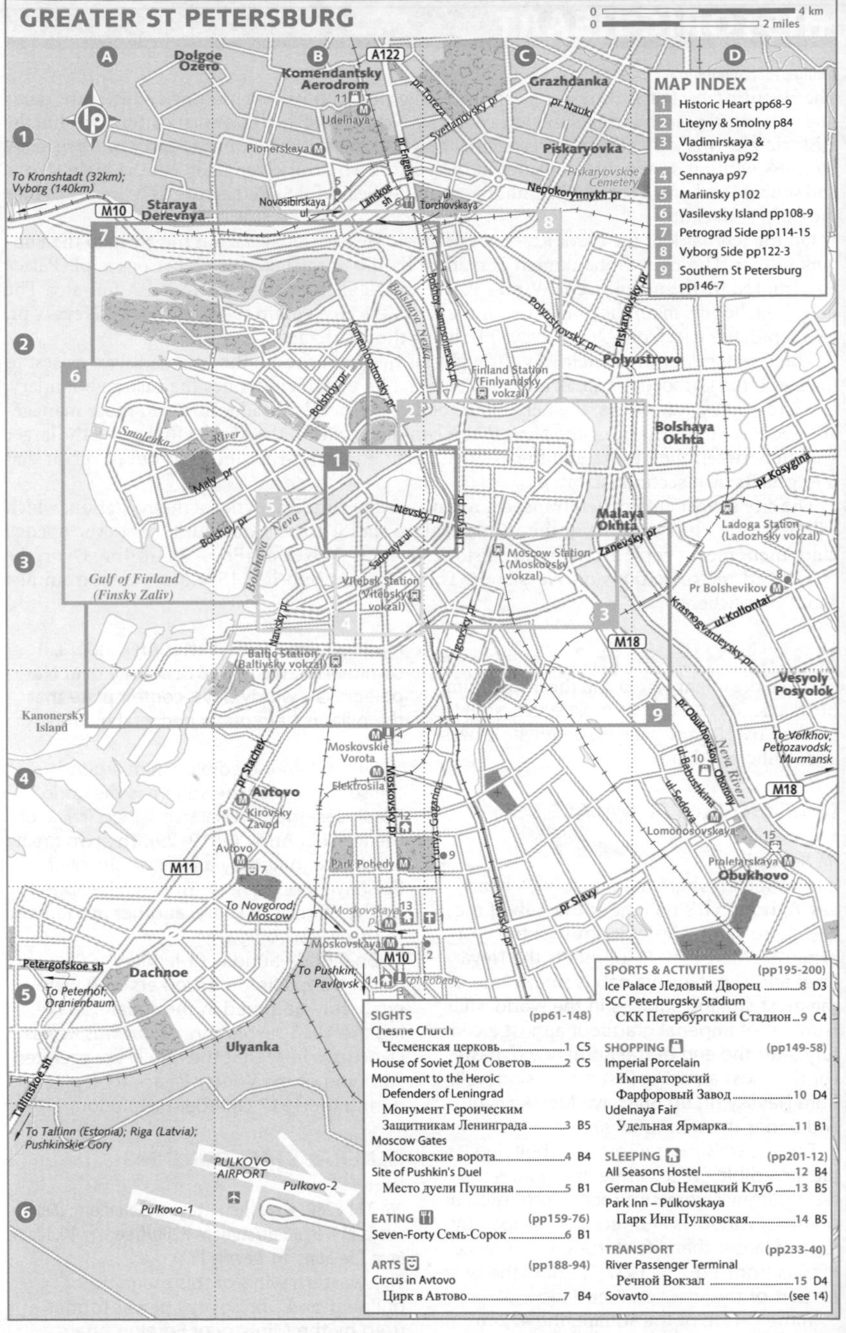
GREATER ST PETERSBURG
0 4 km
0 2 miles
MAP INDEX
1 Historic Heart pp68-9
2 Liteyny & Smolny p84
3 Vladimirskaya & Vosstaniya p92
4 Sennaya p97
5 Mariinsky p102
6 Vasilevsky Island pp108-9
7 Petrograd Side pp114-15
8 Vyborg Side pp122-3
9 Southern St Petersburg pp146-7
Dolgoe Ozero
Komendantsky Aerodrom
Grazhdanka
Piskaryovka
Piskaryovskoe Cemetery
Udelnaya
Pionerskaya
Novosibirskaya ul
Lanskoe sh
pr Engelsa
pr Toreza
Svetlanovsky pr
pr Nauki
ul Torzhovskaya
Nepokorynnykh pr
To Kronshtadt (32km); Vyborg (140km)
M10
A122
Staraya Derevnya
Bolshaya Nevka
Bolshoy Sampsonievsky pr
Kamennoostrovsky pr
Polyustrovsky pr
Piskaryovsky pr
Polyustrovo
Finland Station (Finlyandsky vokzal)
Bolshoy pr
Smolenka River
Maly pr
Bolshaya Okhta
Nevsky pr
Liteyny pr
Sadovaya ul
Bolshaya Neva
Malaya Okhta
Moscow Station (Moskovsky vokzal)
Zanevsky pr
pr Kosygina
Ladoga Station (Ladozhsky vokzal)
Pr Bolshevikov
ul Kollontai
Krasnogvardeysky pr
Gulf of Finland (Finsky Zaliv)
Vitebsk Station (Vitebsky vokzal)
Narvsky pr
Ligovsky pr
M18
Baltic Station (Baltiysky vokzal)
Kanonersky Island
Vesyoly Posyolok
pr Obukhovskoy Oborony
Neva River
ul Babushkina
ul Sedova
To Volkhov; Petrozavodsk; Murmansk
Moskovskie Vorota
Elektrosila
pr Stachek
Avtovo
Kirovsky Zavod
Moskovsky pr
pr Yuriya Gagarina
Park Pobedy
Lomonosovskaya
Proletarskaya
Obukhovo
M11
To Novgorod; Moscow
Moskovskaya Pl
Moskovskaya
pr Slavy
Vitebsky pr
Petergofskoe sh
Dachnoe
To Peterhof; Oranienbaum
To Pushkin; Pavlovsk
pl Pobedy
Ulyanka
Tallinskoe sh
To Tallinn (Estonia); Riga (Latvia); Pushkinskie Gory
PULKOVO AIRPORT
Pulkovo-2
Pulkovo-1
SIGHTS (pp61-148)
Chesme Church Чесменская церковь 1 C5
House of Soviet Дом Советов 2 C5
Monument to the Heroic Defenders of Leningrad Монумент Героическим Защитникам Ленинграда 3 B5
Moscow Gates Московские ворота 4 B4
Site of Pushkin's Duel Место дуели Пушкина 5 B1
EATING (pp159-76)
Seven-Forty Семь-Сорок 6 B1
ARTS (pp188-94)
Circus in Avtovo Цирк в Автово 7 B4
SPORTS & ACTIVITIES (pp195-200)
Ice Palace Ледовый Дворец 8 D3
SCC Peterburgsky Stadium СКК Петербургский Стадион 9 C4
SHOPPING (pp149-58)
Imperial Porcelain Императорский Фарфоровый Завод 10 D4
Udelnaya Fair Удельная Ярмарка 11 B1
SLEEPING (pp201-12)
All Seasons Hostel 12 B4
German Club Немецкий Клуб 13 B5
Park Inn – Pulkovskaya Парк Инн Пулковская 14 B5
TRANSPORT (pp233-40)
River Passenger Terminal Речной Вокзал 15 D4
Sovavto (see 14)

HISTORIC HEART

Eating p163; Shopping p150; Sleeping p203

The Historic Heart of St Petersburg epitomises the city, with its over-the-top architecture, dazzling museums, graceful canals and always-active Nevsky pr. Besides its vast cultural wealth, the Historic Heart is still a thriving residential neighbourhood, where locals carry on their daily business without so much as a glance at the visitors who flock here. Get off the main streets and squares and you'll see old, crumbling, painfully beautiful St Petersburg as it has been since the early 18th century.

On the left bank of the Neva River, the Historic Heart stretches from the Neva to the Fontanka River. The river embankment is marked by the unmistakeable Dvortsovaya pl (Palace Sq), fronted by the magnificent Winter Palace and flanked by the gold-toned Admiralty. The neighbourhood's main thoroughfare (and indeed, the city's main thoroughfare) is Nevsky pr, which radiates east from Dvortsovaya pl, slicing the district in two.

Three waterways wind their way through this neighbourhood: the Moyka River, closest to the Neva; the Griboedov Canal; and the Fontanka River, which defines the eastern boundary. Crisscrossed by waterways, the neighbourhood conveniently divides into two more manageable sections: the strip along the Neva that is contained within the Moyka River; and the larger section between the Moyka and the Fontanka. The Russian Museum, institutional giant that it is, gets its own section (see p76).

The city's most anticipated transport resource is the Admiralteyskaya metro station, which will be located just steps from the Winter Palace and St Isaac's Cathedral (if it ever opens). Until then, most people arrive in the Historic Heart at Ⓜ Nevsky Pr or Ⓜ Gostiny Dvor, the two linked metro stations on Nevsky pr. This transport hub is a 15-minute walk from just about everywhere.

WITHIN THE MOYKA

Between the mighty Neva and the meandering Moyka lie St Petersburg's most stately streets, marked by elegant palaces, exquisite plazas and idyllic parklands.

DVORTSOVAYA PL (PALACE SQ)

Map pp68–9

Ⓜ Nevsky Pr

It is no secret where St Petersburg's heart lies. Although it's no longer the hub of the city, there can be little doubt that the vast expanse where Nevsky pr meets the Neva River and Dvortsovaya nab is simply one of the most striking squares in the world, still redolent of imperial grandeur almost a century after the end of the Romanov dynasty. For the most amazing first impression walk from Nevsky pr, up Bolshaya Morskaya ul and under the triumphal arch.

The square's most impressive building is the incredible green, white and gold Winter Palace (Zimny Dvorets), a rococo profusion of columns, windows and recesses, topped by rows of larger-than-life statues. A residence of tsars from 1762 to 1917, it's now the largest part of the State Hermitage Museum (p125).

In the centre of the square, the 47.5m Alexander Column was designed in 1834 by Montferrand. Named after Alexander I, it commemorates the 1812 victory over Napoleon. On windy days, contemplate that the pillar is held on its pedestal by gravity alone!

Curving an incredible 580m around the south side of the square is the Carlo Rossi–designed General Staff Building (below) of the Russian Army (1819–29). The two great blocks are joined by a triumphal arch over Bolshaya Morskaya ul. The arch is topped by the Chariot of Glory, another monument to the Napoleonic Wars.

On Bloody Sunday (9 January 1905), tsarist troops fired on workers who were peaceably gathered in the square, sparking the 1905 revolution. And it was across Dvortsovaya pl that the much-exaggerated storming of the Winter Palace took place during the 1917 October Revolution.

GENERAL STAFF BUILDING

Map pp68–9

☎ 314 8260; www.hermitagemuseum.org; Dvortsovaya pl 6-8; adult/student R200/free; 🕑 10.30am-6pm Tue-Sun; Ⓜ Nevsky Pr

The western wing of this magnificent building on Dvortsovaya pl was formerly used by the Ministry of Foreign Affairs, including private apartments for the minister

STREET NAMES, SIGNS & FUN WITH CYRILLIC

We use the transliteration of Russian names of streets and squares in this book to help you when deciphering Cyrillic signs and asking locals the way. To save space the following abbreviations are used:

al – alleya аллея (alley)

bul – bulvar бульвар (boulevard)

nab – naberezhnaya набережная (embankment)

per – pereulok переулок (lane or side street)

pl – ploshchad площадь (square)

pr – prospekt проспект (avenue)

ul – ulitsa улица (street)

sh – shosse шоссе (highway)

Cyrillic script is provided for all points of interest (sights, activities, restaurants, clubs, hotels etc) on the maps. So if you can't get a local to understand your Russian pronunciation, just point to the map listing and let them read it. In cases where Cyrillic is not provided, it means that the site is commonly known by its English (or other Latin-language) name.

himself. The fabulous Carlo Rossi–designed interiors have been meticulously maintained, and today house exhibition halls displaying items from the Hermitage collection. Here, the art of 20th-century French painters Pierre Bonnard and Maurice Denis is on permanent display. Monarchists will appreciate the 'heraldic eagle', also featured in 600-plus examples of graphics, paintings and applied arts from Russia and Western Europe.

WINTER PALACE OF PETER I

Map pp68–9

☎ 571 8446; www.hermitagemuseum.org; Dvortsovaya nab 32; adult/student R200/100; 10.30am-5pm Tue-Sun; M Nevsky Pr

Opened as a part of the Hermitage in 1992, this palace on the Neva was the principal residence of Peter the Great, and he died here in 1725. When Giacomo Quarenghi built the Hermitage Theatre on this site between 1783 and 1789, he preserved parts of the palace and grounds. Between 1976 and 1986, excavations beneath the theatre stage uncovered a large fragment of the former state courtyard, as well as several suites of palace apartments. Today, the courtyard is used to display Peter's official carriage and sledge. Some of the chamber rooms have been restored to their appearance during Peter's era, complete with Dutch tiles and parquet floors, and are used to exhibit some of Peter's personal items from the Hermitage collection. The admission price includes a useful audio guide in the language of your choice.

ADMIRALTY Map pp68–9

Admiralteysky proezd 1; closed to the public; M Nevsky Pr

Across the road from Dvortsovaya pl, the gilded spire of the old Admiralty is a prime St Petersburg landmark. It is visible from Gorokhovaya ul, Voznesensky pr and Nevsky pr, as all of these roads radiate outwards from this central point. Despite the spire's solid gold appearance, it's actually made from wood and was almost rotted through before restoration efforts began in 1996. From 1711 to 1917, this spot was the headquarters of the Russian navy; now it houses the country's largest military naval college.

The Admiralty was reconstructed between 1806 and 1823 to the designs of Andreyan Zakharov. With its rows of white columns and its plentiful reliefs and statuary, it is a foremost example of the Russian Empire style. Get a close look at the globe-toting nymphs flanking the main gate. The green gardens, laid out from 1872 to 1874, are dotted with statues of Glinka, Lermontov, Gogol and other cultural figures, as well as a refreshing fountain that dates to 1877.

It's a lovely place to sit and stroll, but the building itself is closed to visitors.

MUSEUM OF THE HISTORY OF POLITICAL POLICE Map pp68–9

☎ 312 2742; www.polithistory.ru in Russian; Gorokhovaya ul 2; adult/student R100/40; 10am-6pm Mon-Fri; M Nevsky Pr

In the very same building that housed the tsarist and the Bolshevik secret police offices, this small museum recounts the history of this controversial institution. An annexe of the Museum of Political History (p117), it includes one room that recreates the office of Felix Dzerzhinsky, founder of the Cheka (Bolshevik secret police). Each of the remaining three rooms is devoted to the

HISTORIC HEART

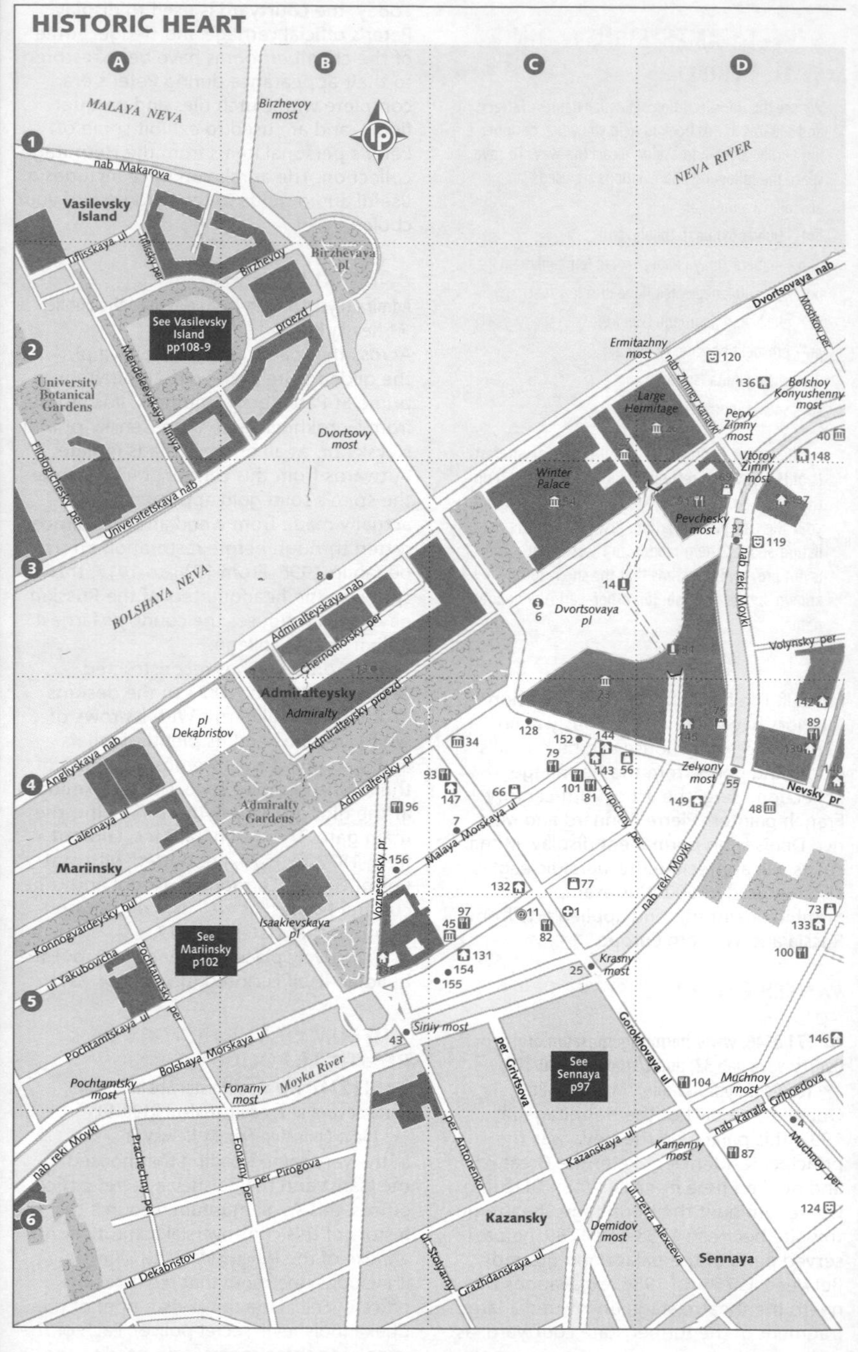

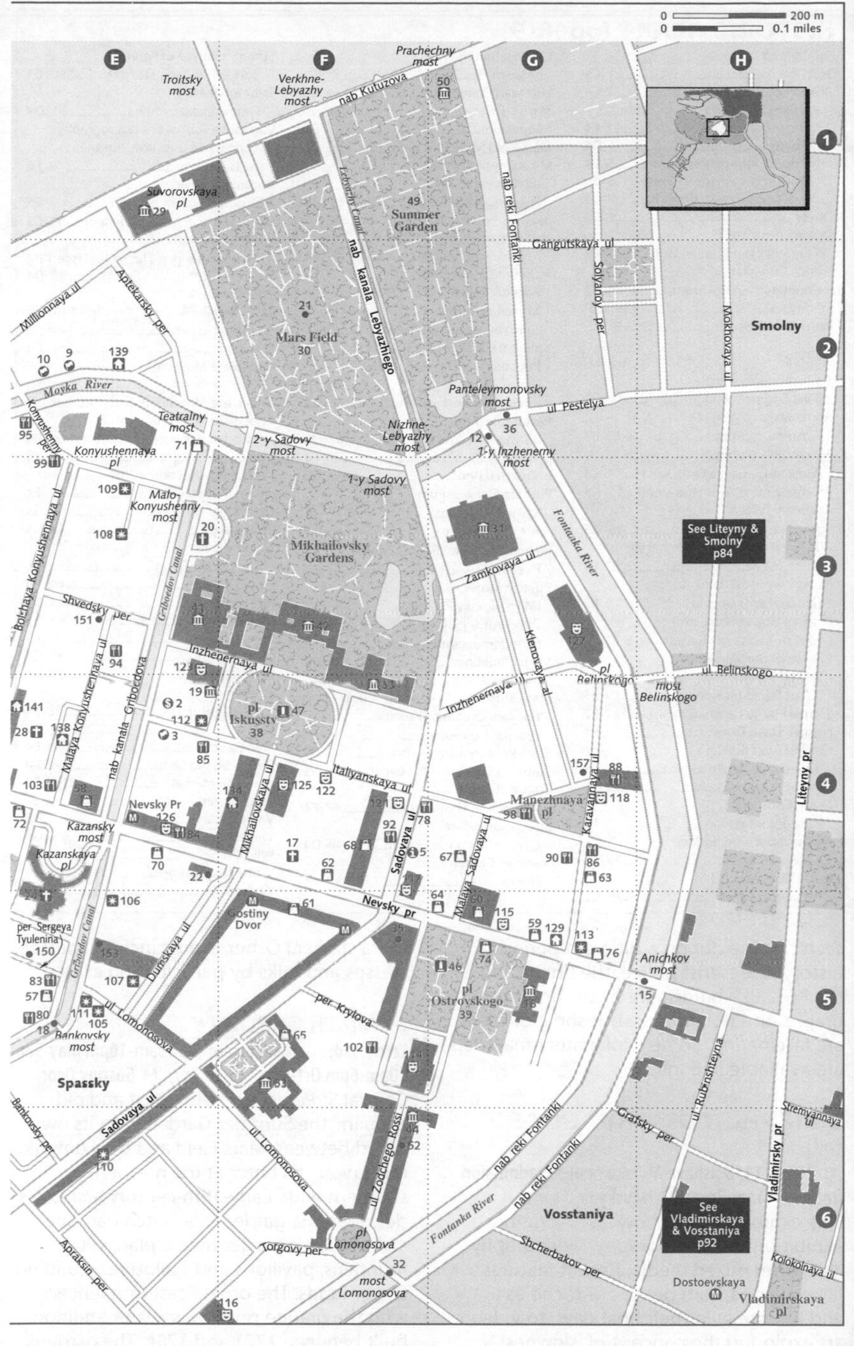

Troitsky most
Verkhne-Lebyazhy most
Prachechny most
nab Kutuzova
Suvorovskaya pl
Summer Garden
Lebyazhy Canal
nab kanala Lebyazhiego
nab reki Fontanki
Gangutskaya ul
Solyanoy per
Mokhovaya ul
Smolny
Millionnaya ul
Aptekarsky per
Mars Field
Moyka River
Panteleymonovsky most
ul Pestelya
Teatralny most
Konyushenny per
Konyushennaya pl
2-y Sadovy most
Nizhne-Lebyazhy most
1-y Inzhenerny most
1-y Sadovy most
Malo-Konyushenny most
Mikhailovsky Gardens
Fontanka River
See Liteyny & Smolny p84
Zamkovaya ul
Bolshaya Konyushennaya ul
Shvedsky per
Griboedov Canal
Klenovaya al
Inzhenernaya ul
pl Belinskogo
most Belinskogo
ul Belinskogo
pl Iskusstv
Malaya Konyushennaya ul
nab kanala Griboedova
Mikhailovskaya ul
Italiyanskaya ul
Sadovaya ul
Karavannaya ul
Manezhnaya pl
Liteyny pr
Nevsky Pr
Kazansky most
Kazanskaya pl
Malaya Sadovaya ul
Nevsky pr
Gostiny Dvor
per Sergeya Tyulenina
Dumskaya ul
Anichkov most
pl Ostrovskogo
per Krylova
ul Lomonosova
Bankovsky most
Spassky
Bankovsky per
ul Rubinshteyna
Grafsky per
Stremyannaya ul
Sadovaya ul
ul Zodchego Rossi
ul Lomonosova
nab reki Fontanki
Vladimirsky pr
Vosstaniya
See Vladimirskaya & Vosstaniya p92
Fontanka River
Apraksin per
Torgovy per
pl Lomonosova
most Lomonosova
Shcherbakov per
Kolokolnaya ul
Dostoevskaya
Vladimirskaya pl
200 m
0.1 miles

HISTORIC HEART (pp68-9)

INFORMATION

36.6 Pharmacy 1 C5
Alfabank 2 E4
Australian Consulate
  Консульство Австралии 3 E4
City Realty 4 D6
City Tourist Information Centre 5 F4
City Tourist Information Centre 6 C3
Cultural Security Department 7 C4
Driver 8 B3
Dutch Consulate
  Консульство Голландии 9 E2
French Consulate
  Консульство Франции 10 E2
Infinity .... (see 135)
Northwest Telecom 11 C5

SIGHTS (pp66-82)

1-y Inzhenerny most
  (First Engineer Bridge) 12 G2
Admiralty
  Адмиралтейство 13 B3
Alexander Column
  Александровская колонна 14 C3
Anichkov most Аничков мост 15 H5
Anichkov Palace
  Аничков дворец 16 G5
Armenian Church of St Catherine
  Церковь св Екатерины 17 F4
Bankovsky most (Bank Bridge)
  Банковский мост 18 E5
Brodsky House-Museum
  Музей-квартира Бродского 19 E4
Church of the Saviour on
  Spilled Blood
  Храм Спас на Крови 20 E3
Eternal Flame Вечный огонь 21 F2
Former Town Duma 22 E4
General Staff Building
  Здание главного штаба 23 C4
Gostiny Dvor .... (see 61)
Kazan Cathedral
  Казанский собор 24 E5
Krasny most (Red Bridge)
  Красный мост 25 C5
Large Hermitage
  Большой Эрмитаж 26 D2
Little Hermitage
  Малый Эрмитаж 27 C2
Lutheran Church 28 E4
Marble Palace
  Мраморный дворец 29 E1
Mars Field Марсово поле 30 F2
Mikhailovsky Castle
  (Engineer's Castle)
  Инженерный замок 31 G3
most Lomonosova 32 F6
Museum of Ethnography
  Музей этнографии 33 F4
Museum of the History of
  Political Police
  Музей истории
  политической полиции 34 C4
National Library of Russia
  Российская Национальная
  Библиотека 35 F5
Panteleymonovsky most 36 G2
Pevchesky most
  (formerly Yellow Bridge) 37 D3
pl Iskusstv 38 F4
pl Ostrovskogo 39 G5
Pushkin Flat-Museum
  Музей-квартира
  А С Пушкина 40 D2
Russian Museum (Benois Wing)
  Русский музей 41 E3
Russian Museum
  (Mikhailovsky Palace)
  Русский музей
  (Михайловский дворец) 42 F3
Singer Building .... (see 58)
Siniy most (Blue Bridge) 43 B5
State Museum of Theatre & Music
  Государственный музей
  театра и музыки 44 F6
State Photography Centre 45 C5
Statue of Catherine the Great 46 G5
Statue of Pushkin
  Памятник Пушкину 47 F4
Stroganov Palace
  Строгановский дворец 48 D4
Summer Garden
  Летний сад 49 F1
Summer Palace of Peter I
  Летний дворец Петра I 50 G1
Triumphal Arch
  Триумфальная арка 51 D3
Vaganova School of Choreography
  Хореографическое училище
  им Ваганова 52 F6
Vorontsov Palace
  Воронцовский дворец 53 F5
Winter Palace Зимний дворец 54 C3
Winter Palace of Peter I
  Зимний дворец Петра I .... (see 120)
Zelyony most (Green Bridge) 55 D4

SHOPPING (pp149-58)

Bon Vin .... (see 80)
Bukvoed 56 C4
Chocolate Museum
  (Gostiny Dvor) .... (see 61)
Chocolate Museum (Passage) .... (see 68)
Chocolate Museum
  (Stroganov Palace) .... (see 48)
Defile 57 E5
Dom Knigi (Nevsky pr 28;
  Singer Building) 58 E4
Dom Knigi (Nevsky pr 62) 59 G5
Eliseevsky 60 G5
Gostiny Dvor
  Гостиный Двор 61 F5
Grand Palace 62 F4
Intendant 63 G4
Mekhlandia 64 G5
Military Shop 65 F5
Open World 66 C4
Parnas 67 G4
Passage
  Универмаг Пассаж 68 F4
Plyos Embassy 69 D3
Rive Gauche 70 E4
Second-hand Shop .... (see 64)
Souvenir Market 71 E2
Stockmann 72 E4
Vanity 73 D5
Versace 74 G5
Wild Orchid 75 D4
Writers' Bookshop 76 G5
Yakhont 77 C4

secret police during a different period of history: the tsarist police, the Cheka and the KGB. Exhibitions are heavy on photographs and documents, but some of them are fascinating. Some explanatory materials are available in English.

STATE PHOTOGRAPHY CENTRE

Map pp68–9

☎ 314 1214; Bolshaya Morskaya ul 35; admission free; 11am-7pm; Ⓜ Nevsky Pr

This exhibition hall showcases rotating exhibitions of photography, videography and other mixed media. Recent features have ranged from photos of Nicholas II and his family in their final days, to video art exploring the concept of 'slowness' in everyday activities. (That last one sounds like a thriller.) Other events include master classes and talks by participating artists.

SUMMER GARDEN Map pp68–9

Letny Sad; admission free; 10am-10pm May-Sep, 10am-6pm Oct-Mar, closed Apr; Ⓜ Gostiny Dvor

Central St Petersburg's loveliest and oldest park, the Summer Garden is on its own island between Mars Field and the Fontanka River (you can enter at the northern or southern end). Early-18th-century architects designed the garden in a Dutch baroque style, following a geometric plan, with fountains, pavilions and sculptures studding the grounds. The ornate cast-iron fence with the granite posts was a later addition, built between 1771 and 1784. The gardens functioned as a private retreat for Peter the

HISTORIC HEART (pp68-9)

EATING (pp159-76)
Baku 78 F4
Bushe 79 C4
Face Café 80 E5
Fat Frier 81 C4
Fidelio Café 82 C5
Garçon Restaurant 83 E5
Il Patio 84 E4
Kalinka Malinka 85 E4
Kavkaz 86 G4
Kilikia 87 D6
Korovabar 88 G4
La Strada 89 D4
Mama Roma 90 G4
NEP 91 D3
Onegin 92 F4
Pelmeny Bar 93 C4
Silk 94 E3
Stolle 95 E2
Tandoori Nights 96 B4
Taverna Oliva 97 C5
Teremok 98 G4
Terrassa (see 73)
The Other Side 99 E3
Tinkoff 100 D5
U Tyoshi na Blinakh 101 C4
Yakitoriya 102 F5
Yolki Palki 103 E4
Zoom Café 104 D5

DRINKING & NIGHTLIFE (pp177-86)
Achtung Baby (see 109)
Belgrad (see 107)
Central Station 105 E5
Coffee Break 106 E5
Datscha 107 E5
Dunes 108 E3
Fidel (see 107)
Mod 109 E3
Revolution 110 E6
Second Floor (see 107)
Sinners 111 E5
Stray Dog Café 112 E4
The Other Side (see 99)
Tinkoff (see 100)
Tribunal Bar 113 G5

ARTS (pp188-94)
Akimova Comedy Theatre Академический театр комедии им Акимова (see 60)
Alexsandrinsky Theatre Александринский театр 114 F5
Avrora 115 G5
Bolshoy Drama Theatre Большой Драматический театр им Товстоногова 116 F6
Demmeni Marionette Theatre Театр марионеток им Деммени 117 F4
Dom Kino Дом кино 118 G4
Glinka Capella House Академическая капелла им Глинки 119 D3
Hermitage Theatre Театр Эрмитаж 120 D2
Komissarzhevskaya Theatre Театр им Комиссаржевской 121 F4
Musical Comedy Theatre Театр музыкальной комедии 122 F4
Mussorgsky-Mikhailovsky Theatre Академический театр оперы и балета им Мусорского 123 E3
Priyut Komedianta Theatre Театр Приют комедианта 124 D6
Shostakovich Philharmonia Bolshoy Zal Большой зал филармонии Шостаковича 125 F4
Shostakovich Philharmonia Maly Zal Малый зал филармонии Шостаковича 126 E4
St Petersburg State Circus Государственный Цирк 127 G3

SPORTS & ACTIVITIES (pp195-200)
Velocity 128 C4

SLEEPING (pp201-12)
Anichkov Pension 129 G5
Belveder Nevsky 130 D4
Casa Leto 131 C5
City Realty (see 4)
Comfort Hotel 132 C4
Cuba Hostel 133 D5
Grand Hotel Europe 134 F4
Herzen Hotel (see 132)
Hotel Astoria 135 B5
Hotel Grifon (see 146)
Hotel Nauka 136 D2
Hotel Sonata (see 93)
Kempinski Hotel Moyka 22 137 D3
Korona 138 E4
Moyka 5 139 E2
Nevsky Deluxe Hotel 140 D4
Nevsky Grand Hotel 141 E4
Nevsky Hotel Aster 142 D4
Nevsky Inn 143 C4
Nevsky Prospekt B&B 144 C4
Nord Hostel 145 D4
Pio on Griboedov 146 D5
Polikoff Hotel (see 129)
Prestige Hotel on Gorokhovaya 147 C4
Pushka Inn 148 D2
Rachmaninov Antique Hotel (see 133)
Solo Hotel (see 93)
Taleon Imperial Hotel 149 D4

TRANSPORT (pp233-40)
Air France (see 156)
Alitalia (see 126)
Austrian Airlines (see 126)
Baltic Airlines (see 152)
Baltic Tours 150 E5
British Airways 151 E3
Central Airline Ticket Office Центральные авиакассы 152 C4
Central Train Ticket Office Центральные железнодорожные кассы 153 E5
CSA Czech Airlines 154 C5
Delta Airlines 155 C5
Finnair (see 151)
Hertz (see 156)
KLM Royal Dutch Airlines 156 B4
LOT Polish Airlines 157 G4
Lufthansa (see 126)
SAS Scandinavian Airlines (see 72)

Great before becoming a strolling place for St Petersburg's 19th-century leisured classes. Only in the 20th century were commoners admitted. The Summer Garden maintains a formal elegance, with hundreds of lime trees shading its straight paths and lines of statues. The park does enjoy a touch of whimsy, however: look for the fountains depicting scenes from Aesop's fables and the monument to children's writer Ivan Krylov.

SUMMER PALACE OF PETER I

Map pp68–9

Muzey Letny Dvorets Petra I; ☎ 314 0456; adult/student R300/150; 10am-5pm Wed-Mon early May–Sep; M Gostiny Dvor

The modest, two-storey Summer Palace in the northeastern corner of the Summer Garden was St Petersburg's first 'palace', which may seem like a slight misnomer for a remarkably small building. The 14-room baroque palace was built for Peter between 1704 and 1714 by Domenico Trezzini. Today it's open as a museum, showing off some simple 18th-century furnishings, porcelain duct work and ornamental painting. The bas-reliefs around the walls depict Russian naval victories.

MARS FIELD Map pp68–9

Marsovo polye; nab kanala Lebyazhiego; M Gostiny Dvor

Once the scene of 19th-century military parades, the grassy Mars Field lies immediately east of the Summer Garden (south of Troitsky most). Formerly known as the Tsarina's

Meadow (Tsaritsyn lug), it's a popular spot for strollers. At its centre, an eternal flame burns for the victims of the 1917 revolution and the ensuing civil war. Don't take a short cut across the grass – you may be walking on the graves of the victims or of later communist luminaries also buried here.

MARBLE PALACE Map pp68–9

☎ 312 9196; www.rusmuseum.ru; Millionnaya ul 5/1; adult/student R270/135; 🕑 10am-5pm Wed-Mon; Ⓜ Nevsky Pr

Between Mars Field and the Neva, this palace is an architectural gem by Antonio Rinaldi, who used 36 kinds of marble, and took pains to bleed them seamlessly into one another. Built between 1768 and 1785, it was a gift from Catherine the Great to Grigory Orlov for suppressing a Moscow rebellion. Formerly the Lenin Museum under the Soviets, it is now a branch of the Russian Museum featuring rotating exhibitions of modern art and a permanent exhibition on foreign artists active in Russia in the 18th and 19th centuries.

An amusing equestrian statue of Alexander III stands plumply in the courtyard outside the main entrance; it became the butt of many jokes after it was erected in 1909 (originally outside Moscow Station). Even his son Nicholas II thought of shipping it off to Irkutsk, but when rumours started that he wanted to send his dad into Siberian exile, he changed his mind. Sculptor Paolo Trubetskoy said of his work, 'I don't care about politics. I simply depicted one animal on another.'

BETWEEN THE MOYKA & THE FONTANKA

The Moyka and Fontanka Rivers provide neat boundaries for this large section of the Historic Heart, with the Griboedov Canal winding between them. Pl Iskusstv (Arts Sq) dominates the north side of Nevsky pr, while Gostiny Dvor and pl Ostrovskogo (Ostrovsky Sq) are the most prominent landmarks on the south side.

CHURCH OF THE SAVIOUR ON SPILLED BLOOD Map pp68–9

Spas na Krovi; ☎ 315 1636; www.cathedral.ru; nab kanala Griboedova 2a; adult/student R300/170; 🕑 11am-7pm Thu-Tue Sep-Apr, 10am-8pm Thu-Tue May-Aug; Ⓜ Nevsky Pr

This multidomed dazzler, partly modelled on St Basil's Cathedral in Moscow, was built between 1883 and 1907 in memory of reformist Tsar Alexander II. On this spot in 1881, a terrorist group known as the People's Will attempted to assassinate the tsar by blowing up his carriage, which did eventually result in his death. Officially called the Church of the Resurrection of Christ, it was intended as a private place of mourning for the life of the tsar.

It was the Bolsheviks who threw the ornate doors of this amazing candy-cake structure open to the people. Not built to withstand the wear and tear caused by thousands of visitors, its interior quickly began to suffer. Following the closure of churches by Stalin in the 1930s, the church was used to store various items from potatoes to theatre sets. Decades of abuse and neglect finally ended in the 1980s, which was surprising given a political climate that was still very cold to religion.

It's now famed as the church that took 24 years to build and 27 to restore, for that's how long it took to refurbish the 7000 sq metres of mosaics that line the walls inside. It reopened in 1997 to much fanfare. In the western apse, the very spot of the assassination is marked by a small but beautiful canopy built out of rhodonite and jasper. The magnificent floor and iconostasis are all Italian marble. These days, it functions as a museum, though services are sometimes held here on special occasions.

If you're on a tight budget, you can still gawk at the superbly polychromatic exterior of this Russian revival marvel, which is unique in the city. The 20 granite plaques on the façade record, in gold letters, the main events of Alexander's reign. The mosaic panels about half-way up detail scenes from the New Testament, and the 144 mosaic coats of arms each represent the provinces, regions and towns of the Russian Empire of Alexander's time, which all joined in mourning the death of the tsar. The whole shebang is crowned by an 81m-high steeple. Photos from the footbridge that crosses the canal are practically required for all visitors to St Petersburg.

PUSHKIN FLAT-MUSEUM Map pp68–9

☎ 314 0007; nab reki Moyki 12; adult/student R200/60; 🕑 11am-5pm Wed-Sun; Ⓜ Nevsky Pr

Alexander Pushkin's last home overlooks one of the prettiest curves of the Moyka

LIFE IMITATING ART

Russian literature is filled with jaded heroes, stubborn heroines, unrequited loves and tragic deaths. None inspires more abhorrence and empathy than Eugene Onegin, the title character in Alexander Pushkin's epic poem.

Eugene Onegin is a world-weary St Petersburg socialite who rejects the love of devoted Tatiana but seduces her sister Olga. Unfortunately, Olga is betrothed to his best friend, Lensky, who challenges our antihero to a duel. Both rivals have misgivings, but pride forces the pair to fight, and Lensky is slain.

Is it a coincidence that Pushkin – the national bard and pride of St Petersburg – was himself slain in a duel? His killer was a French nobleman, Baron Georges d'Anthès, who had publicly courted Pushkin's beautiful wife, Natalya Goncharova.

Oddly enough, d'Anthès married Natalya's sister, Ekaterina – perhaps as a ruse. But Pushkin was not persuaded. After an anonymous letter was circulated, nominating the poet as the 'Grand Master of the Order of Cuckolds', the only honourable response was a fight to the death.

History has not clarified this nasty affair: some still speculate that d'Anthès acted under the influence of Tsar Nicholas I, who found the famed poet's radical politics inconvenient; others imply that the tsar himself may have had a thing for Natalya, a notorious flirt. One thing is for sure: it ended badly for Pushkin.

On a cold night in February 1837, having eaten his final meal at the Literatornoye Kafe on Nevsky pr, Pushkin set off by sled to a remote woodland to meet his adversary (see p124). He was shot and died two days later at his home on the Moyka River (see opposite).

Unlike the remorseful Eugene Onegin, who recognises his foolishness in rejecting Tatiana and must live with his love unrequited and his soul sorrowful, things did not go so badly for d'Anthès. By way of punishment, he was stripped of his rank and forced to leave Russia. He returned to France with his wife (who supposedly never doubted his loyalty), and the two lived out their days in apparent wedded bliss.

This ironic ending does not go over well with Russian romantics. Needless to say, d'Anthès is a much maligned character in Russian history, sometimes dismissed as a tsarist stooge, a hidden homosexual or a French spy (and perhaps all three).

River, north of Nevsky pr. He only lived here four months, but this is where the poet died after his duel in 1837 (see above). The little house is now the Pushkin Flat-Museum, which has been reconstructed to look exactly as it did in the poet's last days. On display are his death mask, a lock of his hair and the waistcoat he wore when he died. Price of admission includes an audio guide.

STROGANOV PALACE Map pp68–9

☎ 117 2360; www.rusmuseum.ru; Nevsky pr 17; adult/student R300/150; 10am-6pm Wed-Mon; M Nevsky Pr

One of the city's loveliest baroque exteriors, the salmon pink Stroganov Palace was designed by court favourite Bartolomeo Rastrelli in 1753 for one of the city's leading aristocratic families. Most famously, the Stroganov's chef created a beef dish served in a sour cream and mushroom sauce that became known to the world as 'beef stroganoff'. The building is now owned by the Russian Museum, which uses the splendidly restored rooms for temporary exhibitions. Also on site are a wacky waxworks museum and a luxury restaurant.

LUTHERAN CHURCH Map pp68–9

☎ 311 2423; Nevsky pr 22; bilingual service 10.30am Sun; M Nevsky Pr

Tucked in a recess between Bolshaya and Malaya Konyushennaya uls is the lovely Lutheran Church that was built for St Petersburg's thriving German community in the 1830s. Distinguished by a four-column portico and topped with a discreet cupola, it was turned into a swimming pool in the 1950s (the high diving board was placed in the apse) – but is that worse than using it to store vegetables, as it had been since the 1930s? The church is open to visitors, having been restored beautifully.

KAZAN CATHEDRAL Map pp68–9

Kazansky Sobor; ☎ 311 4826; www.kazansky.ru in Russian; Kazanskaya pl; admission free; 11am-7pm, services 9am & 6pm daily; M Nevsky Pr

Atypical of St Petersburg churches, the neoclassical Kazan Cathedral was commissioned by Tsar Paul shortly before he was murdered in a coup. It reflects his eccentric desire to unite Catholicism and Orthodoxy in a kind of 'super-Christianity' as well as his fascination with the Knights of Malta, of which he was a member. The cathedral's great, 111m-long colonnaded arms reach out towards Nevsky pr, encircling a pleasant garden that is studded with statues. Look for the victorious Napoleonic War field marshal Mikhail Kutuzov (whose remains are buried inside the cathedral) and his friend and aide Mikhail Barclay de Tolly.

Inside, the cathedral is dark and traditionally orthodox, with a daunting 80m-high dome.

Andrei Voronikhin, a former serf, built the cathedral between 1801 and 1811 and his design was influenced by St Peter's in Rome. His original plan was to build a second, mirror version of the cathedral opposite it on the other side of Nevsky pr, but this never materialised.

SINGER BUILDING Map pp68–9

Nevsky pr 28; Ⓜ Nevsky Pr

Opposite the Kazan Cathedral stands one of St Petersburg's most marvellous buildings, the headquarters of the Singer sewing machine company which opened a factory in the Russian capital in 1904. The building also housed the American consulate for a few years prior to WWI. These days, the Singer Building provides a home to St Petersburg's premier bookstore, Dom Knigi (p151), and an uninspiring coffee shop. The wonderful Singer globe and emblem has now finally been restored after spending all of the 1990s under scaffolding.

PL ISKUSSTV (ARTS SQ) Map pp68–9

Ⓜ Nevsky Pr

Just a block east of the Griboedov Canal is the quiet pl Iskusstv (Arts Sq), named after its cluster of museums and concert halls. In the 1820s and 1830s, Carlo Rossi designed this square and the lovely Mikhailovskaya ul, which joins it to Nevsky pr. A statue of Pushkin, erected in 1957, stands in the middle of the tree-lined square. The square is surrounded by the Shostakovich Philharmonia (p189), Brodsky House-Museum (right), Mussorgsky-Mikhailovsky Theatre (p189), Russian Museum (p76) and Museum of Ethnography (below).

MUSEUM OF ETHNOGRAPHY

Map pp68–9

☎ 313 4420; www.ethnomuseum.ru; Inzhenernaya ul 4/1; adult/student R300/150, English tour R1000; 🕑 10am-6pm Tue-Sun; Ⓜ Gostiny Dvor

In an impressive classical building on pl Iskusstv, this excellent museum displays the traditional crafts, customs and beliefs of more than 150 cultures that make up Russia's fragile ethnic mosaic. There's a bit of leftover Soviet propaganda going on here, but it's a marvellous collection: the sections on Transcaucasia and Central Asia are fascinating, with rugs and two full-size *yurts* (nomads' portable tent-houses). The Special Storeroom has some great weapons and rare devotional objects.

The museum's centrepiece is the magnificent Marble Hall, a 1000-sq-metre gallery surrounded by pink Karelian-marble columns.

BRODSKY HOUSE-MUSEUM

Map pp68–9

☎ 314 3658; pl Iskusstv 3; adult/student R200/100; 🕑 11am-5pm Wed-Sun; Ⓜ Nevsky Pr

This is the former home of Isaak Brodsky, one of the favoured artists of the revolution (not to be confused with Joseph Brodsky, one of the least favourite poets of the same regime). Besides being a painter himself, Brodsky was also an avid collector, and his house-museum contains his collection of thousands of works, including lesser-known works by top 19th-century painters such as Repin, Levitan and Kramskoy. Occasional concerts and contemporary art exhibitions are also held at the museum, which is administered by the Russian Academy of Arts.

MIKHAILOVSKY CASTLE (ENGINEER'S CASTLE) Map pp68–9

Mikhailovsky Zamok; ☎ 570 5112; www.rusmuseum.ru; Sadovaya ul 2; adult/student R300/150, photos R100; 🕑 10am-5pm Wed-Sun, 10am-4pm Mon; Ⓜ Gostiny Dvor

A much greater Summer Palace used to stand at the south end of the Summer Garden. But Rastrelli's fairy-tale wooden creation for Empress Elizabeth was knocked down in the 1790s to make way for the bulky Mikhailovsky Castle. The son of Catherine the Great, Tsar Paul I, was born in the wooden palace and he wanted his own residence on the same spot. He had the current edifice built complete with defensive moat as he (quite rightly) feared assassination. But this erratic, cruel tsar only got 40 days in his new abode before he was suffocated in his bedroom in 1801.

The style is a bizarre take on a medieval castle, quite unlike any other building in the city. In 1823 it became a military engineering school (hence its more common name,

Engineer's Castle, or Inzhenirny Zamok), whose most famous pupil was Fyodor Dostoevsky. There is a movement, however, to use the original name, Mikhailovsky Castle (not to be confused with Mikhailovsky Palace, the Russian Museum's main building).

As a wing of the Russian Museum, the castle is used mainly for temporary exhibitions. A few finely restored state rooms include the lavish burgundy throne room of the Tsar's wife Maria Fyodorovna.

ARMENIAN CHURCH OF ST CATHERINE Map pp68–9

☎ 311 5795; Nevsky pr 42; ⏲ 8am-6.30pm Mon-Fri, 9.30am-1.30pm Sat; Ⓜ Nevsky Pr

Continuing with a tradition of non-Orthodox churches being welcome on Nevsky pr, the Armenian merchant Ovanes Lazarian paid for the city's first Armenian church to be erected here in 1771. It was designed and built by German architect Georg Veldten and completed in 1780. The Soviet regime deemed it reasonable to bash the place to bits and install a 2nd floor, which blocked the view of the cupola. The church has been fully restored now, however, and it's open to visitors.

GOSTINY DVOR Map pp68–9

☎ 110 5200; www.gostinydvor.ru in Russian; Nevsky pr 35; ⏲ 10am-10pm; Ⓜ Gostiny Dvor

The arcades of Gostiny Dvor department store stand facing the clock tower of the former Town Duma (Town Parliament) on Dumskaya ul, which was the seat of the prerevolutionary city government. One of the world's first indoor shopping malls, the 'Merchant Yard' dates from between 1757 and 1785 and stretches 230m along Nevsky pr (its perimeter is over 1km long). This Rastrelli creation is not as elaborate as some of his other work, finished as it was by Vallin de la Mothe in a more sober neoclassical style.

These days, Gostiny Dvor is quite a fashionable shopping spot (see p153). Opposite Gostiny Dvor across Sadovaya ul is the Vorontsov Palace (1749–57), another noble town house by Rastrelli. From 1810 it was the most elite military school in the empire. It's still a military school for young cadets; on weekends you can watch mothers pass food parcels to their sons through the wrought-iron front gates. The palace is occasionally opened for concerts and such, details of which are posted out the front.

PL OSTROVSKOGO (OSTROVSKY SQ)

Map pp68–9

Ⓜ Gostiny Dvor

Ringed with important cultural institutions, pl Ostrovskogo is named for Alexander Ostrovsky (1823–86), a celebrated 19th-century playwright. An enormous statue of Catherine the Great (1873) stands amid the chess, backgammon and mah-jong players that crowd the benches here. At the Empress' heels are renowned statesmen of the 19th century, including her lovers Orlov, Potemkin and Suvorov. This airy square, commonly referred to as Cathy's Garden (Katkin Sad), was created by Carlo Rossi in the 1820s and 1830s.

The most prominent building on the square is Rossi's neoclassical Alexandrinsky Theatre (p190), sometimes called by its Soviet-era name, the Pushkin Theatre. In 1896, at the opening night of Anton Chekhov's *The Seagull*, the play was so badly received here that the playwright fled to wander anonymously among the crowds on Nevsky pr.

The square's west side is taken up by the lavish National Library of Russia, St Petersburg's biggest with some 31 million items, nearly a sixth of which are in foreign languages. Its reading rooms (⏲ 9am-9pm Mon-Fri & 11am-7pm Sat & Sun Sep-Jun, 9am-5pm Tue-Sun & 1-9pm Mon & Wed Jul-Aug) are open to the public, but you must bring your passport to sign in.

Rossi's ensemble continues behind the theatre on ul Zodchego Rossi. It is proportion deified: the buildings are 22m wide, 22m apart and 220m long. The Vaganova School of Choreography at No 2 is the Kirov Ballet's training school, where Pavlova, Nijinsky, Nureyev and others learned their art.

STATE MUSEUM OF THEATRE & MUSIC Map pp68–9

☎ 571 2195; www.theatremuseum.ru; pl Ostrovskogo 6; adult/student R50/25; ⏲ 11am-6pm Thu-Sun & 1-7pm Wed; Ⓜ Gostiny Dvor

Behind the Alexandrinsky Theatre, appropriately enough, this museum is a treasure-trove of items relating to Russian theatre, including model sets, posters and costumes. In a relatively new section aimed at children, there are great models of the Mariinsky stage and antique contraptions used to create stage effects such as wind and rain. The museum also

BRIDGES IN THE BURG

The never-ending network of canals and waterways in St Petersburg has resulted in some innovative designs in the bridges built over the years. With the exception of the new Big Obukhovsky, all of the *mosty* (bridges) across the Neva are drawbridges. They are raised every evening at designated times to let the ships pass, a spectacle that draws starry-eyed lovers and stranded night birds (see p236 for the schedule). But some of the most charming bridges are the smaller structures that span the canals around the city. Of St Petersburg's 340 bridges, here are a few of our favourites:

Anichkov most (Map pp68–9) St Petersburg's most striking bridge features rearing horses at all four corners, symbolising man's struggle with and taming of nature.

Bankovsky most (Bank Bridge; Map pp68–9) This beauty is suspended by cables emerging from the mouths of golden-winged griffins. The name (which does not quite fit this whimsical creation) comes from the Assignment Bank (now a further-education institute) which stands on one side of the bridge.

Most Lomonosova (Map pp68–9) Four Doric towers contain the mechanism that pulls up the moveable central section, allowing boat traffic to pass along the Fontanka underneath.

Lviny most (Bridge of Four Lions; Map p102) Another suspension bridge, this one is supported by two pairs of regal lions, which give the bridge its name.

Panteleymonovsky most (Map pp68–9) At the confluence of the Moyka and the Fontanka, this beauty features lampposts bedecked with the double-headed eagle and railings adorned with the coat of arms.

1-y Inzhenerny most (First Engineer Bridge; Map pp68–9) While there is no shortage of adornment on the cast-iron bridge leading to Mikhailovsky Castle (p74), the highlight is the Chizhik-Pyzhik, the statue of the little bird that hovers over the Moyka.

Siniy most (Blue Bridge), Krasny most (Red Bridge), Zelyony most (Green Bridge) and Pevchesky most (all bridges on Map pp68–9) These colour-coded bridges (the Pevchesky was formerly known as the Yellow Bridge) cross the Moyka at intervals between Isaakievskaya pl and Dvortsovaya pl.

has branches in the Sheremetyev Palace (p87) and the former homes of composer Nikolai Rimsky-Korsakov and singer Fyodor Chaliapin, the Rimsky-Korsakov Flat-Museum (p94) and Chaliapin House Museum (p119) respectively.

ANICHKOV PALACE Map pp68–9

☎ 310 4395; nab reki Fontanki; 🕑 by appointment; Ⓜ Gostiny Dvor

Occupying an entire block between pl Ostrovskogo and the Fontanka River, the Anichkov Palace was built between 1741 and 1750, with input from a slew of architects, including Rastrelli and Rossi. The palace was twice a generous gift for services rendered: Empress Elizabeth gave it to her favourite Count Razumovsky and later Catherine the Great presented it to Potemkin. This was also Tsar Nicholas II's favourite place to stay in St Petersburg – he far preferred the cosy interiors to the vastness of the Winter Palace.

The Anichkov Palace became the city's largest Pioneer Club headquarters after 1936 and to this day it houses more than 100 after-school clubs for over 10,000 children. Today there's a small museum inside, but it is only open sporadically for tours. Call to find out the specific times and dates.

Otherwise, the palace, as a children's club, is off-limits to casual tourists. There is a hokey wax figures exhibition (admission R300; 🕑 11am-7pm) in the courtyard if you are looking for something to do.

RUSSIAN MUSEUM

Even if your time in St Petersburg is limited, try your utmost to accommodate some time for this gem, the Russian Museum (Gosudarstvenny Russky Muzey; ☎ 595 4248; www.rusmuseum.ru; Inzhenernaya ul 4; adult/student R300/150, photos R100, audio guide R200; 🕑 10am-6pm Wed-Sun & 10am-5pm Mon, ticket office closes 1hr before closing time; Ⓜ Nevsky Pr). Your appreciation of Russian culture will be much deepened by it. Moreover, it's easily done in a half-day visit unlike the vast and sometimes overwhelming Hermitage.

While the Hermitage spreads its net across the cultures of the world, the Russian Museum – as its name suggests – focuses solely on Russian art, from primitive Church icons to

top picks

RUSSIAN MUSEUM

If you don't have time for a comprehensive tour, here are the highlights that you won't want to miss.

Mikhailovsky Palace

- Room 14 *The Last Day of Pompeii* by Karl Bryullov and *The Wave* by Ivan Ayvazovsky.
- Room 26 *Peter I Interrogating Tsarevich Alexey in Peterhof* and *The Last Supper*, both works by Nicholas Ghe.
- Rooms 33–35 Works by Ilya Repin, especially *Barge Haulers on the Volga* and *Cossacks Writing a Letter to the Turkish Sultan.*
- Room 36 *Stepan Razin* by Vasily Surikov.
- Room 38 Viktor Vasnetsov's moving *A Knight at the Crossroads.*

Benois Wing

- Room 67 The highly stylised works of Nikolai Roerich, including the *Stroganov Frieze Suite* in the stairwell.
- Room 70 Boris Kustodiev's smug *Merchant's Wife at Tea.*
- Rooms 77–82 The Russian take on 20th-century art, including cubism, futurism and avant-garde.

contemporary commercial art. The collection is magnificent. Although it lacks some of the better-known paintings that can be found in its only real rival, the Tretyakov State Gallery in Moscow, the Russian Museum's range is arguably more even.

Mikhailovsky Palace, the museum's main building, was designed by Carlo Rossi and built between 1819 and 1825. It was a gift for Grand Duke Mikhail (brother of Tsars Alexander I and Nicholas I) as compensation for missing out on his chance on the throne. Nicholas II opened the building as a public gallery on 7 March 1898. The museum originated from the collection begun by Tsar Alexander III, whose bust greets you on the magnificent main staircase.

The Benois Wing was constructed between 1914 and 1919. It is now connected to the original palace and accessible through an entrance on nab kanala Griboedova. In 2002 all 8.7 hectares of the Mikhailovsky Gardens were redesigned according to the original 19th-century plans. The gardens are absolutely lovely and offer the most impressive perspective of Mikhailovsky Palace.

The museum currently boasts over 400,000 items in its collection and now owns three other city palaces where (mostly) temporary exhibitions are also held: the Marble Palace (p72), the Stroganov Palace (p73) and Mikhailovsky Castle (Engineer's Castle) (p74). Joint tickets for all four venues are available for adult/child R600/300.

Mikhailovsky Palace

Enter the museum via the ground floor entrance to the right of the main façade. Pick up a museum map before ascending the magnificent main staircase to the 1st floor, as this is where the chronological ordering of the exhibits begins.

ROOMS 1–4: RELIGIOUS ICONS

The first four rooms of the museum encapsulate a succinct but brilliant history of Russian icon painting over the past eight centuries, including work from the three major schools of Russian icon painting: Novgorod, Muscovy and Pskov. Room 2 has *St George and Scenes of His Life,* while Room 3 features Russian master Andrei Rublev's massive *Peter and Paul* as well as his *Presentation of Christ in the Temple.* Room 4 is notable in its departure from earlier styles. Compare *Old Testament Trinity with Scenes from Genesis* with the completely atypical *Our Father*.

ROOM 5: PETRINE ART

Peter was a great patron of the arts and almost single-handedly brought the Western eye to Russian painting, as witnessed by the massive jump in style from ecclesiastical to secular subjects between Rooms 4 and 5. The room includes three busts of Peter and three portraits, including the creepy *Peter I on His Deathbed.*

ROOMS 6–7: POST-PETRINE ART

Room 6 includes some charmingly odd canvases in very strange shapes as well as mosaic portraits of both Peter and Catherine the Great. There's also a wonderful moulded portrait of Elizabeth I, Peter's daughter. The centre of the room is taken up by a huge portrait of the ill-fated Peter III, although look out for the impressive bust of Prince Menshikov here too. Room 7 has an amazingly ornate ceiling. The room houses a sculpture of *Empress Anna with an Arab Boy* and a few impressive tapestries.

ROOMS 8–10: THE RISE OF THE ACADEMY

These rooms display the early works of the St Petersburg Academy of Arts. These artists borrowed the European classical aesthetic for their work. Look for portraits in Rooms 8 and 10 and biblical themes in Room 9.

ROOM 11: THE WHITE HALL

This Rossi-designed hall was Grand Duke Mikhail's drawing room. Here, the interior is the art – in this case representing the Empire epoch. It's wonderfully ornate and shiny – a perfect place to host musical greats like Strauss and Berlioz, who performed here.

ROOMS 12–17: THE ACADEMY

By the early 19th century the Academy of Arts was more and more influenced by Italian themes given the unfashionability of France. In Room 12 look for Vladimir Borovikovsky's magnificent *Catherine II Promenading in Tsarskoe Selo*. Room 14 is truly spectacular, including enormous canvases such as Ivan Ayvazovsky's *The Wave* and Karl Bryullov's incredible *The Last Day of Pompeii* and *The Crucifixion*.

Some modernity then begins to creep in with Alexander Ivanov's smaller paintings, all of which are grouped together on one side of Room 15. *Four Nude Boys, Old Man Leaning on a Stick* and *Boy Getting out of a Stream* all mark a notable departure in terms of detail and representation. Room 16 is dedicated to drawings, which are considered the basis for all artistic work. And Room 17 pays tribute to the Academy Council.

ROOMS 18–22

At the turn of the 19th century, it became fashionable for 'genre painting' to look to themes from (an incredibly idealised) rural Russia, which you can see in Rooms 18–20. Room 21 contains some enormous canvases: *Phrina at the Poseidon Celebration in Elesium* by Genrikh Semiradsky, *Christian Martyrs at the Colosseum* by Konstantin Flavitsky and *Nero's Death* by Vasily Smirnov. In Room 22 look for the huge rendition of *Pugachev's Judgement* by Vasily Perov.

ROOMS 23–25: THE WANDERERS

The Wanderers (Peredvizhniki) were a group of academy artists who saw their future outside the strict confines of that strict institution. They wandered among the people, painting scenes of realism that had never before been seen in Russian art. Look for brilliant works by Perov, including *Hunters at Rest* and the scathing *Monastery Refectory*.

ROOM 26: NICHOLAS GHE

Ghe's masterpiece, *Peter I Interrogating Tsarevich Alexey in Peterhof,* is one of Russian art's most famous historical paintings. The painting relates to the tumultuous relationship between the despot and his son; Peter could not understand Alexey's character, so different from his own. Alexey foolishly went abroad and sought support from foreign leaders to place him on the throne of Russia. Peter, paranoid by his later years, managed to convince Alexey to return home unpunished if he renounced his right to the succession. While Alexey kept his side of the bargain, Peter had his own son tortured to death as he attempted to extract information about 'plotters' against him. Ghe's other work, such as *The Last Supper,* is equally dark.

ROOMS 27–32: LANDSCAPES

Contemporaries of the Wanderers, landscape artists such as Ivan Shishkin (Room 27) were still popular. These rooms also document the rise of populist art, which had a strong social conscience and sought to educate the public. The best examples of this are Vladimir Makovsky's *The Condemned* and *The Doss House* (Room 30).

ROOMS 33–35: ILYA REPIN

Considered by most Russians to be the greatest artist the nation has ever produced, Ilya Repin (1844–1930) was originally a member of the Wanderers, but he outgrew the movement. He went on to produce key works of Russian realist and populist art. His masterpiece is *Barge Haulers on the Volga,* an unrivalled portrait of human misery and enslavement in rural Russia. Unfortunately it's often on loan abroad, but the Russian Museum is its home. Other Repin highlights here are *Cossacks Writing a Letter to the Turkish Sultan* and his marvellous portrait of a barefoot Leo Tolstoy.

ROOMS 36–38: RUSSIAN HISTORICAL ART

Vasily Surikov was a master at historical painting, which was en vogue in the late 19th century. His portrayals of *Yermak's Conquest of Siberia* and *Suvorov Crossing the Alps* (Room 36) are particularly romantic, but the lifelike rendition of Cossack rebel *Stepan Razin* (Room 37) is undoubtedly his most evocative. Viktor Vasnetsov also specialised in mystical and historical subjects. Check out the moving scene in *A Knight at the Crossroads* (Room 38), where a soldier and horse pause to mourn the loss of an unknown life.

ROOM 39: RUSSIAN ORIENTALISM

The 19th century saw a massive extension of the Russian Empire as vast swathes of Central Asia were tamed and brought under the tsar. This created great interest in the East and its then completely mysterious culture and traditions. Vasily Vereshchagin's work depicts this curiosity, with pieces such as *At the Door of the Mosque.*

ROOMS 40–47: LATE-19TH-CENTURY RUSSIAN ART

These rooms display the large number of complementing and contradictory styles that were fashionable in St Petersburg before the explosion of the avant-garde. These include Arkhip Kuindzhi landscapes (Rooms 40–41), mystical nature scenes with lots of sky and mysterious light; Vladimir Makovsky's marvellously detailed scenes of celebrations like the *Maslenitsa Festival on Admiralteyskaya pl* (Room 42); Appolinary Vasnetsov's dark, beautiful depictions of old Moscow (Room 43); Isaak Levitan's idyllic landscapes, such as *The Lake* and *Silence* (Room 44); big, bold, colourful creations by Andrei Ryabushkin (Room 45); Abram Arkhipov and other artists depicting unromanticised scenes from everyday life (Room 46); and bright paintings of peasants by Filip Mallianvln (Room 47).

ROOMS 48–49

Mark Antokolsky's *Ivan the Terrible* and *Death of Socrates* are on display either side of yet another souvenir stand. From here you enter the Benois Wing to your right or continue straight ahead for the comprehensive account of Russian folk art, featuring everything from kitchen equipment to window frames. The long corridor in Room 49 showcases a series of paintings by Konstantin Korovin.

ROOM 54: ILYA REPIN'S TSARIST PORTRAITS

Room 54 features Repin's enormous rendition of the *Ceremonial Sitting of the State Council on 7th May 1901, Marking the Centenary of Its Foundation.* Around the walls are individual portraits of its members.

ROOMS 55–59

These rooms contain sculptures in storage, but behind glass walls, so still visible. Most interesting here is Etienne Falconet's model for his *Bronze Horseman,* which stands overlooking the Neva on pl Dekabristov.

Benois Wing

The Benois Wing marks the beginning of the modern era in painting – the Russian Museum's superb collection of late-19th-century and early-20th-century avant-garde art is here, while exhibits of contemporary Russian art are held downstairs. Don't miss the massive *Stroganov Frieze Suite,* the four amazing paintings by Nikolai Roerich that hang in the stairwell.

ROOM 66: MIKHAIL VRUBEL & MIKHAIL NESTEROV

Room 66 is normally the home of the father of modern Russian art, Mikhail Vrubel (1856–1910). His ground-breaking works are *Lady in Lilac, Epic Hero* and *Demon in Flight*. Mikhail Nesterov is also astute at combining historical and religious themes.

ROOM 67: NIKOLAI ROERICH

Nikolai Roerich (1874–1947) was a painter, peacenik and spiritual teacher. His philosophical bent is reflected in paintings such as *Three Joys* and *Guests from Overseas*. Roerich's work is prized for its mystical themes and amazingly vibrant colours.

ROOM 68: BALLETS RUSSES ARTISTS

Sergei Diaghilev founded the Ballets Russes in 1909, and he then proceeded to commission theatre sets and costume designs from some of the greatest artists in Russia and – eventually – the world.

Frequent collaborators included Leon Bakst, whose *Portrait of Sergei Diaghilev with his Nanny* (1906) is featured in Room 68. Konstantin Somov and Alexander Benois were also associated with this group.

ROOMS 69–70: VIKTOR SEROV & BORIS KUSTODIEV

Serov's works include portraits of Ida Rubenstein, Princess Yusupova and Olga Orlova. Kustodiev's most famous painting is *Merchant's Wife at Tea,* though some may argue that his scenes of provincial Russian life are more accessible.

ROOMS 71–75

These rooms contain a hodgepodge of painting by artists from the late 19th and early 20th century – many exhibiting impressionist influences. In Room 71, Viktor Vasnetsov plays with religious themes, including the *Mother of God* which occupies an entire wall. Room 72 features several sublime paintings by Konstantin Korovin (1861–1939), including *Northern Idyll* and *Portrait of Shaliapin*. Look also for Mikhail Larionov's wonderful late impressionist *Rose Bush* (1904). Room 73 displays work by Nikolai Miliotti and Victor Borisov-Mussatov, as well as some wonderful sculpture by Mikhail Vrubel. Pavel Kuznetsov and Nikolai Sapunov are also represented here.

ROOM 76: KUZMA PETROV-VODKIN

Spanning two centuries and surviving the Russian Revolution, Kuzma Petrov-Vodkin (1878–1939) was a unique painter. Indeed, he was all but forgotten during the early Soviet period, as his work did not subscribe to socialist realist norms, but he was rediscovered during the 1960s and 70s. His work conveys a dreamlike atmosphere, much of it with homoerotic overtones.

ROOMS 77–79: EARLY AVANT-GARDE

Between 1905 and 1917, the Russian art world experienced an explosion of creative inspiration which defied the stylistic categorisation that had existed before. Nathan Altman was among the brightest stars of the Russian avant-garde. Artist couple Mikhail Larionov and Natalya Goncharova were also leaders of this movement, evidence of which you can see in Room 79.

ROOM 80: CUBISM & FUTURISM

Look for Alexander Rodchenko's famous painting *Black on Black* (1918). Additional work includes pieces by Natalya Goncharova, Lev Bruni and Lyubov Popova.

ROOMS 81–82: LATE AVANT-GARDE PAINTING

Here is an unrivalled selection of Russian art of the late 1920s and early 1930s. Kazimir Malevich's works of great simplicity sit uncomfortably opposite Pavel Filonov's disturbed and crowded representations of Russian life. This is also the permanent home of Malevich's famous *Black Square* (1925), the third of a series of four, although it is often travelling for special exhibitions.

ROOMS 83–85: EARLY SOVIET ART

These rooms are often used for special exhibitions. However, the permanent display features pieces from the early Soviet period, where you can enjoy the tantalising overview of the many interesting directions that Soviet art promised to take before socialist realism became the only acceptable style. And of course there is plenty of the latter, too.

HISTORIC HEART

Walking Tour

1 Dvortsovaya pl Approach the magnificent Dvortsovaya pl (Palace Sq; p66) from Bolshaya Morskaya ul. As you turn the corner from Nevsky pr, behold the Alexander Column (p66), perfectly framed under the triumphal arch. All of the surrounding buildings are part of the State Hermitage Museum (p125).

2 Moyka River From Vtoroy Zimny most, look northwest for a wonderful view of the Neva; way to the south is Bartolomeo Rastrelli's lavish Stroganov Palace (p73). At No 12, the final residence of Russia's most celebrated poet now houses the Pushkin Flat-Museum (p72).

3 Konyushennaya pl This square is dominated by crumbling 18th-century court stables. Extending south from here is Bolshaya Konyushennaya ul (the name comes from *kon*, Russian for 'horse'). One of imperial St Petersburg's most prestigious streets, it was home to writer Ivan Turgenev, musician Nikolai Rimsky-Korsakov and social revolutionary Nikolai Chernyshevsky.

4 Mars Field Formerly the parade grounds for the imperial guard, the wide, open park of Mars Field (p71) later became a burial ground for victims of the revolution and the civil war. An eternal flame burns in their honour. East of here is the shady Summer Garden (p70) and the unusual Mikhailovsky Castle (Engineer's Castle; p74) is to the southeast.

5 Teatralny most Near the intersection of the Moyka and Griboedov Canal, this bridge gives a spectacular perspective on the Church of the Saviour on Spilled Blood (p72). Behind the cacophony of colours, a Style Moderne wrought-iron fence encloses the Mikhailovsky Gardens (p77).

6 Pl Iskusstv Centred around a stoic statue of Pushkin, pretty pl Iskusstv (Arts Sq; p74) is ringed by celebrated cultural institutions. Most notably, the Russian Museum (p76) dominates the north side of the square, which explains the name of the square. Also situated here are the Mussorgsky-Mikhailovsky Theatre (p189) and Shostakovich Philharmonia (p189).

WALK FACTS

Start Dvortsovaya pl at intersection of Bolshaya Morskaya ul and Nevsky pr (M Nevsky Pr)
Finish Pl Ostrovskogo at Fontanka River (M Gostiny Dvor)
Distance 2km
Duration Two hours
Fuel stops Stolle (p167), Coffee Break (p181), Kavkaz (p166)

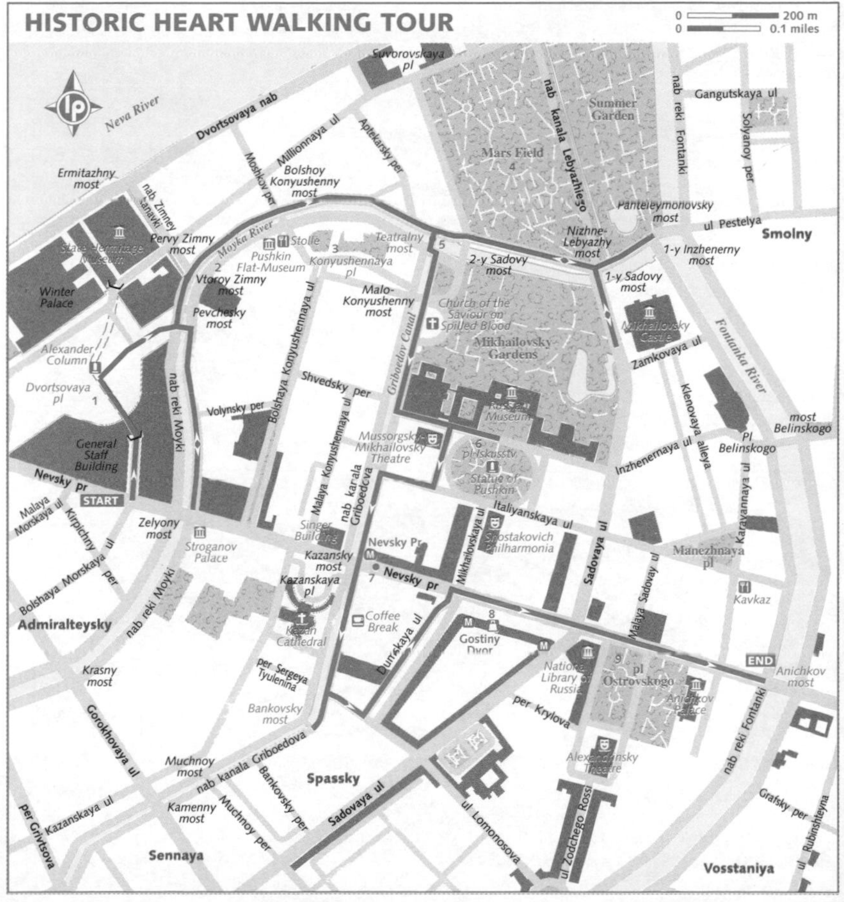

7 Nevsky pr The corner of Nevsky pr and Griboedov Canal is one of the landmark intersections of this infamous avenue. The old Singer building (p74) provides a whimsical contrast to the formidable columned Kazan Cathedral (p73) on the opposite corner. Behind the cathedral, Bankovsky most (p76) is undoubtedly St Petersburg's most picturesque and most photographed bridge.

8 Gostiny Dvor Crowds pour out of the metro station at Gostiny Dvor (p75), the 18th-century trading arcade that's still packed with shoppers. One of the world's first indoor shopping malls, Rastrelli's creation boasts a perimeter over 1km long. The clock tower across the street marks the former Town Duma (Town Parliament).

9 Pl Ostrovskogo Landmarks such as the National Library of Russia (p75), Alexandrinsky Theatre (p190) and Anichkov Palace (p76) surround pl Ostrovskogo (Ostrovsky Sq; p75), named for the famous playwright. The pleasant park is otherwise populated by chess players, young lovers and dowdy drunks. Here, the elaborate Anichkov most (p76), flanked by rearing horses, crosses the Fontanka.

LITEYNY & SMOLNY

Eating p168; Shopping p154; Sleeping p206

The Liteyny and Smolny districts sit side-by-side east of the Historic Heart, tucked inside a swooping curve of the Neva River on its south bank. These neighbourhoods take their names from the industries that once dominated this area: *liteyny* means 'foundry' and *smol* means 'tar'. These evocative names hardly capture the atmosphere of these quaint but quiet neighbourhoods today. Their wide avenues do not see nearly as much traffic as those in the Historic Heart, which makes for a refreshing retreat from the hustle and bustle.

Liteyny is dominated by the commercial street, Liteyny pr, which was once the main road between Nevsky pr and the foundry. The foundry is long gone, but it is still a busy street, heading directly north and crossing the Neva River at Liteyny most (the second permanent bridge in St Petersburg).

Smolny is the city's political and diplomatic centre: Governor Valentina Matvienko's office is at the Smolny Institute (below) and a large number of foreign consulates are located on or around ul Furshtatskaya (see p242).

Otherwise, both of these neighbourhoods are mostly residential, and rather fashionable at that. Over the years, they have been home to many famous residents. The high-society Sheremetyev family built their palatial residence on the Fontanka, and later poet Anna Akhmatova occupied an apartment in the same building (p87). Grigory Potemkin lived in the Horse Guards Palace (now the Tauride Palace; p85). And the young Vladimir Putin spent his youth playing on these streets: his family lived at Baskov per 12. The Sovetskaya Streets – 10 in all, running perpendicular to Suvorovsky pr – were built in the 1930s and are quiet streets pleasant for strolling and soaking up everyday life.

Liteyny and Smolny are bounded on two sides by the Neva River as it flows east from the Gulf of Finland, then turns south. The western border is the Fontanka River and the southern border is Nevsky pr. The main east–west roads are Kirochnaya ul and Shpalernaya ul; Liteyny pr runs north from Nevsky pr, while Suvorovsky pr runs at a diagonal northeast from Nevsky pr.

The area around Liteyny is served by two metro stations: Ⓜ Mayakovskaya, at the intersection of Nevsky pr and ul Marata, and Ⓜ Chernyshevskaya, further north. Smolny suffers from a lack of public transport, although Ⓜ Chernyshevskaya is at its heart. To get to the farthest reaches of the neighbourhood – near the cathedral – it may be easier to hop on one of the *marshrutky* (minibuses) travelling up Suvorovsky pr.

SMOLNY CATHEDRAL Map p84

☎ 271 9182; pl Rastrelli 3/1; adult/student R100/70; 🕑 10am-8pm Thu-Tue; Ⓜ Chernyshevskaya

If baroque is your thing, then look no further than the sky-blue Smolny Cathedral, an unrivalled masterpiece of the genre that ranks among Bartolomeo Rastrelli's most amazing creations. The cathedral is the centrepiece of a convent mostly built to Rastrelli's designs between 1748 and 1757. His inspiration was to combine baroque details with the forest of towers and onion domes typical of an old Russian monastery. There's special genius in the proportions of the cathedral (it gives the impression of soaring upwards), to which the convent buildings are a perfect foil.

In stark contrast, the interior is a disappointingly austere plain white. At the time of research, the interior was closed for renovations to the cupola. But even when it is open, it serves as a concert hall or exhibition space, not as a working church (and indeed, there is not much to see inside).

If you wonder what you are paying for, it is to climb the 63m belfry – all 277 steps – for stupendous views over the city.

SMOLNY INSTITUTE Map p84

☎ 276 1461; pl Proletarskoy Diktatury 3; 🕑 by appointment only 10am-6pm Mon-Fri; Ⓜ Chernyshevskaya

Built by Giacomo Quarenghi between 1806 and 1808 as a school for aristocratic girls, the Smolny Institute was thrust into the limelight in 1917 when it became the headquarters for the Bolshevik Central Committee and the Petrograd Soviet. From here, Trotsky and Lenin directed the October Revolution, and in the Hall of Acts (Aktovy zal) on 25 October, the All-Russian Congress of Soviets conferred power on a Bolshevik government led by Lenin. The Smolny Institute served as the seat of

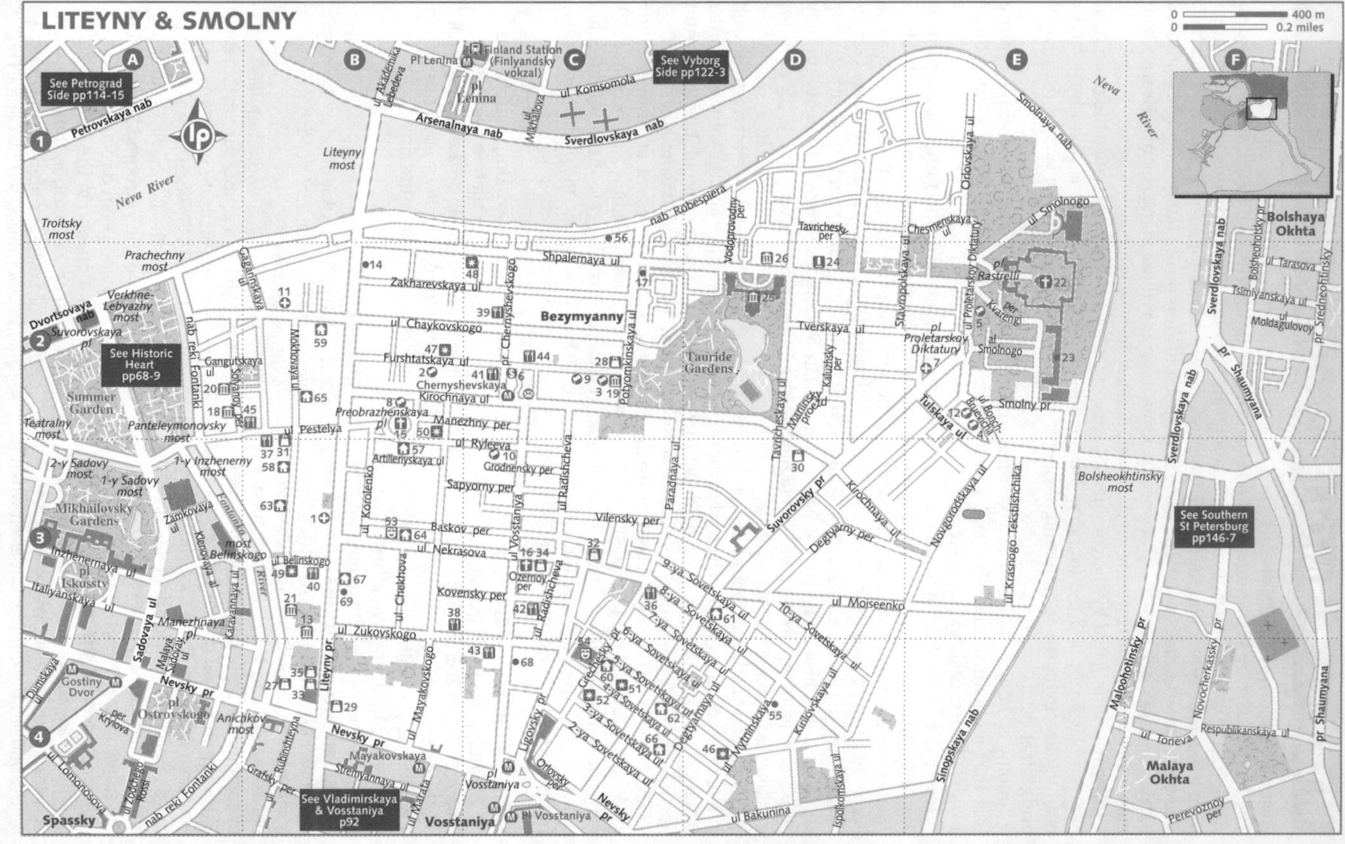
LITEYNY & SMOLNY
0 400 m
0 0.2 miles
See Petrograd Side pp114-15
See Vyborg Side pp122-3
See Historic Heart pp68-9
See Southern St Petersburg pp146-7
See Vladimirskaya & Vosstaniya p92
Finland Station (Finlyandsky vokzal)
Pl Lenina
pl Lenina
ul Akademika Lebedeva
ul Mikhailova
ul Komsomola
Arsenalnaya nab
Sverdlovskaya nab
Petrovskaya nab
Neva River
Liteyny most
Troitsky most
Prachechny most
Verkhne-Lebyazhy most
Dvortsovaya nab
Suvorovskaya pl
Summer Garden
Teatralny most
Panteleymonovsky most
2-y Sadovy most
1-y Sadovy most
1-y Inzhenerny most
Mikhailovsky Gardens
Inzhenernaya ul
pl Iskusstv
Italiyanskaya ul
Sadovaya ul
Manezhnaya pl
Malaya Sadovaya ul
Dumskaya ul
Gostiny Dvor
Nevsky pr
pl Ostrovskogo
per Krylova
ul Lomonosova
ul Zodchego Rossi
nab reki Fontanki
Spassky
Anichkov most
Grafsky per
ul Rubinshteyna
Mayakovskaya
Stremyannaya ul
ul Marata
Vosstaniya
pl Vosstaniya
Pl Vosstaniya
Ligovsky pr
Orlovsky per
Zamkovaya ul
Klenovaya al
Fontanka River
most Belinskogo
Karavannaya ul
ul Belinskogo
Gagarinskaya ul
Gangutskaya ul
Solyanoy per
Mokhovaya ul
ul Pestelya
Liteyny pr
ul Zukovskogo
ul Mayakovskogo
ul Chekhova
Kovensky per
ul Nekrasova
Baskov per
ul Korolenko
Artilleriyskaya ul
Preobrazhenskaya pl
Manezhny per
ul Ryleeva
Grodnensky per
Sapyorny per
ul Vosstaniya
ul Radishcheva
Ozerny per
Vilensky per
Paradnaya ul
Shpalernaya ul
Zakharevskaya ul
ul Chaykovskogo
Furshtatskaya ul
Chernyshevskaya
Kirochnaya ul
pr Chernyshevskogo
Bezymyanny
Potyomkinskaya ul
Tauride Gardens
Vodoprovodny per
nab Robespiera
Tavrichesky per
Tverskaya ul
Kaluzhsky per
Tavricheskaya ul
Mariinsky proezd
Stavropolskaya ul
Chesmenskaya ul
Orlovskaya ul
Smolnaya nab
ul Smolnogo
pl Rastrelli
per Kvarengi
ul Proletarskoy Diktatury
pl Proletarskoy Diktatury
al Smolnogo
Smolny pr
ul Bonch-Bruevicha
Tulskaya ul
Suvorovsky pr
Kirochnaya ul
Degtyarny per
Novgorodskaya ul
ul Krasnogo Tekstilshchika
Bolsheokhtinsky most
ul Moiseenko
9-ya Sovetskaya ul
8-ya Sovetskaya ul
7-ya Sovetskaya ul
6-ya Sovetskaya ul
5-ya Sovetskaya ul
4-ya Sovetskaya ul
3-ya Sovetskaya ul
2-ya Sovetskaya ul
10-ya Sovetskaya ul
Grechesky pr
Degtyarnaya ul
Mytninskaya ul
Kirillovskaya ul
Ispolkomskaya ul
ul Bakunina
Sinopskaya nab
Maloohotinsky pr
Sverdlovskaya nab
pr Shaumyana
Bolsheohotsky pr
ul Tarasova
Tsimlyanskaya ul
ul Moldagulovoy
pr Sredneohtinsky
Bolshaya Okhta
Malaya Okhta
Novocherkassky pr
Respublikanskaya ul
ul Toneva
Perevoznoy per
A
B
C
D
E
F
1
2
3
4

LITEYNY & SMOLNY

power until March 1918. In 1934, Leningrad Party chief Sergei Kirov was assassinated on Stalin's orders as he left the building, sparking the notorious Leningrad purges (see p35). Today St Petersburg governor Valentina Matvienko runs the city from here.

TAURIDE PALACE & GARDENS

Map p84

M Chernyshevskaya

Catherine the Great built this fabulous baroque palace in 1783 for Grigory Potemkin, a famed general and one of her many lovers. The palace takes its name from the Ukrainian region of Crimea (once called Tavria), which Potemkin conquered. The palace was a thank you for that acquisition, amongst other things. Catherine's bitter son, Paul I, turned the palace into a barracks after his ascension to the throne in 1796, which ruined most of the lavish interiors. Between 1906 and 1917 the State Duma, the Provisional Government and the Petrograd Soviet all met here; in the 1930s it housed the All-Union Agricultural Communist University, a fate that would have horrified Catherine the Great. Today it is home to the Parliamentary Assembly of the Member States of the CIS (Commonwealth of Independent States). It is not open to the public.

The gardens, on the other hand, are open to all. Once the romping grounds of the tsarina, the palace gardens have since become – in true Soviet style – a park for the people (also called City Children's Park). The tree-lined dirt paths and picturesque pond make for a pleasant place to stroll, while children can enjoy climbing on the playground equipment or take their chances on some rusty rides.

top picks

IT'S FREE

Here are a few freebies for travellers whose pockets are not so deep:

- **State Hermitage Museum** (p125) Free – and crowded – on the first Thursday of the month.
- **Summer Garden** (p70) Free, thanks to the generous sponsorship of Sberbank in honour of the city's tercentenary.
- **Pushkinskaya 10** (p91) Free to look, not to buy.
- **Cruiser Aurora** (p117) Free Soviet propaganda.
- **Kazan Cathedral** (p73); **Vladimirsky Cathedral** (p91); **Alexander Nevsky Monastery** (p90) Any working church will allow you to enter for free (just say your prayers).
- **Grand Choral Synagogue** (p104) Ditto for working synagogues.
- **Museum of Zoology** (p110) Free on Thursdays.
- **Geological Museum** (p111) Free rocks.
- **Yelagin Island** (p120) Free on weekdays (and still pretty cheap on weekends).
- **Piskaryovskoe Cemetery** (p121)
- **Monument to the Heroic Defenders of Leningrad** (p145)

Just east of the gardens, on Shpalernaya ul, is one of the last remaining **statues of Felix Dzerzhinsky**, founder of the infamous Cheka (Bolshevik secret police), KGB predecessor.

FLORAL EXHIBITION HALL Map p84

☎ 272 5448; Potyomkinskaya ul 2; admission R60; 11am-7pm Tue-Sun; Ⓜ Chernyshevskaya

One of the finest ways to momentarily escape from a St Petersburg winter is to head for the Floral Exhibition Hall, an indoor tropical paradise just northwest of the Tauride Gardens. If you are sufficiently inspired, there is no shortage of flower stalls and florists in the vicinity, so you can take a little piece of paradise back home with you, too.

MUSEUM OF DECORATIVE & APPLIED ARTS Map p84

☎ 273 3258; Solyanoy per 15; adult/student R40/20; 11am-5pm Tue-Sat; Ⓜ Chernyshevskaya

Also known as the Stieglitz Museum, this must-see establishment is as beautiful as you would expect a decorative arts museum to be. A vast array of gorgeous objects is on display, from medieval handcrafted furniture to 18th-century Russian tiled stoves to contemporary works by the students of the Applied Arts School next door. Their surroundings merely match their magnificence. This museum is less visited than some of its counterparts in the city, but the quiet, off-the-beaten-track atmosphere only adds to its appeal.

In 1878 the millionaire Baron Stieglitz founded the School of Technical Design and wanted to surround his students with world-class art to inspire them. He began a collection that was continued by his son and was to include a unique array of European and Oriental glassware, porcelains, tapestries, furniture and paintings. It eventually grew into one of Europe's richest private collections. Between 1885 and 1895, a building designed by architect Maximilian Messmacher was built to house the collection and this building also became a masterpiece. Each hall is decorated in its own unique style, including Italian, Renaissance, Flemish and baroque. The Terem Room, in the style of the medieval Terem Palace of Moscow's Kremlin, is an opulent knockout.

After the revolution the school was closed, the museum's collection redistributed to the Hermitage and the Russian Museum, and most of the lavish interiors brutally painted or plastered over, even destroyed (one room was used as a sports hall). The painstaking renovation continues to this day, despite receiving no funding from the Ministry of Education under whose direction it falls, being connected to the Applied Arts School.

MUSEUM OF THE DEFENCE & BLOCKADE OF LENINGRAD

Map p84

☎ 275 7208; Solyanoy per 9; admission R100; 10am-5pm Thu-Tue, closed last Thu of month; Ⓜ Chernyshevskaya

This museum opened just three months after the blockade was lifted in January 1944 and boasted 37,000 exhibits, including real tanks and aeroplanes. But three years later, during Stalin's repression of the city, the museum was shut, its director shot, and most of the exhibits destroyed or redistributed. Not until 1985's glasnost was an attempt made to once again gather documents to reopen the museum; this happened in 1989. The grim but engrossing displays contain donations from survivors, propaganda posters from the time and many photos depicting life and death during the blockade. Book in advance for an English excursion.

ANNA AKHMATOVA MUSEUM IN THE FOUNTAIN HOUSE Map p84

☎ 272 2211; www.akhmatova.spb.ru; Liteyny pr 53; admission R100, audio tour R100; 10.30am-6.30pm Tue-Sun, 1-9pm Wed; M Gostiny Dvor

Housed in the south wing of the Sheremetyev Palace (1750–55), this touching and fascinating literary museum celebrates the life and work of Anna Akhmatova. St Petersburg's most famous 20th-century poet lived here from 1924 until 1952, as this was the apartment of her common-law husband Nikolai Punin. The apartment is on the 2nd floor and is filled with mementos of the poet and correspondence with other writers. The atmosphere is peaceful and contemplative. It's also an interesting chance to see the interior of an (albeit atypical) apartment from the early to mid-20th century.

Admission also includes the Josef Brodsky 'American Study'. Brodsky did not live here, but his connection with Akhmatova was strong. For lack of a better location, his office has been recreated here, complete with furniture and other 'artefacts' from his adopted home in Massachusetts.

Downstairs is a bookshop and video room where you can watch documentaries on the lives of Akhmatova and her contemporaries while drinking a cup of tea or coffee.

SHEREMETYEV PALACE Map p84

☎ 272 3898; www.theatremuseum.ru; nab reki Fontanki 34; adult/student R180/95; noon-6pm Wed-Sun; M Gostiny Dvor

Splendid wrought-iron gates facing the Fontanka River guard the entrance to the Sheremetyev Palace (1750–55), now a branch of the State Museum of Theatre & Music, which has a collection of musical instruments from the 19th and 20th centuries. The Sheremetyev family was famous for the concerts and theatre performances they hosted at their palace, which was a centre of musical life in the capital in the 18th century. Upstairs, the rooms have been wonderfully restored, which gives an impression of the cultural life of the time. Occasional concerts are still held here.

CATHEDRAL OF THE TRANSFIGURATION OF OUR SAVIOUR Map p84

Spaso-preobrazhensky Sobor; Preobrazhenskaya pl; services 10am & 6pm; M Chernyshevskaya

The interior of this marvellous 1743 cathedral, which has been beautifully restored and repainted both outside and in, is one of the most gilded in the city. The grand gates bear the imperial double-headed eagle in vast golden busts, reflecting the fact that the cathedral was built on the site where the Preobrazhensky Guards (the monarch's personal protection unit) had their headquarters. Architect Vasily Stasov rebuilt the cathedral from 1827 to 1829 in the neoclassical style. It is dedicated to the victory over the Turks in 1828–29; note the captured Turkish guns in the gate surrounding the cathedral.

CHURCH OF ST JOHN THE BAPTIST Map p84

Khram Ioanna Bogoslova; ☎ 273 9619; www.leushino.ru in Russian; ul Nekrasova 31; 9am-6pm; M Mayakovskaya

This extraordinary building has one of the most striking exteriors in the city – its Byzantine façade is totally incongruous with the rest of the street, although few people seem to notice it, hemmed in on both sides by other terraced buildings on ul Nekrasova. The church once had the whole building, but currently it shares the premises with a hospital. Go past the waiting patients to the 2nd floor where you can see the small church and chat with the charming nuns who look after it.

MUSEUM OF EROTICA Map p84

☎ 320 7600; ul Furshtatskaya 47; admission free; 8am-10pm; M Chernyshevskaya

It is odd enough that a museum should be housed in a venereal disease clinic. But even more surprising is the chief attraction of this quirky museum, which is a 30cm-long grey, embalmed penis that allegedly belonged to Rasputin. The chief of the prostate research centre of the Russian Academy of Natural Sciences, Igor Knyazkin, began assembling his collection of sexually themed trinkets his patients had given him over the years. At the very least, it gives patients something to do in the waiting room. Other exhibits include the bone of a sea lion's penis and various statuettes of people and animals in a variety of sexual positions.

WORLD OF WATER MUSEUM

Map p84

Mir Vody; ☎ 275 4325; Shpalernaya ul 56; adult/student R40/15; 🕒 9.30am-6pm Wed-Sun; Ⓜ Chernyshevskaya

The handsomely restored complex of 19th-century brick buildings between Tauride Gardens and the Neva River house St Petersburg's water treatment company Vodokanal and its museum. The 1st floor has an interesting multimedia exhibition about what goes on underneath St Petersburg. The upper floors of the water tower contain historical exhibitions, including the construction of waterways in the city and the water system during the blockade. Displays are slick and informative, though only in Russian.

BOLSHOY DOM Map p84

Liteyny pr 4; 🕒 closed to the public; Ⓜ Chernyshevskaya

Noi Trotsky's monolithic design for the local KGB headquarters (and current Interior Ministry headquarters) is referred to by everyone as the 'Bolshoy Dom' or 'Big House'. It's a fierce-looking block of granite built in 1932 in the late-constructivist style and was once a byword for fear among the people of the city: most people who were taken here during the purges were never heard of again. Employees who have worked here include current president Vladimir Putin during his days as a KGB man.

LITEYNY & SMOLNY

Walking Tour

1 Sheremetyev Palace This spectacular palace on the Fontanka River, built in the mid-18th century, now houses two marvellous museums: the wonderful Anna Akhmatova Museum in the Fountain House (p87), which also hosts

WALK FACTS

Start Nevsky pr at Fontanka River (Ⓜ Gostiny Dvor or Mayakovskaya)
Finish Suvorovsky pr at pl Proletarskoy Diktatury (Ⓜ Chernyshevskaya)
Distance 3km
Duration Two hours
Fuel stops Black Cat, White Cat (p168), Sunduk (p168)

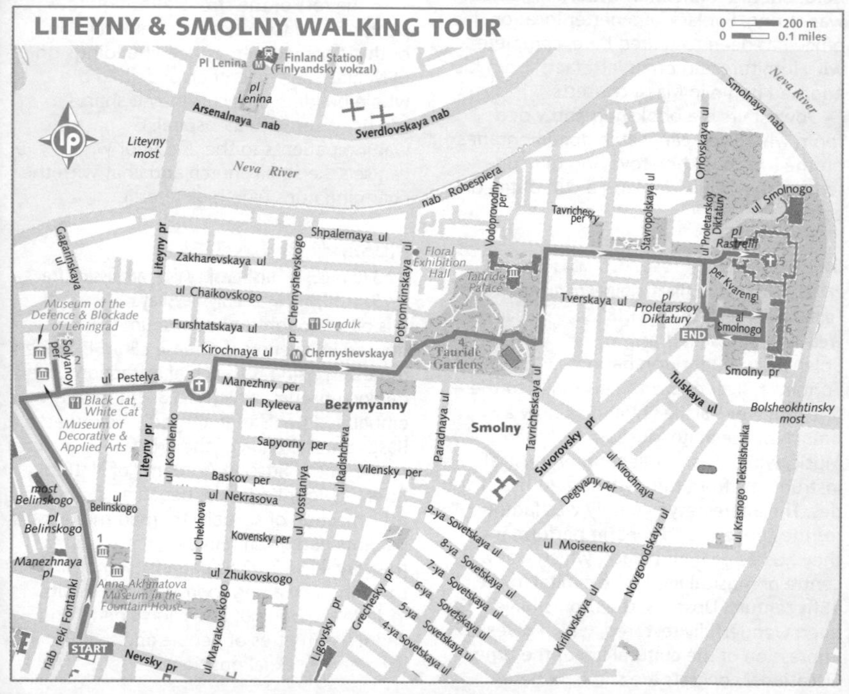

temporary exhibitions of contemporary art, and the 'music' branch of the State Museum of Theatre & Music, often simply called Sheremetyev Palace (p87).

2 Solyanoy per This lane contains two little-known but worthwhile museums: the Museum of Decorative & Applied Arts (p86), housed in an exquisite interior, and the moving Museum of the Defence & Blockade of Leningrad (p86), which remembers the city's heroism during WWII.

3 Cathedral of the Transfiguration of Our Saviour Occupying an island in the middle of ul Pestelya, the Cathedral of the Transfiguration of Our Saviour (p87) is beautifully restored both inside and out.

4 Tauride Gardens Look across the little lake to the fabulous Tauride Palace (p85), gifted by Catherine the Great to her lover, Grigory Potemkin. If the gardens are not blooming, check out the Floral Exhibition Hall (p86) just northwest of the gardens.

5 Smolny Cathedral The baby blue façade and gilt gold domes of Smolny Cathedral (p83), the premier attraction of the neighbourhood, surely represent one of Bartolomeo Rastrelli's proudest moments. The cathedral is no longer functioning as a church, but you can climb 277 steps to the top of the cupola for a fantastic vista.

6 Smolny Institute Just south of the cathedral, the government building of the Smolny Institute (p83) has both historic and contemporary significance. In 1917 the Bolsheviks set up the Petrograd Soviet here, and it continues to be the seat of government today.

VLADIMIRSKAYA & VOSSTANIYA

Eating p169; Shopping p155; Sleeping p208

As Nevsky pr heads east from the Fontanka River, it continues to attract crowds to its shopping centres and street cafés, although the architecture is more urban – less extravagant – than in the Historic Heart (with a few notable exceptions).

On the south side of Nevsky, Vladimirsky pr leads south to Vladimirskaya pl, which is dominated by the grand, gold-domed cathedral of the same name. In the surrounding streets there is the Vladimirskaya metro station (Ⓜ Vladimirskaya) and the shopping centre of Vladimirsky Passage (p156), so you know what neighbourhood you are in.

Ever-lively, Nevsky pr continues east to pl Vosstaniya (Uprising Sq), so called because the February Revolution began here in 1917. Although it is a geographically vast area, large swathes of land are consumed by industrial wasteland, as well as St Petersburg's busiest railway station, Moscow Station (Moskovsky vokzal). Pl Vosstaniya is also the site of the busy connected metro stations, Ⓜ Pl Vosstaniya and Ⓜ Mayakovskaya, which are useful transport options.

The joint districts of Vladimirskaya and Vosstaniya are surrounded by water on three sides, with the Fontanka in the west, the Obvodny Canal running across the south and the Neva looping around to form the eastern border. In the north, the neighbourhood goes up to and includes Nevsky pr.

The quieter, less commercial, easterly end of Nevsky is known locally as Staronevsky (Old Nevsky), despite being no older than Nevsky proper. Nevsky pr ends at pl Alexandra Nevskogo, named after the city's patron saint, who defeated the Swedes in the area during the 12th century. On this square stands the ancient and revered Alexander Nevsky Monastery, the oldest monastery in the city. This end of Nevsky is served by its own metro stop, Ⓜ Pl Alexandra Nevskogo.

ALEXANDER NEVSKY MONASTERY

Map p92

Lavra Alexandra Nevskogo; ☎ 274 0409; www.lavra.spb.ru; pl Alexandra Nevskogo; admission free; ⌚ grounds 6am-10pm; Ⓜ Pl Alexandra Nevskogo

Peter the Great made a mistake when he founded the Alexander Nevsky Monastery on this spot at the far end of Nevsky pr. He wrongly thought that this was where Alexander of Novgorod had beaten the Swedes in 1240. Nonetheless, in 1797 it became a *lavra,* the most senior grade of Russian Orthodox monasteries. And today it is a working monastery that attracts the most devout believers – a revered and holy place – and the gravesite of some of Russia's most famous artistic figures.

You can wander freely around most of the grounds, but you must buy tickets from the kiosk on your right after entering the main gates to enter the graveyards (☎ 271 2635; adult/student R140/70; ⌚ 11am-7pm Fri-Wed Mar-Sep & 11am-3.30pm Fri-Wed Oct-Feb).

The Tikhvin Cemetery (Tikhvinskoe kladbishche), on the right as you enter, contains the most famous graves (see the boxed text, opposite). Now part of the City Sculpture Museum (see following), the former Tikhvin Church contains an exhibition of models of the sculptures and monuments that are scattered around the city.

Facing the Tikhvin across the entrance path, the Lazarus Cemetery (Lazarevskoe kladbishche) contains the graves of several late great St Petersburg architects – among them Andrei Voronikhin, Giacomo Quarenghi, Vasily Stasov and Carlo Rossi. Scholar and polymath Mikhail Lomonosov is also buried here. The St Lazarus Church (admission R30; ⌚ 11am-4.30pm Fri-Wed) is a crypt dating to 1761. It contains the graves of Count Sheremetyev and his serf-actress wife, as well as a few other statesmen, nobles, artists and intellectuals.

In the main *lavra* complex, the first main building on the left is the 1717–22 baroque Annunciation Church (Blagoveshchenskaya Tserkov), now the City Sculpture Museum (☎ 274 2545; adult/student R70/35; ⌚ 11am-5pm Tue & Thu-Sun). Except for the cupola, this interior is hardly recognisable as a church, as only a few fragments of frescoes remain. The exhibition includes the downstairs crypt and some sculptures of headstones upstairs.

About 100m further on is the monastery's 1776–90 classical Trinity Cathedral (Troitsky Sobor; ☎ 274 1612; ⌚ 6am-8pm, services at 7am, 10am & 6pm). Hundreds crowd in here on 12 September to celebrate the feast of St Alexander Nevsky, whose remains are in the silver reliquary by the main iconostasis. Behind the cathedral is the Nicholas Cemetery (⌚ 9am-9pm summer, 9am-6pm winter), a romantically overgrown field where many of the cathedral's priests are buried.

Opposite the cathedral is Metropolitan's House (1775–78), residence of Metropolitan Vladimir, the spiritual leader of St Petersburg's Russian Orthodox community. In the surrounding grounds is a smaller cemetery where leading Communist (ie atheist) Party officials and luminaries are buried. On the far right of the grounds facing the canal is St Petersburg's Orthodox Academy, one of only a handful in Russia (the main one is at Sergiev Posad, near Moscow).

NEW EXHIBITION HALL Map p92

☎ 274 2579; Nevsky pr 179/2; adult/student R150/100; 11am-6pm Sat-Wed; M Pl Alexandra Nevskogo

This small, two-storey exhibition space is one of a few places in the city that are designated for contemporary art. Exhibitions change monthly, usually showcasing local artists, including some edgy, up-and-coming stuff, as well as more conventional works by influential 20th-century artists.

PUSHKINSKAYA 10 Map p92

☎ 764 5258; www.p10.nonmuseum.ru; Ligovsky pr 53; admission free; 3-7pm Wed-Sun; M Pl Vosstaniya

This legendary locale is a required stop for anyone who is interested in the contemporary art and music scene in St Petersburg. The former apartment block – affectionately called by its former street address – contains studio and gallery space, as well as the cool music clubs Fish Fabrique (p184) and Experimental Sound Gallery (GEZ-21) (p184) and an assortment of other shops (see p155). It offers a unique opportunity to hang out with local musicians and artists, who are always eager to talk about their work.

The story of Pushkinskaya 10 goes back to 1988, when a group of artists/squatters took over the condemned apartment block. The decrepit building became 'underground central', as artists and musicians moved in to set up studios, others stopped by to hang out with them, and outsiders became curious about the creative activity going on inside (see the boxed text, p49).

These days, the art centre is a registered nonprofit organisation (officially the Free Culture Society) that is completely on the up-and-up. Some would argue that the place has lost its edge, and the tension between culture and commercial is apparent. But the creative atmosphere here is unparalleled, and the centre is unbeatable as a place to witness art and music being created.

The main galleries, the Museum of Non-Conformist Art and the New Academy of Fine Arts Museum, are on the 4th floor. Smaller galleries are scattered throughout the building, and the artists often open their studios to visitors, especially on Saturday afternoons. A highlight is the Temple of Love, Peace & Music (☎ 764 5353; ground fl; 6-8pm Fri & specially designated 'high holidays'). Collector Kolya Vasin (Russia's most famous Beatles' fan) has an amazing array of John Lennon paraphernalia, which he shares with other fans on designated days.

The centre commonly goes by the name 'Pushkinskaya 10', but note that the entrance is through the archway at Ligovsky pr 53.

VLADIMIRSKY CATHEDRAL Map p92

☎ 312 1938; Vladimirsky pr 20; admission free; 8am-6pm, services 6pm daily; M Vladimirskaya

This fantastic, five-domed cathedral, ascribed to Domenico Trezzini, is the namesake of this neighbourhood. Incorporating both baroque and neoclassical elements, the cathedral was built in the 1760s, with Giacomo Quarenghi's neoclassical bell

GRAVEYARD TO THE GREATS

The Alexander Nevsky Monastery – named for the patron saint of St Petersburg – is the city's most ancient and eminent monastery. So it is appropriate that the attached Tikhvin Cemetery should be the final resting place for so many cultural icons. Like Novodevichy Cemetery in Moscow, this is where visitors pay their respects to the most illustrious individuals in Russian music, literature, art and theatre.

It was in St Petersburg that the 'Group of Five' – Modest Mussorgsky, Nikolai Rimsky-Korsakov, Alexander Borodin, César Cui and Mily Balakirev – so defined Russian music with their folk-influenced themes. And it is here, in Tikhvin Cemetery, that all five are buried, as are Mikhail Glinka and Pyotr Tchaikovsky.

Here is the grave of Ivan Krylov, beloved Russian fabulist. But Tikhvin's most famous literary resident is Fyodor Dostoevsky, whose epitaph is also the epigraph of his final novel, *The Brothers Karamazov*. 'Verily, verily, I say unto you, except a corn of wheat fall into the ground and die, it abideth alone: but if it die, it bringeth forth much fruit.'

VLADIMIRSKAYA & VOSSTANIYA

VLADIMIRSKAYA & VOSSTANIYA

INFORMATION
36.6 Pharmacy ... 1 B2
Anglotourism ... 2 B2
Café Max ... 3 C1
Citibank Nevsky ... 4 B1
FM Club ... 5 B2
Kofe In ... 6 D2
Medem International Clinic & Hospital ... 7 C2
Ost-West Kontaktservice ... 8 D2
Quo Vadis ... 9 B1
Sunday Morning Bike Tour ... (see 64)
Telephone Centre ... 10 C1
Vosstaniya-1 ... 11 C1

SIGHTS (pp90-5)
Alexander Nevsky Monastery Лавра Александра Невского ... 12 E3
Beloselsky-Belozersky Palace Дворец Белосельских-Белозерских ... 13 B1
City Sculpture Museum Городской музей скульптуры ... 14 E3
Dostoevsky Museum Музей Достоевского ... 15 C2
GUVD Museum Музей ГУВД ... 16 D2
Lasarus Cemetery Лазаревское кладбище ... 17 E3
Metropolitan's House ... 18 E3
Museum of Bread ... 19 C2
Museum of the Arctic & Antarctic Музей Арктики и Антарктики ... 20 C2
New Exhibit Hall Новый выставочный зал ... 21 E3
Nicolas Cemetery Никольское кладбище ... 22 F3
Orthodox Academy Духовная Академия ... 23 E3
Pushkinskaya 10 ... 24 C2
Rimsky-Korsakov Flat-Museum Музей-квартира Римского-Корсакова ... 25 B2
Tikhvin Cemetery Тихвинское кладбище ... 26 E3
Trinity Cathedral Троицкий собор ... 27 E3
Vladimirsky Cathedral Владимирский собор ... 28 B2

SHOPPING (pp149-58)
505 ... (see 69)
Art re.flex ... 29 D2
Imperial Porcelain ... 30 D2
Imperial Porcelain ... 31 B1
Kailas ... (see 37)
KultProsvet ... (see 24)
Kuznechny Market Кузнечный рынок ... 32 B2
La Russe ... 33 B1
Lend ... (see 39)
Natalie Kvasova ... 34 B1
Parfionova ... 35 B1
Pushkinskaya 10 ... (see 24)
Rive Gauche ... 36 C2
Spinning Wheel ... 37 C2
Titanik ... 38 C1
Vladimirsky Passage Владимирский пассаж ... 39 B2

EATING (pp159-76)
Baltic Bread ... (see 39)
Bistrot Garçon ... 40 D2
Bliny Domik ... 41 C2
Bushe ... 42 B3
Cat Café ... 43 C2
Chaynaya Lozhka ... 44 C2
Che ... 45 D2
Il Patio ... 46 E3
Imbir ... 47 B2
Matrosskaya Tishina ... 48 B3
Orient Express ... 49 C2
Shinok ... 50 B2
Troitsky Most ... 51 A3
U Tyoshi na Blinakh ... 52 B2
Yolki Palki ... 53 C1

DRINKING & NIGHTLIFE (pp177-86)
Café Rico ... 54 C2
Che ... (see 45)
Experimental Sound Gallery (GEZ-21) ... (see 24)
Fish Fabrique ... (see 24)
Griboedov ... 55 B3
Jazz Philharmonic Hall ... 56 A3
Manhattan ... 57 A2
Ounce ... 58 C1
Pivnaya 0.5 ... 59 A3
Red Club ... 60 D2
Zerno Istiny ... 61 B2

ARTS (pp188-94)
LenSovet Theatre Театр им Ленсовета ... 62 B2
Maly Drama Theatre Малый драматический театр ... 63 B2

SPORTS & ACTIVITIES (pp195-200)
Skat Prokat ... 64 D2

SLEEPING (pp201-12)
Brothers Karamazov ... 65 B3
Fifth Corner ... 66 B2
Helvetia Hotel & Suites ... 67 C2
Hotel Dostoevsky ... 68 B2
Kristoff Hotel ... 69 B2
Nevsky Central Hotel ... 70 C1
Nevsky Express Hotel ... 71 D2
Nevsky Forum ... 72 C1
Oktober Filial Филиал гостиницы Октябрьская ... 73 C2
Oktober Hotel Гостиница Октябрьская ... 74 C1

TRANSPORT (pp233-40)
Aeroflot ... 75 B1
Astoria Service ... 76 B3
Avis ... 77 E3
Cruise Russia ... 78 C3
Rossiya Airlines ... 79 C1

tower added later in the century. Apparently Fyodor Dostoevsky was a parishioner here (convenient, as he lived around the corner). Sadly, the cathedral was closed in 1932 and the Soviets turned it into an underwear factory; but in 1990 it was reconsecrated and reconstructed, and it has resumed its originally intended function. These days it is one of the busiest cathedrals in town, as evidenced by the hordes of babushkas and beggars outside. Nonetheless, it's worth weaving your way through the outstretched hands to admire the cathedral's interiors (upstairs). The baroque iconostasis was originally installed in the private chapel of the Anichkov Palace (p76), but was transferred here in 1808. For an impressive perspective on the onion domes, have a drink in the 7th-floor bar of Hotel Dostoevsky (p209) across the road.

DOSTOEVSKY MUSEUM Map p92

571 4031; www.md.spb.ru; Kuznechny per 5/2; adult/student R120/60, audio tour R70; 11am-6pm Tue-Sun; M Vladimirskaya

Fyodor Dostoevsky lived in flats all over the city, mostly in Sennaya (p96), but his final residence is this 'memorial flat'. Dostoevsky lived here from 1878 until he died in 1881. The apartment remains as it was when the Dostoevsky family lived here, including the study where Fyodor wrote *The Brothers Karamazov,* and the office of Anna Grigorievna, his wife, who recopied, edited and sold all of his books. Two rooms of the museum are devoted to his novels: literature fans will want to pay close attention to the map of Dostoevsky's Petersburg, which details the locations of characters and events in his various works. A rather gloomy likeness of the man himself (as if there's any other kind) is just outside the Vladimirskaya metro station.

RIMSKY-KORSAKOV FLAT-MUSEUM

Map p92

☎ 713 3208; www.theatremuseum.ru; Zagorodny pr 28; adult/student R75/50, Russian tour R200; 11am-6pm Wed-Sun; M Vladimirskaya

Home of Nikolai Rimsky-Korsakov for the last 15 years of his life (1893–1908), this is where he composed 11 of his 15 operas, including the *Fairytale of the Tsar Sultan* and the *Golden Rooster*. The memorial flat (a branch of the State Museum of Theatre & Music) includes four rooms that have been lovingly restored to their original appearance, including the composer's study. A Becker grand piano graces the living room. Rachmaninov, Glazunov, Scriabin, Stravinsky – and of course Rimsky-Korsakov himself – have all tickled these ivories.

The composer maintained a tradition of hosting musical soirees at his home; this tradition continues today, with concerts on Thursday afternoons at 4pm (although you are unlikely to see Chaliapin perform here today). Enter from the courtyard.

GUVD MUSEUM Map p92

☎ 779 7825; Poltavskaya ul 12; tour for up to 20 people R600; 11am-5pm Mon-Fri; M Pl Vosstaniya

For police enthusiasts, the great but little-known GUVD Museum chronicles the history of criminality and law enforcement by the Ministry of Internal Affairs in Leningrad/St Petersburg. This balanced, fascinating exhibition, featuring photos, costumes and weapons in several large halls, will acquaint you with interesting titbits about gang bosses and the Mafia's reign of terror in the 1920s through the fight to control illegal abortions and alcohol production. You'll need to get a guided tour for this, so you will want to book in advance.

BELOSELSKY-BELOZERSKY PALACE

Map p92

☎ 315 5236; Nevsky pr 41; by appointment; M Gostiny Dvor or Mayakovskaya

The salmon pink exterior of the 1840s Beloselsky-Belozersky Palace provides a photogenic backdrop to Anichkov most (p76). The palace was formerly a home of Communist Party officials, and now continues to serve in various official capacities. It is normally closed to the public, although tours of the opulent interior can be arranged and occasional concerts are held in the oak-panelled concert hall. The 1st floor holds the small Anatoly Sobchak Museum on the Establishment of Democracy (☎ 571 1706; 10am-5pm Mon-Fri), which might be interesting for its coverage of recent history.

MUSEUM OF BREAD Map p92

Muzey Khleba; ☎ 764 1110; www.museum.ru/museum/bread in Russian; Ligovsky pr 73; adult/student R100/50; 10am-4pm Mon-Fri; M Pl Vosstaniya

This funky little museum pays tribute to 'our daily bread' and the role it has played in history (of the city and of the world). A model bakery exhibits the equipment that was used to make bread for the city's poorest classes in the 19th century. A special exhibition on the Siege of Leningrad offers an example of a daily ration of bread during WWII. The museum has been open since 1998, but hours of operation are sporadic, so it may be useful to call in advance.

MUSEUM OF THE ARCTIC & ANTARCTIC Map p92

☎ 571 2549; www.polarmuseum.sp.ru; ul Marata 24A; adult/student R100/50; 10am-6pm Wed-Sun; M Vladimirskaya

Inside the former Old Believers' Church of St Nicholas, this little museum is devoted to Soviet polar explorations. The self-proclaimed highlight of the museum is the 'polar philatelic collection' – a huge selection of postcards sent by various expeditions and stamps with polar themes. Apart from stuffed polar bears and the like, the most impressive exhibit is a wooden boat plane hanging from the ceiling.

VLADIMIRSKAYA & VOSSTANIYA

Walking Tour

1 Vladimirskaya Pl Named for the golden-domed Vladimirsky Cathedral (p91), this bustling square is the centre of a commercial district. Indeed, if you like to shop, Vladimirsky Passage (p156) is a nice place to do it. The bronze bust

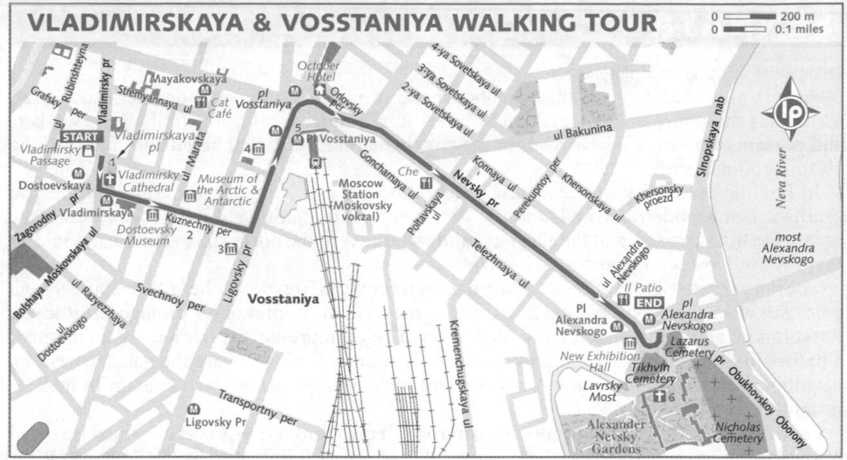

WALK FACTS

Start Vladimirskaya pl ((M) Vladimirskaya)
Finish Pl Alexandra Nevskogo ((M) Pl Alexandra Nevskogo)
Distance 2km
Duration 1½ hours
Fuel stops Cat Café (p170), Che (p170), Il Patio (p170)

of Dostoevsky pays tribute to the fact that the great writer lived nearby.

2 Kuznechny per Though Dostoevsky's best-known novel was set in the streets around Sennaya pl, he also lived in a home on Kuznechny per, which is now the Dostoevsky Museum (p93). Some scenes from *The Idiot* take place in the streets of Vosstaniya, although the descriptions are not quite so vivid as in *Crime and Punishment*. Up the road is the odd little Museum of the Arctic & Antarctic (opposite).

3 Museum of Bread Say what you want about Russian cuisine, but these people know how to bake their bread. The unexpected Museum of Bread (opposite) pays tribute to the staff of life.

4 Pushkinskaya 10 This old-fashioned apartment block houses an eclectic assortment of art galleries, music clubs and studio space. Alive with creative energy and artistic electricity, Pushkinskaya 10 (p91) is a throwback to a time when things were not so predictable.

5 Pl Vosstaniya Inside Moscow Station, St Petersburg's busiest railway station, Peter the Great welcomes visitors to his city. Outside, the sign above the October Hotel (p209) proclaims 'Hero City Leningrad', a designation bestowed upon this city after WWII.

6 Alexander Nevsky Monastery At the far end of Nevsky pr, the important Alexander Nevsky Monastery (p90) dates to 1713. Besides the centrepiece church, the grounds contain three cemeteries – the final resting places of some of Russia's most important cultural figures. Nearby is the New Exhibition Hall (p91) showcasing contemporary art.

SENNAYA

Eating p171; Shopping p156; Sleeping p209

More infamous than famous, this neighbourhood is named for the once derelict Haymarket, which was the centre of Dostoevskian St Petersburg. Sennaya was home to the poor workers and peasants who were new arrivals in the city, living in rat-infested basements and sleeping 10-to-a-room in shifts.

In honour of the city's tercentennial celebrations in 2003, the square received a massive overhaul, being modernised and sanitised almost beyond recognition. But the chaos around the square has not subsided, and the alleyways and waterways to the north still evoke the moodiness that Fyodor Dostoevsky portrayed so vividly.

The border between reality and fantasy has been smudged irrevocably here: Petersburgers will point out where Dostoevsky lived as quickly as they will the homes of his protagonist Rodyon Raskolnikov and the old woman moneylender. The omnipresent stray cats – as permanent a fixture in St Petersburg courtyards as dim light and foul odours – are the gatekeepers to a neighbourhood whose gloominess and squalor have been preserved well enough to make it instantly recognisable.

Sadovaya ul is the neighbourhood's main road. It cuts through Sennaya pl, which is served by two connected metro stations (Ⓜ Sennaya Pl/Sadovaya). It is flanked by the Fontanka River to the south and Griboedov Canal to the north. The Moyka River forms the neighbourhood's northern boundary. Gorokhovaya ul delineates the eastern border with the Historic Heart, and Voznesensky pr marks the western border with Mariinsky. The neighbourhood extends south all the way to Zagorodny pr.

SENNAYA PL Map p97

Ⓜ Sennaya Pl

St Petersburg's Haymarket was the city's filthy underbelly immortalised by Dostoevsky, who lived in the neighbourhood and set *Crime and Punishment* here. Until a recent face-lift, the square was overloaded with makeshift kiosks and market stalls, which made it a magnet for the homeless, beggars, pickpockets and drunks. Despite a big clean-up effort by city authorities in time for the tercentennial in 2003, Sennaya pl retains a fundamental insalubriousness. Be on your guard walking around here at night.

The peripatetic Dostoevsky, who occupied around 20 residences in his 28-year stay in the city, once spent a couple of days in debtors' prison in what is now called the Senior Officers' Barracks, just across the square from the Sennaya pl metro station.

The old woman moneylender from *Crime and Punishment* lived a few blocks west of here, at nab kanala Griboedova 104. Her flat would have been no 74, on the 3rd floor.

DOSTOEVSKY HOUSES Map p97

Kaznacheyskaya ul 7; ⏲ closed to the public; Ⓜ Sennaya Pl

Dostoevsky lived in three flats on this tiny street alone. From 1861 to 1863, he lived at No 1. In 1864, he spent one month living in the faded red building at No 9, before moving to No 7. Here, he lived from 1864 to 1867 and wrote *Crime and Punishment;* indeed, the route taken by the novel's anti-hero Raskolnikov to murder the old woman moneylender passed directly under his window. While this area has changed enormously, it's still possible to catch glimpses of the grim reality of slum life that pervaded this place in the mid-19th century.

RASKOLNIKOV HOUSE Map p97

Dom Roskolnikova; Stolyarny per 5; ⏲ closed to the public; Ⓜ Sennaya Pl

This innocuous house on the corner of Stolyarny per (called 'S… lane' in the book) is one of two possible locations of the attic apartment of Rodyon Raskolnikov, protagonist of Dostoevsky's *Crime and Punishment*. Those who claim this is the place go further, saying that Rodyon retrieved the murder weapon from a street-sweeper's storage bin inside the tunnel leading to the courtyard.

The house is marked by a sculpture of Dostoevsky. The inscription says something to the effect of 'The tragic fate of the people of this area of St Petersburg formed the foundation of Dostoevsky's passionate sermon of goodness for all mankind'.

Other Dostoevsky connoisseurs argue that Raskolnikov's attic apartment would more appropriately be located down the street at No 9, which is otherwise unmarked.

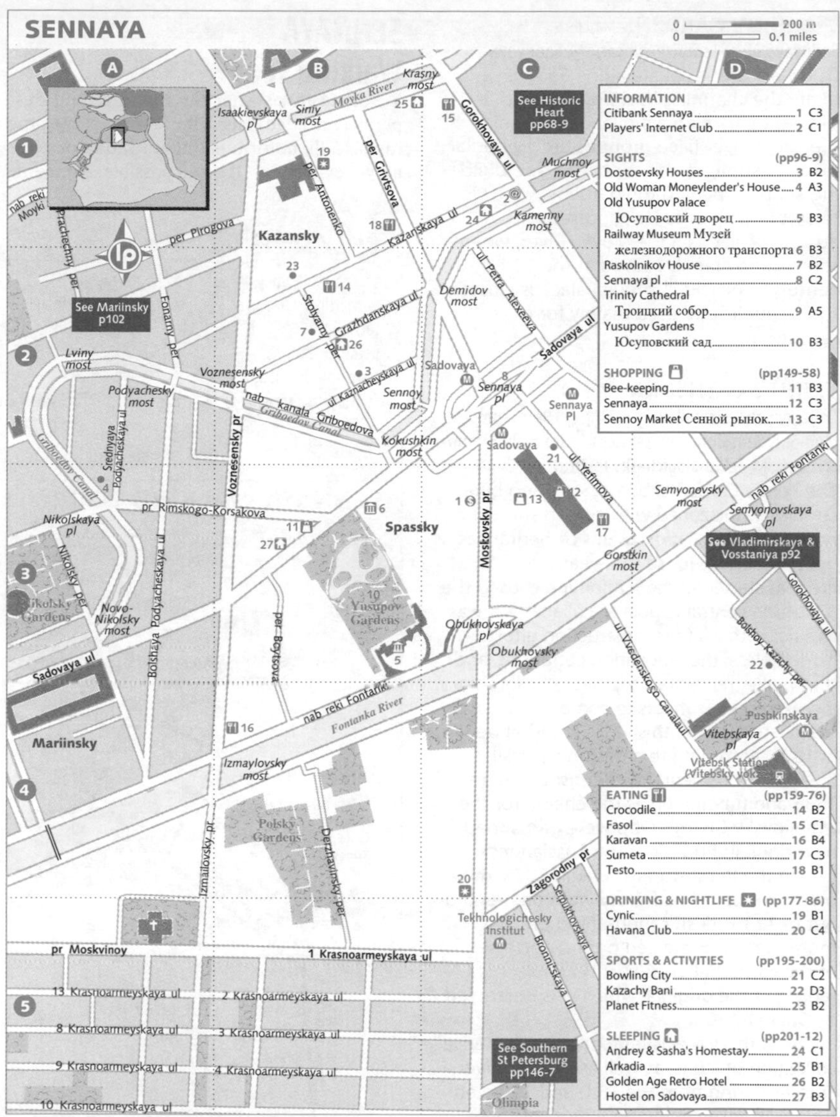

RAILWAY MUSEUM Map p97

☎ 315 1476; www.railroad.ru/cmrt in Russian; Sadovaya ul 50; adult/student/child R70/30/20; 11am-5.30pm Sun-Thu; M Sadovaya

This quirky museum near Sennaya pl houses a collection of scale locomotives and model railway bridges, often made by the same engineers that built the real ones. The oldest such collection in the world, the museum dates to 1809. That's 28 years before Russia had its first working train! It includes models of the *Yenisey Bridge*, the ship that once carried passengers and trains across Lake Baikal. No matter how many overnight trains you have ridden, you are unlikely to recognise the sumptuous 1903 Trans-Siberian wagon, complete with piano salon and bathtub. To see full-size vintage trains, visit the **Museum of Railway Technology** (p146).

YUSUPOV GARDENS Map p97

Sadovaya ul; sunrise-sunset; Sadovaya

Due west of the square along Sadovaya ul are the charming Yusupov Gardens, a pleasant park with a big lake in the middle. The flower-filled grounds are a popular place to stroll, sit and sunbathe. The building set back behind the gardens is the Old Yusupov Palace (not to be confused with the Yusupov Palace on the Moyka River, where the Yusupov family moved in the 18th century). The Old Yusupov Palace is closed to the public and used mainly for official receptions.

TRINITY CATHEDRAL Map p97

Troitsky Sobor; Izmailovsky pr 7A; 9am-7pm Mon-Sat, 8am-8pm Sun, services 10am daily & 5pm Fri-Sun; Tekhnologichesky Institut

The Trinity Cathedral boasts stunning blue cupolas emblazoned with golden stars. Slow but careful restoration of this cathedral has been underway for several years. In 2006, a fire that started in the scaffolding caused the 83m-high central cupola to collapse – it was a major setback to reconstruction efforts. Nonetheless, the renovation continues, and the smaller renovated cupolas act as a shining example of what is to come.

Construction of this vast cathedral began in 1828, according to a design by Vasily Stasov. The cathedral was consecrated in 1835 and functioned as the chapel for the Izmailovsky Guards, who were garrisoned next door. In honour of the Russian victory in the Russo-Turkish War in 1878, the memorial Column of Glory was constructed out of 128 Turkish canons. (The present monument was erected on the north side of the cathedral in 2003: it is an exact replica of the original, which was destroyed by Stalin.)

The cathedral was famed for its immense collection of icons, as well as several silver crosses dating from the 18th and 19th centuries. After the revolution, most of these treasures were looted, the ornate interiors were destroyed and the cathedral was finally closed in 1938.

Trinity Cathedral was returned to the Orthodox Church in 1990, but the interior is decidedly bare, especially compared with its previous appearance. Literature buffs will be interested to know that this is the church where Fyodor Dostoevsky married his second wife, Anna Snitkina, in 1867.

SENNAYA

Walking Tour

1 Sennaya pl After the massive (and desperately needed) face-lift of Sennaya pl (p96), the historically notorious filth and squalor is no longer evident, yet it is still possible to imagine

WALK FACTS

Start Sennaya pl (Sennaya Pl/Sadovaya)
End Trinity Cathedral (Tekhnologichesky Institut)
Distance 1km
Duration One hour
Fuel stops Crocodile (p171), Karavan (p171), Cynic (p179)

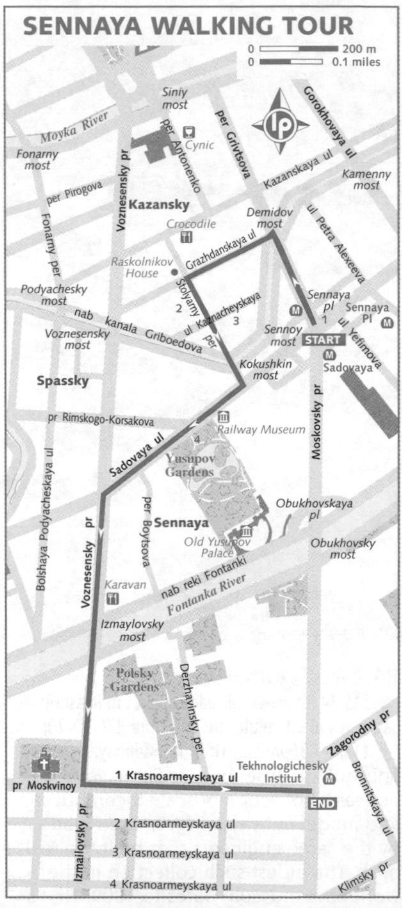

that in Dostoevsky's time it was a teeming madhouse, filled with drunks, beggars, thieves and other sleazy characters.

2 Stolyarny per The house at No 5 Stolyarny per (simply called 'S… lane' in *Crime and Punishment*) is known as Raskolnikov House (p96), as it is one of two possible locations of Raskolnikov's attic room. Many believe that the more likely location is down the street at No 9.

3 Kaznacheyskaya ul Dostoevsky lived in three flats on this tiny street. From 1861 to 1863 he lived at No 1. In 1864 he spent one month at No 9, before moving to No 7, where he would live for three years and write *Crime and Punishment*.

4 Yusupov Gardens Dostoevsky and his characters weren't the only famous residents here. Until the mid 19th-century, the now-infamous Yusupov family lived in the Old Yusupov Palace, which is surrounded by the lovely Yusupov Gardens (opposite). Not far away, the Railway Museum (p97) will delight model-train lovers.

5 Trinity Cathedral Cross the Fontanka River and stroll south to the star-spangled gem of Trinity Cathedral (opposite). Renovation is taking longer than expected because of a 2006 fire that caused the main cupola to collapse.

MARIINSKY

Eating p172; Shopping p157; Sleeping p210

Named after the celebrated Mariinsky Theatre, this neighbourhood is just off the beaten tourist track (assuming you wander away from the theatre itself). The Historic Heart is just next door, but Mariinsky feels far from those crowded streets. Here, the canals that meander through the centre empty into the Gulf of Finland (Finsky Zaliv) and crumbling mansions and forgotten churches gradually give way to the city's docklands. The district houses some of the city's lesser known but most interesting religious buildings, including the recently renovated Grand Choral Synagogue (p104).

Change is in the air, however. Just behind the famous theatre is a huge construction project, better known as Mariinsky II (see p57). Other notable renovation projects are underway, including the long forgotten Palace of Grand Duke Alexey Alexandrovich (p105) and the soon-to-be cultural centre at New Holland (Novaya Gollandiya; p105).

Unfortunately one of the planned improvements is not the introduction of a metro line: the whole area has a somewhat languorous feel, as there's not a single metro station in it. The best way to access this neighbourhood is from Ⓜ Sennaya Pl/Sadovaya, which is a 10- to 20-minute walk from most of the sights. Some sights in the northwestern corner may be more easily accessed from the metro station Ⓜ Vasileostrovskaya, across the river.

The Neva embankment west of the Admiralty is dominated by the golden cupola of St Isaac's Cathedral, which towers over pl Dekabristov and the Admiralty Gardens. Isaakievskaya pl and Voznesensky pr delineate the neighbourhood's eastern boundary with the Historic Heart and Sennaya districts, while the Neva River marks the northern and western boundaries. Voznesensky pr stretches south to the Fontanka River, the southern border of the Mariinsky district.

The Mariinsky Theatre and its namesake Teatralnaya pl are the centrepiece of the neighbourhood. From here, the main drag, ul Dekabristov, heads east and west. A whole network of waterways wind their way around here, including the meandering Moyka, Griboedov and Fontanka, as well as the straight, north–south Kryukov Canal.

ST ISAAC'S CATHEDRAL Map p102

Isaakievsky Sobor; ☎ 315 9732; www.cathedral.ru; Isaakievskaya pl; adult/student cathedral R300/150, colonnade R150/100; ⏲ 11am-6pm Thu-Tue; Ⓜ Sadovaya

The golden dome of St Isaac's Cathedral, looming just south of pl Dekabristov, dominates the St Petersburg skyline. Named after St Isaac of Dalmatia, on whose feast day Peter the Great was born, it is one of the largest domed buildings in the world. More than 100kg of gold leaf was used to cover the 21.8m-high dome alone.

French designer Auguste Montferrand began designing the cathedral in 1818, despite the fact that he was no architect. Indeed, it was Montferrand's contacts at court who ensured that the design was approved by the tsar. Local architects were outraged at the foreign upstart's commission and were quick to point out (correctly) a number of technical flaws in the plan.

The cathedral took so long to build (until 1858) that Nicholas I was able to insist on a more grandiose structure than Montferrand had planned. The long construction period gave rise to a rumour among locals that the Romanov dynasty would fall were the cathedral ever completed – something that in the event happened some 60 years later. Special ships and a railway had to be built to carry the granite from Finland for the huge pillars, which each weigh some 120 tonnes. There's a statue of Montferrand holding a model of the cathedral on the west façade, although Nicholas I denied the architect his dying wish, to be buried here, considering it too high an honour for an artisan.

Since 1990, after a 62-year gap, services have been held here on major religious holidays and St Isaac's may return to full Church control before long. Like the Church of the Saviour on Spilled Blood, St Isaac's is officially classed as a museum and as such lacks any religious atmosphere.

The cathedral's interior is obscenely lavish, covering 4000 sq metres with 600 sq metres of mosaics, 16,000kg of malachite, 14 types of marble and an 816-sq-metre ceiling painting by Karl Bryullov. Among the many displays inside there are some interesting photographs of the cathedral

TO HAVE & TO HOLD

No event gives more cause for celebration than a wedding. Festivities commence when the groom arrives to claim his bride. He is forced to pass a series of tests – physical feats and brain-teasers – before he can see his beloved. Once he proves his devotion, the happy couple proceeds to the department of registry for a simple ceremony, usually attended only by immediate family and close friends. Then the wedding party takes a tour of the city, laying flowers at war memorials to remember the dead, and drinking champagne at other landmarks to celebrate the living.

Newlyweds' most beloved site in St Petersburg is pl Dekabristov. Here, Peter the Great sits astride his horse. And here, brides and grooms, friends and family come to memorialise their wedding day in photographs. More often than not, an amateur band is on hand, playing requests from the wedding parties to earn a few roubles. Everyone is invited to partake of the bubbly, to toast the glad day and the couple's joyful future together.

throughout its history, including one of the park outside being used to grow cabbages during the Nazi blockade.

Finish off your visit by climbing the 262 steps to the *kolonnada* (colonnade) around the drum of the dome. The view to the four corners of the city is sublime. Tickets are sold separately at the kiosk on the north-east side of the cathedral.

BRONZE HORSEMAN Map p102

pl Dekabristov; M Sadovaya

The most famous statue of Peter the Great was immortalised as the Bronze Horseman in the poem by Pushkin. With his mount rearing above the snake of treason, Peter's enormous statue stands at the river end of pl Dekabristov. The statue was sculpted over 12 years for Catherine the Great by Frenchman Etienne Falconet. Its inscription reads 'To Peter I from Catherine II – 1782'. Many have read significance into Catherine's linking of her own name with that of the city's founder: she had no legitimate claim to the throne and this statue is sometimes seen as her attempt to formalise the link (philosophical, if not hereditary) between the two monarchs. The significance of the inscription in both Latin and Cyrillic alphabets would not have been lost on the city's population, which was still in the process of Westernisation during Catherine's reign.

Falconet's original study for the magnificent sculpture can be seen in the Russian Museum (p76). Despite completing his lifework here, Falconet departed Russia a bitter, angry man. Years of arguing with the head of the Academy of Fine Arts over the finer details of the sculpture had taken its toll, and he didn't even bother staying for the unveiling.

The statue has become a much-debated philosophical symbol of the city and the main trademark of the new spirit of St Petersburg.

PL DEKABRISTOV (DECEMBRISTS' SQ)

Map p102

M Sadovaya

Centred on the famed statue of the Bronze Horseman, pl Dekabristov (Decembrists' Sq) is named after the first attempt at a Russian revolution – the Decembrists' Uprising of 14 December 1825. The Decembrists were young officers who were inspired by radical ideas from France during the Napoleonic campaigns and wanted to introduce constitutional monarchy. Ineptly, they set up their protest on the same day as the swearing-in ceremony of the new tsar, Nicholas I. After repeated attempts by Nicholas' ministers to reason with the rebels, they were fired upon. Many officers and bystanders died as a result. Most of the leaders later ended up on the gallows or in Siberia.

The dominant feature of pl Dekabristov is the immense façade of St Isaac's Cathedral (opposite). Most of the west side of the square is occupied by the Central State Historical Archives in the former Senate and Synod buildings, built by Carlo Rossi between 1829 and 1834. These institutions were set up by Peter the Great to run the civil administration and the Orthodox Church.

MARIINSKY THEATRE Map p102

☎ 326 4141, fax 314 1744; www.mariinsky.ru; Teatralnaya pl; box office 11am-7pm, tours by arrangement; M Sadovaya

The pretty green and white Mariinsky Theatre has played a pivotal role in Russian ballet ever since it was built in 1859. Outside performance times you can usually wander into the theatre's foyer and maybe peep into its lovely auditorium. To organise a full

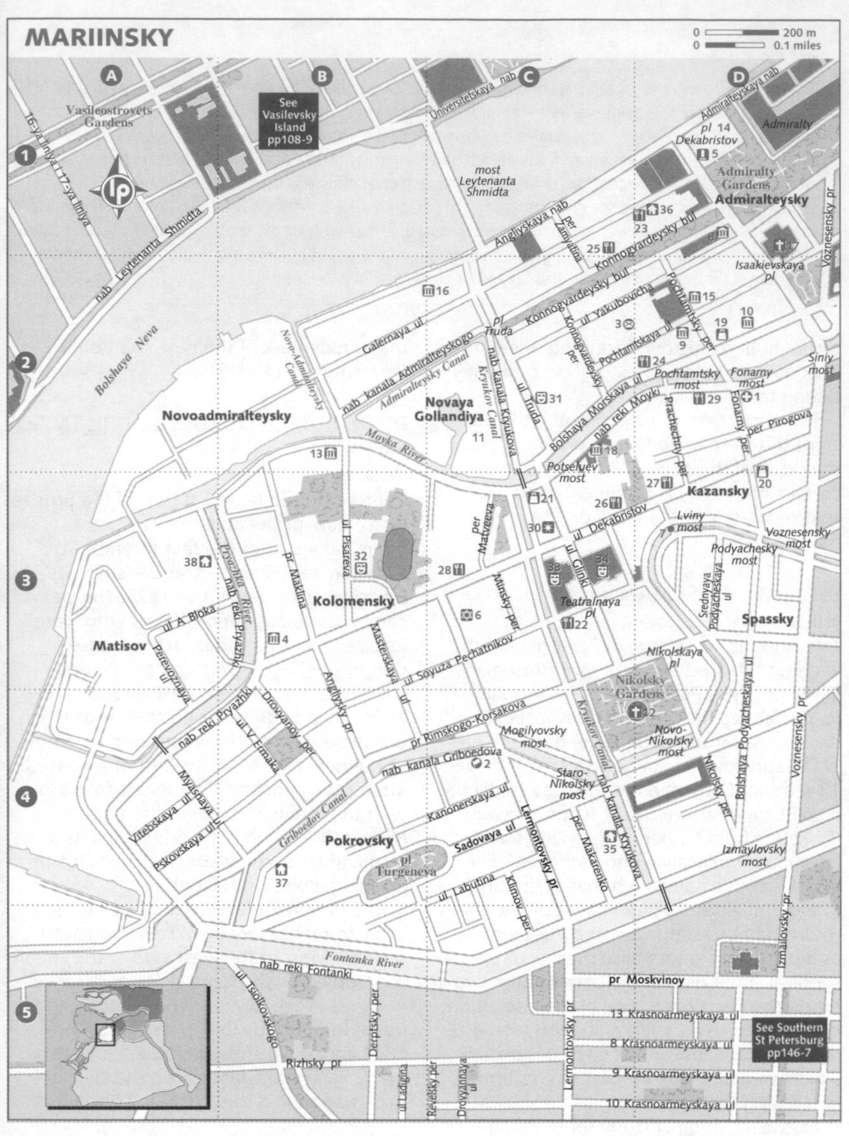

tour, fax a request to Dr Yury Schwartzkopf and call for an answer. For more information about attending performances at the Mariinsky, see p188.

Construction of a new Mariinsky Theatre, known as Mariinsky II, is under way directly west of the original building (see p57). The controversial new building is due to open in 2009. Elsewhere around Teatralnaya pl you will find the illustrious music school, Rimsky-Korsakov Conservatory (p189), which faces the Mariinsky. Surrounding the square is an area of quiet canals and side streets.

YUSUPOV PALACE Map p102

☎ 314 9883; www.yusupov-palace.ru; nab reki Moyki 94; adult/student/child R450/350/250; 11am-5pm; M Sadovaya

This spectacular palace on the Moyka River has some of the most perfectly preserved

MARIINSKY

INFORMATION

American Medical Clinic 1 D2
Chinese Consulate 2 C4
Main Post Office 3 C2

SIGHTS (pp100-06)

Alexander Blok House-Museum Музей-квартира Блока 4 B3
Bronze Horseman Медный всадник 5 D1
Grand Choral Synagogue Большая хоральная синагога 6 C3
Lviny most (Bridge of Four Lions) .. 7 D3
Manege Central Exhibition Hall Манеж центральный выставочный зал 8 D1
Mariinsky Theatre Мариинский театр .... (see 33)
Museum of the History of Religion Музей истории религии 9 D2
Nabokov Museum Музей Набокова 10 D2
New Holland Новая Голландия 11 C2
Nikolsky Cathedral Никольский собор 12 D4
Palace of Grand Duke Alexey Alexandrovich Дворец великого князя Алексея Александровича 13 B2
pl Dekabristov 14 D1
Popov Communications Museum Музей средств связи 15 D2
Rimsky-Korsakov Conservatory .. (see 34)
Rumyantsev Mansion Особняк Румянцева 16 C2
St Isaac's Cathedral Исаакиевский собор 17 D1
Yusupov Palace Юсуповский дворец 18 C2

SHOPPING (pp149-58)

Gallery of Dolls 19 D2
Kosher Shop .... (see 6)
Mariinsky Art Shop .... (see 33)
Mir Espresso 20 D3
St Petersburg Artist 21 C3

EATING (pp159-76)

Backstage 22 C3
Crocodile 23 D1
Le Paris 24 D2
Lechaim .... (see 6)
Lya Rus 25 C1
Noble Nest 26 C3
Stolle (ul Dekabristov 19) 27 D3
Stolle (ul Dekabristov 33) 28 C3
The Idiot 29 D2

DRINKING & NIGHTLIFE (pp177-86)

Shamrock 30 C3

ARTS (pp188-94)

Feel Yourself Russian 31 C2
Mariinsky Concert Hall Мариинский концертный зал 32 B3
Mariinsky Theatre Мариинский театр 33 C3
Rimsky-Korsakov Conservatory Консерватория им Римского-Корсакова 34 C3
Yusupov Palace Theatre Театр Юсуповского дворца .... (see 18)

SLEEPING (p201-12)

Alexander House 35 C4
Guesthouse on Galernaya 36 D1
House in Kolomna 37 B4
Matisov Domik Матисов домик 38 A3

19th-century interiors in the city, in addition to a fascinating history. Admission tickets do sell out, so show up before mid-afternoon to ensure your entry. The admission price to the palace includes an audio tour in English and a number of other languages.

The palace was built by Vallin de la Mothe in the 1760s, but the interiors were redecorated later. It became the residence of the illustrious Yusupov family after they moved from another fine house on Sadovaya ul (which, confusingly, is also sometimes called the Yusupov Palace; see p98). The palace's last Yusupov owner was the eccentric Prince Felix, a high-society darling, enamoured of cross-dressing, who often attended the Mariinsky and society balls as a woman. Most notoriously, the palace is the place where Grigory Rasputin met his gruesome end.

The palace interior is sumptuous and rich, with many halls painted in different styles and decked out with gilded chandeliers, silks, frescoes, tapestries and some fantastic furniture. The tour begins on the 2nd floor, which features an amazing ballroom and banquet hall, where musicians perform short concerts throughout the day. The highlight is the ornate rococo private theatre, which apparently has hosted artists as famed as Fyodor Chaliapin, Mikhail Glinka and Anna Pavlova. The tour continues on the ground floor, where you can't miss the fabulous Turkish Study and Moorish Drawing Room. Of the latter, Felix Yusupov wrote: 'I loved the tender Oriental luxury of this room. I used to dream here… I sat on the sofa with my mother's jewels on me and imagined myself as an Oriental satrap, surrounded by slaves.'

In 1916 Rasputin was murdered here in the grizzliest possible way by Felix Yusupov and some fellow plotters, who considered the 'mad monk' to have become too powerful (see p30). A special 30-minute **Murder of Rasputin Tour** (tour R200; 1.45pm) is conducted once a day in Russian only.

NIKOLSKY CATHEDRAL Map p102

Nikolsky Sobor; Nikolskaya pl 1/3; admission free; 9am-7pm; M Sadovaya

Just south of the Mariinsky Theatre, surrounded on two sides by canals, this ice-blue cathedral is one of the most picture-perfect in the city. The baroque spires and golden domes make the Nikolsky Cathedral one of the city's best-loved churches. It was one of the few that continued to work during the Soviet era when organised religion was effectively banned.

Nicknamed the Sailor's Church (Nicholas is the patron saint of sailors), it contains many 18th-century icons and a fine carved wooden iconostasis. A graceful bell tower overlooks the Griboedov Canal, which is crossed by Staro-Nikolsky most: from this bridge, you can see at least seven bridges, more than from any other spot in the city.

GRAND CHORAL SYNAGOGUE

Map p102

☎ 713 8186; www.jewishpetersburg.ru; Lermontovsky pr 2; admission free; 8am-8pm Sun-Fri, service 10am Sat; M Sadovaya

Designed by Vasily Stasov, the striking Grand Choral Synagogue opened in 1893 to provide a central place of worship for St Petersburg's growing Jewish community. Its lavishness (particularly notable in the 47m-high cupola and the decorative wedding chapel) indicates the pivotal role that Jews played in imperial St Petersburg. The synagogue was fully revamped in 2003 with money donated by an American benefactor. Visitors are welcome except on the Sabbath and other holy days. Men and married women should cover their heads upon entering.

Also on site are the Small Synagogue (11am-4pm Mon-Thu, 11am-1pm Fri & Sun), the Jewish restaurant Lechaim (p172) and the store Kosher Shop (p157). In summer, the synagogue also hosts performances with a Jewish cantor and other musicians performing *chaaznut* and *klezmer* music.

NABOKOV MUSEUM Map p102

☎ 315 4713; www.nabokovmuseum.org; Bolshaya Morskaya ul 47; adult/student R100/20, admission free Thu 11am-3pm; 11am-6pm Tue-Thu, 11am-5pm Fri, noon-5pm Sat & Sun; M Sadovaya

This lovely 19th-century town house was the suitably grand childhood home of Vladimir Nabokov, infamous author of *Lolita* and arguably the most versatile and least classifiable of modern Russian writers. Here Nabokov lived with his wealthy family from his birth in 1899 until the revolution in 1917, when they sensibly left the country. The house features heavily in Nabokov's autobiography *Speak, Memory,* in which he refers to it as a 'paradise lost'. Indeed, he never returned, dying abroad in 1977. There's actually relatively little to see in the museum itself, save for some charming interiors (don't miss the gorgeous stained-glass windows in the stairwell, which are not technically part of the museum, but staff will often allow you to take a peek). Nabokov artefacts on display include family photographs and parts of his extensive butterfly collection. A 30-minute film (in Russian only) features interviews with Vladimir's son and sister, the latter recollecting her time in this house.

MANEGE CENTRAL EXHIBITION HALL

Map p102

☎ 312 2243; www.manege.spb.ru in Russian; Isaakievskaya pl 1; admission varies R50-100; 11am-7pm Fri-Wed; M Sadovaya

Formerly the Horse Guards' Riding School, this large white neoclassical building was constructed between 1804 and 1807 from a design by Giacomo Quarenghi. It now houses rotating art exhibitions, often featuring contemporary and local artists. Particularly interesting is the annual retrospective of painting, sculpture and installation pieces produced by St Petersburg artists, held here each December.

POPOV COMMUNICATIONS MUSEUM

Map p102

Muzey Svyazey imeni Popova; ☎ 315 4873; www.rustelecom-museum.ru in Russian; Pochtamtsky per 4; admission R50; 10.30am-6pm Tue-Sat; M Sadovaya

Housed in the fabulous 18th-century palace of Chancellor Bezborodko, this brand new museum of communications is the perfect addition to Pochtamtskaya ul (Postal St). It is named for Professor AS Popov, inventor of the radio, and it covers all manner of communication, from the Pony Express up through the modern era (on-site computers offer internet access to all museum guests). Exhibits are interactive and interesting, including an antique telephone switchboard that still works; the first civil communications satellite Luch-15, which occupies a prominent place in the atrium; and plenty of multimedia explanations of how things work. Stamp collectors will have a field day admiring the national philatelic collection.

MUSEUM OF THE HISTORY OF RELIGION Map p102

☎ 312 3586; www.relig-museum.ru in Russian; Pochtamtskaya ul 14; adult/student R120/60; 11am-6pm Thu-Tue; M Sadovaya

Back in the day, it was called the Museum of Atheism and it was housed in the Kazan

Cathedral. Now the name has changed, as has the location, but the exhibition remains. It describes the history of various world religions, including the Russian Orthodox Church.

RUMYANTSEV MANSION Map p102

☎ 571 7544; www.spbmuseum.ru; Angliyskaya nab 44; adult/student R60/30; 🕑 11am-5pm Thu-Tue; Ⓜ Vasileostrovskaya

History buffs should not miss this oft-overlooked but superb local museum. It is housed in the majestic 1826 mansion of Count Nikolai Petrovich Rumyantsev, a famous diplomat, politician and statesman, as well as an amateur historian. His personal research library became the basis for the Russian State Library in Moscow. The history of the mansion and its owners is fascinating in itself.

Part of the State Museum of the History of St Petersburg, the bulk of the exhibitions at the mansion address 20th-century history, including displays devoted to the 1921 New Economic Policy (NEP), the industrialisation and development of the 1930s, and the Siege of Leningrad during WWII. Exhibitions are unusual in that they depict everyday life in the city during these historic periods. Ask for the explanatory guide in English at the ticket office downstairs.

ALEXANDER BLOK HOUSE-MUSEUM Map p102

☎ 713 8627; www.spbmuseum.ru; ul Dekabristov 57; adult/student R50/25; 🕑 11am-6pm Thu-Mon & 11am-5pm Tue; Ⓜ Sadovaya

This museum occupies the flat where poet Alexander Blok spent the last eight years of his life (1912–20). The revolutionary Blok believed that individualism had caused a decline in society's ethics, a situation that would only be rectified by a communist revolution.

The 4th floor has been preserved much as it was when Blok lived here with his wife Lyubov (daughter of Mendeleev). After touring the simple but historic home, descend to the 2nd floor, where Blok's mother lived. When the poet fell ill in 1920, his family moved into this apartment where he finally died a year later. Here, a literary exhibition demonstrates the influence of Blok's work, as well as some original copies of his poems. The room where Blok died contains his death mask and a drawing of Blok on his deathbed, sketched on the last page of the poet's pad. Chamber concerts are occasionally performed here – they're worthwhile for the subdued charm of the flats and the lovely views out onto the Pryazhka River.

NEW HOLLAND Map p102

Novaya Gollandiya; cnr nab kanala Kryukova & Bolshaya Morskaya ul; Ⓜ Vasileostrovskaya

Except for one day in 2000 – when an exhibition of avant-garde art was held here – this island has been closed to the public for the nearly three centuries of its existence. The impressive red brick and granite arch, designed by Jean-Baptiste Vallin de la Mothe in the late 18th century, is one of the city's best examples of Russian classicism.

In Peter's time, the complex was used for ship-building (its name refers to the place where he learned the trade). In the 19th century, a large basin was built in the middle of the island. Here, experiments were conducted by scientist Alexey Krylov in an attempt to build a boat that couldn't be capsized. In 1915 the navy built a radio transmitter here – the most powerful in Russia at the time.

The place has since been left to the dogs, but the city has big plans to turn it into a retail and cultural centre (see p57).

PALACE OF GRAND DUKE ALEXEY ALEXANDROVICH Map p102

Dvorets Velikogo Knyazi Alexeya Alexandrovicha; nab reki Moyki 211; 🕑 closed to the public; Ⓜ Vasileostrovskaya

This fabulous derelict mansion at the very far end of the Moyka River belonged to the son of Alexander II. The wrought iron and stone fence is one of its most stunning features, with the Grand Duke's monogram adorning the central gates. The palace was built in 1895 by Maximilian Messmacher, and each façade represents a different architectural style, perhaps reflective of the character of Grand Duke Alexey himself. The interior is equally diverse, although it is not open to the public.

Used as a Pioneers' Palace during the communist era, the building sat empty for years and eventually fell into terrible disrepair. It is now undergoing a badly needed renovation.

MARIINSKY
Walking Tour

1 Pl Dekabristov With the Bronze Horseman (p101) as the centrepiece, Pl Dekabristov (Decembrists' Sq; p101) is surrounded by the Admiralty on the east and Carlo Rossi's Empire-style Senate and Synod buildings on the west.

2 St Isaac's Cathedral The gold dome and neoclassical exterior of St Isaac's Cathedral (p100) house one of the most elaborate marble-filled interiors in the city. St Isaac's Cathedral is the most striking building on the St Petersburg skyline.

3 Isaakievskaya pl A monument to Nicholas I stands at the centre of Isaakievskaya pl (p100), which is often clogged with tour buses. On the south side of the square, the Mariinsky Palace was a gift from Nicholas I to his daughter Maria Nikolaevna. On the west side, the Manege Central Exhibition Hall (p104) hosts exhibitions of contemporary art featuring local artists.

4 Pochtamtskaya ul Through the ornate 1859 archway, 'Postal St' is fresh from a thorough renovation in 2007. Check out the impressive neoclassical façade of the main post office, with a delightful bridge connecting its two buildings. The new Popov Communications Museum (p104) is appropriately located across the street.

5 Yusupov Palace On the south side of the Moyka River, you can't miss the grand but overbearing edifice of the Yusupov Palace (p102), where Rasputin enjoyed his last meal before he was shot and tossed into the freezing river. Today, tourists can gawk at the palace's over-the-top ornate interior.

6 Moyka River This stretch of the Moyka contains a number of beautiful old buildings in states of charming decay and the off-limits island of New Holland (Novaya Gollandiya; p105). Further west, check out the Palace of Grand Duchess Kseniya Alexandrova at No 108 and the Victor Shreter masterpiece at No 112.

7 Teatralnaya pl The pale-green Mariinsky Theatre (p101) dominates its namesake square, with Mariinsky II going up just west. The Rimsky-Korsakov Conservatory stands opposite the theatre. East of the square, the Griboedov Canal runs under another beast-supported suspension bridge, the Lviny most (p76), with chains emerging from the mouths of lions.

8 Nikolsky Gardens Surrounded by canals on three sides, these blooming gardens contain the lovely Nikolsky Cathedral (p103), one of the city's most beloved churches (and one of the few that operated throughout the Soviet period).

WALK FACTS
Start Pl Dekabristov (M Sadovaya)
End Sennaya pl (M Sadovaya)
Distance 2km
Duration 1½ hours
Fuel stops The Idiot (p172), Stolle (p173)

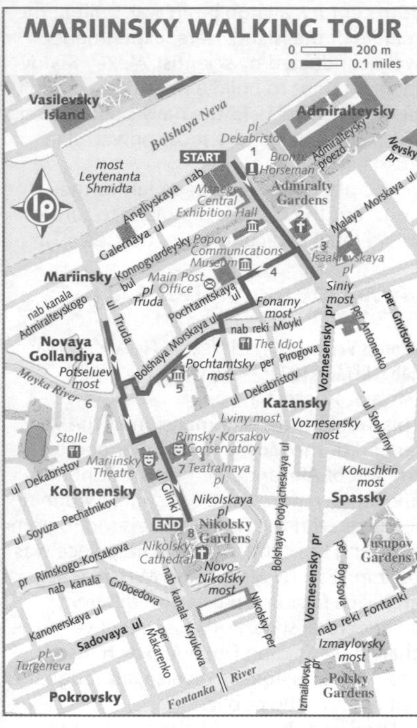

VASILEVSKY ISLAND

Eating p173; Sleeping p211

Peter the Great originally intended that this triangular island would be the heart of his city. As such, it is among the oldest neighbourhoods in St Petersburg, especially the eastern tip known as the Strelka (tongue of land). Peter wanted the Strelka as his city's administrative and intellectual centre, which is why it's crammed with buildings of historical and cultural significance, a 'museum ghetto' as it were. There's no metro station nearby, but it's a pleasant stroll across Dvortsovy most (Palace Bridge) from the square of the same name. Alternatively, Ⓜ Sportivnaya is on the Petrograd Side, a short walk over Tuchkov most. Today, the island is still the intellectual centre of the city, thanks to the presence of St Petersburg State University, along the river embankment. The area behind the campus maintains a distinct academic atmosphere and is bustling with cafés and clubs. This part of the island is easy to access, as it is served by a designated metro station (Ⓜ Vasileostrovskaya).

The streets are numbered lines *(linii)*, which ascend as you head west. So the metro station is on 6-ya liniya i 7-ya liniya, the next street is 8-ya liniya i 9-ya liniya, and so on, up to 24-ya liniya i 25-ya liniya. The east–west thoroughfares are Bolshoy, Sredny and Maly prs (Big, Middle and Small Aves), so the whole island is very well organised.

There are very few reasons to go out to the far northern and western edges of the island (though there's a metro station out there, Ⓜ Primorskaya). Unless your cruise ship is docked at the *morskoy vokzal* (sea station), you're unlikely to want to visit this strangely empty end of the island.

STRELKA Map pp108–9

Among the oldest parts of Vasilevsky Island, this eastern tip is where Peter the Great wanted his new city's administrative and intellectual centre. In fact, the Strelka became the focus of St Petersburg's maritime trade, symbolised by the colonnaded Customs House (now the Pushkin House, p110). The two Rostral Columns, archetypal St Petersburg landmarks, are studded with ships' prows and four seated sculptures representing four of Russia's great rivers: the Neva, the Volga, the Dnieper and the Volkhov. These were oil-fired navigation beacons in the 1800s (their gas torches are still lit on some holidays).

The Strelka has one of the best views in the city, with the Peter & Paul Fortress to the left and the Hermitage, the Admiralty and St Isaac's Cathedral to the right. The Neva is adorned with a fantastic dancing fountain (🕑 30-min 'performances' at noon & 8pm-midnight on the hr Wed-Thu & 8am-midnight on the hr Fri-Sun), perched midway between the Strelka and Zayachy Island. In summer, classical music blasts from the loudspeakers, while the shoots of water are choreographed to spray, sputter and spurt in time to the music.

KUNSTKAMERA Map pp108–9

Museum of Anthropology & Ethnography; ☎ 328 1412; www.kunstkamera.ru; Universitetskaya nab 3; admission R200; 🕑 11am-6pm Tue-Sun, closed last Tue of the month; Ⓜ Vasileostrovskaya

The city's first museum was founded in 1714 by Peter himself. It is famous for its ghoulish collection of monstrosities, preserved 'freaks', two-headed mutant foeti, deformed animals and odd body parts, all collected by Peter with the aim of educating the notoriously superstitious Russian people. He wanted to demonstrate that the malformations were not the result of the evil eye or sorcery, but rather caused by 'internal damage as well as fear and the beliefs of the mother during pregnancy' – a slightly more enlightened interpretation. This fascinating place is an essential St Petersburg sight, although not one for the faint-hearted. Think twice about bringing young children here and definitely give Kunstkamera a wide berth if you are pregnant yourself.

Most people rush to see the sad specimens, largely ignoring the other interesting exhibitions on native peoples from around the world. Wonderfully kitsch dioramas exhibit rare objects and cultural practices from Asia, Oceania, Africa and the Americas. The 3rd floor houses an exhibition devoted to Mikhail Lomonosov, with a re-creation of his study laboratory.

The top floors of the tower contain the Academy of Science's first astronomical observatory (tour R1200), and the great Gottorp Globe (1654–64), a rotating globe and planetarium all in one. This special exhibition is open only as part of a guided tour, which is not included in your admission price. Entrance to the museum is on Tamozhenny per.

VASILEVSKY ISLAND

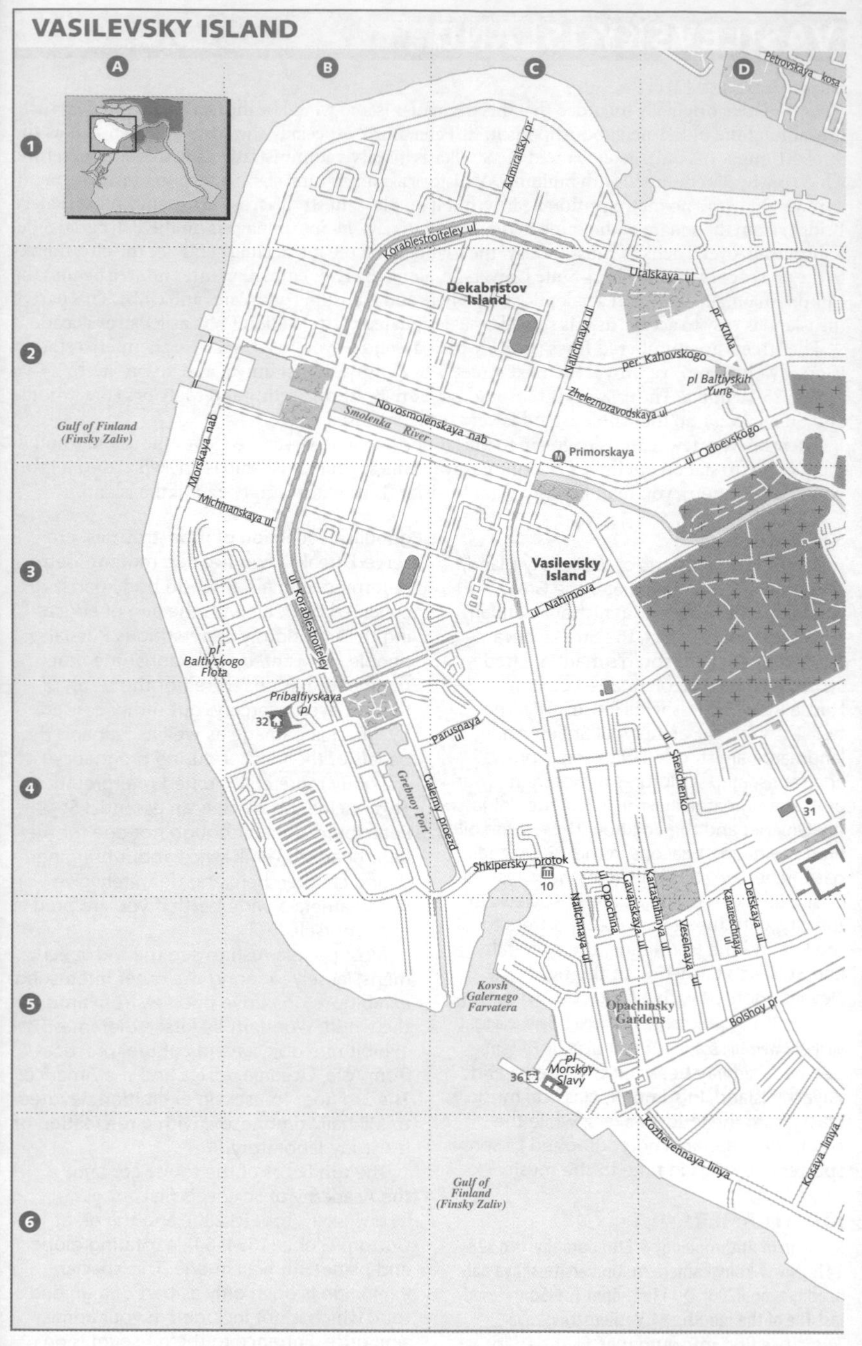

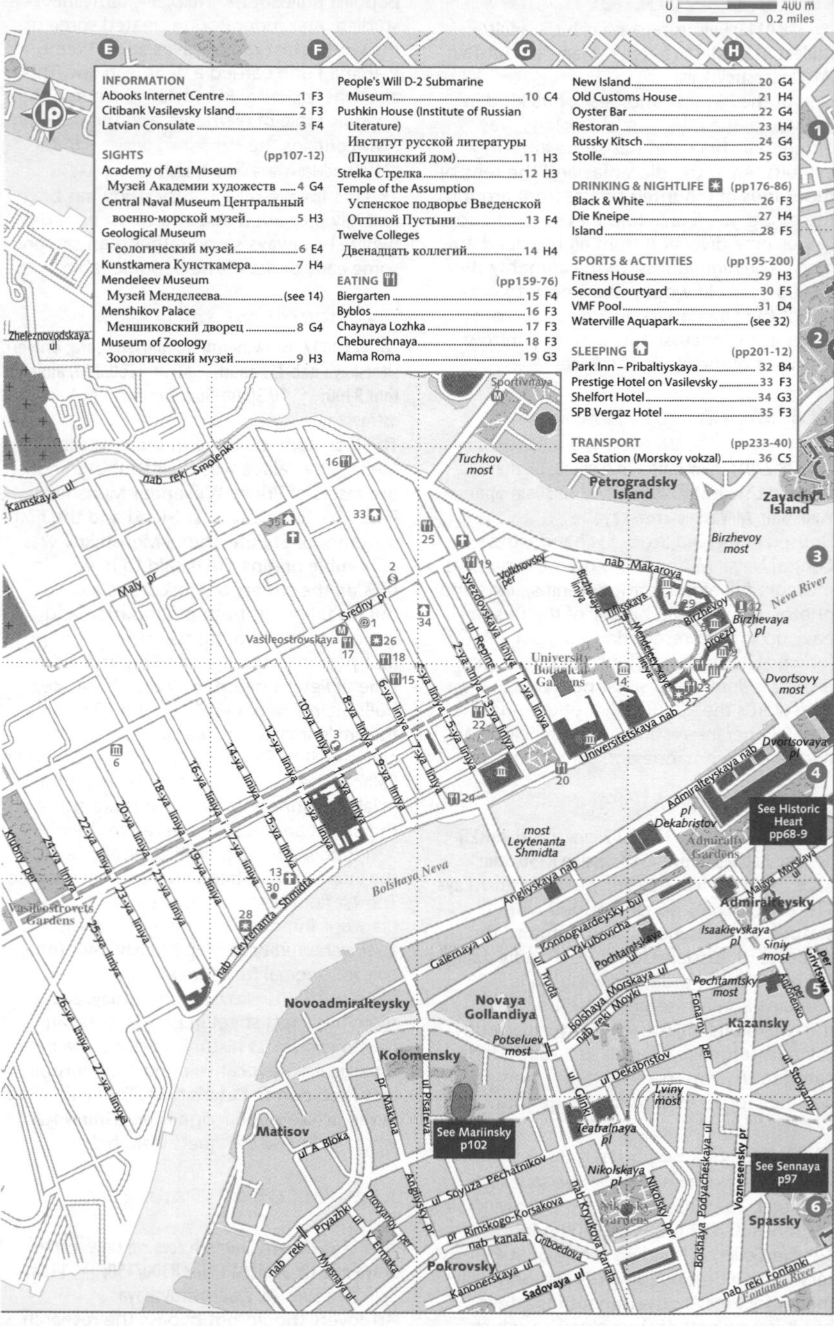
0 400 m
0 0.2 miles
E
F
G
H
1
2
3
4
5
6
INFORMATION
Abooks Internet Centre 1 F3
Citibank Vasilevsky Island 2 F3
Latvian Consulate 3 F4
SIGHTS (pp107-12)
Academy of Arts Museum Музей Академии художеств 4 G4
Central Naval Museum Центральный военно-морской музей 5 H3
Geological Museum Геологический музей 6 E4
Kunstkamera Кунсткамера 7 H4
Mendeleev Museum Музей Менделеева (see 14)
Menshikov Palace Меншиковский дворец 8 G4
Museum of Zoology Зоологический музей 9 H3
People's Will D-2 Submarine Museum 10 C4
Pushkin House (Institute of Russian Literature) Институт русской литературы (Пушкинский дом) 11 H3
Strelka Стрелка 12 H3
Temple of the Assumption Успенское подворье Введенской Оптиной Пустыни 13 F4
Twelve Colleges Двенадцать коллегий 14 H4
EATING (pp159-76)
Biergarten 15 F4
Byblos 16 F3
Chaynaya Lozhka 17 F3
Cheburechnaya 18 F3
Mama Roma 19 G3
New Island 20 G4
Old Customs House 21 H4
Oyster Bar 22 G4
Restoran 23 H4
Russky Kitsch 24 G4
Stolle 25 G3
DRINKING & NIGHTLIFE (pp176-86)
Black & White 26 F3
Die Kneipe 27 H4
Island 28 F5
SPORTS & ACTIVITIES (pp195-200)
Fitness House 29 H3
Second Courtyard 30 F5
VMF Pool 31 D4
Waterville Aquapark (see 32)
SLEEPING (pp201-12)
Park Inn – Pribaltiyskaya 32 B4
Prestige Hotel on Vasilevsky 33 F3
Shelfort Hotel 34 G3
SPB Vergaz Hotel 35 F3
TRANSPORT (pp233-40)
Sea Station (Morskoy vokzal) 36 C5
Zheleznovodskaya ul
Sportivnaya
Tuchkov most
Petrogradsky Island
Zayachy Island
Birzhevoy most
Neva River
nab reki Smolenki
Kamskaya ul
Maly pr
Sredny pr
Vasileostrovskaya
Volkhovsky per
nab Makarova
Birzhevaya liniya
Tiflisskaya
Birzhevoy proezd
Mendeleevskaya liniya
Birzhevaya pl
Syezdovskaya liniya
ul Repina
University Botanical Gardens
Dvortsovy most
Universitetskaya nab
Dvortsovaya pl
Admiralteyskaya nab
pl Dekabristov
See Historic Heart pp68-9
Admiralty Gardens
Malaya Morskaya ul
Admiralteysky
Isaakievskaya pl
Siniy most
per Grivtsova
Pochtamtsky most
Kazansky
most Leytenanta Shmidta
Angliyskaya nab
Bolshaya Neva
Konnogvardeysky bul
ul Yakubovicha
Pochtamtskaya ul
Galernaya ul
Truda
Bolshaya Morskaya ul
nab reki Moyki
Fonarny per
Novoadmiralteysky
Novaya Gollandiya
Potseluev most
Kolomensky
ul Dekabristov
Lviny most
ul Stolyarny
ul Glinki
Teatralnaya pl
pr Maklina
ul Pisareva
See Mariinsky p102
Matisov
ul A Bloka
ul Soyuza Pechatnikov
Nikolskaya pl
Nikolsky per
Nikolsky Gardens
Bolshaya Podyacheskaya ul
Voznesensky pr
See Sennaya p97
Spassky
Angliysky pr
Pryazhki
Drovyanoy per
ul V Ermaka
Myasnaya ul
nab reki Pryazhki
pr Rimskogo-Korsakova
nab kanala Griboedova
nab Kryukova kanala
Pokrovsky
Kanonerskaya ul
Sadovaya ul
nab reki Fontanki
Fontanka River
Vasileostrovets Gardens
Klubny per
nab Leytenanta Shmidta
1-ya liniya
2-ya liniya
3-ya liniya
4-ya liniya
5-ya liniya
6-ya liniya
7-ya liniya
8-ya liniya
9-ya liniya
10-ya liniya
11-ya liniya
12-ya liniya
13-ya liniya
14-ya liniya
15-ya liniya
16-ya liniya
17-ya liniya
18-ya liniya
19-ya liniya
20-ya liniya
21-ya liniya
22-ya liniya
23-ya liniya
24-ya liniya
25-ya liniya
26-ya Liniya
27-ya liniya

MUSEUM OF ZOOLOGY Map pp108–9

☎ 218 0112; Universitetskaya nab 1/3; adult/student R150/50, Thu free; 🕒 11am-5pm Sat-Thu; Ⓜ Vasileostrovskaya

One of the biggest and best of its kind in the world, the Museum of Zoology was founded in 1832 and has some amazing exhibits. Amid the dioramas and the tens of thousands of mounted beasts from around the globe, you'll also find a live insect zoo (a welcome diversion from all the dead animals). The highlight is unquestionably the 44,000-year-old woolly mammoth thawed out of the Siberian ice in 1902. Buy your ticket at the microscopic cashier window just west of the main entrance.

CENTRAL NAVAL MUSEUM

Map pp108–9

☎ 328 2701; www.museum.navy.ru; Birzhevaya pl 4; adult/student R320/110; 🕒 10.30am-6pm Wed-Sun; Ⓜ Vasileostrovskaya

Housed in the Old Stock Exchange, the Central Naval Museum is a grand, expansive museum full of maps, model ships, flags and photos. It covers the history of the Russian navy up to the present day – a must-see for naval enthusiasts. The highlight of the display is *Botik,* Peter's first boat and in his own words the 'grandfather of the Russian Navy'. Other interesting exhibits include a two-seater submarine and some big oars.

PUSHKIN HOUSE Map pp108–9

Pushkinsky Dom; ☎ 328 0502; www.pushkinskijdom.ru; nab Makarova 4; admission R150, tour R120; 🕒 10am-4pm Mon-Fri; Ⓜ Vasileostrovskaya

The old customs house, topped with statues and a dome, is now home to the Institute of Russian Literature. Fondly called Pushkin House, the handsome building contains a small literary museum with dusty exhibits on Tolstoy, Gogol, Lermontov and Turgenev, as well as a room dedicated to the writers of the Silver Age. Call in advance for an English-language tour.

TWELVE COLLEGES Map pp108–9

Mendeleevskaya liniya 2; Ⓜ Vasileostrovskaya

Marked by a statue of scientist-poet Mikhail Lomonosov (1711–65), the 400m-long Twelve Colleges building is one of St Petersburg's oldest buildings. It was originally meant for Peter's government ministries, but it is now part of the university, which stretches out behind it. Within these walls populist philosopher Nikolai Chernyshevsky studied, Alexander Popov created some of the world's first radio waves and a young Vladimir Putin earned a degree in law. This is also where Dmitry Mendeleev invented the periodic table of elements, and the building now contains the Mendeleev Museum (☎ 328 9744; Mendeleevskaya liniya 2; adult/student R60/30; 🕒 11am-4pm Mon-Fri). His cosy study has been lovingly preserved and you can see his desk (where he always stood rather than sat) and some early drafts of the periodic table.

MENSHIKOV PALACE Map pp108–9

☎ 323 1112; www.hermitagemuseum.org; Universitetskaya nab 15; adult/student R200/100, audio tour R100; 🕒 10.30am-5pm Tue-Sun; Ⓜ Vasileostrovskaya

The first stone building in the city, the Menshikov Palace was built to the grandiose tastes of Prince Alexander Menshikov, Peter the Great's closest friend and the first governor of St Petersburg. Menshikov was of humble origins (he is said to have sold pies on the streets of Moscow as a child), but his talent for both organisation and intrigue made him the second-most important person in the Russian Empire by the time of Peter's death in 1725. His palace, built mainly between 1710 and 1714, was the city's smartest residence at the time: compare it to Peter the Great's tiny Summer Palace! The palace was used by Peter for official functions and its interiors are some of the oldest and best-preserved in the city.

It is now a branch of the Hermitage and the interiors have been impressively restored. The 1st floor displays some stunning Dutch tile work, intended to fortify the rooms against humidity to help Menshikov's tuberculosis. Original furniture and the personal effects of Menshikov are on display. Each room has a fact sheet in English you can borrow to explain its history. Vavara's Chamber is particularly evocative of how the aristocracy lived during Peter's time. The main room in the palace is the magnificent Grand Hall, where balls and banquets were held.

ACADEMY OF ARTS MUSEUM

Map pp108–9

☎ 213 3578; www.nimrah.com.ru; Universitetskaya nab 17; adult/student R300/150; 🕒 11am-6pm Wed-Sun; Ⓜ Vasileostrovskaya

Art-lovers should not bypass the research museum of the Russian Academy of Arts, which contains works by students and faculty since the founding of this institution in 1857. Two 3500-year-old sphinx monuments guard the entrance of this time-tested institution. This is the original location of the academy, where boys would live from the age of five until they graduated at age 15. It was an experiment to create a new species of human: the artist. For the most part, it worked; many great Russian artists were trained here, including Ilya Repin, Karl Bryullov and Anton Losenko. But the curriculum was designed with the idea that the artist must serve the state, and this conservatism led to a reaction against it. In 1863, some 14 students left to found a new movement which became known as the Wanderers (Peredvizhniki).

Nonetheless, the Academy of Arts has many achievements to show off, including numerous studies, drawings and paintings by academy members. On the 3rd floor, you can examine the models for the original versions of Smolny Cathedral, St Isaac's Cathedral and the Alexander Nevsky Monastery. And if you had any doubt that the Academy of Arts is an august academic institution, take a peek into the fabulous old library.

GEOLOGICAL MUSEUM Map pp108–9

☎ 312 5399, excursions 328 9248; Sredny pr 74; admission free; 🕑 10am-5pm Mon-Fri; Ⓜ Vasileostrovskaya

Located in the upper floors of the geology faculty of the university, this huge room contains several kilometres of fossils, rocks and gems – a veritable treasure chest of geological finds. The precious and semiprecious stones will certainly have you gawking at Mother Nature's handiwork: sparkling amethyst crystals (one from the Altai mountains that is 1.5m long!); huge chunks of malachite from the Urals; and a gorgeous gypsum 'rose' from Astrakhan. Also on display are prehistoric rocks and fossils, dinosaur fragments, animal skulls and mammoth tusks.

The centrepiece of the museum is a huge map of the Soviet Union made entirely of precious gems. The winner of the Paris World Exposition Grand Prix in 1937, this 26.6-sq-metre, 3.2-tonne mosaic took more than 700 people to create, combining amethysts, diamonds, granite, rubies and other gems from 500 different places in the USSR. This masterpiece was on display in St George's Hall in the Hermitage for 34 years. There's a similarly constructed hammer and sickle nearby.

PEOPLE'S WILL D-2 SUBMARINE MUSEUM Map pp108–9

☎ 356 5277; Shkipersky protok 10; adult/student R300/150; 🕑 11am-5pm Wed-Sun

Opened as a fun, unique museum, the *People's Will (Narodovolets)* D-2 Submarine was one of the first six (diesel-fuelled) submarines built in the Soviet Union. It was in action between 1931 and 1956, and proudly sank five German ships. Mandatory tours (in Russian) depart on the hour to take you through the sub to see how the crew of 53 lived and worked.

TEMPLE OF THE ASSUMPTION Map pp108–9

Uspenskoe Podvore Optina Pustin; ☎ 321 7473; cnr nab Leytenanta Shmidta & 14-ya liniya i 15-ya liniya; admission free; 🕑 daily; Ⓜ Vasileostrovskaya

This stunning 1895 neo-Byzantine church was built by architect Vasily Kosyakov on the site of a previous monastery. It was closed during the Soviet period, and from 1957 the building became the city's first – and very popular – year-round skating rink. The 7.7m, 861kg metal cross on the roof was only replaced in 1998. The exterior was under scaffolding at the time of research, but the church continued to hold services. Women should cover their heads before entering.

VASILEVSKY ISLAND

Walking Tour

1 Strelka The eastern nose of Vasilevsky Island, the Strelka (p107) boasts an unparalleled panorama, looking out over the Peter & Paul Fortress, the Hermitage, the Admiralty and St Isaac's Cathedral. A recent addition is the dancing fountain in the middle of the Neva. Overlooking the park, the old stock exchange now houses the Central Naval Museum (opposite).

2 Kunstkamera The Museum of Anthropology & Ethnography, Kunstkamera (p107) was Russia's first museum, set up by Peter to dispel common superstitions about illness and disease. The collection of deformed foeti and animals is impressive, if a little disturbing. Next door is the equally impressive Museum of Zoology (opposite).

3 St Petersburg State University At Peter's behest, Domenico Trezzini built the magnificent Twelve Colleges (p110) in 1722. The emperor based his bureaucracy here: separate entrances for each ministry signified their independence, while the unified façade highlighted collective goals. It is now part of the university, housing the Mendeleev Museum (p110) amongst others. Behind these buildings, the grounds contain the beautiful university botanical gardens.

4 Menshikov Palace Peter originally gifted the entirety of Vasilevsky Island to his best friend, Prince Menshikov, who proceeded to build the fabulous Menshikov Palace (p110) on the north bank of the Neva. Menshikov's humble origins gave him a taste for opulence, and the interior is the best-preserved Petrine décor in the city.

5 Academy of Arts Museum Two Egyptian sphinx monuments mark the entrance to the institutional Academy of Arts Museum (p110), which houses 250 years of artistic expressions. On display are works by academy students and faculty over the years, as well as temporary exhibitions. A beautiful old library – lined with dusty volumes and packed with dark wood furniture – is open for visiting researchers.

6 6-ya liniya i 7-ya liniya This pedestrian-friendly street is one of the city's most pleasant places to sit at a sidewalk café and watch the world go by. Check out the charming Church of St Andrew, before sampling the goods at one of the sweet sidewalk cafés (see p173).

WALK FACTS

Start Strelka (Ⓜ Nevsky Pr)
End 6-ya liniya i 7-ya liniya (Ⓜ Vasileostrovskaya)
Distance 2km
Duration Two hours
Fuel stops Die Kneipe (p180), Cheburechnaya (p174), Black & White (p181)

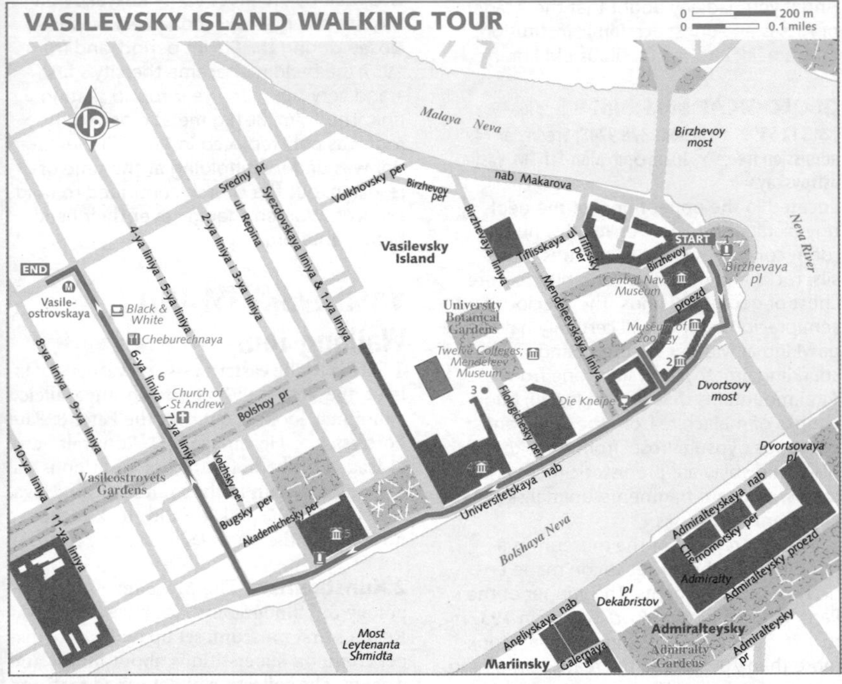

PETROGRAD SIDE

Eating p174; Shopping p157; Sleeping p211

The Petrograd Side (Petrogradskaya Storona) is a cluster of delta islands, of which five are significant: Zayachy (Hare), Petrogradsky, Krestovsky, Kamenny (Stone) and Yelagin Islands. The Bolshaya and Malaya Neva and the Bolshaya, Srednaya and Malaya Nevka channels weave around them.

ZAYACHY ISLAND

On little Zayachy Island, Peter the Great first broke ground for St Petersburg and built the Peter & Paul Fortress in 1703. Having captured the formerly Swedish outpost on the Neva, he thus staked his claim to the northwestern region and then set to turn the outpost into a modern Western city. Although the city grew from here, today there is only room for the ancient fortress and not much more. It is surrounded by a moat and accessible only by boat or bridge from Petrogradsky Island. There is no metro station on Zayachy Island, but Ⓜ Gorkovskaya is just across the bridge in Alexandrovsky Park.

PETER & PAUL FORTRESS Map pp114–15

Petropavlovskaya krepost; ☎ 230 0329; www.spbmuseum.ru; grounds free; ⏰ grounds 6am-10pm daily, exhibitions 11am-6pm Thu-Tue; Ⓜ Gorkovskaya

Founded in 1703, the Peter & Paul Fortress is the oldest major building in St Petersburg. It was built as a defence against the Swedes, but they were defeated before the fortress was finished. In fact, it has never been utilised in the city's defence – unless you count incarceration of political 'criminals' as national defence.

Up until 1917, the main use of the structure was as a prison. One of the first and most famous inmates was Peter's own son Alexey, who was tortured and killed for his betrayal of his father. Other famous residents were Fyodor Dostoevsky, Maxim Gorky, Noi Trotsky, Mikhail Bakunin and Alexander Lenin (Vlad's older brother).

Enter the fortress from the eastern side of the island. Just inside the main gate is a useful information office, where you can pick up a map and buy tickets. You can also buy an overall ticket (adult/student R250/130), which allows access to all of the exhibitions on the island (except the bell tower) for 10 days. While there are loads of various and changing exhibitions, make a point to pay your respects at the SS Peter & Paul Cathedral, with its landmark needle-thin spire, and at the Trubetskoy Bastion, which was closed for renovation at the time of research.

The SS Peter & Paul Cathedral (adult/student R150/70; ⏰ 10am-7pm May-Sep) has a magnificent baroque interior, quite different from other Orthodox churches. All of Russia's prerevolutionary rulers from Peter the Great onwards (except Peter II and Ivan VI) are buried here. Peter I's grave is at the front on the right. Nicholas II and his family – minus Alexey and Maria – were the latest most controversial additions in 1998 (see p34).

The 122.5m-high bell tower (☎ 498 0505; adult/student R100/60; ⏰ tours noon, 1.30pm, 3.30pm & 4pm May-Sep) remains the city's tallest structure. It offers a small exhibition about the renovation of the tower, as well as an up-close inspection of the bell-ringing mechanism. The main reason to climb all these steps, of course, is for the magnificent 360-degree panorama. The bell tower is open only with a guided tour, so call in advance or check the information office for the schedule, which is likely to change. Tickets are sold at the boathouse.

Between the cathedral and the Senior Officers' Barracks is Mikhail Shemyakin's statue of a seated Peter the Great, with strangely proportioned head and hands. When the statue was unveiled in 1991 it caused outrage among the citizens of St Petersburg, for whom Peter remains a saintly figure. Local lore has it that rubbing his right forefinger will bring good luck.

The Commandant's House (adult/student R60/40; ⏰ 11am-7pm Thu-Tue) contains an exhibition on the history of the St Petersburg region from medieval times to 1917. The Engineers' House (☎ 498 0607; adult/student R60/40; ⏰ 11am-7pm Thu-Tue) also has a museum with rotating exhibitions.

In the fort's southwest corner are reconstructions of the grim cells of the Trubetskoy Bastion, where Peter supervised the torture to death of his son. The cells were used by later tsars to keep a lid on original thinking in the empire.

PETROGRAD SIDE

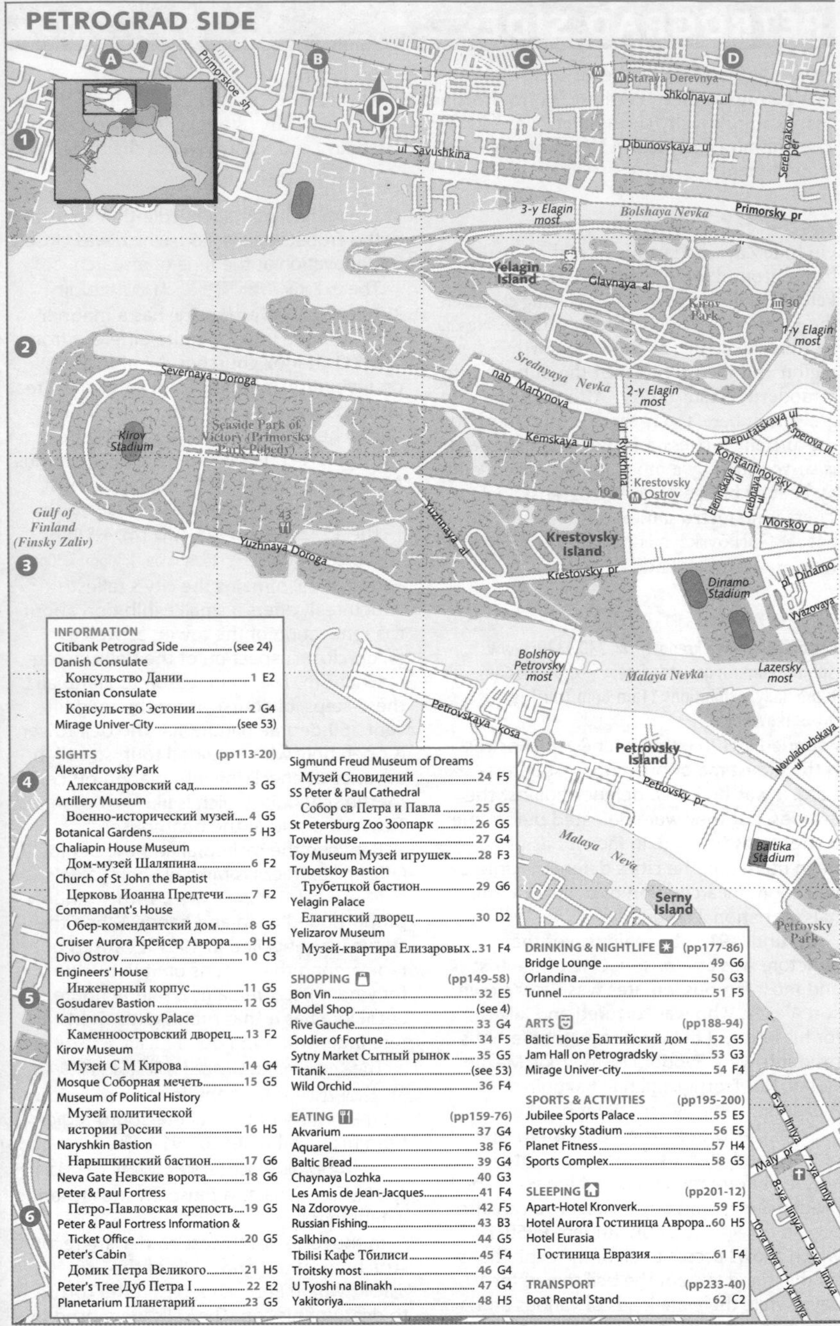

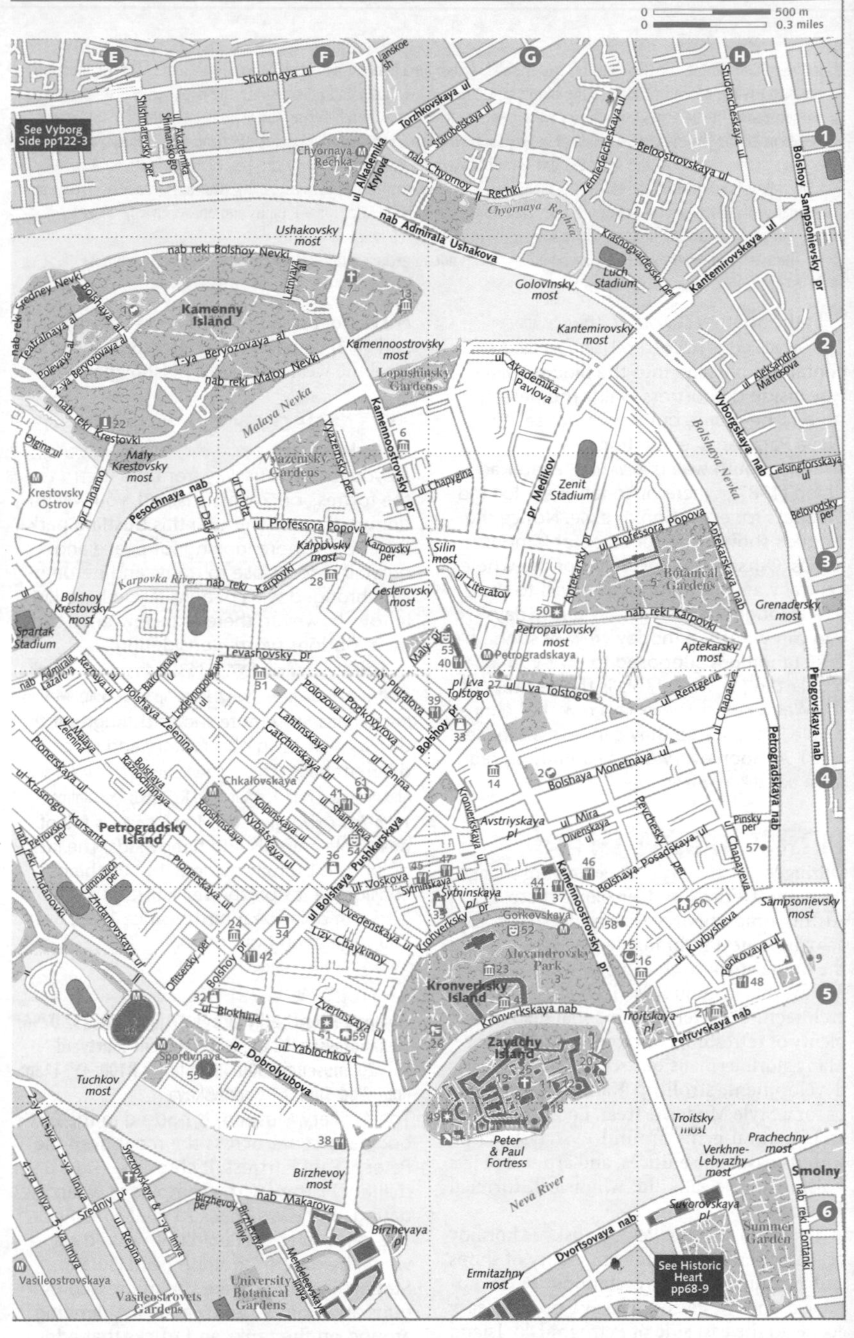

500 m
0.3 miles
See Vyborg Side pp122-3
Kamenny Island
Petrogradsky Island
Kronverksky Island
Zayachy Island
Peter & Paul Fortress
Neva River
Malaya Nevka
Bolshaya Nevka
Karpovka River
Chyornaya Rechka
Zenit Stadium
Luch Stadium
Spartak Stadium
Botanical Gardens
Alexandrovsky Park
Summer Garden
University Botanical Gardens
Vasileostrovets Gardens
Lopushinsky Gardens
Vyazemsky Gardens
Troitsky most
See Historic Heart pp68-9

WALRUS CLUB

In the cold of winter, the Neva River is frozen solid, except for a pool formed by a 12-sq-metre hole in the ice. Ignoring the bitter wind, an enthusiastic young man strips down to his shorts and plunges into the pool, while a small crowd gathers round. He emerges from the icy waters and stands proudly with his arms above his head in the sign for Victory. Welcome to the Walrus Club, a group of hearty souls who exhort the health benefits of taking a daily dip.

This scene unfolds at the southeastern corner of Zayachy Island, in front of the Peter & Paul Fortress. A friendly blue walrus is painted on the fortress wall. Many of the ice swimmers, known as *morzhi* (walruses), have been paying regular visits to this spot for decades. They claim the practice eliminates muscle pains and boosts energy. More than a few *morzhi* – advancing in age – claim the icy dip improves their libido.

There is good news for all walrus wannabes: this is not an exclusive club. All are invited to take the plunge!

In the southeast corner, the Gosudarev Bastion (adult/child R60/40; 11am-7pm Thu-Tue) contains a passage into the hidden walkway inside the fortress walls. The passage used to be secret, but now it houses the 'Neva Panorama' exhibition.

In the south wall is Neva Gate, a later addition (1787), where prisoners were loaded on boats for execution or exile. Notice the plaques showing water levels of famous floods. Outside are fine views of the whole central waterfront. Along the wall to the left, throughout the year on sunny days, you can witness a motley crew of sunbathers (standing is supposed to give you a *proper* tan); in winter this is the territory of the Walrus Club, the crazy crew that chops a hole in the ice so they can take a dip (see above). At noon every day a cannon is fired from Naryshkin Bastion.

PETROGRADSKY ISLAND

During WWI, the city of St Petersburg changed its name to the less Germanic 'Petrograd'. At this time, the large island north of Zayachy became a fashionable place to live, and the name stuck to the island, if not the city. Today, this fabulous district boasts sparkling architecture, a lively commercial district and plenty of refreshing, uncrowded, green space. Many glorious mansions remain from its early development: stroll up Kamennoostrovsky pr for a Style Moderne treat. Look closely for architectural gems around Avstriyskaya pl, with its castlelike edifices, and around pl Lva Tolstogo, especially the whimsical, turreted Tower House.

The main street of Petrogradsky is Bolshoy pr, a happening avenue with plenty of shops and restaurants. Metro stations M Gorkovskaya and M Petrogradskaya provide easy access to the east side of Petrogradsky Island (including Kamennoostrovsky pr and the eastern end of Bolshoy pr), while M Chkalovskaya and M Sportivnaya are better for the west side (and the western end of Bolshoy pr).

ALEXANDROVSKY PARK Map pp114–15

M Gorkovskaya

As you make your way from the metro to the fortress on Zayachy Island, you will undoubtedly pass through this bustling park. Don't come here looking for peace and quiet: it is too close to traffic and perpetually thronged with people. If you have kids in tow, however, there are a few entertainment options worth considering.

The Planetarium (☎ 233 5312; Alexandrovsky Park 4; adult/child R100/free; 12.30am-5pm Tue-Sun; M Gorkovskaya) has 50-minute shows throughout the day, as well as an observatory and several different halls. The St Petersburg Zoo (☎ 232 4828; Alexandrovsky Park 1; adult/child R250/60; summer 10am-7pm daily, winter 10am-4pm Tue-Sun) is full of miserable animals and happy kids. The lack of funds is pitifully evident, but all things considered it's pretty well kept. It's the world leader in polar bear births (since 1993, over 100 have been born here).

ARTILLERY MUSEUM Map pp114–15

Voyenno-istorichesky Muzey Artilerii; ☎ 232 0296; Alexandrovsky Park 7; adult/student courtyard R50/20, museum R300/150, photos R100; 11am-6pm Wed-Sun; M Gorkovskaya

The Artillery Museum is housed in the fort's original arsenal, across the moat from the Peter & Paul Fortress. It chronicles Russia's military history, with examples of weapons dating all the way back to the Stone Age. The centrepiece is Lenin's armoured car, which he rode in triumph from Finland Station. Even if you are not impressed by guns and bombs, who can resist climbing around on the tanks and trucks that adorn the courtyard?

CRUISER AURORA Map pp114–15

☎ 230 8440; Petrovskaya nab; admission free; 🕓 10.30am-4pm Tue-Thu, Sat & Sun; Ⓜ Gorkovskaya

In the Bolshaya Nevka opposite the Hotel St Petersburg is the *Aurora,* a mothballed cruiser from the Russo-Japanese War, built in 1900. From a downstream mooring on the night of 25 October 1917, its crew fired a blank round from the forward gun, demoralising the Winter Palace's defenders and marking the start of the October Revolution. During WWII, the Soviets sank it to protect it from German bombs. Now, restored and painted in pretty colours, it's a living museum that swarms with kids on weekends. It's possible to see the crew's quarters as well as endless communist propaganda and a collection of friendship banners from around the world.

PETER'S CABIN Map pp114–15

Domik Petra Velikogo; ☎ 314 0374; Petrovskaya nab 6; admission R200; 🕓 10am-5pm Wed-Mon; Ⓜ Gorkovskaya

In a patch of trees east of the fortress is a little stone building known as Peter's Cabin, St Petersburg's oldest surviving structure. This log cabin was supposedly built in three days in May 1703 for Peter to live in while he supervised the construction of the fortress and city. During Catherine the Great's time, the house was protected by a bricklayer.

The cabin has always been a sentimental site for St Petersburg. During WWII, Soviet soldiers would take an oath of allegiance to the city here, vowing to protect it from the Germans, before disappearing to the front. After the Siege of Leningrad, this was the first museum to reopen to the public.

The little cabin feels more like a shrine than a museum, but confirms Peter's love for the simple life with its unpretentious, homely feel, visibly influenced by the time he spent in Holland. Look out for the bronze bust of Peter by Parmen Zabello in the garden.

MUSEUM OF POLITICAL HISTORY

Map pp114–15

☎ 233 7052; www.polithistory.ru in Russian; ul Kuybysheva 4; adult/student R150/70, English guide R700 (maximum 5 people); 🕓 10am-5pm Fri-Wed; Ⓜ Gorkovskaya

East of Kamennoostrovsky pr, the 1904 Kshesinskaya Palace contains the Museum of Political History. Indeed, the building *is* political history – it was the headquarters of the Bolsheviks and Lenin often gave speeches from the balcony. The elegant Style Moderne palace had previously belonged to Mathilda Kshesinskaya, famous ballet dancer and one-time lover of Nicholas II in his pre-tsar days. It is worth a visit to see the house itself, as well as the best Soviet kitsch in town.

Of special note are the rare satirical caricatures of Lenin that were published in magazines between the 1917 revolutions (the same drawings a few months later would have got the artist imprisoned or worse). By contrast, the Lenin memorial room is unchanged since Soviet days, with an almost religious atmosphere. You can visit Lenin's one-time office where he worked between the February and October Revolutions.

The main exhibition tackles Russian politics from the Brezhnev era to the present day. It's excellently curated, with explanations in English. Elsewhere, both the pre- and post-revolutionary period are covered in scrupulous (almost forensic) detail.

top picks

FOR CHILDREN

Here's how you can keep your kids happy in St Petersburg:

- **Hermitage** (p125) Call in advance for a special kid-focused tour.
- **Russian Museum** (p76) Call ahead for a tour for children.
- **Kunstkamera** (p107) Inspire your kid to start a new collection.
- **Museum of Zoology** (p110) Snuggle up with some stuffed animals.
- **People's Will D-2 Submarine Museum** (p111) Give new meaning to the song 'Under the Sea'.
- **Artillery Museum** (opposite) Drive tanks and shoot guns (or at least pretend).
- **Kirov Museum** (p118) See how children lived in the Soviet era.
- **Alexandrovsky Park** (opposite) Take your pick between the zoo, the planetarium and the wide open spaces.
- **Krestovsky Island** (p120) Give them some thrills on the roller coasters at Divo Ostrov.
- **Museum of Railway Technology** (p146) Ride the train or drive the train, whichever suits your fancy.

MOSQUE Map pp114–15

☎ 233 9819; Kronverksky pr 7; Ⓜ Gorkovskaya

East of Alexandrovsky Park, this beautiful working mosque (1910–14) was modelled on Samarkand's Gur Emir Mausoleum. Its fluted azure dome and minarets have emerged from a painstaking renovation and are stunning. It is not really open to the public: *jamat* (congregation) members are highly protective of their mosque, which is a serious place of worship and not a tourist attraction. However, if you are respectfully dressed (women should wear a head covering), you can walk through the gate at the northeast side and politely ask the guard for entry. It might help if you say you are a student of religion or architecture. If you are asked in, remove your shoes, do not talk and do not take photos.

KIROV MUSEUM Map pp114–15

☎ 346 0217; www.kirovmuseum.spb.ru; Kamennoostrovsky pr 26/28; adult/student R70/40, tour R200; 🕑 11am-6pm Thu-Tue; Ⓜ Petrogradskaya

Sergei Kirov, Communist Party leader and celebrated Soviet henchman, spent 10 years of his life at this decidedly unproletarian apartment, until his murder in 1934 sparked a wave of deadly repression in the country. The apartment is now a fascinating museum showing how the Bolshevik elite really lived: take a quick journey back to the days of Soviet glory, including choice examples of 1920s technology (the first ever Soviet typewriter is here) and books (20,000 of them).

Many of Kirov's personal items are on display, including gifts from Leningrad workers, such as a portrait made completely out of feathers. His office from the Smolny Institute has been fully reconstructed in one of the halls downstairs.

A gory but reverential display shows the clothes that Kirov wore when he was killed. The tiny hole in the back of his cap was where he was shot (blood stains intact!) and the torn seam on his jacket's left breast was where doctors tried to revive his heart.

BOTANICAL GARDENS Map pp114–15

☎ 346 3639; ul Professora Popova 2; admission grounds free, greenhouse R50; 🕑 11am-4pm Sat-Thu; Ⓜ Petrogradskaya

On eastern Aptekarsky (Apothecary) Island, this quiet jungle was once a garden of medicinal plants that gave the island its name. The gardens date to 1714, when they were founded by Peter the Great himself. The botanical gardens contain 26 greenhouses on a 22-hectare site. It is a lovely place to stroll and a fascinating place to visit – and not just for botanists. At the turn of the 20th century, these were the second-biggest botanical gardens in the world, behind London's Kew Gardens. However, 90% of the plants died during WWII, which makes the present collection all the more impressive (you will recognise the 'veterans' by their war medals!).

A highlight is the *tsaritsa nochi (Selenicereus pteranthus),* a flowering cactus that blossoms only one night a year, usually in mid-June. On this night, the gardens stay open until morning for visitors to gawk at the marvel and sip champagne.

SIGMUND FREUD MUSEUM OF DREAMS Map pp114–15

☎ 380 7650; www.freud.ru; Bolshoy pr 18A; 🕑 noon-5pm Tue & Sun; Ⓜ Sportivnaya

An odd conceptual exhibition – based on abstractions and ideas, not artefacts – this unusual museum is an outgrowth of the Psychoanalytic Institute that houses it. The two-room exhibition aims to stimulate your subconscious as you struggle to read the display symbolising what Freud himself would have dreamt. Illustrations to Freud's patients' dreams and other quotations line the dimly lit, incense-scented hall.

TOY MUSEUM Map pp114–15

Muzey Igrushki; ☎ 234 4312; nab reki Karpovki 32; 🕑 11am-6pm Tue-Sun; Ⓜ Petrogradskaya

Since 1997, this privately run museum has been collecting toys from all over Russia and presenting them in three sections – folk toys, factory toys and artisanal toys. Examples of the latter include toys made in Sergiev Posad, home of the ubiquitous *matryoshka* (nesting doll), a creation often assumed to be far older than it is, being created for the first time only in the 19th century. The Toy Museum is charming and often has very interesting temporary exhibitions too.

YELIZAROV MUSEUM Map pp114–15

☎ 235 3778; ul Lenina 52, flat 24; adult/student R200/50; 🕑 10am-6pm Mon-Tue & Thu-Sat; Ⓜ Chkalovskaya

This unique building (known locally as the 'boat house' due to its uncanny similarities externally to a large cruise liner) was built in 1913 at the height of St Petersburg's lust for Style Moderne. It would otherwise be unremarkable were it not for the fact that Lenin's wife's family lived here and the great revolutionary himself laid low here before the revolution while organising the workers.

The flat's delightful turn-of-the-20th-century fittings have been preserved intact, and by the look of things, Lenin had a very bourgeois time of it. See the bathroom, where Vladimir Ilyich had a daily splash and the telephone that today still bears Lenin's home phone number.

CHALIAPIN HOUSE MUSEUM

Map pp114–15

☎ 234 1056; www.theatremuseum.ru; ul Graftio 2B; admission R40; ⌚ noon-6pm Wed-Sun; Ⓜ Petrogradskaya

Opera buffs will want to make the trek out to this house-museum (a branch of the State Museum of Theatre & Music) where the great singer Fyodor Chaliapin lived before fleeing the Soviet Union in 1922. The kindly babushkas (clearly music-lovers themselves) will probably play some of the singer's recordings for you as you peruse his personal effects.

ZAYACHY & PETROGRADSKY Walking Tour

1 Zayachy Island The city known as Sankt Pieter Burkh was founded on Zayachy Island (p113), within the walls of the city's first defensive installation, the Peter & Paul Fortress (p113). Make sure you check out the SS Peter & Paul Cathedral (p113), the last resting place of Peter the Great and almost every tsar since.

2 Alexandrovsky Park The circular Alexandrovsky Park (p116) surrounds Zayachy Island on three sides, so you'll have to pass through it on your way. It contains a small amusement park, a zoo, a planetarium and plenty of other fun for all ages.

3 Artillery Museum Hawks flock to the massive Artillery Museum (p116), appropriately placed along the moat opposite the fortress. Its enormous exhibition features weapons through the ages, as well as plenty of tanks and bombers to climb on in the courtyard.

4 Troitskaya pl The central square of Peter's early city, Troitskaya pl (Trinity Sq) formerly had as its centrepiece the enormous Trinity Cathedral, where Peter attended Mass. The cathedral was destroyed and now the square's most striking building is the Mosque (opposite). The palace of ballerina Mathilda Kshesinskaya now houses the Museum of Political History (p117).

5 Petrovskaya nab This embankment is home to two historic landmarks. Peter's Cabin (p117) is considered the oldest structure in the city and the city's soul. Off the islands eastern tip, the Cruiser Aurora (p117) is a legendary battleship surviving since the Russo-Japanese War.

6 Kamennoostrovsky pr Stroll up this stylish street to get a sense of Petrograd's ever-growing vibrancy. It is packed with shops (see p157), theatres and restaurants (see p174), not to mention the ever-popular Kirov Museum (opposite).

WALK FACTS

Start Peter & Paul Fortress (Ⓜ Gorkovskaya)
End Kamennoostrovsky pr (Ⓜ Petrogradskaya)
Distance 3km
Time Two hours
Fuel stops Troitsky Most (p175), Yakitoriya (p175)

ZAYACHY & PETROGRADSKY WALKING TOUR

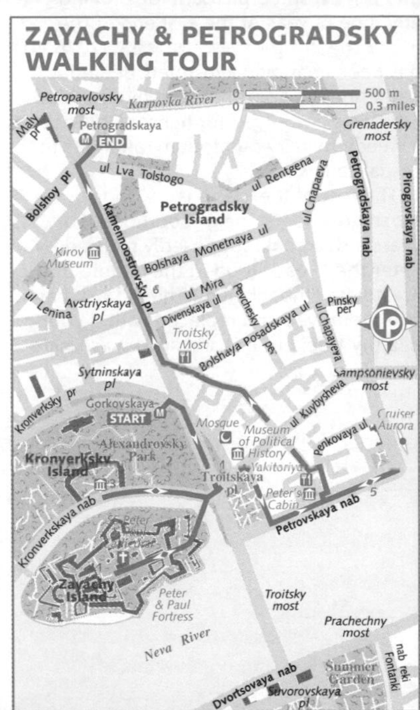

KIROVSKY ISLANDS

This is the collective name for the three outer delta islands of the Petrograd Side – Kamenny, Yelagin and Krestovsky. Once marshy jungles, the islands were granted to 18th- and 19th-century court favourites and developed into elegant playgrounds. Still mostly parkland, they are leafy venues for picnics, river sports and White Nights' cavorting.

Yelagin Island is an especially attractive oasis, as it is closed to cars. Krestovsky and Kamenny Islands are also pleasant places to stroll, as there is plenty of parkland, as well as a sort of New Russian suburbia. The metro station Ⓜ Krestovsky Ostrov provides easy access to both Krestovsky and Yelagin Islands; for Kamenny you can walk across the bridge from Ⓜ Chyornaya Rechka on the Vyborg Side.

KAMENNY ISLAND Map pp114–15

Ⓜ Chyornaya Rechka

Century-old *dachas* (country cottages; now inhabited by wealthy New Russians) line the lanes that twist their way around Kamenny (Stone) Island. The wooded island is punctuated by a series of canals, lakes and ponds, and is pleasant for strolling any time of year. At the east end of the island the Church of St John the Baptist (1776–81) has been charmingly restored. Behind it, Catherine the Great built the big, classical Kamennoostrovsky Palace for her son; it is now a weedy military sanatorium (off limits to casual callers).

The rest of the island is a woodsy, mostly residential neighbourhood. For years a dead oak, supposedly planted by Peter the Great, stood in the middle of the Krestovka embankment. The old oak has been removed and replaced with a young, healthy tree; but it is still known as Peter's Tree.

YELAGIN ISLAND Map pp114–15

☎ 430 0911; www.elaginpark.spb.ru in Russian; admission Mon-Fri free, adult/student Sat & Sun R30/10; 🕑 6am-midnight; Ⓜ Krestovsky Ostrov

This island is basically a giant park, a delightful car-free zone that is a fantastic place to wander. It was landscaped by the architect Carlo Rossi, so you can expect the loveliest of settings. The centrepiece is the Yelagin Palace (☎ 430 1130; Yelagin ostrov 1; admission R100; 🕑 10am-6pm Wed-Sun), also by Rossi, which Alexander I built for his mother Empress Maria. The very beautiful restored interiors of the main house include old furnishings on loan from the Grand Europe and Astoria Hotels; don't miss the stupendous 1890s carved-walnut ensemble in the study and the incredible inlaid-wood floors. Other nearby estate buildings sometimes host temporary exhibitions too.

The rest of the island is a lovely network of paths, greenery, lakes and channels. At the northern end of the island, you can rent rowing boats (per hour R160) to explore the ponds or in-line skates to explore the paths; in winter it's an ideal setting for sledding, skiing and skating (see p198). At the west end, a plaza looks out to the Gulf of Finland: sunsets are resplendent from here.

KRESTOVSKY ISLAND Map pp114–15

Ⓜ Krestovsky Ostrov

The biggest of the three northern islands, Krestovsky consists mostly of the vast Seaside Park of Victory (Primorsky Park Pobedy), dotted with sports fields. Not far from the metro station, Divo Ostrov (☎ 323 9705; www.divo-ostrov.ru; admission free, rides R40-70; 🕑 11am-8pm daily Jun-Aug, 11am-8pm Sat-Sun Sep-May; Ⓜ Krestovsky Ostrov) is a low-rent Disney-style amusement park with thrill rides kids will adore. You can rent bikes and in-line skates here. At the island's far western end, the 80,000-seat Kirov Stadium is set for demolition and reconstruction.

VYBORG SIDE

Eating p175; Sleeping p212

Peter the Great had no apparent interest in the far side of the Neva and today, beyond the embankment and Finland Station (Finlyandsky vokzal), among the factories and railway lines, there are few attractions. But there is more than meets the eye, including some excellent, unusual restaurants and a few unexpected and off-beat sights.

Take a tour of Russia's oldest working prison, Kresty Prison. Pay your respect to the blockade victims at the mass graves at Piskaryovskoe Cemetery. Haggle for trash and treasure at the city's largest flea market, Udelnaya Fair (Udelnaya Yarmarka; p158). Say a prayer at the wonderful Sampsonievsky Cathedral or recite a mantra at the world's most northerly Buddhist temple. Or follow in the footsteps of generations of pilgrims and poetry-lovers who lay flowers at the site where Alexander Pushkin fought the duel that would end his life.

Distances are vast on the Vyborg Side: despite two metro lines and some 14 stations, there are often big distances to cover on foot. Most useful are the stations Ⓜ Staraya Derevnya and Ⓜ Pl Lenina, both near the Neva.

HERMITAGE STORAGE FACILITY

Map pp122–3

☎ 334 9226; www.hermitagemuseum.com; Zausadebnaya ul 37a; admission R200; ⏲ tours 11am, 1pm, 1.30pm & 3.30pm Wed-Sun; Ⓜ Staraya Derevnya

In case you did not see enough stuff at the museum in town, the storage facility of the Hermitage provides a superb reason for dragging yourself out to northern St Petersburg. Inside the state of the art complex you'll be led through a handful of rooms housing but a fraction of the museum's collection. This is not a formal exhibition as such, but the guides are knowledgeable and the examples chosen for display – paintings, furniture, carriages – are wonderful. The highlight is undoubtedly the gorgeous wool and silk embroidered Turkish ceremonial tent, presented to Catherine the Great by the Sultan Slim III in 1793. Beside it stands an equally impressive modern diplomatic gift: a massive wood carving of the mythical garuda bird, given by Indonesia to the city for its 300th anniversary.

The Hermitage (p125) has big plans for this site; by 2010, it is meant to be the largest facility of this kind in the world, with eight buildings open to the public. The storage facility is directly behind the big shopping centre opposite the metro station.

PISKARYOVSKOE CEMETERY

Map p65

Piskaryovskoe Kladbishche; ☎ 247 5716; pr Nepokoryonnikh 72; ⏲ 10am-5pm; Ⓜ Lesnaya or Pl Muzhestva

It's hard work getting to this rather remote cemetery, but as the main burial place for the victims of the Nazi blockade in WWII, it is a poignant memorial to the tragedy (see the boxed text, below).

Originally, this area was just an enormous pit where unnamed and unmarked bodies were dumped. Some half a million people were laid to rest here between 1941 and 1943. In 1960 the remodelled cemetery was opened and has been an integral part of the city's soul ever since. Every year on Victory Day (9 May) the cemetery is packed out with mourners, many of whom survived the blockade or lost close relatives to starvation.

From Lesnaya metro station turn right and walk down the street about 100m and

HERE LIE THE PEOPLE OF LENINGRAD

No place in present-day St Petersburg better captures the horror of the holocaust of wartime Leningrad than Piskaryovskoe Cemetery. Defiant yet moving music emanates from the speakers; a devastated Mother Russia casts her eyes over the destruction. The inscription on the wall behind the sculpture reads:

Here lie the people of Leningrad
Here are the citizens – men, women and children
And besides them the Red Army soldiers
Who gave their lives
Defending you, Leningrad,
Cradle of the Revolution,
Their noble names we cannot number
So many lie beneath the eternal granite
But of those honoured by this stone
Let no one forget
Let nothing be forgotten.

Olga Bergolts, Siege survivor

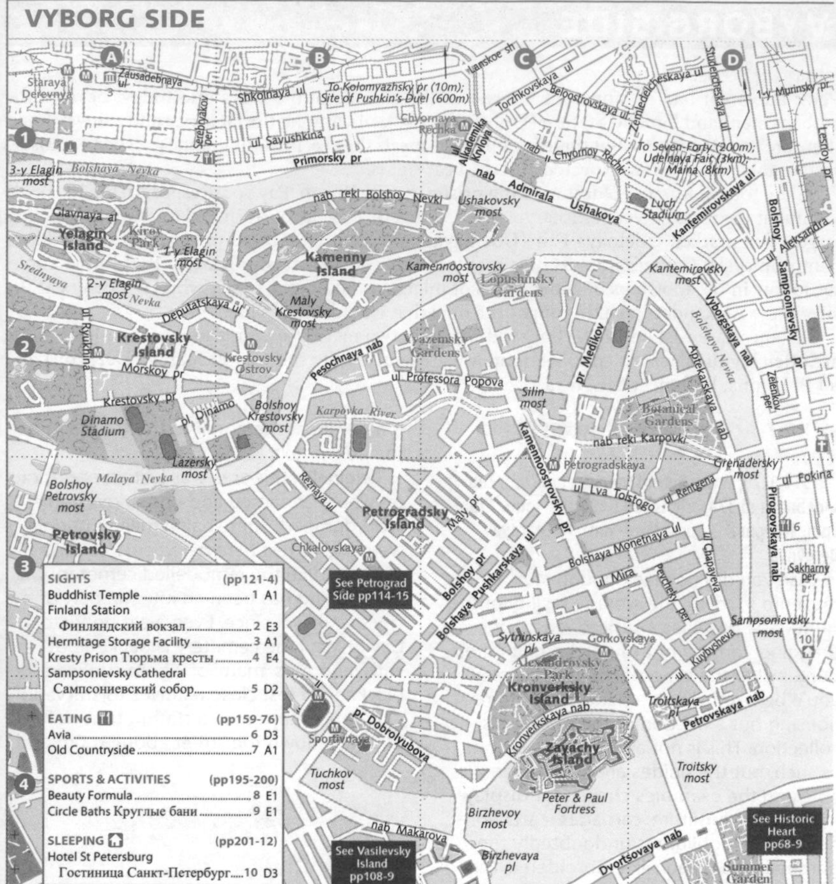

take bus 123, K-385 or K-33. These go to the Piskaryovka train station, from where it's a further 10 to 15 minutes to walk to the cemetery itself. It may be easier to take a cab from Lesnaya station (reckon on about R150 each way).

FINLAND STATION Map pp122–3

Finlyandsky vokzal; pl Lenina 6; Ⓜ Pl Lenina

Finland Station is where Lenin finally arrived in 1917 after 17 years in exile abroad. Here, in the square where his statue now stands, he gave his legendary speech from the top of an armoured car to a crowd who had only heard of but never seen the man. After fleeing a second time he again arrived here from Finland, this time disguised as a railway fireman, and the locomotive he rode in is displayed on the platform. It's not really the same station, as it was rebuilt in the 1970s in the drabbest possible Soviet style. However, its historic significance remains. Walk out onto the square that still bears Lenin's name and you'll see a marvellous statue of the man himself at the far end.

KRESTY PRISON Map pp122–3

☎ 542 6861, 542 4735; www.kresty.ru; Arsenalnaya nab 7; admission R300; 🕑 tours noon, 1.30pm, 3pm Sat & Sun year-round, plus 4.30pm Sat & Sun May-Oct; Ⓜ Pl Lenina

Kresty is St Petersburg's main holding prison; if you're busted here, Kresty's where they take you to await whatever it is that awaits you. You wouldn't want to find out: conditions are much better now than when

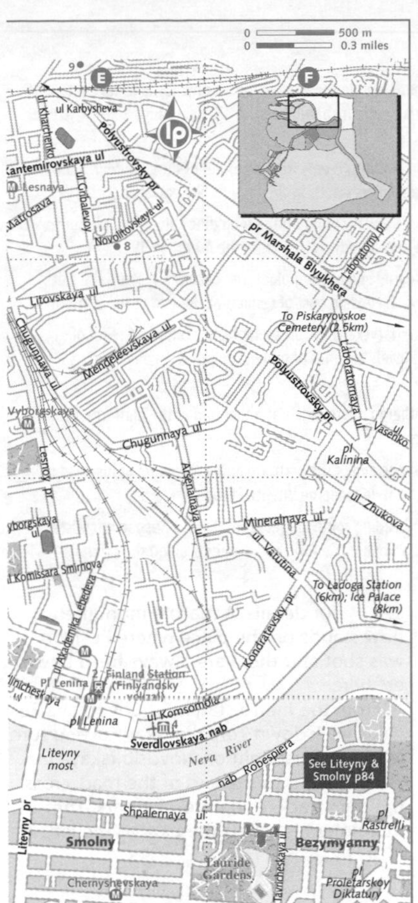

the prison was at its most crowded, but it is still hardly a pleasant place.

Kresty is the oldest working prison in Russia, built in 1892. Tours visit the holding areas, the grounds and a small museum. This definitely constitutes a unique day out in the city. You will have a chance to see the six-bunk cells and the frightening solitary-confinement closets. Inmates are on site – working, walking or peeking out at you through slats in their cells. Guests are advised not to interact with them. The little museum has exhibitions on past residents (like Noi Trotsky and the entire Provisional Government from 1917), as well as art made by prisoners with lots of time on their hands.

Each tour can accommodate up to 25 people, so it's worth arriving early and claiming your spot in the queue (your passport must be shown on entry). Tours are in Russian only, although several tour operators organise excursions in English (see p247).

BUDDHIST TEMPLE Map pp122–3

☎ 239 0341, 430 0341; Primorsky pr 91; service 10am; M Staraya Derevnya

This beautiful *datsan* (temple) was built between 1909 and 1915 at the instigation of Pyotr Badmaev, a Buddhist physician to Tsar Nicholas II. Money was raised from all over Russia, and as far afield as Thailand and England, by various Buddhist organisations; it even gained the support of the Dalai Lama in Lhasa.

The communists shut the temple, arrested many of the monks and used the building as a military radio station. In the 1960s it was taken over by the Zoological Institute and used as laboratories (the Soviets thrived on using religious buildings for purposes that were particularly humiliating). Thankfully, however, the damage was not particularly profound and the *datsan* was returned to the city's small Buddhist community in 1990, since when it has been renovated. Visitors are welcome, though it's best to avoid the services unless you're a Buddhist.

SAMPSONIEVSKY CATHEDRAL

Map pp122–3

☎ 294 5751; Bolshoy Sampsonievsky pr 41; adult/student R200/100; 10am-8pm Thu-Tue May-Sep, 11am-6pm Thu-Tue Oct-Apr; M Vyborgskaya

This fascinating pea-green baroque cathedral dates from 1740 and is a beautiful highlight of a remarkably dull industrial area of the Vyborg Side – it's well worth the trip out here. It is believed to be the church where Catherine the Great married her one-eyed lover Grigory Potemkin in a secret ceremony in 1774.

Today it's a delightful place, having been repainted and restored to its original glory on the outside. Restoration on the inside continues and it looks marvellous. The cathedral's most interesting feature is the calendar of saints, two enormous panels on either side of the nave, each representing six months of the year and every day decorated with a mini-icon of its saint(s). The enormous silver chandelier above the altar is also something to behold, as is the stunning baroque, green and golden iconostasis.

UNDERGROUND ART

If you've had your fill of museums and palaces in St Petersburg, an ideal way to spend a rainy day is to take a tour of underground art. Metro line 1 (that's the red line on the official metro map) between Ⓜ Pl Vosstaniya and Ⓜ Avtovo is striking for its station designs:

Avtovo (Map p65) The red and gold mosaic at the end of the platform is only the beginning of the grandeur. Marble and cut-glass clad columns hold up the roof, while a relief of soldiers stands in the temple-like entrance.

Baltiyskaya (Map pp146–7) Look for a naval theme here, with a wavy motif on the mouldings along the platform ceiling and a vivid marble mosaic at the end of the platform depicting the volley from the *Aurora* in 1917.

Kirovsky Zavod (Map p65) This station is named after the nearby engineering plant; the decoration along the platform also takes its inspiration from the oil wells and industry. A scowling bust of Lenin is at the end of the platform.

Narvskaya (Map pp146–7) Perhaps the city's coolest station, Narvskaya features a fantastic sculptured relief of Lenin and rejoicing proletariat over the escalators, as well as lovely carvings of miners, engineers, sailors, artists and teachers on the platform columns.

Pl Vosstaniya (Map p92) Lenin and Stalin are depicted together in the roundels at either end of the platform. Look out for Lenin on a tank and Lenin with the Kronshtadt sailors.

Pushkinskaya (Map pp146–7) A statue of the poet stands at the end of the platform and a moulding of his head is above the escalators. Nip out of the station to view the nearby Style Moderne Vitebsk Station.

Tekhnologichesky Institut (Map pp146–7) On the platform heading south are reliefs of famous Russian scientists, while the northbound platform announces the dates of Russia's major scientific achievements along the columns.

SITE OF PUSHKIN'S DUEL Map p65

Mesto duela AS Pushkina; Kolomyazhsky pr; Ⓜ Chyornaya Rechka

This is a point of literary pilgrimage for those who mourn the loss of Russia's poetic genius, Alexander Pushkin, who was senselessly killed in a duel with the Frenchman Georges d'Anthès on 8 February 1837. The story has developed a certain mythology around it in the past two centuries: see p73 for details. A marble monument now stands on the place where Pushkin was shot and there are always fresh flowers here.

From the metro station at Chyornaya Rechka, walk down Torzhkovskaya ul and turn left at the first light on Novosibirskaya ul. Walk straight to the end of the road, cross the train tracks and enter the park. The monument is across the park to the left.

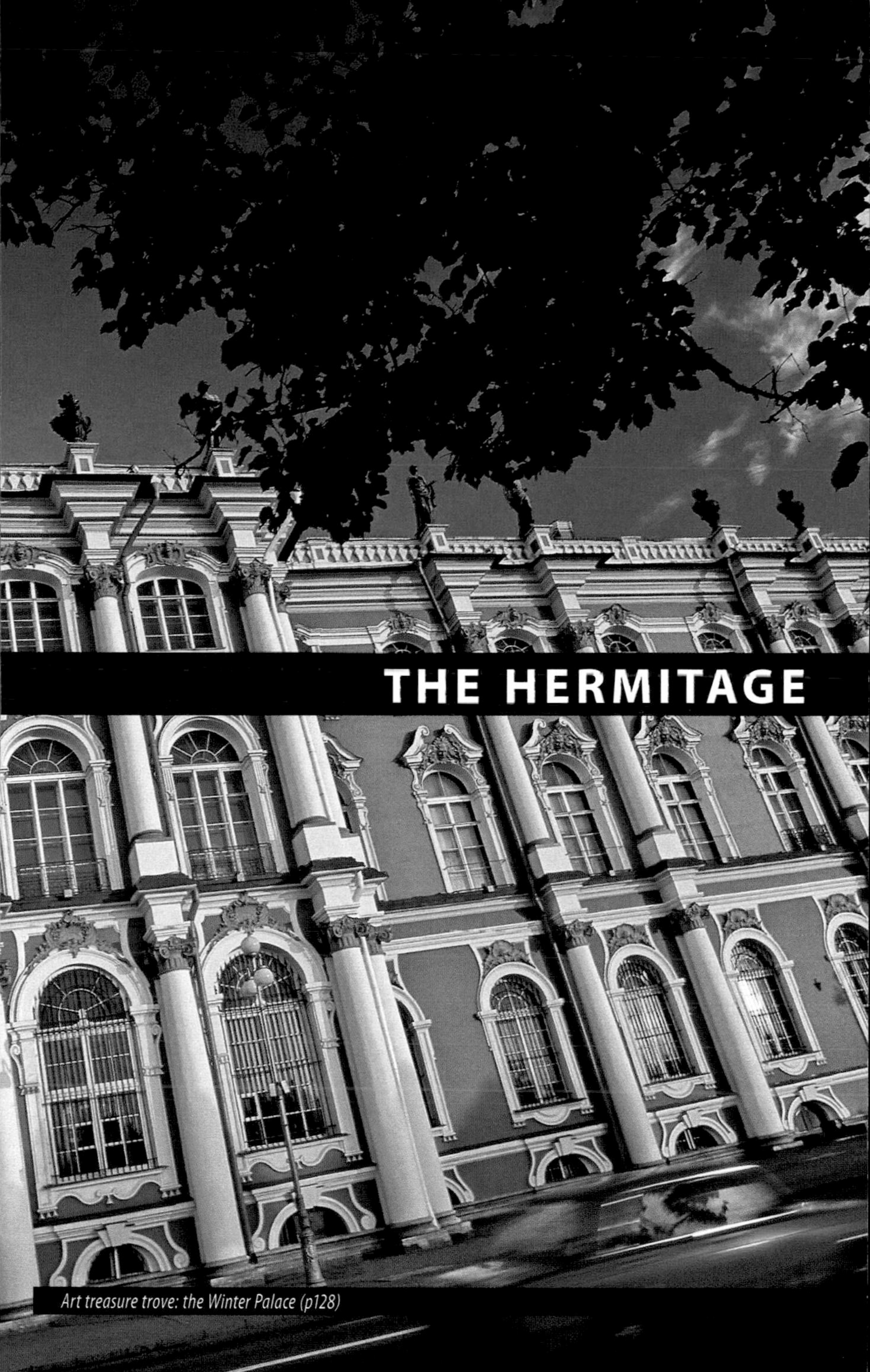

THE HERMITAGE

Art treasure trove: the Winter Palace (p128)

STATE HERMITAGE MUSEUM

The Hermitage's imperious Winter Palace façade

top picks

HERMITAGE HIGHLIGHTS

- **Ancient Egypt (Room 100)** p134
- **Jordan Staircase** p139
- **19th- and 20th-century French Painting (Rooms 143–146)** p138
- **Imperial staterooms and apartments, including the Malachite Hall, Nicholas Hall, Armorial Hall and Hall of St George (Rooms 178–198)** p139
- **Pavilion Hall (Room 204)** p138
- **Leonardo da Vinci (Room 214)** p137
- **Master of Light, Rembrandt (Room 254)** p138
- **Dreamy impressionists and postimpressionists (Rooms 316–320)** p142
- **Russian Avant-Garde (Room 333)** p143
- **The Many Facets of Matisse and Picasso (Rooms 343–350)** p144

In 1764 Empress Catherine II purchased the art collection of Johann Gotzkowski and put it on display in the 'small hermitage' where she entertained guests. This collection would grow into one of the world's most celebrated art museums, eventually filling the original building, as well as the classical Large Hermitage and the baroque Winter Palace, with millions of artistic masterpieces from around the world. Today, it comprises the State Hermitage Museum, the geographic and tourism centrepiece of St Petersburg.

No other institution so embodies the opulence and extravagance of the tsarist regime which ruled from the Winter Palace for more than a century. But today – for the price of admission – anybody can parade down the grand staircases and across parquet floors, gawking at crystal chandeliers and gilded furniture.

More importantly, all are invited to peruse the glorious artwork. Each year, millions of art lovers flock to the Hermitage to feast their eyes on the Western European collection – which spans history from the Middle Ages through to the modern period – appropriate for this city which was built to be Russia's 'window to the West.' Occupying more than 120 rooms, the collection does not miss much: Spanish, Flemish, Dutch, French, English and German art are all covered from the 15th to the 18th centuries, while the Italian collection goes back all the way to the 13th century, including the Florentine and Venetian Renaissance.

An undeniable highlight is the French and German paintings from the 19th and 20th centuries. The collection of impressionist and postimpressionist paintings is arguably the best in the world, especially considering recent additions. Much of this artwork was displayed for the first time in the 1990s, when the Hermitage revealed some fabulous art hoards kept secret since seizure by the Red Army from Germany at the end of WWII.

The Western European art is remarkable – and highly recommended – but the Hermitage collection is broader still. Prehistoric pieces date back to the Palaeolithic and Neolithic Ages. Egyptian mummies, Greek artefacts and Roman sculpture recall those ancient cultures. And in the furthest, seemingly forgotten corners of the museum, the Oriental collection covers the Middle East, China and Japan. The wealth of the collection itself is limitless: vast as the amount of artwork on display in the museums is, there's about 20 times more in its vaults.

THE RUSSIAN ARK

Film director Alexander Sokurov celebrates the Hermitage's history and artistry in his highly lauded film *The Russian Ark*. The viewer sees through the eyes of an unnamed narrator, a ghost who resides in the Winter Palace. The other character is a 19th-century visitor, the Marquis de Custine, who wrote extensively about his travels to Russia. In one unedited sweep, the narrator guides the 'European' through 33 rooms of the Winter Palace and 300 years of Russian history. The film premiered for St Petersburg's tercentenary in 2003.

The main complex of the Hermitage – covered in this chapter – consists of five linked buildings along Dvortsovaya nab: the massive green and white, glittering façade of the Winter Palace; the original Little Hermitage; the Old and New Hermitages, which are usually grouped together as the Large Hermitage; and the Hermitage Theatre (p188), which is open only for special events and performances. Other facilities that are technically part of the State Hermitage Museum are covered elsewhere in this book, including the General Staff Building (p66), the Winter Palace of Peter I (p67), Menshikov Palace (p110), the Hermitage Storage Facility (p121) and the Imperial Porcelain factory (p158).

An additional special collection known as the Golden Rooms (☎ 571 8446; admission R350) is open only by guided tour. The focus is a hoard of fabulous Scythian and Greek gold and silver from the Caucasus, Crimea and Ukraine, dating from the 7th to 2nd centuries BC.

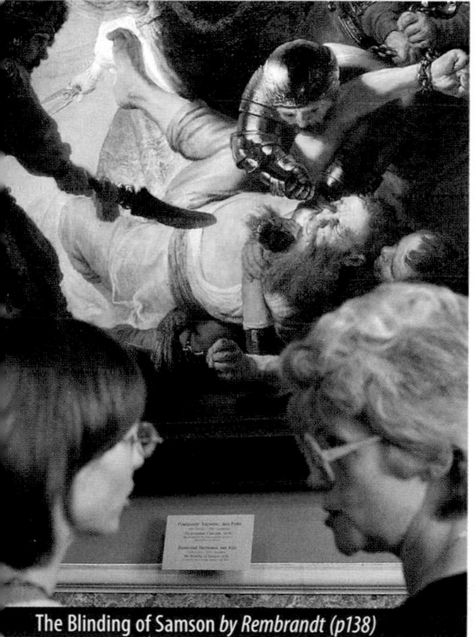
The Blinding of Samson *by Rembrandt (p138)*

Hot-footing it past a statue outside the Hermitage

The baroque Winter Palace (right)

The imperial rulers occupied this spot overlooking the Neva ever since the days of Peter the Great.

His first, relatively modest mansion stood on the site of the Hermitage Theatre (see Winter Palace of Peter I, p67).

A NEW WINTER PALACE

It was Empress Anna who first engaged a young Bartolomeo Rastrelli to incorporate the existing structures into a proper palace in the 1730s. But even this effort would not satisfy the whims of ever-extravagant Empress Elizabeth. In 1754 she signed a decree ordering the creation of a Winter Palace, and she closely supervised its design and construction. Her inopportune death in 1761 occurred only a few months before the Winter Palace was finally completed to her plans.

Visitors and residents were wowed by the capital's newest addition, 'visible from a distance, rising above the rooftops, the upper storey of the new winter palace, adorned with a host of statues,' as described by one 18th-century visitor to the capital. But the palace – of course – was a private residence. After the death of Empress Elizabeth, Peter III lived here for only three months before he was overthrown in a palace coup and replaced by Catherine the Great. This grand baroque building thenceforth became the official residence of the imperial family.

THE IMPERIAL ART COLLECTION

Catherine and her successors didn't much care for Rastrelli's baroque interiors and had most of the rooms completely remodelled in classical style. Catherine also built the Little Hermitage next door – and later the so-called Old Hermitage – to house her growing art collection. In the 1780s Giacomo Quarenghi added the Hermitage Theatre, which served as the private theatre for the imperial family.

In December 1837 a devastating fire broke out in the heating shaft of the Field Marshals' Hall; it burned for over 30 hours and destroyed a large portion of the interior. Most of the imperial belongings were saved, thrown out of windows or dragged outside to sit in the snow. Nicholas I vowed to restore the palace as quickly as possible, employing architect Vasily Stasov and thousands of workers to toil around the clock. Their efforts were not in vain, as the project was completed in a little over a year.

Arch your neck and take in the long view

Most of the classical interiors in the ceremonial rooms that we see today – including the Grand Hall, the Throne Room and the Armorial Hall – were designed by Stasov.

RUSSIA'S FIRST PUBLIC MUSEUM

Nicholas I was the first ruler to open the collection to the public. During a visit to Germany in 1838 he was impressed by the museums he saw in Munich – specifically, by the idea of buildings that were architectural masterpieces in themselves, designed specifically to house and preserve artistic masterpieces. He employed German architect Leo von Klenze and local boy Vasily Stasov to carry out such a project in the proximity of the Winter Palace. The result was the 'neo-Grecian' New Hermitage, adorned by statues and bas-relief depicting great artists, writers and other cultural figures. After 11 years of work, the museum was opened to the public in 1852.

THE STORMING OF THE WINTER PALACE

After the February Revolution in 1917, Alexander Kerensky and the Provisional Government occupied the Winter Palace. However, the 26 October 'storming' of the Winter Palace was not nearly as dramatic as history makes it out to be. The cruiser *Aurora* fired a blank shot to signal the start of the assault; and the Red Guards – led by Lenin – moved in on the Winter Palace, which was being guarded by the 'Women's Battalion of Death'. Three shells struck the building, bullet holes riddled the square side of the palace and a window was shattered on the 3rd floor before the Provisional Government was arrested in the Small Dining Room behind the Malachite Hall. This largely bloodless battle would be celebrated for 70 years as the most glorious moment in history.

GROWING THE COLLECTION

Since Catherine the Great made her first significant artistic purchase in 1764, the imperial art collection had grown consistently, as each new ruler procured paintings, sculpture and artefacts to add to the store of treasures. But it was the postrevolutionary period that saw a threefold increase in the collection. In 1917 the Winter Palace and the Hermitage were declared to be state museums. And throughout the 1920s and 1930s, the new Soviet state seized and nationalised countless valuable private collections, namely those of the Stroganovs, Sheremetyevs, Shuvalovs, Yusupovs and the Baron Stieglitz. In 1948 it incorporated the renowned collections

Fine ceiling detail puts art in a higher place

ART UNDER SIEGE

'The empty Hermitage was like a house from which a corpse has been carried out.' Such was the description of one local artist, who laboured for weeks on end, packing away artwork in anticipation of a Nazi attack on Leningrad.

On a grim day in the summer of 1941 the Hermitage staff received an emergency summons to the museum. They immediately went to work, taking down paintings, rolling canvasses, packing precious artwork away into boxes and crates. Artists, professors, historians and art-lovers – even those with no official affiliation with the museum – showed up to lend a hand. They worked around the clock, taking care to preserve the treasures. Two trains carried over 1,118,000 pieces of artwork, evacuating them to the safety of the Ural Mountains.

And none too soon. In September 1941, the command came from the highest ranks of the Nazi party: 'The Fuehrer has decided to wipe the city of Leningrad from the face of the earth.' More than 2000 people – Hermitage employees, artists and their families – moved into the basement of the Winter Palace, which had been converted into a bomb shelter.

Conditions were bleak, to say the least. Yet somehow – even when food was nonexistent and temperatures were well below freezing – cultural life endured. Professors engaged in scholarly debate to pass the time; artists painted poignant depictions of their surroundings; and residents kept a daily toll of the damage done. On 10 December, the literati gathered to celebrate the 500th anniversary of the Uzbek poet Nava'i. 'When Nava'i's verses were being read, the air shook with the explosions of German shells,' recalled one participant. In June 1942, artists organised the first exhibition of works rendering the defence of Leningrad.

Before the siege was lifted, two bombs exploded on Dvortsovaya pl, and more than 30 shells blasted the beleaguered building. All of the windows were shattered, and snow and ice filled the rooms, causing extensive damage to the ornamental walls, ceilings and floors. Eighty museum workers died of starvation.

Immediately after the war ended, the Hermitage staff set to work to organise an exhibition. The majority of the most valuable artwork was still in the Urals, but other pieces were brought out of storage and a few rooms were hastily repaired. The exhibition opened in July 1944 – a demonstration of the triumph of art and beauty. According to one worker, 'The inhabitants of Leningrad perceived the chance to walk the clean, warm floors of the Hermitage...as a real proof of the brilliant victories over the enemy.'

of postimpressionist and impressionist paintings from of Moscow industrialists Sergei Shchukin and Ivan Morozov. The coffers of the Hermitage swelled.

In 1995 the Hermitage displayed some of the 20th century's sweetest war booty. The exhibition, called 'Hidden Treasures Revealed', consisted entirely of art captured from German private collections by the Red Army in 1945, including works by Monet, Degas, Renoir, Cézanne, Picasso and Matisse – almost all of which had never been publicly displayed.

A river runs through it: the Neva alongside the Hermitage

ADMISSION & TOURS

The Jordan Staircase (p139)

The main entrance to the Hermitage for individuals is through the courtyard of the Winter Palace from Palace Sq.

At the information kiosk of the State Hermitage Museum (☎ 571 3420; www.hermitagemuseum.org; Dvortsovaya nab 34; adult/student/child R350/free/free; 10.30am-6pm Tue-Sat & 10.30am-5pm Sun) you can pick up a free colour map of the museum, available in most European languages. Immediately after ticket inspection you can hire an audio guide (R250) with recorded tours in English, German, French, Italian or Russian. Groups enter from the river side of the Winter Palace.

One way to avoid the queues – and get a decent introduction to the sometimes overwhelming museum – is to join a tour. Most official tours whiz through the main sites in about 1½ hours; but it's easy enough to 'lose' the group and stay until closing time. To book a tour, contact the excursion office (☎ 571 8446; 11.30am-1pm & 2-4pm), who can tell you the times of tours in English, German or French.

Much of the Hermitage is now wheelchair-accessible, and there are wheelchairs available on site. Note that the wheelchair entrance is on the square side of the building. It's best to call in advance (☎ 710 9079) if you require any assistance, so that someone will be there to open the gates.

Make an entrance via Palace Sq (above)

QUICK TIP

Avoid the massive queues at the Hermitage by purchasing your ticket online at www.hermitagemuseum.org. Order your tickets in advance, and you will receive an electronic voucher within one to three days. The voucher allows you to jump to the front of the line, but you must bring a photo ID to pick up your ticket. The one-day simple entrance (US$18) covers admission to the main complex on Dvortsovaya pl. A two-day combo ticket (US$26) allows for admission to the main complex, as well as the General Staff Building, Menshikov Palace, the Winter Palace of Peter I and the Imperial Porcelain Museum. Both tickets include permission to take photography and – most importantly – to jump the queue. Priceless.

VISITING THE HERMITAGE

Gilt and chandeliers adorn the stately Armorial Hall (p140)

The Hermitage is a dynamic institution: displays change, specific pieces go on tour, and temporary exhibitions occupy particular rooms, displacing whatever normally resides there. Furthermore, this being Russia, the museum occasionally closes rooms without warning, for maintenance or other mysterious reasons. Use the following room-by-room description as a guideline; but don't be surprised when every painting is not exactly in its place. As per the Russian system of numbering floors, the ground floor is called the 1st floor, followed by the 2nd floor, 3rd floor etc.

WINTER PALACE: 1ST FLOOR

You can actually escape some of the crowds by ducking into the western wing of the Winter Palace, which many visitors bypass.

Rooms 1–26: Prehistoric Artefacts

The prehistoric collection at the Hermitage contains thousands of artefacts dating from as far back as the Palaeolithic era (500,000 to 12,000 BC). Most of the items were excavated from different regions around Russia in recent years. Here we list some of the highlights.

Room 12 Carved petroglyphs (dating to 2000 BC) were taken from the northeastern shores of Lake Onega after archaeological expeditions in 1935.

Rooms 13–14 Excavations of a burial mound in the northern Caucasus uncovered the corpse of a nomadic chief, lavishly dressed and covered in jewels. Inside the grave, archaeologists found gold and silver vessels – as well as the elaborate jewel-studded canopy that covered his body.

Rooms 15–18 The Scythians lived in the southern part of present-day Russia from the 7th to 3rd centuries BC. The display includes a few examples of the 'Scythian animal style', including the Kelermes panther and Kostromsky stag, both golden plaques that were ornaments on an iron shield. If you like this, you should check out the special exhibition in the Golden Rooms (p127).

Rooms 21–23 & 26 Conditions in the Altai Mountain region were ideal for preserving tribal tombs. Room 26 contains human corpses that are more than 2000 years old, including a tribal chief who is completely covered in tattoos.

HERMITAGE – 1st FLOOR

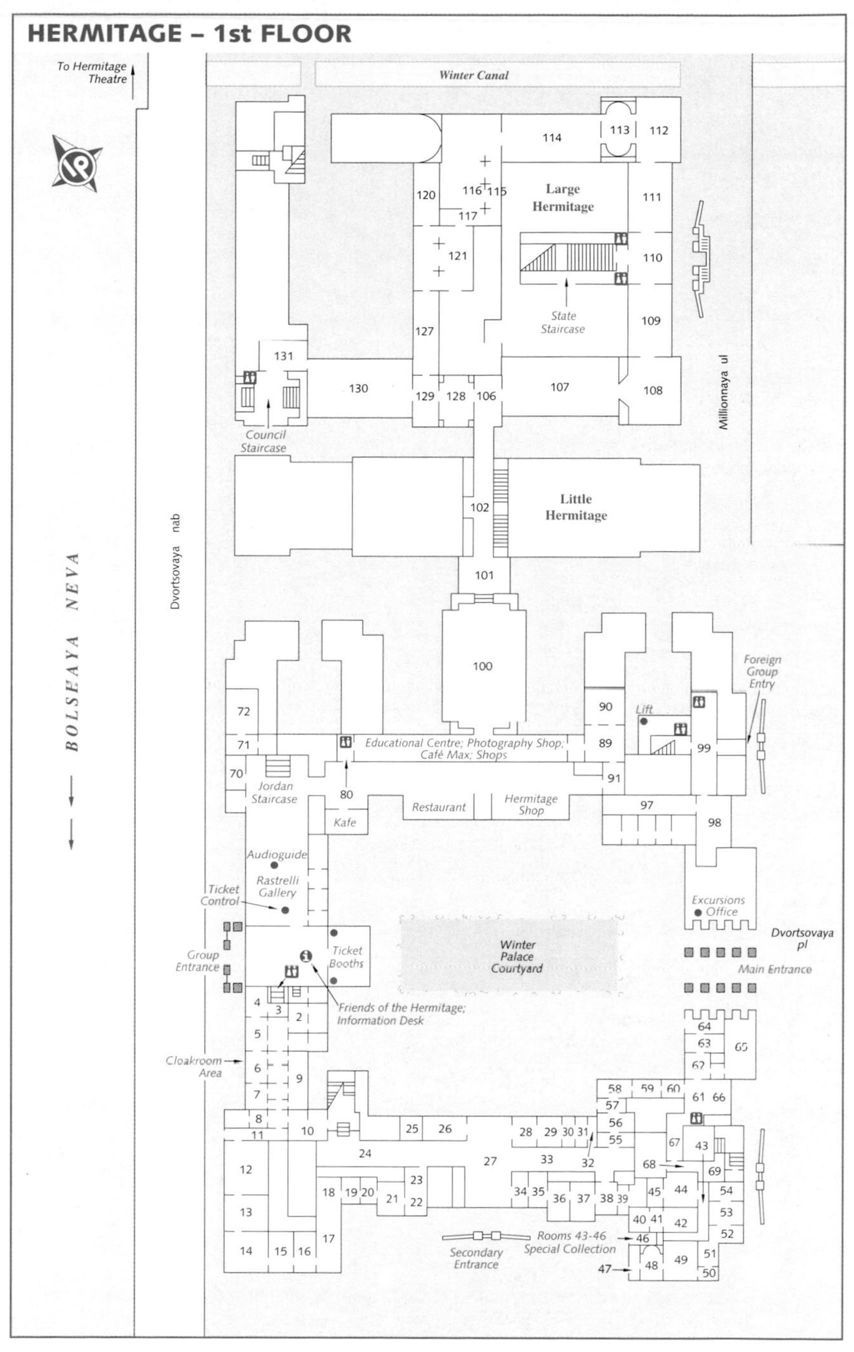

Re-creating da Vinci's Benois Madonna (p137)

Rooms 27–40 & 46–69: Ancient East

These rooms were closed at the time of research, but they normally contain artefacts from Central Asia and the Caucasus, dating as far back as the 10th century BC. Rooms 67–69 usually feature art and artefacts of the Golden Horde, who swept through Russia in the 13th and 14th centuries.

Room 100: Ancient Egypt

In the east wing of the Winter Palace (leading to the Little Hermitage) you will find the incredible artefacts of Ancient Egypt. This excellent collection, uncovered by Russian archaeologists, spans the Egyptian era from the Old Kingdom (3000–2400 BC) to the New Empire (1580–1050 BC). The ancient papyrus texts are amazing, including *The Shipwrecked Sailor*, a secular text that dates to 1900 BC. There are many painted sarcophagi and tombstones carved with hieroglyphics, as well as an intriguing (and disturbing) mummy from the 10th century BC.

LITTLE HERMITAGE: 1ST FLOOR

The little staircase at the end of Room 100 will bring you into the Little Hermitage, which used to house the palace stables and riding school. Most of this building is off-limits, but you can continue through Rooms 101 and 102 to the Large Hermitage.

LARGE HERMITAGE: 1ST FLOOR

Rooms 106–131: Antiquity

The Hermitage has over 100,000 items from Ancient Greece and Rome, including thousands of painted vases, antique gemstones, Roman sculpture and Greek gold. The space, designed by Leo von Klenze in the classical style, is particularly appropriate for this collection:

Room 107 Jupiter Hall is a sumptuous space with portraits of sculptors on the ceiling.

Room 108 Designed by von Klenze to imitate a courtyard in a Roman house.

Room 109 Peter I acquired the sculpture *Tauride Venus* from Pope Clement XI. This piece – a Roman copy of a Greek original – was the first antique sculpture ever brought to Russia.

Room 111 Another impressive design by von Klenze, this one was intended to be a library (which explains the philosophers' portraits).

Room 130 Hall of Twenty Columns.

LARGE HERMITAGE: 2ND FLOOR

From Room 131, head up the Council Staircase (Sovietskaya Lestnitsa), which derives its name from the members of the State Council who used it in the 19th century. At the top is Room 206 where a marble, malachite and glass triumphal arch announces the beginning of the Italian section.

Rooms 207–238: Italian Art

Covering 30-plus rooms, the Hermitage's collection of Italian art traverses the 13th to the 18th centuries. The highlights are certainly the works by the Renaissance artists: Leonardo da Vinci, Raphael, Giorgione and Titian. Look also for Botticelli, Caravaggio and Tiepolo.

Room 207 The earliest example in this collection is *The Crucifixion,* painted by Ugolino Di Tedice in the first half of the 13th century.

The Loggia of Raphael (p137), Giacomo Quarenghi's copy of the Vatican gallery

HERMITAGE – 2nd FLOOR

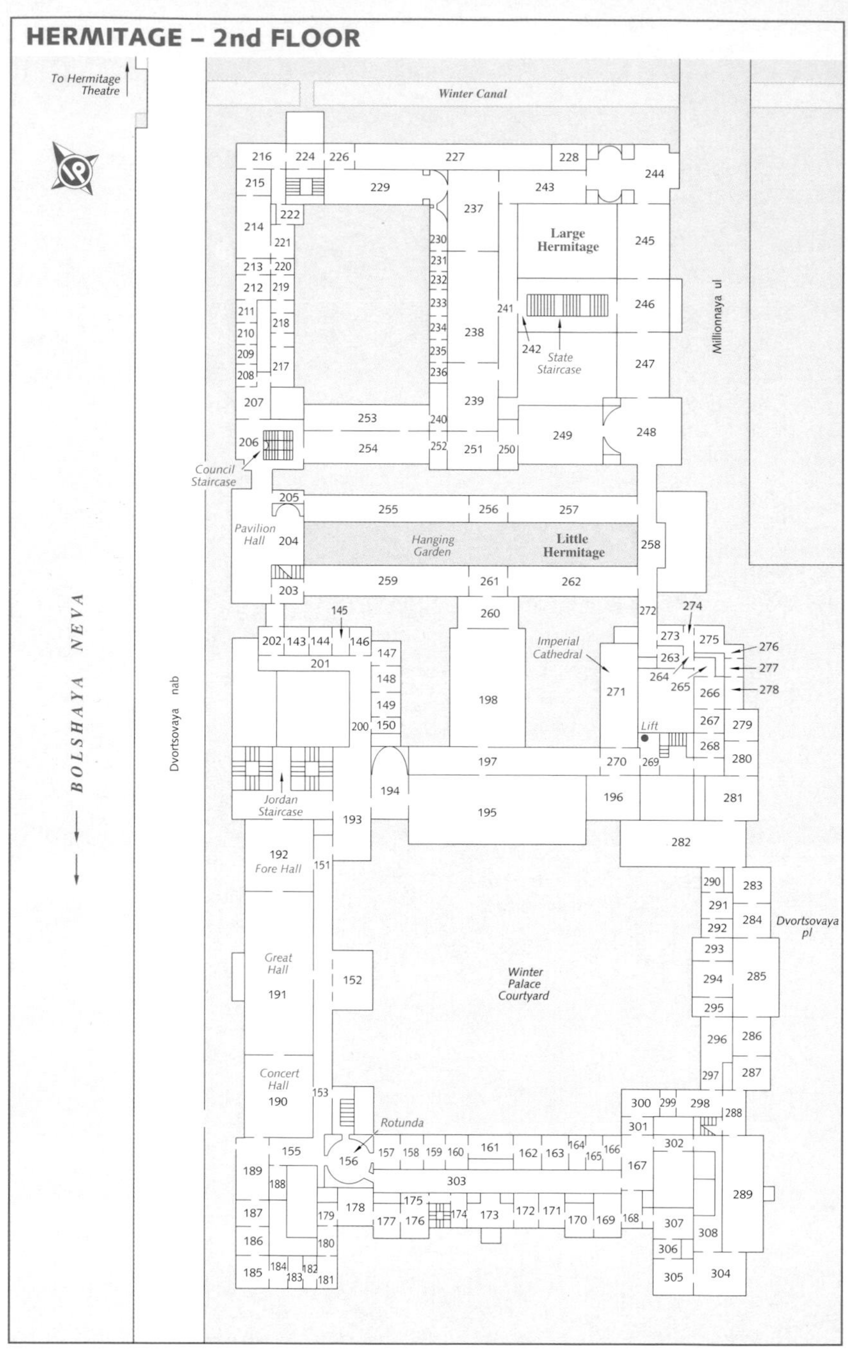

Room 214 Of a dozen or so original paintings by Leonardo that exist in the world, two of them are here. Note the contrast between the *Benois Madonna* (1478) and the *Madonna Litta* (1490), both named after their last owners. For years, the Benois Madonna (also called *Madonna with Flowers*) was considered lost. Only in 1909, the architect Leon Benois surprised the art world when he revealed that it was part of his father-in-law's collection. The Madonna's toothless smile is sometimes taken as evidence that the painting was unfinished.

Room 217 Giorgione is one of the most mysterious painters of the Renaissance, as only a few paintings exist that are known for certain to be his work. A portrait of idealised beauty, *Judith* is said to portray the inseparability of life and death.

The Union of Earth and Water *by Rubens (below)*

Rooms 219–221 Follow the development of Titian, the best representative of the Venetian school during the 16th century. *Portrait of a Young Woman* and *Flight into Egypt* reflect his early style, while his later works such as *Dana* and *St Sebastian* are more widely accepted as masterpieces. *St Sebastian* (1575) tells in part the story of the saint who attempted to convert Emperor Diocletian to Christianity, who was tied to a tree, shot with arrows and left for dead. According to the Catholic tradition, Sebastian survived his ordeal and returned to Rome to preach to Diocletian, who had him beaten to death then and there.

Rooms 226–227: Loggia of Raphael When Catherine the Great visited the Vatican she was so impressed that she decided to bring a little piece home with her. In the 1780s she commissioned Quarenghi to create this copy of a Vatican gallery; a team of Raphael's students re-created the master's murals on canvas. Note the occasional Russification on these versions: the two-headed eagle of the Romanov dynasty replaces the papal coat-of-arms.

Room 229 Features two original pieces by Raphael, *Dana* and *St Sebastian,* as well as many pieces by his disciples. This room also normally contains the Hermitage's only piece by Michelangelo, a marble statue of a crouching boy.

Rooms 237–238 Italian Skylight Halls, bathed in natural light, which highlights the ornately painted ceilings.

Rooms 239–240: Spanish Art

Ranging from the 16th to the 18th centuries, this collection is small by comparison with some of the other countries, occupying the Small Skylight Hall and the Spanish Room. But the most noteworthy artists of this 'Golden Age' of Spanish painting are represented, including Murillo, Ribera and of course Velazquez. The collection also includes two remarkable paintings from the 16th century: the marvellous *St Peter and St Paul,* by El Greco; and *Nailing Christ to the Cross,* by realist painter Ribalta.

Room 243: Knights' Hall

Walk through several rooms filled with marble and sculpture and bypass the grand State Staircase, until you arrive at Knights' Hall. Nicholas I started collecting artistic weapons and armaments from around the world. Here is the Western European collection, featuring four impressive 16th-century German knights sitting atop their armoured horses.

Rooms 245–247: Flemish Art

These three rooms dedicated to 17th-century Flanders are almost entirely consumed by three artists: Peter Paul Rubens, Anthony Van Dyck and Frans Snyders (all of whom were favourites of Catherine the Great). While the numbers here are a little overwhelming, look for *Bacchus* and *Portrait of a Lady-in-Waiting to the Infanta Isabella,* which are considered among Rubens' masterpieces.

Rooms 249–254: Dutch Art

Dating from the 17th and 18th centuries, the Dutch collection contains over 1000 pieces. The 26 paintings by Rembrandt nearly outshine anything else in this collection, but don't miss two wonderful paintings by Frans Hals and other excellent genre paintings in the Tent Hall (Room 249). Art from the Netherlands from the 15th and 16th centuries can be found in rooms 258–262 in the Little Hermitage.

Room 254 It's possible to spend hours in this room dedicated to Rembrandt and his pupils. The collection traces his career, starting with *Flora* and *The Descent from the Cross,* which are noticeably lighter but more detailed. His later work tends to be darker and more penetrating, such as the celebrated *The Return of the Prodigal Son.* Painted in 1669, it arguably represents the height of Rembrandt's mastery of psychology in his paintings. The solemn baroque masterpiece is a moving portrait of unquestioning parental love and mercy.

Pure white-and-gold: the Pavilion Hall (below)

LITTLE HERMITAGE: 2ND FLOOR

Apart from the amazing ornamental Pavilion Hall, the rooms on the 2nd floor of the Hermitage are a hodgepodge, including paintings from the Netherlands and applied art from Western Europe.

Room 204: Pavilion Hall

A highlight of the Hermitage, this ceremonial hall is an airy white-and-gold room sparkling with 28 chandeliers. The south windows look on to Catherine the Great's hanging garden (closed at the time of research), while the north overlooks the Neva. The amazing floor mosaic in front of the windows is copied from a Roman bath. The centrepiece, though, is the amazing Peacock Clock, created by James Fox in 1772. A revolving dial in one of the toadstools tells the time, and on the hour (when it's working) the peacock spreads its wings and the toadstools, owl and cock come to life. The Peacock Clock is exercised on a monthly basis, but otherwise it's retired.

WINTER PALACE: 2ND FLOOR

Back in the Winter Palace, the amazing baroque and classical interiors are on full display in the ceremonial rooms, known as the Neva Enfilade and the Great Enfilade, as well as in the private apartments of the last imperial family.

Rooms 143–146: French Painting

Formerly called 'Hidden Treasures Revealed', this exhibition of 19th- and 20th-century French oil paintings consists of pieces that were confiscated by the Red Army from private collections in Germany. First exhibited in 1995, many of these pieces had never before been publicly displayed. The collection is stunning, including works by Monet, Degas, Renoir, Cézanne, Picasso, Matisse and Van Gogh. If you like this, there is more on the 3rd floor (see p142).

Rooms 147–189: Russian Culture & Art

While the Hermitage is famous for its European art, it goes without saying that what started as an imperial art collection would have a fair amount of Russian pieces. Most of the western wing of the Winter Palace contains the huge collection from ancient Rus (10th to 15th centuries) up through the 18th century, including artefacts, icons, portraits and furniture.

Rembrandt takes centre stage in the display of Dutch art (opposite)

Rooms 155–156 Moorish Dining Room and Rotunda.

Rooms 157–162 The Petrovsky Gallery displays personal effects and equipment used by Peter the Great, as well as some beautiful early 18th-century furniture. Look for the ivory chandelier that was partly built by Peter himself.

Room 161 In 1880 there was an attempt on the life of Alexander II in this room. A young revolutionary, Khalturin, planted a bomb in the room below. It killed 11 soldiers when it went off, although the tsar had wandered into another room at the time. Khalturin was executed, but he received belated tribute for his great deed by the Soviets, who renamed Millionnaya ul after him.

Rooms 175–187: Imperial Apartments

This series of rooms represent the private apartments of the last imperial family, Nicholas II and Alexandra et al. Many of these rooms were completed in 1894, and they now show off wonderful 19th-century interiors, as well as acting as a sort of tribute to the last tsar.

Room 178 Nicholas II spent much of his time in this wonderful Gothic library, topped with a sublime walnut ceiling.

Room 181 Pompeii dining room.

Room 187 The griffin-motif furniture in this palace drawing room dates from 1805.

Aim for the tsars: the Jordan Staircase (right)

THE JORDAN STAIRCASE

The main staircase of the Winter Palace – a magnificent creation of Bartolomeo Rastrelli – is a great introduction to the opulence of the tsars. Ten solid-granite columns support the marble staircase, which is lined with Italian sculptures purchased by Peter the Great. During the 18th century the staircase was known as the Ambassadorial Staircase, as visiting foreign dignitaries would enter the palace here for audiences with the tsar. However, in the 19th century it became known as the Jordan Staircase. Every year, on 6 January, the imperial family would use this staircase to descend to the Neva River for the celebration of Christ's baptism in the River Jordan. The tradition was to cut a hole in the ice and ladle out a cup of water, which was then blessed by the Metropolitan of St Petersburg and ceremoniously drunk by the emperor.

Room 188 This small dining room is where the Provisional Government was arrested by the Bolsheviks in 1917.

Room 189 Two tonnes of gorgeous green columns, boxes, bowls and urns earn this room the name 'Malachite Hall', one of the most striking rooms in the entire palace. It is the handiwork of Bryullov, who completed this room in 1839. Three figurines on the wall represent Day, Night and Poetry. This was where the last meeting of the 1917 Provisional Government occurred, on the fateful nights of 25 and 26 October 1917; they were arrested soon after, in the Small Dining Room next door.

Rooms 190–192: Neva Enfilade

You can say one thing about the Winter Palace. There is no shortage of places to entertain. These days, the ceremonial halls are used for temporary exhibitions.

Room 190 This Concert Hall was used for small soirées. The enormous ornate silver tomb was commissioned by Empress Elizabeth for the remains of Alexander Nevsky.

Room 191 As many as 5000 guests could be entertained in the Great Hall (also called Nicholas Hall). The palace's largest room was the scene of imperial winter balls.

Room 192 Fore Hall was used for pre-ball champagne buffets.

Rooms 193–198: Great Enfilade

More staterooms.

Room 193 Field Marshals' Hall is known for its military-themed chandelier and coach. This is where the disastrous fire of 1837 broke out.

Room 194 The Hall of Peter the Great contains his none-too-comfy oak-and-silver throne.

Room 195 This gilt Armorial Hall contains chandeliers engraved with the coat-of-arms of all the Russian provinces.

Room 197 The 1812 War Gallery is hung with 332 portraits of Russian and allied Napoleonic war leaders.

Room 198 St George's Hall was the staterooms where the imperial throne used to sit (indeed, it was also known as the Great Throne Room). With white Carrara marble imported from Italy and floors crafted from the wood of 16 different tree species, it is a splendid affair. Its 800 sq metres are now used for temporary exhibitions.

Rooms 263–268: German Art

This small collection of German art ranges from the 15th to the 18th centuries. Among the earliest works there are five paintings by Lucas Cranach the Elder. The Prussian court painter Hans von Aachen is responsible for the *Allegory of Peace, Art & Abundance,* which is considered a

Hold the steely gaze of a war leader in the 1812 War Gallery at Room 197 (above)

Arabesques on a wooden floor at the Hermitage

All that glitters…the Golden Drawing Room (p142)

prime example from the 17th century. Also note the pieces by Anton Mengs, a famous master of neoclassicism, and Angelica Kauffman, a rare example of a female artist who was accepted by her peers in the 18th century.

Room 271: Imperial Cathedral

The private imperial cathedral was the site of many royal weddings, funerals and other ceremonies, including the wedding of Nicholas II to Alexandra in 1894.

Rooms 272–288 & 290–297: French Art

These rooms trace the development of French art from the 15th to the 18th centuries, including tapestries, ceramics, metalwork and paintings. Look for rooms devoted to Nicholas Poussin, founder of French Classicism, and Claude Lorrain, master of the Classical landscape. Antoine Watteau is also a highlight, especially *Savoyard with a Marmot*. Room 282, Alexander Hall, is another testament to the victory over Napoleon in 1812.

Rooms 298–300: English Art

These rooms were closed at the time of research, but they normally showcase English art from the 15th to the 18th centuries. There are plenty of portraits, including a few examples by England's leading portrait painter, Sir Godfrey Kneller. Highlights of the collection include several historical pieces by Sir Joshua Reynolds, especially *The Infant Hercules Strangling the Serpents*. Commissioned by Catherine the Great, the piece was meant to symbolise the growing strength of the Russian nation. *Portrait of a Lady in Blue,* by Thomas Gainsborough, is perhaps the most famous piece in the collection. The woman is unknown, although she is rumoured to be the Duchess of Beaufort (Gainsborough was married to the illegitimate daughter of the Duke of Beaufort). Up close it is possible to observe the feathery brushstrokes that create the overall effect; step back and all the strokes have faded magically.

Rooms 289 & 304–308: Private Rooms of Alexander II & Maria Alexandrovna

This series of rooms comprised the private apartments of Tsar Alexander II. His wife Maria Alexandrovna had most of them redesigned to her liking when she moved here in the 1840s. Named according to their colour scheme, they are easy to recognise.

Room 289 Using a Roman bath as a model, Bryullov designed the White Hall for the wedding of Alexander II and Maria Alexandrovna. Besides the superb moulded ceiling, the room now displays 18th-century furniture and accessories.

Room 304 The Golden Drawing Room features a fabulous gilt ceiling and a marble fireplace with an intricate mosaic over the mantle. Note the monogram of Maria Alexandrovna, which has been incorporated into the design scheme.

Room 305–308 Rooms such as the Blue Bedroom and the Crimson Study compete to outdo each other with their rich colours and lavish designs.

WINTER PALACE: 3RD FLOOR

Although the rooms are not numbered chronologically, the artwork is actually arranged in approximate chronological order. Start at Room 314 near the stairs and lift in the northeast corner, continue from 332 to 328, then 325 to 315, ending with 343 to 350. The rest of the rooms on this floor house the Oriental and Middle Eastern collection.

Rooms 316–320: Impressionists & Postimpressionists

Inspired by Romanticism, a group of painters in the 1860s began experimenting with painting modern life and landscapes, endeavouring to capture the overall effect of a scene instead of being overly concerned with details. The new trend – radical in its time – was known as impressionism. After impressionism, artists continued to use thick brush strokes, vivid colours and real-life subject matter, but they were more likely to use sharp lines and distorted shapes.

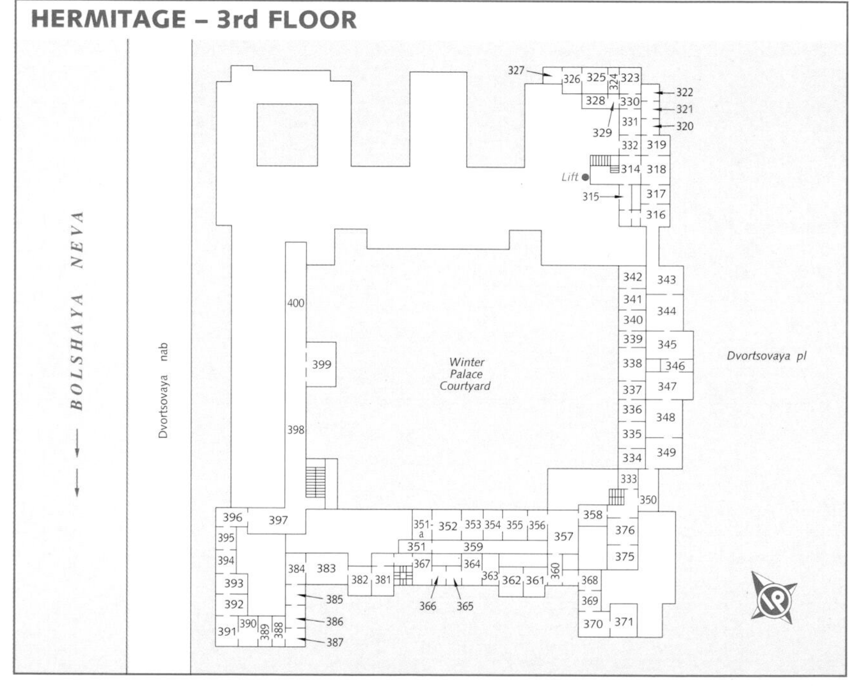

Locked in embrace: Cupid and Psyche statue at the Winter Palace entrance

Rooms 316–317 Gauqin is famed for the primitive paintings that he carried out in Tahiti. While it is impossible to assess the relative greatness of paintings by Vincent Van Gogh, *The Lilac Bush* is surely among his most magical. There is more Van Gogh next door in Room 343.

Rooms 318–319 Besides the magnificent impressionist paintings, including Cézanne and Pissarro, don't miss Rodin's sensuous sculptures.

Room 319 Feast your eyes on the paintings by Claude Monet, including his early work *Lady in a Garden.* One of the most extraordinary paintings in the entire Hermitage collection is his later work, *Waterloo Bridge, Effect of Mist* (1903). This wonderfully melancholic depiction of light diffused in the London fog over the Thames is a stunning example of his subtle mastery of colour. It depicts the view from Monet's room at the Savoy Hotel in 1903, looking towards Waterloo Bridge.

Room 320 Six paintings by Renoir include the celebrated *Portrait of the Actress Jeanne Samary* (1878).

Rooms 321–331: Barbizon School & Romanticism

Romanticism was the prevailing school of art in the 19th century and Delacroix is the most celebrated French Romantic painter. See what we mean by 'romantic' in his paintings of *Moroccan Saddling a Horse* or *Lion Hunt in Morocco* (Room 331).

The Barbizon School, named for the village where this group of artists settled, reacted against this romanticism, making a move toward realism. Gustav Courbet, Jean-Baptiste Camille Corot, Théôdore Rousseau and Jean-François Millet are all represented (Rooms 321–322).

Room 333: Russian Avant-Garde

This is the only room in the entire Hermitage to feature 20th-century Russian art, most of which is housed in the Russian Museum. Look for some examples of Kandinsky's early work, as well as paintings by Kazimir Malevich. This is the permanent home of the *Black Square* (1915), the most striking painting of the Petrograd avant-garde. Malevich created several variants of the simple black square against a white background throughout his career, of which this is the fourth and last. It was taken by many as a nihilistic declaration of the 'end of painting', causing both awe and outrage. The painting went missing during the Soviet period, mysteriously reappearing in southern Russia in 1993. Oligarch Vladimir Potanin bought the painting for $1 million and donated it to the Hermitage in 2002.

Rooms 334–342: 19th-Century European Art

Squeezed in among the French, you'll find a handful of rooms dedicated to other European artists, especially German. There are examples from the Berlin School and the Dusseldorf School, as well as some landscapes by Caspar David Friedrich. Note the paintings by von Klenze, architect of the New Hermitage.

Rooms 343–350: 20th Century

Arguably, the collection culminates in these rooms, where you can see as many as 37 paintings by Matisse and almost as many by Picasso. Henri Matisse was initially classified as a Fauvist: indeed you can see work by his contemporaries in Room 350. But he continued to paint in his own particular style, even as Fauvism declined in the early 20th century. Around this time, Matisse met Pablo Picasso and the two became lifelong friends. Picasso is best known as the founder and master of cubism; but again, his work spanned many styles.

Rooms 343–345 A turning point for Matisse – and perhaps his most famous work – is *The Dance* (1910). The intense colours and the dancing nudes convey intense feelings of freedom. This panel – along with the accompanying *The Music* – was painted specifically for Russian businessman Sergei Shchukin. While these panels are certainly commanding, don't miss *The Red Room* and *Portrait of the Artist's Wife.*

Rooms 348–349 Picasso's blue period is characterised by sombre paintings in shades of blue. When he was only 22, he painted *The Absinthe Drinker,* a haunting portrait of loneliness and isolation. The sensuous *Dance with Veils* (1907) and *Woman with a Fan* (1908) are excellent representations of his cubist work, as are the ceramics on display here.

Rooms 351–400: Oriental & Middle Eastern Culture & Art

These 50 rooms display ancient art from the Far East, including China and Tibet, Indonesia, Mongolia and India. Also on display are art and artefacts from Syria, Iran, Iraq, Egypt and Turkey.

Rooms 381–382 This is one of the world's best collections of Byzantine art – look for the amazing ivory diptych of men fighting beasts from AD 500.

Rooms 383–387 & 391–394 Apparently, ancient merchants from the Ural Mountains traded with travellers from Iran and the Middle East. Excavations in the Urals uncovered the world's largest collection of Sasanide silver (vases, plates, ornamental wine glasses) from the 3rd to the 7th centuries.

Rooms 398 & 400 The numismatic collection boasts over 90,000 coins and medals.

Revelling in the freedom of The Dance *(above) by Henri Matisse*

SOUTHERN ST PETERSBURG

Sleeping p212

Stalin chose Southern St Petersburg to be the centre of his new Leningrad: he hated the tsarist associations of the Historic Heart, and starting in the 1930s, new planning and construction began in earnest.

The process was interrupted by WWII and the reconstruction that was necessary afterwards, and the plans were finally shelved after Stalin's death in 1953. As such, the proposed 'southern' city centre was never completed. But evidence of this grand scheme remains, most notably in buildings like the bombastic House of Soviets, which occupies a prominent position on the main drag.

While the area of southern St Petersburg is vast, it is not too hard to access the most important sights, all of which lie along the north–south avenue, Moskovsky pr, which is the start of the main road to Moscow. This is also the road to Pulkovo Airport.

As one of the primary entryways into the city, Moskovsky pr was designed to be visually striking. The Monument to the Heroic Defenders of Leningrad at pl Pobedy (Victory Sq) is one of the first sights that welcomes visitors to the city. Just north of here, the aforementioned House of Soviets is fronted by hundreds of fountains and a stoic statue of Lenin. Further north, the Moscow Triumphal Arches span the road at Moskovskie Vorota.

The south of St Petersburg is far from the centre of the city, but it is well served by three metro lines and some 18 stations, making it extremely easy to get there. Most useful for the sights listed here are Ⓜ Moskovskaya and Ⓜ Park Pobedy.

MONUMENT TO THE HEROIC DEFENDERS OF LENINGRAD

Map p65

☎ 293 6036; www.spbmuseum.ru; pl Pobedy; admission free; 🕑 10am-5pm Thu-Tue; Ⓜ Moskovskaya

Pl Pobedy (Victory Sq) is one of the first sights of the city that visitors see on the road from the airport to the city centre, making a deeply Soviet impression for a town as imperial as St Petersburg! The square now houses the vast Monument to the Heroic Defenders of Leningrad, which is the city's most moving monument. The front line was only 9km from this spot.

Centred around a 48m-high obelisk, the monument (unveiled in 1975) is a sculptural ensemble of bronze statues symbolising the plight and eventual victory in WWII. On a lower level, a bronze ring 40m in diameter symbolises the city's encirclement; a very moving sculpture stands in the centre. Haunting symphonic music creates a sombre atmosphere to guide you downstairs to the underground exhibition in a huge, mausoleum-like interior. Here, the glow of 900 bronze lamps creates an eeriness matched by the sound of a metronome (the only sound heard by Leningraders on their radios throughout the war save for emergency announcements), showing that the city's heart was still beating. Large bronze sheets form the Chronicle; changed daily, these are engraved with the events in Leningrad on each day of the blockade. Twelve thematically assembled showcases feature items from the war and siege. An electrified relief map in the centre of the room shows the shifting front lines of the war. Ask to see the two seven-minute documentary films.

HOUSE OF SOVIETS Map p65

Moskovsky pr 212; 🕑 closed to the public; Ⓜ Moskovskaya

No building in the city can compare in terms of sheer staggering bombast to this Stalinist beauty (or beast, depending on your take). Planned to be the central administrative building of Stalin's Leningrad, it was built with the leader's neoclassical tastes in mind. Begun by Noi Trotsky in 1936, it was not finished until after the war, by which time Trotsky had been purged. Nonetheless, this magnificently sinister building is a great example of Stalinist design, with its columns and bas-reliefs and an enormous frieze running across the top.

The House of Soviets dominates the vast square (Moskovskaya pl) before it, which features a 1970 bronze statue of Lenin and a seemingly endless array of fountains. The House of Soviets was never used as the Leningrad government building, as the plan was shelved after Stalin's death in 1953. Today it houses the Moskovsky Region's local administration.

SOUTHERN ST PETERSBURG

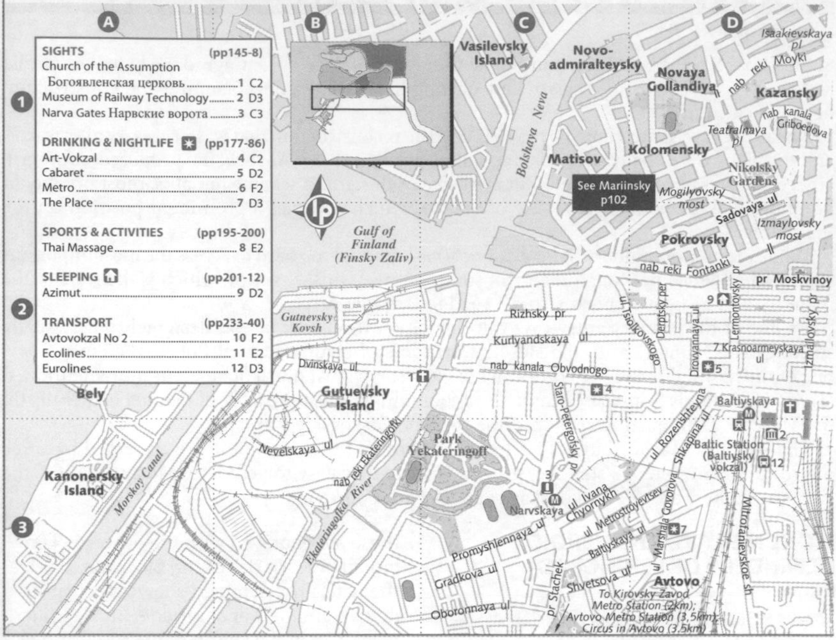

SIGHTS (pp145-8)
Church of the Assumption Богоявленская церковь 1 C2
Museum of Railway Technology 2 D3
Narva Gates Нарвские ворота 3 C3

DRINKING & NIGHTLIFE (pp177-86)
Art-Vokzal 4 C2
Cabaret 5 D2
Metro 6 F2
The Place 7 D3

SPORTS & ACTIVITIES (pp195-200)
Thai Massage 8 E2

SLEEPING (pp201-12)
Azimut 9 D2

TRANSPORT (pp233-40)
Avtovokzal No 2 .... 10 F2
Ecolines 11 E2
Eurolines 12 D3

CHESME CHURCH Map p65

☎ 373 6114; ul Lensoveta 12; admission free; ⏲ 10am-7pm; Ⓜ Moskovskaya

One of the city's most wonderful buildings, this red-and-white Gothic beauty looks not unlike a candy cane, with long, vertical white stripes giving the impression that it's rising straight up from the earth like a mirage and shooting upwards.

Designed by Yury Felten, it was built between 1777 and 1780 in honour of the Battle of Chesme (1770).

The church's remote location is due to the fact that Catherine was on this spot when news arrived of her great victory over the Turks. Ever capricious, Catherine ordered that a shrine be built on the spot to preserve this great moment in Russian history. It now seems particularly incongruous with its surroundings, as Stalin's ill-fated city centre has since grown up around it.

While the Chesme Church is definitely more visually impressive from the outside, do go inside to see some of the icons, including a beautiful painting of Christ's arrival in Nazareth.

MOSCOW GATES Map p65

pl Moskovskie Vorota; Ⓜ Moskovskie Vorota

About 4km south of Sennaya pl, the iron Triumphal Arch looks much like Berlin's Brandenburg Gate, though it is somewhat less than grand in its surroundings. The arch was built by Vasily Stasov in 1838 to mark victories over Turks, Persians and Poles. Demolished in 1936, it was rebuilt between 1959 and 1961. Local legend has it that the gate is built on the spot where the earliest travellers entering the city had to show that they had brought bricks or stones to be used in the construction of buildings.

MUSEUM OF RAILWAY TECHNOLOGY Map pp146–7

☎ 768 2063; nab kanala Obvodnogo 118; adult/child R150/80; ⏲ 11am-5.30pm Tue-Sun; Ⓜ Baltiyskaya

A huge treat for trainspotters lurks in a forgotten lot behind the former Warsaw Station (now a fancy shopping mall). This museum has a wonderful collection of Russian locomotives from the 19th and 20th centuries, including a dining carriage

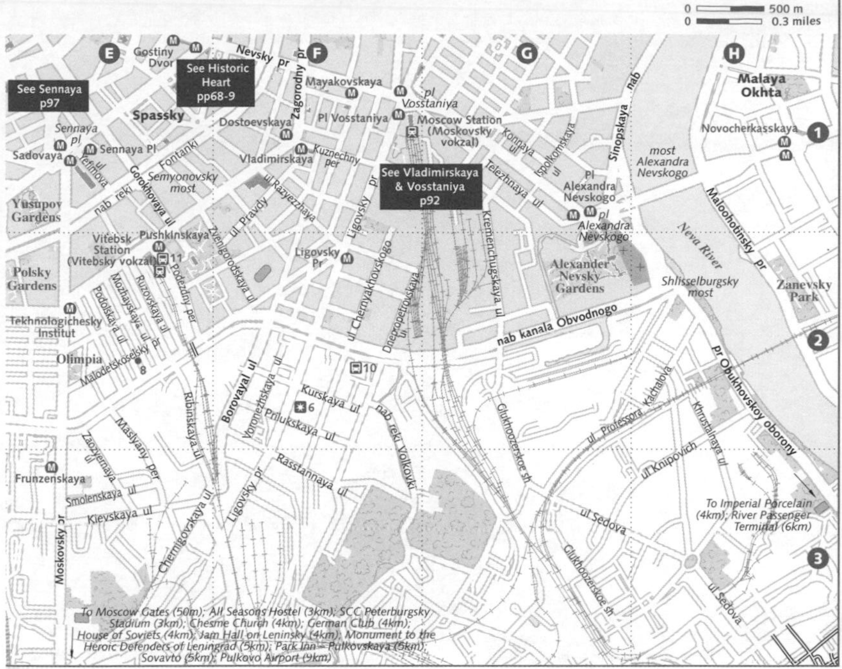

you can go into and some ancient steam engines. This is a fantastic option for kids.

NARVA GATES Map pp146–7

Narvskaya pl; Ⓜ Narvskaya

Just outside the Narvskaya metro station, the Narva Gates were built between 1827 and 1834 by Vasily Stasov as a tribute to the defeat of Napoleon in 1812. Standing proudly at one of the city's old gates, this 12-columned monolith is crowned with an angel of victory and decorated with an assembly of valiant warriors.

CHURCH OF THE ASSUMPTION Map pp146–7

Dvinskaya ul 7; admission free; 9am-6pm; Ⓜ Narvskaya

When Tsarevich Nikolai (later Nicholas II, the last Romanov tsar) was attacked by a Japanese fanatic while on a tour of Asia in 1891, he sustained a serious blow to the head but miraculously survived. The customs officers of St Petersburg's docklands gathered money and constructed a bell tower in thanks for the survival of the heir to the throne.

The church was sanctified in 1899, and the imperial family would annually come here to attend a service of thanksgiving for Nicholas' deliverance. The church was shut from 1935 to 1991. Restoration is ongoing since then, with fantastic results. The impressive portico and shimmering golden domes are particularly (and incongruously) beautiful in this, one of St Petersburg's most industrial suburbs.

KANONERSKY ISLAND Map pp146–7

An original option for a day's outing is to head to the remote, grassy tip of this island in the city's southwest to watch the big boats head out into the Gulf of Finland. The island once served as part of the city's defence and a shooting training ground; since 1883 a ship-repairing factory has been located here. Taking taxi bus 115 outside Sadovaya ul 39 (at Sennaya pl), you get to go under the only tunnel linking two islands in the city. After the last stop, walk for 40 minutes to the very tip of the island. You'll need good shoes, as there's a bit of climbing over rocks involved, but the views are worth it.

SHOPPING

top picks

- **Souvenir Market** (p153)
- **Vanity** (p151)
- **Eliseevsky** (p152)
- **Dom Knigi** (p151)
- **Sol-Art** (p154)
- **La Russe** (p155)
- **Pushkinskaya 10** (p155)
- **Kailas** (p156)
- **Udelnaya Fair** (p158)

SHOPPING

Back in the old days, the only place to buy a tin of caviar or a painted box was at an elite Beriozka store. Entry was restricted to foreigners and people with foreign currency, every store carried the same dull stuff and prices were high. The only other options were the sad selection at the State Department Store or the notorious black market. Russia has come a long way – basic toiletries are no longer luxuries, and one no longer need defy the law to bring home a decent souvenir.

That said, shopping is not among Russia's main attractions. Foreign goods cost the same as (if not more than) they do at home – and that includes items in the top-tier designer stores that line Nevsky pr. If the item seems like a steal, then it's very likely to be a bargain-basement counterfeit. Local items are often of low quality, although this situation is improving.

A small but enterprising fashion industry is up-and-coming in St Petersburg. A few local designers are blazing this trail, selling classy and creative clothing designs. There is also no shortage of shops selling fur and leather at all levels of quality.

The selection of souvenir-type items is always changing and growing, as artisans unleash long-dormant creativity and collectors uncover long-hidden treasures. Russia flagrantly ignores international copyright laws much to the delight of Western shoppers who snap up CDs and DVDs at prices unthinkable at home. As is appropriate for a city of literati, St Petersburg has no shortage of booksellers, including delightful second-hand shops that can be found in unlikely locations.

Unless stated otherwise, all shops work a roughly 9am to 8pm regime throughout the week, sometimes curtailing hours slightly on Saturday and/or Sunday. Lunch breaks are not uncommon, usually from 1pm to 2pm, although times vary hugely. Unless otherwise stated, all supermarkets are open 24 hours.

top picks

SHOPPING STRIPS

- **Nevsky pr** (below) Main street, St Pete. You'll not find any bargains, but you will find everything else.
- **Pushkinskaya ul** (p155) In addition to the funky collection of art galleries at Pushkinskaya 10 (which you enter from Ligovsky pr), Pushkinskaya ul is home to intriguing shops selling music, clothing, jewellery and more.
- **Vladimirsky pr** (p155)
- **Bolshoy pr** (p157) The Petrograd Side is its own little world, all the way across the Bolshaya Nevka. That's why it has its own little shopping strip, lined with all the Western and Russian retail outlets you'll find on Nevsky pr.

HISTORIC HEART

Not only the historic heart, but also the commercial heart, this district is bursting with credit-maxing designer digs, swanky shopping malls, eye-catching boutiques, filled-to-the-brim bookstores and run-of-the-mill souvenir shops. A stroll down Nevsky pr will send serious shoppers to seventh heaven, although the real gems and best bargains are hidden away in the smaller surrounding streets.

PLYOS EMBASSY Map pp68–9 Art

Polsolstvo Plyos; ☎ 315 4363; embplios@mail.ru; nab reki Moyki 35; Ⓜ Nevsky Pr

Plyos is a town on the Volga River, celebrated as the inspiration for Isaak Levitan, Russia's greatest landscape artist. This little gallery acts as the town's unofficial representative in St Petersburg, exhibiting landscape paintings by local and national artists. While the work is not particularly innovative, it is indeed beautiful, capturing the most magnificent moments in the Russian countryside.

BUKVOED Map pp68–9 Books

☎ 312 6734; Nevsky pr 13; 🕑 9am-10pm Mon-Sat, 10am-10pm Sun; Ⓜ Nevsky Pr

These bookshops are popping up all over St Petersburg. This is one of the smaller outlets, but it is centrally located and it carries a good selection of maps, art books, posters, calendars and postcards, as well as a smaller selection of English-language literature.

DOM KNIGI Map pp68–9 Books

☎ 448 2355; www.spbdk.ru in Russian; Nevsky pr 28; 9am-midnight; M Nevsky Pr;

The stalwart of the city's bookshops is Dom Knigi, housed in the wonderful, whimsical Singer Building (p74). For years, this was the only place in the city that carried a decent selection of literature, and it is still an inviting place to browse. On the 1st floor, you'll find lots of souvenir-type coffee-table books with colourful pictures, and – bonus – free internet access. Another bigger outlet is down the street at Nevsky pr 62 (Map pp68–9; ☎ 314 1422; 9am-midnight; M Gostiny Dvor).

WRITERS' BOOKSHOP

Map pp68–9 Books

Knizhnaya Lavka Pisateley; ☎ 716 2429; nevskiy66@mail.ru; Nevsky pr 66; M Gostiny Dvor

Specialising in foreign literature, this place is one of the few that carries titles by your favourite Lonely Planet authors. Besides top-notch travel guides, you'll also find an excellent selection of English-language literature, including English translations of Russian classics and contemporary bestsellers.

DEFILE Map pp68–9 Clothing & Accessories

☎ 571 9010; www.kisselenko.ru; nab kanala Griboedova 27; 11am-8pm Mon-Sat, noon-7pm Sun; M Nevsky Pr

If you are into fashion and you are in search of a uniquely Russian souvenir, this sweet boutique is the place to come. Owned by designer Lilia Kisselenko, of Kisselenko Fashion Salon (p154), Defile carries elegant and eclectic clothing and accessories – almost exclusively by Russian designers. This shop also hosts the biannual fashion event, Defile on the Neva (p19).

MEKHLANDIA

Map pp68–9 Clothing & Accessories

☎ 571 3700; Nevsky pr 54; 10am-9pm; M Gostiny Dvor

The Russian word *mekh* means 'fur', so the name of this place translates as Fur-land, evoking a sort of animal-run amusement park. Alas, this place is no fun for animals, as it contains a huge selection of fur and leather clothing, especially coats, hats and handbags. (We know it's not nice to kill animals, but it gets you through the brutal Russian winter.)

CLOTHING SIZES

Women's clothing

Aus/UK	8	10	12	14	16	18
Europe	36	38	40	42	44	46
Japan	5	7	9	11	13	15
USA	6	8	10	12	14	16

Women's shoes

Aus/USA	5	6	7	8	9	10
Europe	35	36	37	38	39	40
France only	35	36	38	39	40	42
Japan	22	23	24	25	26	27
UK	3½	4½	5½	6½	7½	8½

Men's clothing

Aus	92	96	100	104	108	112
Europe	46	48	50	52	54	56
Japan	S		M	M		L
UK/USA	35	36	37	38	39	40

Men's shirts (collar sizes)

Aus/Japan	38	39	40	41	42	43
Europe	38	39	40	41	42	43
UK/USA	15	15½	16	16½	17	17½

Men's shoes

Aus/UK	7	8	9	10	11	12
Europe	41	42	43	44½	46	47
Japan	26	27	27½	28	29	30
USA	7½	8½	9½	10½	11½	12½

Measurements approximate only, try before you buy

VANITY Map pp68–9 Clothing & Accessories

☎ 438 5548; www.vanity-fashion.com; Kazanskaya ul 3; 11am-9pm; M Nevsky Pr

Vanity has been around for more than a decade, with boutiques inside the city's finer hotels and shopping centres. In 2007 this name in fashion became a name in architecture, dining and culture. Vanity's latest endeavour is its largest store yet, housed in a modern structure of glass and steel, tucked behind Kazan Cathedral. Everything here is jaw-dropping gorgeous, from the all-designer-all-the-time fashions for sale, to the perfectly-coiffed beauties selling them. Stop by the 5th-floor Terrassa (p165) for a cocktail or coffee before you hit your credit limit.

VERSACE Map pp68–9 Clothing & Accessories

☎ 713 4933; Nevsky pr 39; M Gostiny Dvor

Versace have definitely bagged one of the best retail premises in town: the sumptuous Rossi pavilion of the Anichkov Palace, overlooking Nevsky pr and the palace grounds.

WILD ORCHID

Map pp68–9 Clothing & Accessories

Dikaya Orkhideya; ☎ 571 2979; www.wildorchid.ru; nab reki Moyki 55; 🕑 10am-10pm; Ⓜ Nevsky Pr

Underwear is yet another measure of Russia's amazing transition to capitalism. Gone are the days of one-size-fits-all, baggy cotton briefs; sensational, sexy lingerie is on sale all over St Petersburg (and often modelled by women on the street). This top-of-the-line store carries lingerie by European designers that is devastatingly sensual (and devastatingly expensive). There are several other outlets around town, including one in **Grand Palace** (opposite) and one on the **Petrograd Side** (Map pp114–15; ☎ 233 8775; Bolshoy pr 29; 🕑 10am-10pm; Ⓜ Petrogradskaya).

STOCKMANN Map pp68–9 Department Store

☎ 326 2636; www.stockmann.ru; Nevsky pr 25; 🕑 10am-9pm Sun-Thu, 10am-7pm Fri & Sat; Ⓜ Nevsky Pr

Once a lifeline for foreign residents, this Finnish department store is now hardly distinguishable from its Russian counterparts. Nonetheless, it's not a bad place to shop for clothing, homewares and other miscellany, even though it's not exactly the same stuff you would find in Helsinki. At the time of research, a huge new Stockmann department store was being built at pl Vosstaniya.

BON VIN Map pp68–9 Food & Drink

☎ 571 3405; www.bonvin.ru; nab kanala Griboedova 29; 🕑 10am-9pm Mon-Sat; Ⓜ Nevsky Pr

With low ceilings and exposed brick, this little wine cellar is an atmospheric place to pick out a *bon vin*. There is no shortage of *grands crus* and pricey reserves if you are shopping for a special occasion, but head to the sale rack in the centre of the store for excellent French, Spanish and Italian wines that you can afford to drink every day. There is another outlet in **Smolny** (Map p84; ☎ 272 1067; Furshtatskaya ul 62; Ⓜ Chernyshevskaya) and one on the **Petrograd Side** (Map pp114–15; ☎ 498 7413; Bolshoy pr 1; Ⓜ Sportivnaya).

CHOCOLATE MUSEUM

Map pp68–9 Food & Drink

☎ 315 1348; www.concord-catering.ru; Nevsky pr 17; 🕑 11am-9pm; Ⓜ Nevsky Pr

Despite the misnomer, this place is not a museum. While you are welcome to come inside to peruse the artistic pieces, it is unlikely you will leave without procuring your very own chocolate chess set or chocolate 'Fabergé' egg. This outlet is in the basement of the Stroganov Palace, but there are others inside **Gostiny Dvor** (opposite) and **Passage** (opposite). So rest assured, you'll have no trouble finding that chocolate bust of Vladimir Ilych.

ELISEEVSKY Map pp68–9 Food & Drink

☎ 312 1865; Nevsky pr 56; 🕑 10am-9pm; Ⓜ Gostiny Dvor

How many supermarkets can boast being mentioned in *Anna Karenina*? This luxury food store is a stunner, with 20m ceilings, huge windows and *fin de siècle* fittings. It feels a little strange to pop in for a quart of milk, but it's a fine place to shop for speciality items such as alcohol, chocolate and caviar.

INTENDANT Map pp68–9 Food & Drink

☎ 571 1510; www.intendant-salon.ru in Russian; Karavannaya ul 18; 🕑 11am-11pm; Ⓜ Gostiny Dvor

Showcasing an enormous selection of wines from around the world, Intendant is an expensive place to shop (and not a little snooty about it). But they know their stuff. So if you're in the market for a full-bodied Bordeaux or a peppery Pinot, this upscale vintner will not disappoint.

RIVE GAUCHE

Map pp68–9 Jewellery & Cosmetics

☎ 314 3149; www.rivegauche.ru in Russian; Nevsky pr 27; 🕑 10am-9pm Sun-Thu, 10am-10pm Fri & Sat; Ⓜ Nevsky Pr

Yves Saint-Laurent does not seem to mind that this Russian company has stolen the name of its well-known perfume and used it to set up an extensive network of shops selling brand-name cosmetics. With more than 30 shops around the city, you're never far from a new bottle of Chanel No 5. There are additional outlets near **pl Vosstaniya** (p156) and on the **Petrograd Side** (p157).

YAKHONT Map pp68–9 Jewellery & Cosmetics

☎ 314 6415; Bolshaya Morskaya ul 24; Ⓜ Nevsky Pr

From this building, Carl Fabergé dazzled the imperial family and the rest of the world with his extraordinary bespoke designs. Yakhont has no link to the Fabergé family, but it is carrying on the tradition anyway. This long, dark salon provides an impressive showcase of their work.

MILITARY SHOP Map pp68–9 Military

Tovar dlya Voennikh; ☎ 310 1814; Sadovaya ul 26; 10am-7pm; Ⓜ Gostiny Dvor

In a city with men in uniform on every street corner, this is where you can get yours (the uniform that is!). Buy stripy sailor tops, embroidered badges, big boots, camouflage jackets and snappy caps at decent prices. Look for the circular green and gold sign with 'Military Shop' written in English; the entrance is in the courtyard.

OPEN WORLD Map pp68–9 Music

Otkrity Mir; ☎ 715 8939; Malaya Morskaya ul 13; 10am-10pm; Ⓜ Nevsky Pr

Melodies waft from the speakers out onto the sidewalks, enticing music-lovers into this little shop. It sells a huge range of classical, jazz and world music, all licensed but still very reasonably priced. The staff is delightfully friendly and helpful, and you are free to browse the enormous selection at your leisure.

GOSTINY DVOR Map pp68–9 Shopping Centre

☎ 110 5200; www.gostinydvor.ru in Russian; Nevsky pr 35; 10am-10pm; Ⓜ Gostiny Dvor

One of the oldest shopping arcades in the world, Gostiny Dvor (Merchant Yard) was built in the mid-18th century. After a decade-long renovation, the exterior looks smart, while the interior retains a largely Soviet feel. On the ground floor, endless corridors of counters showcase everything from stereos to souvenirs. Upstairs you will find some fancier fashion outlets, which are definitely an improvement.

GRAND PALACE

Map pp68–9 Shopping Centre

☎ 449 9411; Nevsky pr 44; 11am-9pm; Ⓜ Gostiny Dvor

For once the rather uppity title is well deserved – this palatial shopping centre was created for the New Russian shopping classes, who expect nothing less than grand and glittering. The biggest names in fashion are here, including Max Mara, Dior and Lacroix, not to mention the fanciest free toilets in the city.

PASSAGE Map pp68–9 Shopping Centre

Passazh; ☎ 311 7084; www.passage.spb.ru in Russian; Nevsky pr 48; 11am-9pm; Ⓜ Gostiny Dvor

This old-fashioned arcade, lined with boutiques and souvenir shops, runs between Nevsky pr and Italiyanskaya ul. The shopping here is not particularly unique, but it is a pleasant, atmospheric place to stroll, similar to Moscow's world-famous GUM.

SOUVENIR MARKET

Map pp68–9 Souvenirs

☎ 962 2613; nab kanala Griboedova 2; sunrise-sunset; Ⓜ Nevsky Pr

You're unlikely to find any incredible bargains at the sanitised market behind the Church of the Saviour on Spilled Blood, but you will find a great selection of handicrafts, Soviet paraphernalia and other souvenirs. And you are encouraged to haggle with the vendors, some of whom are also the artists. The vendors speak enough English to barter back.

ROE TO RUIN

Caviar: the very word evokes glamorous lifestyles, exotic travel and glittering festivities. But the sturgeon, the source of this luxury item, is in grave danger. Although they have survived since dinosaurs roamed the earth, the question now is whether these 'living fossils' can withstand the relentless fishing pressure, pollution and habitat destruction that have brought many sturgeon species to the brink of extinction. Surveys show that the population of osetra sturgeon is less than half the size it was in 1978, while the beluga sturgeon population has declined by 45% since 2004.

Sturgeon today face several major obstacles to survival. Primarily, the global caviar market has placed a premium on sturgeon, prompting overfishing and poaching. Political turmoil in sturgeon-producing countries, including Russia, has resulted in a flourishing black-market trade. Many sturgeon migrate through the waters of different states and countries, resulting in a lack of effective management of their populations. Coupled with an ongoing loss of habitat and a slow pace of reproduction, the sturgeon are facing an upstream swim.

Contrary to many conservationist recommendations, a 2007 international conference on endangered species (Cites) declined to pass emergency measures to protect the Russian sturgeon population. But it did take important steps to improve monitoring of the caviar trade. Most importantly for travellers, governments are encouraged to reduce the amount that individuals are allowed to carry across borders, from 250g to 125g of caviar per person.

For more information on the plight of the sturgeon, see www.caviaremptor.org.

PARNAS Map pp68–9 Supermarket

Malaya Sadovaya ul 3; M Gostiny Dvor

A chain of supermarkets that operates throughout the city. Conveniently located just off Nevsky pr, this outlet is not a bad place to stock up on basic foodstuffs. Or, you can do like the locals and buy a few beers to drink while you sit on pedestrian-friendly Malaya Sadovaya and soak up the atmosphere.

LITEYNY & SMOLNY

This mostly residential neighbourhood does not offer too much in the way of shopping, but it is an arty, intellectual place, as evidenced by the proliferation of galleries and bookstores.

BOREY ART CENTRE Map p84 Art

☎ 275 3837; Liteyny pr 58; 10am-6pm; M Mayakovskaya

There is never a dull moment at this underground (in both senses of the word) art gallery. In the front room, you'll see some fairly mainstream stuff for sale, but the back rooms always house creative and cutting-edge exhibitions by local artists. The bookshop is one of the best in town for books on art and architecture.

LIBERTY ART GALLERY Map p84 Art

☎ 579 4410; www.sovietart.ru; ul Pestelya 17/25; 11am-8pm Tue-Sun; M Chernyshevskaya

'Liberty' may be an odd name for a gallery specialising in art of the Soviet period, but nonetheless, here it is. Exhibitions highlight art from the 1930s to the 1980s.

SEKUNDA Map p84 Art

☎ 275 7524; Liteyny pr 61; 11am-7pm Mon-Sat; M Mayakovskaya

Sekunda – as in 'second-hand' – is a small bric-a-brac place where you might find an unusual souvenir, whether an old postcard or a stuffed moose head. Enter through the courtyard.

SOL-ART Map p84 Art

☎ 327 3082; www.solartgallery.com; Solyanoy per 15; 10am-6pm; M Chernyshevskaya

In the sumptuous surroundings of the Museum of Decorative & Applied Arts (p86), this is a great place to buy contemporary local art. Styles include classical realism, avant-garde and everything in between.

ANGLIA BOOKS Map p84 Books

☎ 579 8284; www.anglophile.ru; nab reki Fontanki 38; M Gostiny Dvor

The city's only English-language bookshop has a large selection of contemporary literature, history and travel writing. It also hosts small art and photography displays, organises book readings and generally is a cornerstone of expat life in St Petersburg.

KISSELENKO FASHION SALON

Map p84 Clothing & Accessories

☎ 271 2552; www.kisselenko.ru; Kirochnaya ul 47; M Chernyshevskaya

Designer Lilia Kisselenko uses sublimely simple fabrics to create women's clothing that is at once linear and flatteringly feminine. This is a name to watch out for – she's not quite flashy enough to appeal to the New Russian nouveau riche (who don't care for Russian products anyway), but rather caters to connoisseurs with a discerning eye and upper-class fashion sensibility. If you like this place, check out Kisselenko's other boutique, Defile (p151).

MALTEVSKY MARKET Map p84 Market

ul Nekrasova 52; 8am-8pm; M Pl Vosstaniya

Bargaining is encouraged at this bright spacious market, packed with vendors selling exotic fruits and vegetables, mounds of multicoloured spices, and fresh meats, fish and fowl. In some cases, the meat is so fresh it is still being hacked off its carcass. Don't miss free samples of honey straight from the hive.

SOLDIER OF FORTUNE Map p84 Military

Soldat Udachi; ☎ 579 1850; www.soldat.spb.ru in Russian; ul Nekrasova 37; M Pl Vosstaniya

The extensive selection of guns and knives at this little shop is impressive, if a little frightening. Check out the knives with intricately carved handles; penknives straight out of James Bond; and machetes with names such as 'Predator Axe'. The place also carries more mundane equipment like binoculars and water bottles, as well as all manner of camouflage clothing and military souvenirs.

SPORTIVNY ON LITEYNY

Map p84 Sportswear

☎ 272 2170; Liteyny pr 57; M Mayakovskaya

This is a huge store selling sports clothes, running shoes, camping and hunting equipment, skis and even the occasional mosquito-net hat (which could come in handy in the city, even if it looks a tad odd!). With an excellent selection (including Russian and imported products) and competitive pricing, this sports shop is a great place for active types to stock up for their urban or outdoor adventures.

VLADIMIRSKAYA & VOSSTANIYA

This bustling commercial district is really just an extension of the Historic Heart. Vladimirsky pr, which turns into Zagorodny pr, is one of the city's slickest shopping streets, lined with boutiques and overlooked by the Vladimirsky Passage shopping centre. As Nevsky pr continues east past the Fontanka River, it is also lined with stores big and small, catering to tourists, residents and everyone in between. A smaller side street, Pushkinskaya ul, houses a cluster of eclectic, arty shops, not to mention the avant-garde art centre at Pushkinskaya 10. Only east of pl Vosstaniya does the activity start to peter out.

LA RUSSE Map p92 Antiques

☎ 572 2043; www.larusse.ru; Stremyannaya ul 3; 11am-8pm; M Mayakovskaya

Lots of rustic old whatnots and genuine antiques are piled into this quirky arty antique store. You might unearth anything from a battered old samovar to an intricately painted sleigh. Enquire about occasional excursions into the countryside, where most of these items are procured.

ART RE.FLEX Map p92 Art

☎ 332 3343; www.artreflex.ru; pr Bakunina 5; 11am-8pm; M Mayakovskaya

This contemporary gallery is unique in that it showcases artists of all ages, genres and experience levels. So its exhibitions mix the work of up-and-coming artists with more established masters, including their painting, graphics and sculpture, in an attempt to highlight the most interesting trends in contemporary art.

PUSHKINSKAYA 10 Map p92 Art

☎ 764 5258; www.p10.nonmuseum.ru; Ligovsky pr 53; admission free; 3-7pm Wed-Sun; M Pl Vosstaniya

Officially known as the Free Culture Society, this contemporary art mecca (see p91) is guaranteed to turn up something weird and wonderful. There are lots of separate studios and galleries spread throughout the complex. On the ground level there is also a small bookshop, KultProsvet (☎ 764 5240; 11am-8pm). Note that despite the name, the entrance is actually through the arch from Ligovsky pr.

NATALIE KVASOVA

Map p92 Clothing & Accessories

☎ 703 5406; Vladimirsky pr 1; M Vladimirskaya

When it comes to winter hats, Russian fashion really comes into its own. Nowhere in the world are women so expressive with their headgear as on the snowy streets of St Petersburg and Moscow. The designs of Natalie Kvasova are up there with the best of them, sporting feathers and fur, bows and brims. This boutique also carries a small selection of fur coats and wraps warm enough to get you through any winter.

PARFIONOVA Map p92 Clothing & Accessories

☎ 713 1415; www.parfionova.ru; Nevsky pr 51; M Mayakovskaya

Tatyana Parfionova was the first St Petersburg couturier to have her own fashion house back In the 1990s, when the New Russians turned up their noses at anything that was not straight from Paris or Milan. Now this local celebrity showcases her stuff at her Nevsky pr boutique, where you'll find her striking monochromatic *prêt-à-porter* designs as well as her famous crimson scarves.

SPINNING WHEEL

Map p92 Clothing & Accessories

Pryalka; ☎ 571 6889; Pushkinskaya ul 10; M Pl Vosstaniya

A lovely little store selling handmade sweaters, gloves and hats, all made from downy wool, as well as linen dresses and blouses. Blankets, tablecloths and other household linens are also for sale. The stuff is simple but lovely, and prices are reasonable.

IMPERIAL PORCELAIN

Map p92 Homewares

☎ 713 1513; www.ipm.ru; Vladimirsky pr 7; 10am-8pm; M Vladimirskaya

This is the more convenient location of the famous porcelain factory. There is another IPM shop (Map p92; ☎ 717 4838; Nevsky pr 160; 10am-8pm; M Pl Vosstaniya) midway between pl Vosstaniya and pl Alexandra

Nevskogo. Prices are marked up slightly from the factory outlet (p158).

RIVE GAUCHE Map p92 Jewellery & Cosmetics
☎ 717 0187; www.rivegauche.ru; Nevsky pr 81; 10am-9pm; M Mayakovskaya
This fast-growing chain carries perfumes, make-up and other cosmetics from top international names. Outlets are all over the city – see p152 for a full review.

KUZNECHNY MARKET Map p92 Market
☎ 312 4161; Kuznechny per 3; 8am-8pm; M Vladimirskaya
The colours and atmosphere of the city's largest fruit and vegetable market are quite the sensory experience. And the vendors – mostly from the Caucasus and Central Asia – will ply you with free samples of fresh fruits, homemade *smetana* (sour cream) and sweet honey.

505 Map p92 Music
☎ 315 1815; Zagorodny pr 9; 10am-11pm; M Vladimirskaya
Excellent range of CDs, DVDs and computer games, and the added novelty of being able to handle the goods yourself (albeit while being watched by about 14 security guards at one time).

KAILAS Map p92 Music
☎ 764 2668; www.kailas.sp.ru in Russian; Pushkinskaya ul 10; 11am-9pm Mon-Sat, 11am-6pm Sun; M Pl Vosstaniya
Principally a music shop, Kailas has an impressive selection of contemporary and classical music from around the world, which covers all genres; the specialities seem to be classical, jazz, indie-Russian and 'ethnic' music. Oddly enough, the store also has an 'Eastern department', which sells incense, jewellery and clothing from the exotic East.

TITANIK Map p92 Music
☎ 310 4929; Nevsky pr 63; 24hr; M Mayakovskaya
The chain store Titanik has a great selection of CDs and DVDs – the only drawback is that they are all behind glass and if your Russian isn't good it's very hard to tell what things are just by reading the spines. There are outlets all over the city, including one on the Petrograd Side (Map pp114–15; Bolshoy pr 35; M Petrogradskaya).

VLADIMIRSKY PASSAGE
Map p92 Shopping Centre
Vladimirsky Passazh; ☎ 331 3232; www.vladimirskiy.ru in Russian; Vladimirsky pr 19; M Vladimirskaya
Walking into this centre from the chaotic street outside you'll be forgiven for thinking you've passed through a portal to another world. Over 100 stores sell designer clothing, imported food products and other fancy stuff. Shoppers linger at sushi bars and coffee shops, including an outlet of Baltic Bread (p169).

LEND Map p92 Supermarket
☎ 331 3233; Vladimirsky pr 19; M Vladimirskaya
This is the best supermarket in the city centre, located under the giant Vladimirsky Passage (above) shopping centre. You can get everything from fresh pasta and Italian pesto to a reasonably priced bottle of Sancerre. There's also sushi available, not to mention an aquarium full of perch and pike waiting to be someone's supper.

SENNAYA

It's said that you can buy almost anything on Sennaya pl and its seedy side streets, although in the 1990s the suggestion was more about the availability of drugs rather than any particularly amazing consumer opportunities. Since the tercentennial cleanup though, lots of smart shops have opened up, particularly in and around the brand spanking new Sennaya shopping centre.

BEE-KEEPING Map p97 Food & Drink
Pchelovodstvo; ☎ 315 4252; Sadovaya ul 51; M Sadovaya/Sennaya Pl
Step into this sweet shop and you won't be able to resist taking home some honey to your honey (or for yourself). You can sample many different flavours of honey from all over Russia, and there are also natural remedies, creams and teas made from beeswax and pollen. If you are so inspired, you can also buy the necessary equipment to set up your own *pchelovodstvo*.

SENNOY MARKET Map p97 Market
☎ 310 1209; Moskovsky pr 4; 8am-7pm; M Sadovaya/Sennaya Pl
Cheaper and less atmospheric than Kuznechny Market (left), Sennoy Market is also centrally located. You'll find fruit and veggies, as well as fresh-caught fish and fresh-cut meat.

SENNAYA Map p97 Shopping Centre

☎ 740 4640; www.sennaya.ru in Russian; ul Yefimova 3; Ⓜ Sadovaya/Sennaya Pl

An unnervingly American-style mall a short walk from Sennaya pl, this huge centre is mainly for fashion, but includes a food hall, a bowling alley (p199) and the Patterson department store.

MARIINSKY

Mariinsky is more of a cultural district than a commercial centre, but there are a handful of art galleries and speciality souvenir shops you might want to check out. If you're in the market for speciality food and drink items, it's definitely worth making a special trip.

ST PETERSBURG ARTIST Map p102 Art

Peterburgsky Khudozhnik; ☎ 337 1339; www.piter-art.com; nab reki Moyki 100; Ⓜ Sadovaya

Dedicated to preserving and promoting the tradition of realist art, this museum and exhibition centre showcases local artists who painted from the 1950s to the 1990s. Most featured artists have been exhibited in venues as famous as the Russian Museum and Moscow's Tretyakov. The gallery also publishes the magazine *St Petersburg Artist* and hosts occasional concerts.

KOSHER SHOP Map p102 Food & Drink

☎ 713 8186; www.jewishpetersburg.ru; Lermontovsky pr 2; Ⓜ Sennaya Pl

Serving St Petersburg's Jewish community, the Kosher Shop is conveniently located next to the Grand Choral Synagogue (p104). Although its emphasis is on kosher food, the shop also sells books about Judaism in many languages, Jewish music and art.

MIR ESPRESSO Map p102 Food & Drink

☎ 315 1370; ul Dekabristov 12/10; Ⓜ Sadovaya

Come for the aroma and stay for the amazing coffee from all over the world. There's espresso machines and every type of coffee maker and caffeine-related accessory.

GALLERY OF DOLLS Map p102 Souvenirs

Galereya Kukol; ☎ 314 4934; Bolshaya Morskaya ul 53/8; Ⓜ Sadovaya/Sennaya Pl

Featuring ballerinas and babushkas, clowns and knights, this gallery depicts just about every fairy-tale character and political persona in doll form. The highly creative figures are more like art than toys. Our personal favourite is the miniature babushka mopping the floor in the corner.

MARIINSKY ART SHOP

Map p102 Souvenirs

☎ 326 4197; Mariinsky Theatre, Teatralnaya pl 1; ⏲ 11am-6pm on performance days, also open during interval; Ⓜ Sadovaya/Sennaya Pl

Opera- and ballet-lovers will delight at the theatre-themed souvenirs for sale in the Mariinsky gift shop. None of it is cheap, but where else can you get a 'Property of Kirov Ballet' T-shirt? Also on sale: a comprehensive collection of CDs, DVDs, books and posters that you won't find elsewhere.

PETROGRAD SIDE

Bolshoy pr is not quite Nevsky pr. It is nonetheless an inviting place to shop, its sidewalks lined with food stores, clothing boutiques and speciality shops. The Petrograd Side does not see nearly as many people as the Historic Heart, so it's an excellent destination if you prefer to avoid crowds. Besides the places listed here, many chain stores have outlets on Bolshoy pr, including Rive Gauche (p152), Wild Orchid (p152), Titanik (opposite) and Bon Vin (p152).

RIVE GAUCHE

Map pp114–15 Jewellery & Cosmetics

☎ 346 2515; Bolshoy pr 69; Ⓜ Petrogradskaya

One of many in a chain of cosmetics stores scattered around the city. See p152 for a full review.

SOLDIER OF FORTUNE

Map pp114–15 Military

Soldat Udachi; ☎ 232 2003; www.soldatudachi.com; Bolshoy pr 17; ⏲ 10am-9pm; Ⓜ Sportivnaya

Strangely, this weaponry store seems unrelated to the store of the same name in Vosstaniya (p154), and frankly, you have to wonder about a town that has enough demand to support two such stores. Nonetheless, here is another place that has everything a modern-day Rambo could wish for, including GPS devices, Swiss army knives and camping gizmos.

SYTNY MARKET

Map pp114–15 Market

☎ 233 2293; Sytninskaya pl 3/5; ⏲ 8am-6pm; Ⓜ Gorkovskaya

This colourful market on the Petrograd Side sells almost everything from vegetables, fruit, meat and fish inside to electronics, clothing and knick-knacks outside. Its name means 'sated' market, quite understandably.

MODEL SHOP

Map pp114–15 Souvenirs

☎ 716 9077; Artillery Museum, Alexandrovsky Park 7; Ⓜ Gorkovskaya

Inside the Artillery Museum (p116; you don't need to pay for entry to get access to the shop), this is a must for model plane, train and automobile fans. There's a huge range of mainly Russian models in stock and the staff is extremely helpful.

OUT OF TOWN

There are a few places on the outskirts which are worth a trip out of town.

IMPERIAL PORCELAIN

Map p65 Homewares

☎ 560 8544; www.ipm.ru; pr Obukhovskoy Oborony 151; Ⓜ Lomonosovskaya

Dating back to the mid-18th century, this is the company that used to make tea sets for the royal family. Formerly known as Lomonosov China, the company continues to produce innovative designs – the speciality being contemporary takes on traditional themes. The stuff is expensive, but the quality is high and the designs are spectacular. This factory outlet offers discounted prices that are significantly cheaper than you will see at stores in the city centre (p155). To get there, turn left from the metro station and walk under the bridge. Turn left on the embankment and you will see the factory ahead.

UDELNAYA FAIR

Map p65 Market

Udelnaya Yarmarka; Vyborg Side; 🕒 9am-6pm; Ⓜ Udelnaya

Bargain-hunters, antique-lovers and second-hand scavengers will love Udelnaya Fair, a vast, informal flea market. Stalls are filled with cheap clothing and other goods from Europe, but outside, loads of people bring their old stuff to see if they can find any takers for the trash and treasures. To get there, exit the metro station to the right and cross the train tracks.

EATING

top picks

- **The Other Side** (p165)
- **Terrassa** (p165)
- **Imbir** (p170)
- **Restoran** (p173)
- **Zoom Café** (p166)
- **Onegin** (p164)

EATING

In the past few years, St Petersburg has blossomed into a culinary capital. Foodies will be thrilled by the plethora of dining options, from old-fashioned *haute russe* to contemporary fusion. Young chefs are breaking down Soviet stereotypes and showing the world how creative they can be. They are importing exotic ingredients, rediscovering ancient cooking techniques and inventing new-fangled ones.

And St Petersburg diners are eating it up. Literally. Restaurants are packed with patrons eager to sample world cuisines, sip expensive wines, share small plates, eat raw fish, taste exotic fruits and smoke hookah pipes. Gone are the days when only the New Russian nouveau riche could afford to eat out: these days the new middle class also enjoys the pleasures of the palette.

When you tire of borscht (beetroot soup) and beef stroganoff, you will be able to find excellent European, American and Asian cuisine. Italian fare is popular and sushi is everywhere. Cuisine from former Soviet republics – especially Georgia and Armenia – is also ubiquitous and delicious.

If sampling the local delicacies is on your list of things to do in St Petersburg, you will not be disappointed (and if it is not on your list, it should be). For Russian food has undergone its own revolution since the end of Soviet rule: the bliny (crepes) are tastier, the *smetana* (sour cream) creamier, and the caviar more plentiful…

The *St Petersburg Times* has an online dining guide (www.sptimes.ru), as does the city's official tourist information site (www.visit-petersburg.ru). Additional online reviews can be found at any of the tourism portals listed on p20.

HISTORY

Seventy years of mistreatment by the Soviets has given Russian cuisine a bad rap. Today, many restaurants in St Petersburg allow the diner to experience Russian food as it is meant to be – exquisite *haute russe* masterpieces once served at fancy feasts and extravagant balls, as well as the tasty and filling meals that have for centuries been prepared in peasant kitchens with garden ingredients.

Options for dining out during the Soviet period were so limited that Russians hardly ever did it. They might have taken lunch at the local *stolovaya* (cafeteria) but otherwise they cooked at home, they ate at home and they drank at home. And home-cooked meals tasted far better than the slab of meat and lump of potatoes that came on the plate in most restaurants.

The past decade has done wonders for dining in St Petersburg. Now the options seem limitless, not only for traditional Russian fare, but also for sushi, pasta, coffee and more. Clever restaurateurs are inventing more interesting ways to present food. Likewise, Petersburgers are changing the way they eat. They may still take lunch at the *stolovaya,* but it is a modern *stolovaya* with a funky theme or an all-you-can-eat buffet. They go out for business lunches, for after-work drinks, for celebratory occasions and even just for dinner.

ETIQUETTE

Just because the restaurant scene in St Petersburg has exploded in recent years, it does not mean that Petersburgers no longer entertain at home: Russian hospitality has deep roots. If you visit a St Petersburg home, you can expect to be regaled with stories, to be drowned in vodka, to receive many toasts and to offer a few yourself. You can also expect to eat an enormous amount of food off a tiny plate. Once the festivities begin, it is difficult to refuse any food or drink: you will go home stuffed, drunk and happy.

Should you be lucky enough to be invited to a Russian's home, bring a gift. Wine, confectionery and cake are all appropriate. Keep in mind that food items are a matter of national pride, so unless you bring something really exotic (eg all the way from home), a Russian brand will be better appreciated. Flowers are also popular – make certain there's an odd number because even numbers are for funerals.

SPECIALITIES

Zavtrak (breakfast) in hotels can range from a large help-yourself buffet to a few pieces of bread with jam and tea. Traditional Russian breakfast favourites include bliny and *kasha* (porridge).

Russians have a preference for a fairly heavy *obied* (early-afternoon meal) and a lighter *uzhyn* (evening meal). Meals, and menus, are divided into various courses such as *zakuski* (appetisers), often grouped into either hot or cold; first courses (usually soups); second courses (or mains), also called hot courses; and desserts.

Appetisers

A typical Russian meal starts with a few *zakuski,* which are often the most interesting items on the menu. The fancier *zakuski* rival main courses for price.

Russia is famous for its *ikra* (caviar), the snack of tsars and New Russians. Caviar in Russia is no longer the bargain it once was, due to declining sturgeon populations and the good old market economy (see p153). The best is *chyornaya ikra* or *zirnistaya* – black (sturgeon) caviar. Much cheaper and saltier is *krasnaya ikra* or *ketovaya* – red (salmon) caviar. Russians spread it on buttered bread or bliny and wash it down with a slug of vodka or a toast of champagne. Vegetarians can try ersatz caviar made entirely from eggplant or other vegetables.

Most restaurant menus offer a truly mind-boggling array of *salati* (salads), including standards such as *ovoshnoy salat* (vegetable salad) containing tomatoes and cucumbers, or *stolichny salat* (capital salad) with beef, potatoes and eggs in mayonnaise. Even if you read Russian, the salads are usually not identifiable by their often nonsensical names.

First Course

Rich soups may well be the pinnacle of Slavic cooking. There are dozens of varieties, often served with a dollop of sour cream. Most are made from meat stock. The most common soups include borscht (delicious beetroot soup), *shchi* (cabbage or sauerkraut soup), *okroskha* (cucumber soup with a *kvas* – a beer-like drink – base) and *solyanka* (a tasty fish or meat soup with salty vegetables and a hint of lemon).

Second Course

The second course can be *ptitsa* (poultry), *myaso* (meat) or *ryba* (fish), which might be prepared in a few different ways. Russian *pelmeni* (dumplings) are usually filled with meat, although they may also come with potatoes, cabbage or mushrooms. Other staples include *zharkoye* (hot pot) – a meat stew served up piping hot in a little jug, *kotleta po kievsky* (better known as chicken Kiev) and *shashlyk* (meat kebab), all of which will usually be found on any restaurant menu. Fish is extremely popular and freshly caught in St Petersburg, either from the Baltic or from Lake Ladoga. The range is enormous, but common staples include *osyetrina* (sturgeon), *shchuka* (pike), *losos/syomga* (salmon) and *treska* (cod).

Often you must order a *garnir* (side dish) or you will just get a hunk of meat on the plate. Options here are usually *kartoshki* (potatoes), *ris* (rice) or undefined *ovoshchi* (vegetables). *Khleb* (bread) is served with every meal. The Russian black bread – a vitamin-rich sour rye – is delicious and uniquely Russian.

Desserts

Perhaps most Russians are exhausted or drunk by dessert time, since this is the least imaginative course. The most common options are *morozhenoe* (ice cream), super sweet *tort* (cake) or *shokolat* (chocolate).

VEGETARIANS & VEGANS

Russian is a heavy, meat-dependent cuisine. Soups are usually made with beef or chicken stock; all traditional meals revolve around a meaty main course; and even salads usually

CATCH OF THE DAY

Every year, shortly after the ice melts on the Neva River, the *koryushki* (freshwater smelt) swim up the river to spawn. To local Petersburgers, this annual event – usually in early May – is a time of celebration, symbolising the end of a long, dark winter and the beginning of gorging on fish, whether fried, dried, smoked or pickled.

The *koryushka* is sometimes called the 'cucumber fish' for its distinctive smell (which disappears after cooking). For a few short weeks, this delicious fish appears on restaurant menus and in private homes. The city hosts an annual *koryushki* festival at the Peter & Paul Fortress. Across the city, cooks get busy: breading this mild-flavoured fish with flour, salt and sunflower oil, frying it up in a pan, and serving it with a slightly sweet tomato sauce or straight up. It's a popular snack *k pivu* (with beer) or, of course, with vodka.

have dead animals mixed in with a few veggies. Most frustrating is the lack of fresh fruits and vegetables. Until recently, vegetarians in St Petersburg had a pretty tough time of it.

Fortunately, the culinary revolution has opened up some new options for vegetarians and vegans. Most restaurants now recognise the need to offer at least one vegetarian choice on their menu. Additionally, there is no shortage of Indian and Italian restaurants, which offer plenty of meat-free options. St Petersburg even supports an excellent (and popular) all-vegetarian chain, Troitsky Most (see p171 or p175).

When dining at traditional Russian restaurants, veggies should keep in mind the following. Fish is plentiful and fresh in St Petersburg, so it offers an excellent alternative for seafood-eaters. Fresh vegetables are rare, but pickled vegetables are not: learn to love sauerkraut, beets and salty cucumbers. Most importantly, there is no shortage of starch in Russia. Bread, bliny and potatoes are always on the menu; and they are filling. During the 40 days before Orthodox Easter (Lent; *veliky post* in Russian), many restaurants offer a menu that is happily animal-free. If you are serious about your vegetarianism, timing your trip with this period will give you extra options when eating out. Ask for the *postniy menyu* (Lenten menu).

PRACTICALITIES

Opening Hours

Most places are open from 11am or noon to 11pm or midnight daily, often with later hours on Friday and Saturday. In this guide, hours are listed only when they vary from this standard.

Restaurants rarely close between lunch and dinner, as the late lunch or afternoon snack is a popular custom. Discounts of up to 25% are often available before 4pm or 5pm. Alternatively, many places offer a fixed price 'business lunch' during this time, which is a great way to sample some of the pricier restaurants' dishes around town.

How Much?

Prices have been rising steadily but inexorably in St Petersburg and it's now standard to pay at least R600 per main course in an upscale restaurant, and about R200 to R300 in midrange outfits. If you are on a budget, you'll be very well taken care of (not to mention in good company) at the fast-food joints and *stolovye* (cafeterias) that cater to locals; see p167 for some recommendations. Many restaurants offer a fixed midday menu (business lunch) for R150 to R350 – a great way to sample the fare of some expensive restaurants.

Some restaurants set their menu prices in *uslovie yedenitsiy* (standard units; often abbreviated as y.e.), which is equivalent to euros (although you will have to pay in roubles calculated at the exchange rate of the day). Prices in this chapter are quoted in roubles, regardless of the currency quoted on the menu. Credit cards are widely accepted, especially at upscale restaurants.

Booking Tables

Booking tables is rarely required in St Petersburg, although it can't hurt to reserve your spot at a popular restaurant, especially on a Friday or Saturday night or during the busy tourist season (mid-June and early July). At upscale restaurants, you will always be welcomed more warmly if you book in advance.

Tipping

The standard for tipping in St Petersburg is 10%, while a lesser amount is acceptable at more casual restaurants. Self-service cafés and *stolovye* do not require any tip. Occasionally, the service charge is included in the bill, in which case an additional tip is not necessary.

Self-Catering

If you want to eat like an old-time Petersburger, you'll buy your food and cook it at home. Even if cooking in St Petersburg is not feasible, exotic foods and drinks are among the most interesting and affordable souvenirs by which to remember Russia. See the Shopping chapter (p150) for suggestions about where to buy such delicacies. Most characteristic are vodka and caviar, *zakuski* of the tsar's court and the Soviet politburo. High-quality vodka is often packaged in a wide variety of decorative bottles, some with historical or regional themes. Vodka connoisseurs admire the design and shape of the bottles almost as much as the fiery brew itself.

PRICE GUIDE

$$$	over R600 a meal
$$	R300-600 a meal
$	under R300 a meal

top picks

COOKBOOKS

- *Please, To the Table* (Anya Von Bremzen) A tried and true authority on Russian cooking. Learn to make bliny (and just about every other Russian dish) like the babushkas.
- *Tastes and Tales from Russia* (Alla Danishevsky) Each recipe is accompanied by a folktale: a great way to introduce children to Russian cooking.
- *The Georgian Feast* (Darra Goldstein) One of the few English-language cookbooks focusing on this spicy Caucasian cuisine.
- *A Year of Russian Feasts* (Catherine Cheremeteff Jones) Part cookbook and part travelogue, Jones writes of her experiences with Russian traditions, culinary celebrations and day-to-day life.
- *Classic Russian Cooking: Elena Molokhovets' A Gift to Young Housewives* (Joyce Toomre) More of a history lesson than a recipe book, this tome is based on the most popular cookbook from the 19th century.

The Russian sweet tooth is notorious (a fact that's evidenced by the profusion of gold teeth). Russians adore confections and chocolate, and without fail, prefer locally produced treats over any old Belgian or Swiss chocolate. Never mind that the major Russian confectionaries are largely owned by Cadbury or Nestlé, Russian chocolate is a matter of national pride. (Keep this in mind when buying chocolate for Russian friends.) Many companies produce beautiful pieces with fancy wrapping and colourful boxes in honour of local events, holidays or historical places.

FARMERS MARKETS

The Russian *rynok* (market) is a busy, bustling place, full of activity and colour. Even if you are not shopping, it is entertaining to peruse the tables piled high with multicoloured produce; homemade cheese and jam; golden honey straight from the hive; vibrantly coloured spices pouring out of plastic bags; slippery, silver fish posing on beds of ice; and huge slabs of meat hanging from the ceiling. Many vendors bring their products up from the Caucasus to sell them in the capital. Prices are lower and the quality of product is often higher than in the supermarkets. Bring your own bag and don't be afraid to haggle.

For reviews of the following markets, see the Shopping chapter: Kuznechny Market (p156), Sennoy Market (p156), Sytny Market (p157) or Maltevsky Market (p154).

SUPERMARKETS

Gone are the days when food shopping required waiting in a different line for each food item. These days, St Petersburg boasts many Western-style supermarkets, complete with prepackaged foods, Western brands and shopping carts. The selection is impressive compared to what stocked the shelves a decade ago. Unless you stick to Russian brands, prices tend to be at least as high as prices in the West.

Once a Scandinavian haven, Stockmann (see p152) has a pricey foreign goods supermarket in the basement. Other more affordable supermarket chains include Parnas (p154) and Lend (p156).

Peak inside Eliseevsky (p152) for a glimpse of prerevolutionary grandeur, as the store is set in the former mansion of the successful merchant Eliseev. It now houses an upscale market selling caviar and other delicacies.

HISTORIC HEART

The historic heart of St Petersburg is also its culinary heart: the range of eating options is immense and ever-expanding. Choose from modern or traditional Russian, various ethnic cuisines, fast food and more. In general, the best places are not on Nevsky pr – you are better off exploring the back roads if you are in search of a satisfying, savoury meal.

WITHIN THE MOYKA

This inner circle of the Historic Heart is so packed with palaces, museums and churches that there is hardly any room left for regular places such as restaurants. But you'll find a few gems on the smaller streets, especially Gorokhovaya, Malaya Morskaya and Bolshaya Morskaya.

NEP Map pp68–9 Russian $$$

☎ 571 7591; www.neprestoran.ru; nab reki Moyki 37; meals R600-800; Ⓜ Nevsky Pr

Unlike most communist-theme restaurants in the city, NEP celebrates the early 1920s, a period of entrepreneurial activity and relative liberalism under Lenin's New Economic Policy. The restaurant's hip 1920s style evokes a kind of vaudevillian luxury, as does the delicious Russian menu. Live music and cabaret plays from 8.30pm from Wednesday to Sunday.

TANDOORI NIGHTS Map pp68–9 Indian $$

☎ 312 3886; Voznesensky pr 4; meals R400-600; Ⓜ Nevsky Pr

The city's most stylish Indian restaurant is also among its most authentic, offering a mix of traditional and modern recipes road-tested by a top London Indian chef. Great choice for vegetarians.

TAVERNA OLIVA Map pp68–9 Greek $$

☎ 314 6563; www.tavernaoliva.ru; Bolshaya Morskaya ul 31; meals R300-500; Ⓜ Nevsky Pr

Greek-themed photographs and folkloric art bring the requisite Mediterranean atmosphere to this cavernous hall. (The atmosphere is also 'enhanced' by live music, which can be a bit much.) Nonetheless, the place is extremely popular, and with good reason. The traditional Greek cooking is excellent, as attested to the Greek expats who seem to frequent this place. There is also a pleasant sidewalk café which offers a partial menu.

FIDELIO CAFÉ Map pp68–9 Italian $$

☎ 314 8444; Gorokhovaya ul 13; business lunch R200, meals R300-400; Ⓜ Nevsky Pr

Pressed white linens and serious scrubbed waitstaff lend an upscale atmosphere to this surprisingly affordable café. The menu is not extensive, but what the café does, it does well: crispy pizzas and pastas with various tomato- and cream-based sauces. The three-course business lunch is a steal.

FAT FRIER Map pp68–9 Russian $

Tolstiy Frayer; ☎ 314 5921; www.tolstiy-fraer.ru; Kirpichny per 1; meals R200-400; 🕑 10am-1am Sun-Thu, 10am-3am Fri & Sat; Ⓜ Nevsky Pr

Now with branches around the city, this beer hall on the back streets of the Historic Heart provides a fun hideaway for some comfort food and a Baltika beer. The nostalgic communist paraphernalia recalls the days of Leonid Brezhnev, but thankfully the staff do not – there are smiles all round and good service.

PELMENY BAR Map pp68–9 Russian $

☎ 570 0405; Gorokhovaya ul 3; meals R200-400; Ⓜ Nevsky Pr

Specialising in the old Siberian standard *pelmeni* (dumplings), this cute café serves them up with beef, pork, salmon or mushrooms. Choose a soup or a salad as a starter, and you've got an immensely satisfying meal. The setting feels like a Russian *dacha* (country cottage), with its wood interior and whimsical dolls floating near the ceiling. Also an excellent place for solo travellers, as you can take the wolf as your dinner companion.

top picks

RUSSIAN CUISINE

- **Molokhovets' Dream** (p168) Time-tested recipes from the Martha Stewart of Old Russia.
- **Old Countryside** (p175) The next best thing to home cooking.
- **Na Zdorovye** (p175) Enjoy the cuisine of Russian tsars and Soviet dictators in a hokey setting.
- **Kalinka Malinka** (opposite) Old-fashioned country cooking.
- **Yolki Palki** (p167) An easy and affordable way to sample some Russian favourites.

BUSHE Map pp68–9 Bakery $

☎ 764 2927; www.bushe-bakery.ru; Malaya Morskaya ul 7; breakfast or snacks R50-100; 🕑 9am-9pm; Ⓜ Nevsky Pr

Local Bushe devotees wait for the doors to open so they can enjoy a hot cup of coffee, a fresh-squeezed fruit juice or flaky pastry before heading to work. Sweet and savoury pastries run the gamut, filled with cream, fruit, meat, mushrooms and more. The bakery is Austrian, but it's Soviet in style (meaning not particularly efficient and certainly not overly friendly). But the baked goods are to die for, so who needs chitchat?

BETWEEN THE MOYKA & THE FONTANKA

The network of streets between the Moyka and Fontanka Rivers contain some of St Petersburg's finest dining. Nevsky pr is lined with restaurants, but your options are more plentiful (and more cost effective) if you get away from the main drag.

ONEGIN Map pp68–9 Russian $$$

☎ 571 8384; Sadovaya ul 11; meals R800-1500; 🕑 5pm-2am; Ⓜ Gostiny Dvor

You have to be in the know to know about Onegin, the hippest of places to see and be seen. Down a small staircase from Sadovaya ul – and barely marked at street level – the restaurant has an interior that is an incredibly over-the-top display of New Russia. Antique and plastic furniture sit side by side, swathed in purple velvet and overhung by crystal chandeliers. Even with all this excess, the menu really delivers. Look out for decadent Russian dishes such as duck fillet with glazed forest berries in grape sauce or marble steak with foie gras and fresh asparagus. Reservations are recommended.

KALINKA MALINKA

Map pp68–9 Russian $$$

☎ 314 2681; Italiyanskaya ul 5; meals R600-800; Ⓜ Nevsky Pr

Kitsch but charming, this long-standing folkloric restaurant is in a basement on pl Iskusstv (Arts Sq). It specialises in country cooking, just as the peasants used to prepare, and the interior resembles a cosy country house. So try hot, homemade *solyanka* or rabbit à la Russe for a great introduction to unembellished Russian cuisine. Live folk music will accompany your evening meal.

GARÇON RESTAURANT

Map pp68–9 French $$$

☎ 570 0348; nab kanala Griboedova 25; meals R600-800; Ⓜ Nevsky Pr

While most French restaurants in town are painfully upscale, this gorgeous little bistro is both smart and unpretentious, and prices are reasonable given the excellent standard of the cooking. The interior is quaint yet romantic, but on a summer evening you can't beat the lovely outdoor patio overlooking the Griboedov Canal. Incidentally, the patio opens early on Sunday, making this an excellent choice for brunch.

SILK Map pp68–9 Asian Fusion $$$

Shyolk; ☎ 571 5078; Malaya Konyushennaya ul 4/2; meals R600-800; Ⓜ Nevsky Pr

Dreamy and decadent, this place is done up with gauze drapes, soft lighting and lounge-all-night sofas. It looks fabulous, and the food tastes pretty good too. This is fusion in the truest sense, as the mostly Japanese menu also features a few representatives from Europe. If you must eat sushi while in St Petersburg, this is a good place to do it.

TERRASSA Map pp68–9 European $$

☎ 337 6837; www.terrassa.ru; Kazanskaya ul 3; lunch R300-500, dinner R500-700; Ⓜ Nevsky Pr

On the top floor of chic Vanity (p151) shopping centre, this too-cool café and bistro is the latest and greatest on offer by St Pete's culinary creatives. The centrepiece is the namesake terrace, a wide porch boasting unbelievable views of Kazan Cathedral, Nevsky pr and the Church of the Saviour on Spilled Blood. It is a spectacular setting. And indeed, at the time of research, reservations were necessary to sit on the terrace any time of day, any time of week. Inside, the atmosphere is Old World but understated. The focus is clearly on the food; if you have any doubt, take a peak inside the open kitchen, where chefs are busy preparing fresh fusion cuisine, exhibiting influences from Italy, Asia and beyond.

KOROVABAR Map pp68–9 Steakhouse $$

☎ 314 7348; Karavannaya ul 8; meals R500-700; ⏲ noon-1am Sun-Thu, 1pm-3am Fri & Sat; Ⓜ Gostiny Dvor

In case you could not tell from the Holstein décor, *korova* means 'cow'. And this so-called cow-bar milks this theme for all its worth. Cow hides hang from the ceilings and adorn the booths. Yet somehow, it works: the place is way more hip than it is hokey. The sophisticated menu features an excellent selection of steaks, among other things, and an incredible wine list. And if all that black and white has you longing for greener pastures, take a seat on the pleasant porch.

BAKU Map pp68–9 Uzbek $$

☎ 571 9123; Sadovaya ul 12/23; meals R400-600; Ⓜ Gostiny Dvor

The amazing mosque-like interior is reason enough to stop at this new addition. Tiled walls, arched doorways and throw pillows whisk you to Azerbaijan – exactly what's intended. And there you can indulge in *plov*, the traditional dish of rice and lamb, subtly spiced with cumin and sprinkled with raisins, as well as grilled meats and vegetables. This is an experience to delight all of your senses.

THE OTHER SIDE

Map pp68–9 International $$

Drugaya Storona; ☎ 312 9554; www.theotherside.ru; Bolshaya Konyushennaya ul 1; meals R300-600; Ⓜ Nevsky Pr

Calling itself a 'gastro bar and refuge', this newish place is attracting fans for its friendly atmosphere, its innovative, international menu and its schedule of live music (see p184 for details). Take a seat on the patio on the pleasant pedestrian-only street or head into the cosy interior. The diverse menu hits just about every continent, with dishes ranging from rack of lamb served on a bed of couscous to grilled salmon on soba noodles. There is a range of sandwiches and other lighter fare available for the cost conscious.

TINKOFF Map pp68–9 German $$

☎ 718 5566; www.tinkoff.ru; Kazanskaya ul 7; business lunch R250, meals R300-600; ⌚ noon-2am; Ⓜ Nevsky Pr

St Petersburg's most fashionable – and arguably most delicious – beer comes from this huge factory-like bar and microbrewery. At its centre is a German-style beer hall,, serving excellent schnitzel, sauerkraut and other specialities, including a hard-to-resist metre-long sausage. The boisterous and sociable dining area has great atmosphere and – of course – great beer. See p180 for more information about evening entertainment. Most importantly, pay no attention to the ́sushi bar in the middle of the restaurant.

KAVKAZ Map pp68–9 Georgian $$

☎ 312 1665; Karavannaya ul 18; meals R300-500; Ⓜ Gostiny Dvor

Another long-standing favourite, Kavkaz means 'Caucasus' and features excellent Georgian fare. It's a casual affair: the basement digs are not so impressive to look at, but the portions are generous and the food – served on large wooden platters – is consistently delectable. This is the place to experience the legendary Georgian hospitality (and shashlyk and wine etc).

LA STRADA Map pp68–9 Italian $$

☎ 312 4700; www.lastrada.com.ru; Bolshaya Konyushennaya ul 27; meals R400-600; Ⓜ Nevsky Pr

The atrium-style dining room, accented with tile floors, streetlights and mural-painted walls, evokes *la dolce vita*. And somehow, the otherwise Soviet-looking buildings that are visible through the glass ceiling are rendered more romantic in this context. It's an exceedingly pleasant atmosphere to feast on fresh pasta and delectable pizza – not too trendy and certainly not too cheap, but so satisfying.

YAKITORIYA Map pp68–9 Japanese $$

☎ 315 8343; www.yakitoriya.spb.ru; pl Ostrovskogo 5/7; meals R300-500; ⌚ 11am-6am; Ⓜ Gostiny Dvor

With its efficient service and excellent fresh fish, it's easy to see why this chain has been so successful in St Petersburg and – indeed – across the country. This location off Nevsky pr is the most central of many locations. It features an actual sushi bar, which is ideal for solo diners. The woody interior is slick and modern, with a slightly upscale atmosphere.

MAMA ROMA Map pp68–9 Italian $$

☎ 314 0347; www.mamaroma.ru; Karavannaya ul 3/35; meals R300-500; ⌚ 8am-11pm; Ⓜ Gostiny Dvor

Mama's menu is almost too long, as it's hard to choose between the grilled meats and fish, the hardy homemade pastas drowning in delicious sauces and the crispy thin pizzas topped with your favourite meats and cheeses. The latter is the hands-down favourite because it is so affordable, but all of Mama Roma's offerings are fresh and delicious and prepared to order.

FACE CAFÉ Map pp68–9 European $$

☎ 571 9695; www.facecafe.ru; nab kanala Griboedova 29; meals R200-500; ⌚ 9am-midnight; Ⓜ Nevsky Pr; ☒

Despite the name, this little café on the banks of the canal does not exercise face control; indeed, it is one of the city's more welcoming venues – especially notable considering its cool minimalist décor and excellent menu. The subterranean space is well lit, with arched doorways and an unusual engraved Art Deco bar. The menu offers a little bit of everything, but the food is well prepared and artistically presented. It's highly recommended for breakfast, with homemade *kasha* and hearty omelettes that will keep you sated throughout the day.

ZOOM CAFÉ Map pp68–9 European $$

☎ 448 5001; www.cafezoom.ru; Gorokhovaya ul 22; meals R200-400; ⌚ 10am-10.30pm; Ⓜ Sennaya Pl; 💻 wi-fi

Leather-bound menus include several pages dedicated to maps and geographic descriptions before they get to the goods. And they are good: Russian and European soups, salads and sandwiches, as well as fresh-squeezed juices, exotic coffee drinks and a seemingly endless tea list. Light pink

FAST FOOD: RUSSIAN-STYLE

Now that Russians are part of the capitalist world, they sometimes need to eat on the go just like the rest of us. There is no shortage of American fast-food chains around St Petersburg, but there are also a few uniquely Russian chains that are every bit as popular as their Western counterparts. Perfect for travellers who are short on time and/or short on cash, these options for *bystraya yeda* (fast food) offer an authentic Russian experience at a faster pace and lower price. Outlets are located around the city:

Blin Donalt's (Map p84; ul Zhukovskogo 18; meals R60-100; 10am-10pm; M Pl Vosstaniya) This funny fast-food joint has somehow avoided legal action from a certain well-known American chain. Here you get fast-food bliny (crepes), chicken Kiev and borscht (beetroot soup) – all as far from the real thing as McDonald's apple pie, but a fascinating comment on post–Soviet Russia.

Chaynaya Lozhka (Tea Spoon; meals R150-250; 9am-9pm); Smolny (Map p84; pr Chernyshevskogo 9; M Chernyshevskaya); Vosstaniya (Map p92; ul Marata 3; M Mayakovskaya); Vasilevsky Island (Map pp108–9; Sredny pr 32/44; M Vasileostrovskaya); Petrograd Side (Map pp114–15; Kamennoostrovsky pr 40; M Petrogradskaya) Chaynaya Lozhka is an excellent bliny, soup and salad joint that has become a citywide phenomenon. It's serve yourself cafeteria-style, but the bliny are made to order and the soups and salads are fresh and delicious.

Teremok (Map pp68–9; www.teremok.ru; cnr Malaya Sadovaya & Italiyanskaya ul; bliny R40-100; 10am-10pm; M Gostiny Dvor) Sprinkled all over the city, these kiosks are superb value, serving up fresh bliny with the fillings of your choice. There is no seating, so grab your snack to go and eat it at the standing-room-only tables in the vicinity. Besides this central location in the Historic Heart, there are Teremok outlets outside many metro stations.

U Tyoshi na Blinakh (meals R200-300; 24hr); Historic Heart (Map pp68–9; Malaya Morskaya ul 4/1); Vosstaniya (Map p92; Zagorodny pr 18; M Vladimirskaya); Petrograd Side (Map pp114–15; Sytninskaya ul 16; M Gorkovskaya) 'Auntie's pancakes' are being served up in so many locations now that it's a wonder she's not dropped dead yet. This cafeteria-style chain is a great place to fill up quickly and cheaply. Besides the tired-looking bliny, you can also sample hot soups, fresh salads and a variety of tasty pre-prepared mains.

walls are adorned with B&W photos, while well-stocked bookshelves and a range of board games (not to mention wi-fi access) encourage lingering. This is the kind of place where it's easy to become a regular.

IL PATIO Map pp68–9 Italian $$

☎ 314 8215; http://il-patio.rosinter.com; Nevsky pr 30; meals R300-500; M Nevsky Pr

Patio Pizza was one of the first post-Soviet restaurants to gain widespread popularity for its tasty pizza and extensive salad bar, all at prices that were manageable for Olga and Ivan Russian. Branches quickly spread around Moscow, and then across the country. Now this tried-and-true favourite has gone slightly upscale, with a new, more Italian name, and a new, more stylish look. Wood-oven pizzas and fresh salad bars are still the highlights of the menu.

KILIKIA Map pp68–9 Armenian $$

☎ 327 2208; Gorokhovaya ul 26/40; meals R200-400; noon-3am; M Sennaya Pl

An excellent option for the late-night munchies, the Kilikia is famous for its shashlyk, which sates the appetite of the post-clubbing crowd. Otherwise, it's a popular spot for St Petersburg's Armenian community, which should tell you something about the authentic and delicious food. Live music plays most nights.

YOLKI PALKI Map pp68–9 Russian $

☎ 571 0385; www.elki-palki.ru; Malaya Konyushennaya ul 9; meals R200-400; 24hr; M Nevsky Pr

Another chain restaurant that made it big in Moscow, Yolki Palki is now attempting to woo the St Petersburg diners – and having some success of it. Its wooden interior is decorated with stuffed animals and fake trees, reminiscent of the Russian countryside, and its menu specialises in reliable, affordable Russian country classics. The salad bar is the main drawcard here – a huge selection for one fixed price, with no waiting and no deciphering Russian menus. It's an excellent option for vegetarians.

STOLLE Map pp68–9 Russian $

☎ 312 1862; www.stolle.ru; Konyushenny per 1/6; meals R100-300; 9am-11pm; M Nevsky pr; ⊠

This is one of St Petersburg's coolest places to come for coffee, although you'd be a fool to leave without sampling one of its magnificent *pirogi* (pies). In fact, the entire menu is excellent, but the pies are irresistible. A 'stolle' is a traditional Saxon Christmas cake: the selection of sweets and savouries sits on the counter, fresh from the oven. It may be difficult to decide (mushroom or meat; apricot or apple?) but you really can't go wrong. This outlet on Konyushennaya pl is one of the city's largest, and it comes with a separate non-smoking room.

LITEYNY & SMOLNY

This is a largely residential and institutional neighbourhood which does not have a wide selection of restaurants. There are a few noteworthy exceptions located near the metro station (M Chernyshevskaya) and on ul Pestelya.

MOLOKHOVETS' DREAM

Map p84 Russian $$$

Mechta Molokhovets; ☎ 929 2247; www.molokhovets.ru; ul Radishcheva 10; meals R800-1500; M Pl Vosstaniya

Inspired by the cookbook of Elena Molokhovets (see A Gift to Young Housewives, opposite), the Russian Martha Stewart, the menu here covers all the classics from borscht to beef stroganoff, as well as some more exotic fare. Start with berry kissel, a delicious sweet soup of brambles and wine, and don't bypass the speciality, *koulibiaca*, a golden pastry pie of fish or rabbit.

VOX Map p84 Italian $$$

☎ 273 1469; ul Pestelya 4; meals R800-1200; 🕑 11am-1am; M Chernyshevskaya

On a quaint corner of the pedestrian-friendly Stolyarny per and ul Pestelya, Vox has a prime spot for a sidewalk café. It's a delightful setting to sip a cool drink on a summer afternoon, especially when the Museum of Decorative & Applied Arts has a street exhibition, as it is sometimes prone to do. The interior is equally appealing and very upscale. Dim lighting, white linens and stripped-down décor provide a suitably sexy environment for antipastos, pastas, meats and seafood. This place maintains a cool ambience, despite the constant crowds. Reservations recommended.

BLACK CAT, WHITE CAT

Map p84 International $$$

Chyornaya Koshka, Bely Kot; ☎ 279 7430; ul Pestelya 13/15; meals R600-800; M Chernyshevskaya

This super-sleek place wins plaudits for contemporary design: exposed brick walls are hung with posters, light streams in through huge bay windows, and chiffon sheets hang between the tables for privacy. The place is named after the Serbian film *Black Cat, White Cat*. The menu features an eclectic mix of grilled meats, fresh salads and homemade soups, perhaps with a Serbian twist, though it's hard to pinpoint.

GIN NO TAKI

Map p84 Japanese $$

☎ 272 0958; www.ginnotaki.ru; pr Chernyshevskogo 17; meals R500-700; 🕑 11am-6am; M Chernyshevskaya

In a city awash with wannabe Japanese restaurants, this large and lively operation is one of the most authentic, with a wide range of sushi, sashimi, kebabs, tempura and bento box lunches. Unnervingly, the entire staff greets you very loudly in Japanese as you walk in the door. That exuberance aside, Gin No Taki makes for an excellent Japanese dining experience. Should you be inspired by the cooking, there is a Japanese grocery store next door.

SUNDUK Map p84 International $$

☎ 272 3100; www.cafesunduk.ru; Furshtatskaya ul 42; meals R400-600; M Chernyshevskaya

Calling itself an 'art café', Sunduk is tucked into a tiny basement, its two rooms crowded with mismatched furniture, musical instruments, carefully posed mannequins and lots of other junk (or 'art') that creates a bohemian atmosphere. The European menu has a good selection of meat and fish, with plenty of Russian classics, all of which is pretty tasty. Live music nightly – see p185.

FAT FRIER Map p84 Russian $

Tolstiy Frayer; ☎ 272 7943; www.tolstiy-fraer.ru; ul Belinskogo 13; meals R200-400; 🕑 10am-1am Sun-Thu, 10am-3am Fri & Sat; M Mayakovskaya

The original branch of this citywide chain is a great place for late-night dining. See p164 for a full review.

A GIFT TO YOUNG HOUSEWIVES

The most popular cookbook in 19th-century Russia was called *A Gift to Young Housewives,* a collection of favourite recipes and household management tips that turned into a bestseller. The author, Elena Molokhovets, a housewife herself, was dedicated to her 10 children, to the Orthodox Church, and to her inexperienced 'female compatriots' who might need assistance keeping their homes running smoothly.

This book was reprinted 28 times between 1861 and 1914, and Molokhovets added new recipes and helpful hints to each new edition. The last edition included literally thousands of recipes, as well as pointers on how to organise an efficient kitchen, how to set a proper table and how to clean a cast-iron pot. ('To clean a burned pan, strew five kopeks' worth of chloride of lime into the pot, fill with water, and boil this liquid until the pot is bleached white...then strain into a bottle. After yellowed linen is washed it may be soaked in this water for fifteen minutes or longer until it whitens.')

Molokhovets received an enormously positive response from readers who credited her with no less than preserving their family life. The popular perception of the time was that a wife's primary responsibility was to keep her family together, and keeping her husband well fed seemed to be the key. As one reader wrote, 'a good kitchen is...not an object of luxury. It is a token of the health and well-being of the family, upon which all the remaining conditions of life depend.' Molokhovets included some of these letters in later editions as testimony to her work.

The classic cookbook was never reprinted during the Soviet period. The details of sumptuous dishes and fine table settings – let alone questions of etiquette and style – would certainly have been considered petty and bourgeois by the Soviet regime. Yet still, copies of this ancient tome survived, passed down from mother to daughter like a family heirloom. Today, the book reads not only as a cookbook, but also as a lesson in history and sociology.

At the end of the 20th century, Molokhovets' 'gift' was bestowed upon the modern world, when Joyce Toomre, a culinary historian, translated and reprinted this historical masterpiece. The 1992 version, *Classic Russian Cooking: Elena Molokhovets' A Gift to Young Housewives,* includes Toomre's detailed analysis of mealtimes, menus, ingredients, cooking techniques etc. The hundreds of pages of recipes range from instructions for making wheat starch to details on stringing an eel by its eyes before frying. (As Toomre notes, some are included purely for historical value.)

PRAVDA Map p84 — Russian $

☎ 579 8902; www.pravda.salons.su; ul Zhukovskogo 45; meals R100-300; Ⓜ Mayakovskaya

There is nothing new about a retro Soviet-themed restaurant, but somehow it never grows tired: the propaganda posters, the portraits of Lenin, the *Internationale*. This so-called 'art café' actually promises 'communist lunches', which is rarely the object of such nostalgia. But the place is fun, as is the menu of old-fashioned Soviet favourites (and its prices really do hark back to the Soviet period!).

BALTIC BREAD Map p84 — Bakery $

Baltiisky Khleb; www.baltic-bread.ru; Grechesky pr 25; meals R100-300; 🕑 10am-9pm; Ⓜ Pl Vosstaniya

This outstanding bakery-café is an excellent place to stop for breakfast, lunch or a late-afternoon coffee break. Seating is limited, so take your order *soboy* ('to go') and head to Tauride Gardens (p85). There is another outlet in Vladimirsky Passage (p171) and one on the Petrograd Side (p175).

VLADIMIRSKAYA & VOSSTANIYA

Plenty of places to eat are clustered around the metro stations at pl Vosstaniya and Vladimirskaya, as well as along Nevsky pr. Zagorodny pr is also becoming something of an 'eat street', with plenty of restaurants to suit all price ranges.

MATROSSKAYA TISHINA Map p92 — Russian $$$

☎ 764 4413; ul Marata 54/34; meals R600-800; Ⓜ Ligovsky Pr

Generally accepted by all to be the city's finest seafood restaurant, this place is often completely full. The curious metallic maritime design complements the excellent menu of grilled, baked and fried fish.

top picks

FOR KIDS

Here are some suggestions for family-friendly feeding:

- **Fat Frier** (p164 or p168)
- **Il Patio** (p167 or right)
- **Tinkoff** (p166)
- **Yolki Palki** (p167 or opposite)
- **Shinok** (right)
- **Bliny Domik** (opposite)
- **Russky Kitsch** (p173)
- **Na Zdorovye** (p175)

You can even pick which trout or perch you want to end up on your plate.

BISTROT GARÇON Map p92 French $$$

☎ 717 2467; Nevsky pr 95; meals R600-800; 9am-1am; M Pl Vosstaniya

The more casual of two outlets, this gorgeous little bistro is smart and unpretentious, with low lighting, upscale but still charming décor, and professional staff. Prices are reasonable given the excellent standard of the cooking (and Parisian chef). See p165 for a review of the other Garçon.

IMBIR Map p92 Russian $$

☎ 713 3215; Zagorodny pr 15; meals R400-600; noon-2am; M Dostoevskaya

Effortlessly cool, Imbir combines ornate tsarist décor with contemporary design to brilliant effect. With a great atmosphere, it's always full. The hip local crowd come here for dark coffee and creative cooking, all of which is reasonably priced. The staff aims to please, which is a welcome change of pace from the typically cooler-than-thou attitude at trendy places.

ORIENT EXPRESS Map p92 Russian $$

Vostochny Ekspress; ☎ 314 5096; www.orient-express.spb.ru; ul Marata 21; meals R400-600; M Mayakovskaya

All aboard for a taste of the romance, mystery and history of the legendary train line. Decked out like a luxury locomotive, this fun restaurant features booths that resemble train cabins and all the railway paraphernalia you can imagine. It's an absolute must for train spotters and anybody who is about to board the Trans-Siberian. Rest assured, you won't get food like this once on board the real thing, so enjoy the Eastern-influenced menu, especially the selection of meats grilled over hot coals.

CHE Map p92 International $$

☎ 716 7608; www.cafeclubche.ru; Poltavskaya ul 3; meals R300-500; M Pl Vosstaniya; wi-fi

Few places are cooler to hang out than Che. Come by day for good lunch specials and wi-fi access or come by night for cold beer and live music. Either way, you will enjoy the loungy furniture, friendly service and laidback atmosphere. The mostly Russian menu features rotating 'specials' suggested by the chef, as well as standard soups, salads and other European fare.

SHINOK Map p92 Ukrainian $$

☎ 571 8262; Zagorodny pr 13; meals R400-600; 24hr; M Dostoevskaya

Tucked into a folksy interior filled with embroidered linens and painted wooden handicrafts, Shinok is a fun, friendly place to sample Ukrainian fare. The waitstaff may look like Ukrainian peasants, but they speak English and are eager to please. Country cooking like hearty soups and meat-filled *vareniki* (dumplings) will sate your appetite, and there is live folk music nightly at 7pm.

CAT CAFÉ Map p92 Georgian $$

☎ 571 3377; Stremyannaya ul 22/3; meals R300-500; M Mayakovskaya

With vines hanging from the ceiling to evoke the Caucasian countryside, this popular restaurant dishes up Georgian favourites: hearty *khinkali* (meat dumplings), decadent *khachapuri* (cheese bread), grilled eggplant and zucchini. At the time of research, Russia and Georgia were ironing out their trade differences, so hopefully you can also wash it down with a delicious Georgian red wine.

IL PATIO Map p92 Italian $$

☎ 271 3177; Nevsky pr 182; meals R300-500; M Pl Alexandra Nevskogo

There are not too many places to eat at the far end of Nevsky pr. Fortunately, Russia's favourite pizza place comes through for hungry travellers who want to grab lunch after visiting the monastery. See p167 for a full review.

YOLKI PALKI Map p92 Russian $

☎ 273 1594; www.elki-palki.ru; Nevsky pr 88; meals R200-300; 🕑 24hr; Ⓜ Mayakovskaya

Prominently placed on this busy strip of Nevsky pr, this is one of several outlets of the favourite Russian chain. See p167 for a full review.

BLINY DOMIK Map p92 Russian $

☎ 315 9915; Kolokolnaya ul 8; meals R200-400; 🕑 10.30am-11.30pm; Ⓜ Vladimirskaya

There is more than just bliny on the menu at this long-running favourite. Besides sweet and savoury pancakes of every kind, there are also soups, salads and other snacks. The place is set up like a cosy and welcoming country home. It gets very busy at noon, so come for breakfast or a late lunch.

TROITSKY MOST Map p92 Vegetarian $

☎ 715 1998; Zagorodny pr 38; meals R200-300; Ⓜ Pushkinskaya

The Zagorodny pr branch is by far the nicest of this chain of vegetarian cafés, with the Indian spiritual-style Trang Café attached, and overlooking a small park. A huge selection of soups and salads, excellent pasta (including unbeatable lasagne) and other meat-free treats round out the daily-changing menu.

BALTIC BREAD Map p92 Bakery $

Baltiisky Khleb; ☎ 331 3220; Vladimirsky pr 19; meals R100-300; Ⓜ Dostoevskaya

Strangely enough, despite the name this is a British bakery. This branch is located in the Vladimirsky Passage shopping centre, where you can pick up fresh bread, cakes and even ready-made sandwiches on the run. You can take away or eat in the small café area provided.

BUSHE Map p92 Bakery $

☎ 312 3578; ul Razyezzhaya 13; breakfast or snacks R50-100; Ⓜ Vladimirskaya

This Austrian bakery has developed a huge number of local devotees, thanks to fresh-baked pastries and delicious coffee drinks. See p164 for a full review.

SENNAYA

There are loads of fast-food restaurants around Sennaya pl, including Chaynaya Lozhka (see boxed text, p167). For something a bit more upscale, there are some worthwhile restaurants on Gorokhovaya ul and Kazanskaya ul.

KARAVAN Map p97 Central Asian $$$

☎ 310 5678; Voznesensky pr 46; meals R600-800; Ⓜ Sadovaya

Despite the kitschy décor (epitomised by the camel in the corner), Karavan is a superb Central Asian restaurant with a lovely location overlooking the Fontanka River. Open grills line the dining room, giving an optimum view (and scent) of the kebabs that are on the menu. The grilled meats and vegetables are guaranteed to make your mouth water, while the wine list offers some excellent and unusual complements. Service is attentive and efficient.

CROCODILE Map p97 International $$

Krokodil; ☎ 570 4240; Kazanskaya ul 46; meals R300-500; Ⓜ Sennaya Pl

Service can be slow at this underground hideaway, but the unusual and highly edible food is worth the wait. Look for innovative combinations that produce a delicious effect: mostly European fare with some international flare. The menu offers rich homemade soups, hearty salads that double as main courses, traditional pasta dishes and some excellent, unusual vegetarian options. The interior is almost as eclectic as the menu, but it's inviting and a bit arty and – again – the overall result is appealing.

TESTO Map p97 Italian $$

☎ 310 8270; per Grivtsova 5/29; meals R300-500; Ⓜ Sennaya Pl

Take your pick from a wide range of homemade pastas and top them with your favourite sauce, whether tomato-based bolognese or a rich, creamy salmon sauce. A few options for soup, salad and pizza round out the menu, but the pasta is the main drawcard. The modern space is not too fancy, but low light and Italian accents provide just enough ambience that you could bring a date here.

FASOL Map p97 Russian-European $$

☎ 571 0907; www.fasolcafe.ru; Gorokhovaya ul 17; meals R300-500; Ⓜ Sennaya Pl

A few of the modern dishes at this chic minimalist café feature the namesake beans (fasol), but that is not actually the reason to come here. (The name is actually supposed to be a play on the name of the street, which means 'Pea Street.') Whatever it's called, the updated Russian cuisine is creative and cost-effective. Try the herring salad with freshly fried potato pancakes.

SUMETA Map p97 Caucasian $

☎ 310 2411; ul Yefimova 5; meals R200-300; Ⓜ Sadovaya

Even if you've never had Dagestani food, you'll see plenty of familiar Caucasian dishes in this quiet but friendly place, from Lula kebab (minced-meat kebab) to fried eggplant with garlic and walnuts in sour cream. Try the pumpkin *chudu* (large pancake) or the selection of Caucasian wines for something new.

MARIINSKY

Decidedly quiet, the Mariinsky district does nevertheless have a few excellent restaurants clustered around the theatre. Look out for the expatriate mainstay The Idiot and the Mariinsky's fashionable restaurant, Backstage (Za Stsenoy).

NOBLE NEST Map p102 Russian-French $$$

Dvoryanskoye Gnezdo; ☎ 312 0911; ul Dekabristov 21; meals R1000-1500; Ⓜ Sennaya Pl/Sadovaya

This is the doyenne of the St Petersburg *haute cuisine* world, housed in the Trianon of the Yusupov Palace (p102). It's exceptionally stuffy (men shouldn't even think of entering without a tie), but – as previous diners such as Bill Clinton will no doubt tell you – the Russian-French cuisine is exceptional. Reservations recommended.

LE PARIS Map p102 French $$$

☎ 571 9545; www.leparis.ru; Bolshaya Morskaya ul 63; meals R800-1200; Ⓜ Sennaya Pl/Sadovaya

Sumptuous yet understated, this French restaurant sits just across the Moyka River from the Yusupov Palace. The three rooms include the main wood-panelled dining room and a smaller, simpler wine and cheese tasting room. No matter where you choose to indulge, you will not be disappointed by the excellent French fare and wine list. Apparently, this class act is a favourite with city governor Valentina Matvienko among other local dignitaries. Reservations recommended.

BACKSTAGE Map p102 Russian $$$

Za Stsenoy; ☎ 327 0684; Teatralnaya pl 18/10; meals R600-1000; 🕑 noon-2am; Ⓜ Sennaya Pl/Sadovaya

The Mariinsky's official restaurant is tucked away rather out of sight on one corner of Teatralnaya pl. The décor is stage-worthy, and the food is excellent. Service sometimes comes with a sniff, but that somehow befits an institution so celebrated as the Mariinsky. Apparently, famous opera singers and ballet dancers are welcome to write all over the walls. Probably best to refrain unless you count yourself among the stars.

LECHAIM Map p102 Jewish $$

☎ 972 2774; www.lehaim-spb.ru; Lermontovsky pr 2; meals R300-600; 🕑 noon-11pm Sun-Fri; Ⓜ Sennaya Pl/Sadovaya

Hidden away beneath the Grand Choral Synagogue (p104), this classy kosher restaurant is the city's best place for traditional Jewish cooking. You'll probably have the place to yourself, which detracts a bit from the otherwise authentic atmosphere.

THE IDIOT Map p102 Vegetarian $$

☎ 315 1675; nab reki Moyki 82; meals R400-600; 🕑 11am-1am; Ⓜ Sennaya Pl/Sadovaya; 💻 wi-fi

'Dostoevsky loved this place!' boasts an advertisement for this atmospheric expat institution. And why wouldn't he? The food is nothing to write novels about, but vegetarians are likely to disagree, as there is not a single animal on the menu. In any case, the cosy subterranean space, the antique furnishings and crowded bookshelves, plus the ever-amiable crowd, make it an extremely pleasant place to come to eat or drink.

CROCODILE Map p102 International $$

Krokodil; ☎ 314 9437; Galernaya ul 18; meals R300-500; Ⓜ Sennaya Pl/Sadovaya

The original (and perhaps more interesting) restaurant by this name, this bar and restaurant is a top choice for lunch or dinner, as long as you are not in a rush. Enjoy a dimly lit but artsy interior and an interesting, eclectic menu. See p171 for a full review.

LYA RUS Map p102 Russian $$

☎ 571 2946; Konnogvardeysky bul 15; meals R300-400; Ⓜ Sennaya Pl

Another kitschy Russian country house, this is a sweet place to sample hearty peasant

top picks

BREAKFAST

- **City Bar** (p179) For late nights and early mornings.
- **Stolle** (p167) Get your pie for the big pie fight.
- **Face Café** (p166) Real Russian breakfast, featuring bliny, *kasha* and more.
- **Bistrot Garçon** (p170) Hearty omelettes and rich, dark coffee.
- **Marius Pub** (p208) Inside the Helvetia Hotel & Suites.

soups and sip vodka while you watch traditional Russian song and dance. Typical for this type of place, the décor is folksy and the food is filling.

STOLLE Map p102 Bakery $

☎ 714 2571; www.stolle.ru; ul Dekabristov 33; meals R100-300; 🕑 9am-11pm; Ⓜ Sadovaya; 💻 wi-fi

One of several outlets throughout the city, Stolle is a great place to come for coffee or dessert after an evening at the theatre. Black-and-white photos adorn the light-coloured walls, while jazz music wafts in the air. There is another outlet further up ul Dekabristov (☎ 315 2383; ul Dekabristov 19; 🕑 9am-9pm), although its basement setting is not quite as inviting. See p167 for a full review.

VASILEVSKY ISLAND

One of the city's most interesting areas for dining, Vasilevsky Island offers river cruises, ethnic cuisine, and some of the classiest and most innovative Russian restaurants in town. Look around the metro station at Ⓜ Vasileostrovskaya and near the Strelka.

OLD CUSTOMS HOUSE Map pp108–9 Russian $$$

Staraya Tamozhnya; ☎ 327 8980; www.concord-catering.ru; Tamozhenny per 1; meals R800-1200; 🕑 1pm-1am; Ⓜ Nevsky Pr

This restaurant is not actually set in the old customs house, although it is around the corner in the historic building that houses St Petersburg's first museum (Kunstkamera). Costume-clad doormen and mannequins posing as customs officials ensure that you don't mistake the theme of this otherwise classy restaurant. Famous for its wine list and excellent food, this restaurant is where you will see St Petersburg's uppermost classes partaking of filet mignon and caviar crepes.

OYSTER BAR Map pp108–9 French $$$

Ustrichny Bar; ☎ 323 2279; www.oysters.spb.ru; Bolshoy pr 8; oysters per half-dozen R800-1000, meals R600-1000; Ⓜ Vasileostrovskaya

Four kinds of oysters are on the menu at this rather unlikely basement bar, along with complementary wines (which your knowledgeable server will recommend) and other seafood specialities. If you are yearning for a truly decadent and ostensibly aphrodisiac experience, look no further.

NEW ISLAND Map pp108–9 International $$$

☎ 320 2120; www.concord-catering.ru; Universitetskaya nab 13; meals R800-1200; 🕑 2pm, 6pm, 8pm & 10.30pm late Apr-Oct; Ⓜ Vasileostrovskaya

The list of diners on this smartest of boat restaurants is dizzying – George W Bush, Jacques Chirac and the Queen of Spain have all dined here, while Putin is a regular. These heavies come for the sumptuous décor and beautifully presented international menu, not to mention the fantastic city views from the two-hour cruise. Reservations required.

RESTORAN Map pp108–9 Russian $$

☎ 327 8979; Tamozhenny per 2; meals R400-600; Ⓜ Nevsky Pr

Natural light filters in through large street-level windows, filling the spacious hall. Cream-coloured linens and hardwood floors make for a chic, contemporary décor. It's an interesting contrast to the name of the restaurant (the old-fashioned Russian spelling harks back to the days of Romanov splendour). The menu manages to combine the best of *haute russe* cuisine with enough modern flare to keep things interesting.

RUSSKY KITSCH Map pp108–9 Russian $$

☎ 325 1122; www.concord-catering.ru; Universitetskaya nab 25; meals R400-600; Ⓜ Vasileostrovskaya

The centrepiece of this crazy café is a ceiling fresco featuring a shameless Fidel Castro and Leonid Brezhnev entwined in a passionate embrace. It's the biggest and best example of a venue laden with kitsch, just as the name promises. The walls and ceilings are plastered with funny photo collages, featuring scenes from Soviet socialist realism alongside other anachronisms; mismatched tapestries cover Victorian furniture; and menus are fashioned from butchered copies of Lenin's selected works. Whether or not this is your style, you're sure to find something that pleases in the diverse (and delicious) menu, and the glass-enclosed porch overlooking the Neva River is an absolutely delightful place to sip a coffee.

BIERGARTEN Map pp108–9 German $$
☎ 329 0895; 6-ya liniya i 7-ya liniya 15; meals R400-600; 24hr; M Vasileostrovskaya
Dark wood furnishings and beamed ceilings enhance the Bavarian atmosphere at this German beer hall. Select a table in the dark, inviting interior or on the porch overlooking Vasilevsky Island's main thoroughfare. Both are ideal spots to enjoy traditional German biergarten fare and a nice selection of beers.

MAMA ROMA Map pp108–9 Italian $$
☎ 328 0639; www.mamaroma.ru; Sredny pr 6; meals R300-500; 8am-11pm; M Vasileostrovskaya
Reliable Italian fare from decent pizza to risotto and pasta, not to mention an excellent breakfast. See p166 for a full review.

BYBLOS Map pp108–9 Lebanese $$
☎ 325 8564; Maly pr 5; meals R300-500; M Vasileostrovskaya
The only Lebanese place in town, this Vasilevsky Island hideaway attracts a large crowd for its excellent-value lunch, as well as a more relaxed evening clientele. Here you'll find delicious mezze, hummus, *kibbeh* (minced meat with bulgur wheat), tabbouleh, *kofta* (spicy meatballs of lamb or beef) and of course hookahs and Lebanese wine.

STOLLE Map pp108–9 Russian $
☎ 328 7860; www.stolle.ru; Syezdovskaya & 1-ya liniya 50; meals R100-300; M Vasileostrovskaya
This cosy café is the original Stolle – apt, as this is the historic location of the city's Saxon quarter. See p167 for a full review.

CHEBURECHNAYA Map pp108–9 Cafeteria $
☎ 323 8028; 6-ya liniya i 7-ya liniya 19; meals R100-200; M Vasileostrovskaya
This is not one of the many restaurants trying to be 'retro'; this *stolovaya* (cafeteria) just continues to do what it has been doing for decades. Bypass the sit-down restaurant and head straight into the nondescript cafeteria (on the right), where you can place your order at the cash register. Nowadays, there are a few other items on the menu, but you'll want to order the namesake *cheburechka*, a delicious Georgian meat-stuffed pastry. Take your receipt and pick up your food at the window. It may be the tastiest – and surely the cheapest – meal you will eat in St Pete.

PETROGRAD SIDE

The excellent restaurants on the Petrograd Side are not so easy to find if you don't know they are there, but it's worth seeking them out for the city's best Chinese and Georgian fare, not to mention a few interesting Russian restaurants. Look also for branches of some of the better Russian chains.

AQUAREL Map pp114–15 Fusion $$$
☎ 320 8600; moored off Birzhevoy most; meals R800-1200; M Sportivnaya
Aquarel combines a wonderful setting with fantastic fusion cuisine. Indeed, this is the place that pioneered fusion cuisine in the city, and the kitchen continues to artfully combine Russian, Mediterranean and Asian elements into some uniquely delicious dishes. This food fest takes place on a slickly decked-out boat, moored on the Neva River, offering amazing views of the façade of the Hermitage and the lights of Birzhevoy most. Unfortunately, service can be snooty and – even worse – slow, which is unacceptable for an otherwise high-class (and high-price) joint. There is a cheaper café on the top floor serving pasta and pizza and other simple fare.

RUSSIAN FISHING
Map pp114–15 Seafood $$$
Russkaya Rybalka; ☎ 323 9813; www.russian-fishing.ru; Yuzhnaya Doroga 11, Krestovsky Island; meals R800-1200; noon-9pm; M Krestovsky Ostrov
History has it that this was Prince Menshikov's favourite fishing ground. The folks at Russian Fishing want you to be able to experience the same joy as the prince, so when you arrive you will be given a rod and some bait and you can (hopefully) catch your own dinner. The pond is stocked with trout, sterlet and other types of sturgeon (but only expert fishers can be picky about their choice); the

chef will bake, smoke or grill your catch to order. If you are not up for the fishing adventure, you can order from the menu (and there are some nonfish options).

AKVARIUM

Map pp114–15 Chinese $$$

☎ 326 8286; Kamennoostrovsky pr 10; meals R600-800; M Gorkovskaya

Tucked into a funny location behind Lenfilm, Akvarium maintains the serene aura of a Chinese garden, complete with swimming fish and flowing fountains. It's a perfect atmosphere to indulge in St Petersburg's most authentic Chinese fare, including – appropriately for a place called 'Aquarium' – an excellent range of seafood.

LES AMIS DE JEAN-JACQUES

Map pp114–15 French $$

☎ 232 9981; Bolshoy pr 54/2; meals R400-600; 10am-midnight Sun-Thu, 24hr Fri & Sat; M Petrogradskaya

You can't beat this delightful wine bar for eating and drinking like they do in Paris. The menu boasts excellent, affordable bistro fare, including breakfast (served all day on weekends), as well as a huge selection of French wines. The cosy, comfortable interior and the sidewalk seating are equally inviting, so take a seat and pour yourself a glass of Bordeaux.

TBILISI

Map pp114–15 Georgian $$

☎ 232 9391; Sytninskaya ul 10; meals R400-600; M Gorkovskaya

Decidedly upscale as far as Georgian restaurants go, Tbilisi has a great interior with tiled tables and big booths, made more private by intricate latticework between them. This place is a beloved St Petersburg institution, thanks to its top-notch cooking 'prepared by real Georgian chefs'. Classics such as *khachapuri* (cheese bread) receive rave reviews. It's also an excellent place to sample some nice Georgian wines.

NA ZDOROVYE

Map pp114–15 Russian $$

☎ 232 4039; www.concord-catering.ru; Bolshoy pr 13; meals R400-600; M Sportivnaya

Na Zdorovye means 'To your health', the generic Russian toast that is emitted before clinking glasses and throwing back a shot. Indeed, this playful restaurant is as good a place as any to indulge in that long-standing tradition. Drawing on both pre- and post-revolutionary folklore, Na Zdorovye promises that you can still eat like 'the tsars and the Soviet dictators'. But it is mostly old Russian recipes that have been recreated here, including veal stuffed with cherries and trout in almond sauce. It's definitely a place to try some more unusual Russian dishes in a *very* Russian setting.

SALKHINO

Map pp114–15 Georgian $$

☎ 232 7891; Kronverksky pr 25; meals R300-500; M Gorkovskaya

Another justly popular Georgian restaurant, Salkhino serves big portions of delicious food in a convivial, arty setting. Pastel-coloured walls are adorned with paintings by local artists, which is not your typical Georgian décor. But the overall atmosphere *is* typically Georgian, which means doting service and warm hospitality.

YAKITORIYA

Map pp114–15 Japanese $$

☎ 970 4858; www.yakitoriya.spb.ru; Petrovskaya nab 4; meals R300-500; M Gorkovskaya

A second branch of Moscow's favourite sushi chain is on Petrogradsky Island. See p166 for a full review.

TROITSKY MOST

Map pp114–15 Vegetarian $

☎ 232 6693; Kamennoostrovsky pr 9/2; meals R200-300; 9am-11pm; M Gorkovskaya

The original branch of the vegetarian chain is located on Petrogradsky Island, just a few blocks north of the bridge for which it is named. See p171 for a full review.

BALTIC BREAD

Map pp114–15 Bakery $

☎ 498 0440; www.baltic-bread.ru; Bolshoy pr 80; meals R100-300; 9am-10pm; M Petrogradskaya

For a great breakfast option or maybe a late-afternoon pick-me-up, head to the Petrograd outlet of this St Petersburg favourite. See p169 for a full review.

VYBORG SIDE

The restaurants on the Vyborg Side are few and far between. We have included a handful that are heartily recommended for their filling fare and unique atmosphere.

OLD COUNTRYSIDE

Map pp122–3 Russian $$

Staraya Derevnya; ☎ 431 0000; ul Savushkina 72; meals R400-600; 1-10pm; M Chyornaya Rechka

This tiny, family-run hideaway is well off the beaten track, but its intimate atmosphere and delectable food are one-of-a-kind. Try old Russian recipes such as beef in plum and nut sauce or ham in oranges. The small size of the restaurant guarantees personal service, but reservations are a must. From the metro station, take any tram down ul Savushkina and get off at the third stop.

SEVEN-FORTY Map p65 Jewish $$

Sem-Sorok; ☎ 492 3444; www.740spb.ru; Bolshoy Sampsonievsky pr 108; meals R400-600; Ⓜ Chyornaya Rechka

For traditional Jewish home cooking in a delightful, folksy setting, Seven-Forty is worth the trip out of the city centre. Set on two levels, the warm, welcoming interior is scattered with artefacts that may have been scavenged from your Jewish grandmother's basement. The menu is not kosher, but its carefully crafted cuisine is delicious and different. Seven-Forty can be tricky to reach: take tram 40 or catch a cab from the metro station.

AIVA Map pp122–3 International $$

☎ 320 4929; Pirogovskaya nab 17; meals R400-600; 🕑 24hr; Ⓜ Vyborgskaya

Aiva may seem out of the way, but all the cool kids come here to sit on the covered terrace and sip sophisticated cocktails. Rag-rug pillows accent the rustic décor, giving the place an exotic Eastern ambience. The menu is a mixed bag, with dishes from Europe and Asia, as well as Russian and Georgian standards. The service at this trendy café gets decidedly mixed reviews, but everyone agrees that the setting is super fine.

DRINKING & NIGHTLIFE

top picks

- **Griboedov** (p184)
- **Cynic** (p179)
- **Datscha** (p182)
- **The Other Side** (p184)
- **Fish Fabrique** (p184)
- **Mod** (p183)
- **Stray Dog Café** (p181)

DRINKING

'Drinking is the joy of the Rus. We cannot live without it.' With these words Vladimir of Kiev, father of the Russian state, is said to have rejected abstinent Islam on his people's behalf in the 10th century. And the grateful Russian people have confirmed old Vlad's assessment, as drinking remains an integral part of Russian culture and society.

SPECIALITIES

The word 'vodka' is the diminutive of *voda*, the Russian word for water, so it means something like 'a wee drop'. Russians sometimes drink vodka in moderation, but more often it's tipped down in swift shots, often followed by a pickle. Russky Standard and Stolichnaya are two good brands of vodka that are commonly available. It's very rare to get bad vodka in a restaurant, so do not fear if you don't recognise the brand name, as there are many. In shops it's a different story, though: always buy vodka from a respectable-looking store (avoid street kiosks if possible) and always check for an unbroken seal.

Many visitors to Russia are surprised to learn that *pivo* (beer) is actually Russia's most popular alcoholic drink. The market leader is Baltika, a Scandinavian joint-venture with Russian management, based in St Petersburg. It makes no less than 12 excellent brews. No 3 and 7 are the most popular standard lagers, but there is also a wheat beer (No 8), dark beers (No 4 and 6) and a 'strong beer' (No 9), which at 8% proof is extremely popular. Tinkoff (p180) is a national chain of microbreweries that has begun bottling its potent brews for retail sale. Other leading Russian beers are Bochkarev, Nevskoye, Stepan Razin and Tri Medvedi.

Russians drink *Sovietskoe shampanskoe* (sparkling wine) to toast special occasions and to sip during intermission at the theatre. It tends to be sickeningly sweet: look for the label that says *sukhoe* (dry).

Kvas is a mildly alcoholic fermented rye-bread water. Cool and refreshing, it is a popular summer drink that tastes something like ginger beer. In the olden days it was dispensed on the street from big wheeled tanks. Patrons would bring their own bottles or plastic bags and fill up. The *kvas* truck is a rare sight these days, but this cool tasty treat is still available from Russian restaurants.

ETIQUETTE

Few traditions in Russia are as sacrosanct as the drinking of vodka, the national drink. Forget any foreign notions of drinking vodka mixed with tonic or orange juice – this is anathema to your average Russian. If you need something to wash it down, you can chase with a lemon or a pickle or, perhaps, a mixer in a separate glass.

Vodka is served chilled. One person makes a toast, then everyone clinks glasses and knocks it back. Women can usually get away with sipping, but men will be scoffed at if they don't drink up – at least the first round. Back in the day, vodka bottles rarely had resealable caps, which meant that once opened it must be finished. Times have changed, however; these days, finishing off the bottle is not technically necessary.

It is bad luck to place an empty bottle on the table – it must be placed on the floor. Most importantly of all, snack between shots; Russians swear that by doing this you'll *never* get drunk…

Many visitors are surprised by the ubiquity of drinking, meaning that people will crack open a beer anywhere. It is not illegal to drink in public places, so it's not unusual to see young people sipping beers on the sidewalk or in the park. It was only recently that consuming alcohol on the metro was prohibited.

WHERE TO DRINK

Back in the day, the equivalent of the local pub was a *ryumochnaya*, which comes from the word *ryumka* (shot). These were pretty grim places, serving up *sto grammov* (100 grams), but not much else. Most people preferred to drink at home, surrounded by friends and family.

In recent years, St Petersburg's drinking possibilities have expanded exponentially (although there are still a few old-school *ryumochnye* around town; see p180). Now, drink-

NA ZDOROVYE!

'To your health!' is what Russians say when they throw back a shot of vodka. But this pronouncement hardly suffices as a proper toast in a public forum or an intimate drinking session among friends. A proper toast requires thoughtfulness and sincerity.

A few themes prevail. The first toast of the night often acknowledges the generosity of the host, while the second usually recognises the beauty of the ladies present. In mixed company, you can't go wrong raising your glass to international friendship or world peace. But in all cases, the toast requires a personal anecdote or a profound insight, as well as a bit of rambling preamble to make it meaningful.

In Russia, drinking vodka is a celebration of life in all its complexity – the triumph, the tragedy and the triviality. A toast is a vocalisation of that celebration, so say it like you mean it. And drink it in the same way – *zalpom* – bottoms up!

ers can take their pick from wine bars, whisky bars, Irish pubs, sports bars, microbreweries and more. In summer months, there is also an assortment of *letny sady* (summer gardens) scattered around town.

PRACTICALITIES

Opening Hours

Most Russians prefer to drink with meals, so almost all bars and pubs double as restaurants. As such, they generally have the same opening hours as eating venues (from 11am or noon to 11pm or midnight). Popular drinking spots are more likely to stay open later – usually until 2am – though the kitchen may close. Some hot spots stay open for drinking until 5am or 6am.

How Much?

Prices for alcohol vary widely depending on where you are drinking. Expect to pay anywhere from R60 to R150 for a pint of beer, and between R50 and R200 for 50g of vodka. Don't forget a 10% tip for the bartender.

BARS & PUBS

You'll get the chance to drink almost anywhere you look – from the café at the theatre to the kiosk in the park. Almost all restaurants and cafés offer alcoholic beverages on their menus. We have listed some of the city's choice drinking venues below, but you will likely find your own favourite, especially if you explore the streets of the Historic Heart, Liteyny, Smolny, Vladimirskaya and Vosstaniya. The city's official tourist information site (www.visit-petersburg.ru) has an online drinking guide. You might also consider joining the highly recommended Friday-night pub crawl offered by Peter's Walking Tours (p247).

BRIDGE LOUNGE Map pp114–15

☎ 910 0000; www.bridgelounge.ru; Zayachy Island; ⌚ noon-last customer; Ⓜ Gorkovskaya

This swank spot is part restaurant, part lounge and 100% upper-class. Set within the western bastion of the Peter & Paul Fortress, this see-and-be-seen spot boasts an atmospheric location and awesome vista. Its white tent-roof interior is gorgeous, with plush pillows and drapes adorning the otherwise sparse space. Face control ensures that the clientele looks as good as their surroundings.

CITY BAR Map p84

☎ 448 5837; www.citybar.ru; Furshtatskaya ul 20; ⌚ 11am-2am; Ⓜ Chernyshevskaya; 💻 wi-fi

A sort of St Petersburg celebrity, co-owner Aileen has presided over this popular place since 1996. It's busy every night of the week with expats and travellers and locals who enjoy their company. They come for free wi-fi access, outrageously good food (especially breakfast and burgers) and live entertainment. Music, poetry readings and stand-up comedy are all on the agenda, depending on the day. Also available: English-language books and DVDs from the lending library.

CYNIC Map p97

Tsynik; ☎ 312 9526; www.cinic.spb.ru; per Antonenko 4; ⌚ 1pm-3am Sun-Thu, 1pm-7am Fri & Sat; Ⓜ Sennaya Pl/Sadovaya; 💻 wi-fi

Calling itself a 'trash-café-club', Cynic holds a very special place in the hearts of the St Petersburg underground. Rumour has it that this divey place is struggling for survival, but the student-slacker crowd has not abandoned its no-frills cellar bar. Arty types still come to nurse cheap beers and indulge in the famously delicious *grenki*

EAT & DRINK, DRINK & EAT

Want some more places to drink? Check out the following eating venues, which draw a frothy beer or mix a strong cocktail in addition to serving food:

- NEP (p163)
- Fidelio Café (p164)
- Fat Frier (p164 or p168)
- Onegin (p164)
- Korovabar (p165)
- Face Café (p166)
- Zoom Café (p166)
- Black Cat, White Cat (p168)
- Imbir (p170)
- Crocodile (p171 or p172)
- Fasol (p171)
- The Idiot (p172)
- Russky Kitsch (p173)
- Biergarten (p174)
- Aquarel (p174)
- Les Amis de Jean-Jacques (p175)
- Aiva (p176)

(black bread fried in garlic). Literature fans of the male persuasion can peruse Pushkin in the toilet.

DIE KNEIPE Map pp108–9

Grad Petrov; ☎ 326 0137; www.die-kneipe.ru; Universitetskaya nab 5; 🕑 noon-last customer; Ⓜ Vasileostrovskaya

Fresh-brewed lager, Weiss, pilsner, Dunkel and Hefe-Weiss – it's reason enough to stop by this newish microbrewery on Vasilevsky Island. The incredible happy-hour specials (from 4pm until 9pm) are added incentive. To top it off, the outdoor tables offer amazing views of St Isaac's Cathedral and the Admiralty across the Neva River.

DUNES Map pp68–9

Dyuni; ☎ 7-901-303 7122; www.summerkiosk.spb.ru; Konyushennaya pl 2; 🕑 11am-1am Mar-Sep; Ⓜ Nevsky Pr

Feel like lounging on the beach with a fruity cocktail, catching some rays or playing some badminton? Then visit Dunes, St Petersburg's first beach bar, complete with sand, hammocks and beach chairs. That this outdoor café is located in a crumbling courtyard (with no sea in sight) only adds to the charm. The place is hard to find: go through the unmarked archway off Konyushennaya pl and proceed to the second courtyard.

PIVNAYA 0.5 Map p92

☎ 315 1038; www.piv05.ru; Zagorodny pr 44/2; 🕑 11am-2am; Ⓜ Vladimirskaya

With Soviet films playing on the big screen, this classic place recalls the days when the local *pivnaya* (beer bar) was the only choice for a brew. This particular *pivnaya* has gone upscale. The retro-chic atmosphere is heavy on the chic, however, with its dark wood and copper décor, sumptuous leather furniture and electronica music.

PROBKA Map p84

☎ 273 4904; www.probka.org; ul Belinskogo 5; 🕑 1pm-1am; Ⓜ Gostiny Dvor

Romantic and sophisticated, serving wines from around the world…what more do you want from your wine bar? Tile floors and terracotta walls recall an Italian *enoteca*, with its shelves stocked with wine bottles and liqueurs. Several wines are available by the glass or half-bottle, and there is a menu of light snacks, salads and pastas.

RYUMOCHNAYA Map p84

4-ya Sovetskaya ul 10; 🕑 7am-11pm; Ⓜ Pl Vosstaniya

This is a hold-over from the days when a drinking establishment needed no special name. The *ryumochnaya* was the generic place where comrades stopped on their way to or from work to toss back a shot or two before continuing on their way. It's hard to say how long this particular *ryumochnaya* has been around, but you can be sure that if you order *sto grammov* (100 grams), they will know what you are talking about.

SHAMROCK Map p102

☎ 318 4625; www.shamrock.spb.ru; ul Dekabristov 27; 🕑 9am-2am; Ⓜ Sadovaya

It may seem odd to pop in for a pint after watching ballerinas dance across *Swan Lake*, but that is what many theatre-goers do. This friendly Irish-owned pub opposite the Mariinsky Theatre attracts a steady stream of foreigners and locals. Not all of them are coming from the theatre: some make a special trip to feast on shepherd's pie, drink Guinness and enjoy the *craic*.

TINKOFF Map pp68–9

☎ 718 5566; www.tinkoff.ru; Kazanskaya ul 7; 🕑 noon-2am; Ⓜ Nevsky Pr

Set inside a gigantic contemporary brewery, Tinkoff is a great place to sample one of eight freshly brewed beers and enjoy live entertainment. There's stand-up comedy at 10pm Thursday nights, and live music or DJs from 9pm Friday through Sunday. And if you get hungry, you're in luck (see p166 for a restaurant review).

TRIBUNAL BAR Map pp68–9

☎ 314 2423; Karavannaya ul 26; 9am-6am; M Gostiny Dvor

This used to be a kind of legendary place, famous for the debauchery and decadence that would set in as soon as the crowd had enough to drink. It's now in a new location. And while ads promise that 'the legend continues', the debauchery feels a little over-programmed. Nonetheless, scantily clad women dancing on the bar are practically guaranteed.

CAFÉS

St Petersburg temperatures occasionally call for a warming drink, so it's nice to know you're never far from a fresh-brewed cup o' joe. Indeed, who can be surprised about the blossoming of a café culture in this city of artists, intellectuals and philosophers? A few of the Russian chains have followed their Western counterparts and opened up outlets on every corner. Rest assured, you will never be far from a Coffee House (Kofe Khaus), Ideal Cup (Idealnaya Chashka) or Shokoladnitsa. But the independent cafés listed here earn higher marks for atmosphere and artistry. They're recommended for coffee, tea and perhaps something to sate your sweet tooth. Many cafés have full menus, and these are reviewed in the Eating chapter (p160).

BLACK & WHITE Map pp108–9

☎ 323 3881; www.blackwhite.ru; 6-ya liniya i 7-ya liniya 25; 8.30am-1am; M Vasileostrovskaya

So perhaps the black and white décor is a little predictable, but the location on Vasilevsky's Island main strip is unbeatable.

top picks

GAY ST PETE

- Sinners (p183)
- Cabaret (p182)
- 3L (p182)
- Central Station (p182)

The sidewalk seating offers a perfect place to sip your joe and watch the world go by. Also serving breakfast and business lunch.

CAFÉ RICO Map p92

☎ 764 7214; Nevsky pr 77/1; 9am-10pm; M Pl Vosstaniya

Evoking Columbia, or maybe Brazil, the décor of this long-standing favourite raises expectations about the quality of the coffee. And Café Rico does not disappoint, serving roasts from around the world, as well as coffee cocktails and irresistible sweets. The entrance is actually from Pushkinskaya ul.

COFFEE BREAK Map pp68–9

☎ 314 6729; nab kanala Griboedova; 7.30am-11pm; M Nevsky Pr

Not just a café, but also an art gallery. Infused with the sounds of chill-out music and the aromas of fresh-brewed java, this modern space is a delightful place to get your daily dose and admire the local artwork. The choice of coffees, teas and other drinks is impressive.

OUNCE Map p92

Untslya; ☎ 315 5786; Nevsky pr 63; 10am-10pm; M Mayakovskaya

Hiding behind the tea shop, a chic salon overlooks a quiet courtyard. Twinkling lights and comfy couches make for a sublime setting to sip your tea. Sample from hundreds of varieties of black, green and herbal.

STRAY DOG CAFÉ Map pp68–9

☎ 315 7764; pl Iskusstv 5; 11.30am-midnight; M Nevsky Pr

Back in the day, this underground café was the gathering place for poets and playwrights ('the day' meaning 1912 and 'poets and playwrights' meaning the likes of Anna Akhmatova, Osip Mandelstam and Vladimir Mayakovsky). These days, the crowd isn't so bohemian, but the café still hosts occasional poetry readings and acoustic music performances. Prominently placed on pl Iskusstv (Arts Sq), it's a convenient and cosy place to stop for a drink before or after the theatre.

ZERNO ISTINY Map p92

☎ 712 5319; www.zerno-istiny.ru; Zagorodny pr 20; 24hr; M Vladimirskaya;

While the décor is nothing special, this cosy café has friendly service, decent coffee and – bonus – free internet access. Bring your own computer or borrow one from the bar. Thirty minutes free with the purchase of a cup of coffee.

CLUBBING

Dance and music clubs might open at 10pm or 11pm, but they don't get hopping until after midnight. On weekends, all St Petersburg clubs stay open until the very early hours (usually 6am or 7am). Most operate every night of the week, although some are open only on weekends (specified in the listings). Check the *St Petersburg Times* for updates. Also, look out for posters around town advertising club events and one-off parties with famous DJs or good local groups playing. Many of the city's clubs charge an admission fee of R100 to R400. Nearly all clubs serve food, although be aware that a 'crazy menu' is not for ordering food but for choosing women (and sometimes men).

3L Map p84 — Lesbian

Tri El; ☎ 710 2016; www.triel.spb.ru; 5-ya Sovetskaya ul 45; cover R0-150; 🕔 5pm-midnight Tue, 10pm-6am Wed-Sun; Ⓜ Pl Vosstaniya

Russia's first (and only?) lesbian club opened in 2002 and is still a fun, laidback place with dancing, live music at 7pm Thursday and billiards. The multicoloured paint job and oddly shaped apertures give the interior a dreamy, almost space-age atmosphere. But the crowd is pretty down-to-earth and very diverse (aside from being mostly women, of course). Tuesday, Wednesday and Saturday are women-only.

CABARET Map pp146–7 — Gay

Kabare; ☎ 575 4512; www.cabarespb.ru; nab kanala Obvodnogo 181; men/women R200/400; Ⓜ Baltiyskaya

Now in a new location near Baltic Station, this cabaret and karaoke club has a fun, friendly vibe, open to anyone who is entertained by a little gender-bending. The highlight of the night is the 2am drag show, which is among the best in the city if you enjoy seeing men dressed as ageing Soviet pop stars.

CENTRAL STATION Map pp68–9 — Gay

☎ 312 3600; www.centralstation.ru; ul Lomonosova 1/28; admission before midnight free, after midnight R100-300; 🕔 6pm-6am; Ⓜ Gostiny Dvor

Right behind Sinners, this newer, flashier gay club is huge, featuring countless bars and dance floors, in addition to the café and souvenir shop (in case you have such a good time that you need to have a pair of Central Station boxer shorts). There seems to be something special going on every night, including guest DJs, dance contests and many, many men. Thursday is student night; Saturday is a weekly 'pop' party.

HAVANA CLUB Map p97 — Latin

☎ 259 1155; Moskovsky pr 21; cover R100-250; 🕔 noon-6am; Ⓜ Tekhnologichesky Institut

Enduringly popular, Havana is the only club that plays a consistent mix of salsa, merengue and Latin-infused jazz. There is usually live music on at least one of the three dance floors. So put your dancing shoes on (no trainers allowed!) and let

BEAT STREET

If you are up for a night of bar-hopping, you can't do better than **Dumskaya ul** (Map pp68–9; Dumskaya ul 9; cover R100-300; 🕔 8pm-6am; Ⓜ Gostiny Dvor), where four of St Petersburg's hottest spots for drinking and music are crammed into a crumbling, classical façade. A couple of these places are (or were) owned by Anton Belyankin and Andrei Gradovich – two members of the local ska band Dva Samolyota – which pretty much guarantees great music and a cool vibe.

Sadly, rumours are running rampant that Dumskaya ul is slated as the city's next big renovation project. So this strip of deliciously divey clubs is not long for this world, or at least not this location. So come now, while you still can. Look for a casual crowd, cheap drinks and a good time:

Datscha Shabby chic décor, cheap drinks and a strict 'no house or techno' policy.

Fidel (www.barfidel.ru) This funky place is a sort of musical and alcoholic tribute to the ruler who 'outlived six presidents of America and six leaders of the Soviet Union and Russia'.

Belgrad (http://belgrad-club.livejournal.com) *Bel*-yankin and *Grad*-ovich. Get it? This is your best bet for live music. DJs start playing at 10pm while bands start at midnight.

Second Floor You guessed it: there's more fun upstairs.

loose your inner Ricky Ricardo. Wednesday night is free for 'real Latinos' so make sure you bring your passport if you hail from a Spanish-speaking country.

ISLAND Map pp108–9 Dance

Ostrov; ☎ 328 4857; nab Leytenanta Shmidta 37; cover R300-400; 10pm-6am Fri & Sat; M Vasileostrovskaya

The Island club is on a rather hard-to-reach embankment location on Vasilevsky Island. It is professionally run and aimed at a well-off, fashionable crowd without being pointlessly elitist. There are some superb shows on the revolving dance floors. Music is mainly pop and techno, although big-name DJs occasionally visit.

METRO Map pp146–7 Dance

☎ 776 0210; www.metroclub.ru; 174 Ligovsky pr; cover before 11pm R180-240, after 11pm R240-360; 10pm-6am; M Ligovsky Pr

St Petersburg's most popular spot for teenagers, Metro is a giant venue with three dance floors, featuring Russian and European music downstairs, techno and house on the 2nd floor and the poppiest pop on the top floor. At 2am four nights a week (Monday, Wednesday, Friday and Saturday), male and female dancers clad in leather (at least at the beginning) put on an erotic show. Student nights – Monday and Wednesday – are packed.

MOD Map pp68–9 Live Music & Dance

☎ 881 8371; Konyushennaya pl 2; cover Fri & Sat R150-200; 6pm-6am; M Nevsky Pr

A popular spot for students and other indie types who appreciate the fun and friendly atmosphere, the groovy mix of music (live and spun) and the added entertainment. *Novus,* anyone? (It's like billiards, but not.) If you don't find something you like, head next door to the new (and promising) Achtung Baby.

REVOLUTION Map pp68–9 Dance

☎ 571 2391; www.revolutionclub.ru; Sadovaya ul 28; men/women R300/150; 10pm-6am; M Gostiny Dvor

There's no better place to watch the sunrise than from the top floor of Revolution. The glass-enclosed 'winter garden' is higher than most other buildings in the vicinity, giving a wonderful 360-degree view of the surrounding city. And if you are here at sunrise, it means you have been dancing all night – easy to do with DJs spinning tunes on two dance floors.

SINNERS Map pp68–9 Gay

Greshniki; ☎ 570 4291; www.greshniki.ru; nab kanala Griboedova 28/1; cover men R0-150, women R300-500; 10pm-6am; M Gostiny Dvor;

Sinners is St Petersburg's gay mainstay – sleazy but fun – featuring male striptease, drag shows and an intriguing on-stage shower show. The décor is leather and chains, evoking a dark dungeon. Three floors include a mirrored dance floor, a balcony overlooking it and a chill-out lounge. The club functions on a card system – you pay for everything when you leave.

TUNNEL CLUB Map pp114–15 Dance

☎ 233 4015; www.tunnelclub.ru; cover R100-230; cnr Zverinskaya ul & Lybansky per; midnight-6am Thu-Sat; M Sportivnaya

Back in the 1990s, Tunnel pioneered techno music in this bastion of old-school rock-and-roll. Closed for several years, the military-themed club reopened in the bomb shelter where it was first born. The setting is spooky but somehow appropriate for the electronica that goes down here.

LIVE MUSIC

St Petersburg is widely considered Russia's best music city – the best place to hear great music, and the best place to be a musician. For local insight, read the interview on p46. Otherwise, check out the many music clubs around the city. Vosstaniya seems to be a centre for contemporary music, but there are venues all around town, and even in the outskirts.

ART-VOKZAL Map pp146–7

☎ 495 9004; www.artvokzal.ru; nab kanala Obvodnogo 138; cover R250-400; 11am-6am; M Baltiyskaya

This innovative new club has retained much of the structure of the factory that formerly occupied this space, so the atmosphere is industrial, gritty and modern. It's a no-frills space for cutting-edge performance art and music. In some cases, 'cutting-edge' might mean adult puppet theatre, in other cases, it could be experimental jazz music: so check the programme before you commit.

CHE Map p92

☎ 277 7600; www.cafeclubche.ru; Poltavskaya ul 3; 🕑 24hr; Ⓜ Pl Vosstaniya

Coffee lounge by day; jam-packed bar by night. This is where you'll find the smart set, slumped in comfy sofas and listening to live music. Art 'happenings' are diverse, ranging from world music to jiving jazz to DJ spins. The food is also excellent (see p170).

EXPERIMENTAL SOUND GALLERY (GEZ-21) Map p92

☎ 764 5258; www.tac.spb.ru; Ligovsky pr 53, 3rd fl; cover R100-150; 🕑 concerts from 9pm; Ⓜ Pl Vosstaniya

You know that a place called 'experimental' is going to be out there, especially as it is part of the alternative art complex at Pushkinskaya 10 (p91). Music ranges from jazz to rock to undefinable, and there are also film screenings, readings and other expressions of creativity. The toilet contains quite an interesting gallery (of sorts).

FISH FABRIQUE Map p92

☎ 164 4857; www.fishfabrique.spb.ru; Ligovsky pr 53, ground fl; 🕑 3pm-6am, concerts from 9pm Thu-Sun; Ⓜ Pl Vosstaniya

You don't get any more scruffy than this museum of local boho life. Here, in the dark underbelly of Pushkinskaya 10 (p91), artists, musicians and wannabes of all ages meet to drink beer and listen to music. Playing table football is also something of a rite of passage for anyone wanting to join the local arts scene. DJs or bands play in the evenings, making this one of the best places to hear punk and other alternative music.

GRIBOEDOV Map p92

☎ 764 4355; www.griboedovclub.ru; Voronezhskaya ul 2a; cover R200; 🕑 noon-6am, concerts 10pm; Ⓜ Ligovsky Pr; 💻 wi-fi

Griboedov is hands-down the longest-standing and most respected music club in the city. Another club in a bomb shelter, this one was founded by the blokes from the local ska band Dva Samolyota. It's a low-key bar in the early evening, gradually morphing into a rowdy club later in the night. Excellent music acts run the gamut from russky rock to reggae to electronica to trance. Upstairs, Griboedov Hill functions as a cool café by day with occasional concerts by night.

MAINA Map p65

☎ 332 0044; www.maina-spb.ru; pr Engelsa 154; cover R100-200; 🕑 concerts 9pm & 11pm; Ⓜ Pr Prosveshcheniya

Maina is out there, geographically speaking. But that does not seem to stop hordes of music-lovers from showing up, feasting on modern, fusion fare and jamming to trendy tunes. Local bands and DJs are on the programme, and the music runs the gamut, including some styles we've never heard of (intelligent lounge? femme-punk?). But it's a daring, innovative place, and the fact that it's out in the docklands makes it all the edgier.

MANHATTAN Map p92

☎ 713 1945; www.manhattanclub.ru; nab reki Fontanki 90; cover R0-200; 🕑 2pm-5am daily, concerts 8pm Wed-Sun; Ⓜ Vladimirskaya; 💻

This 'art-club' features live music and artistic expositions, all in a spacious but run-down basement near the Fontanka River. The atmosphere is laidback and bohemian, although these arty types can get raucous late in the evening, depending on the music. There are often a couple of bands doing sets each evening.

ORLANDINA Map pp114–15

☎ 234 8046; www.orlandina.ru; nab reki Karpovki 5/2; cover R120-300; 🕑 10am-11pm Mon-Fri, 10am-6am Sat, noon-11pm Sun; Ⓜ Petrogradskaya

Opened and owned by the small indie record label, Caravan records, this underground club is perhaps a venue to promote its bands. Nonetheless, it's a pretty slick spot, now in its second location, with a café, bar and music store downstairs, and a concert hall upstairs. The music runs the gamut, with punk, ska, reggae and everything in between.

THE OTHER SIDE Map pp68–9

Drugaya Storona; ☎ 312 9554; www.theotherside.ru; Bolshaya Konyushennaya ul 1; 🕑 noon-last customer, concerts 8pm Sun-Thu, 10pm or 11pm Fri & Sat; Ⓜ Nevsky Pr

What is not to love about this fun and funky 'refuge'? The food is incredibly diverse and uncommonly delicious (see p165 for a full review). And for that matter, so is the nightly entertainment, which ranges from acoustic to jazz to afro to ska, all in the course of a week.

THE PLACE Map pp146–7

☎ 252 4683; www.placeclub.ru; ul Marshala Govorova 47; Ⓜ Baltiyskaya

This area around Baltiyskaya metro is up and coming: while it used to be considered the boonies, it now hosts some of the hippest and most happening venues for art and music. The Place is no exception. Music ranges from folk to funk, while readings, film screenings and art exhibitions are also in the works. The space itself is more upmarket than other such bohemian clubs. With balconies overlooking the stage and an inviting veranda, the Place may appeal to the artsy-fartsy type with upscale tastes.

RED CLUB Map p92

☎ 717 0000; www.clubred.ru; Poltavskaya ul 7; cover R100-350; 🕑 6pm-6am, concerts from 8pm; Ⓜ Pl Vosstaniya

At the end of an alley near the train tracks, this old warehouse is a great venue for all kinds of music – both local groups and lesser-known European bands. The place is pretty barren in terms of décor: the focus is clearly on the music. Concerts take place early in the evening, then the place turns into a dance club, playing R&B and house music until all hours.

ZOCCOLO Map p84

Tsokol; ☎ 274 9467; www.zoccolo.ru; 3-ya Sovetskaya ul 2/3; cover R200-250; 🕑 7pm-midnight Sun-Thu, 7pm-6am Fri & Sat, concerts 8pm; Ⓜ Pl Vosstaniya

The former St Petersburg musical institution Moloko was forced to move and, apparently, changed name as well. Now Zoccolo, it still has a very positive vibe and a great line up of music: indie rock, pop rock, world music, folk, synth-goth-creation, funk-fusion-bossa, latin-hiphop-reggae and, even, 'if-Radiohead-played-punk'. This all goes down in the new urgently orange and green underground space near pl Vosstaniya.

JAZZ CLUBS

During the Soviet period, jazz music was a form of rebellion. Always valuing culture over politics (at least conservative politics), Petersburgers have a particular fondness for this elevated art form. Most of the city's jazz clubs are located in Smolny; besides the places listed here, you can often hear live jazz at Art-Vokzal (p183) and Che (opposite). The annual festival, Jazz Spring, provides a great introduction to jazz in the city.

JAZZ PHILHARMONIC HALL Map p92

☎ 764 8565; www.jazz-hall.spb.ru; Zagorodny pr 27; cover R100-200; 🕑 concerts 7pm Wed-Sun, Ellington Hall concerts 8pm Tue, Fri & Sat; Ⓜ Vladimirskaya

Founded by legendary jazz violinist and composer David Goloshchokin, this venue represents the more traditional side of jazz. Two resident bands perform straight jazz and Dixieland in the big hall, which seats up to 200 people. The smaller Ellington Hall is used for occasional acoustic performances. Foreign guests also appear doing mainstream and modern jazz. Drinks and light snacks available.

JFC JAZZ CLUB Map p84

☎ 272 9850; www.jfc.sp.ru; Shpalernaya ul 33; cover R150-300; 🕑 concerts 7pm; Ⓜ Chernyshevskaya

Very small and very New York, this cool club is the best place in the city to hear modern, innovative jazz music, as well as the occasional blues, bluegrass, funk, fusion and even folk. The space is tiny, so book a table if you want to sit down. Otherwise, you can always stand at the bar (which is less expensive). The menu is limited to drinks and snacks.

RED FOX JAZZ CAFÉ Map p84

Krasniy Lis; ☎ 275 4214; www.rfjc.ru; ul Mayakovskogo 50; cover R60-100; 🕑 10.30am-11pm Mon-Fri, 2-11pm Sat & Sun; Ⓜ Chernyshevskaya

The newest addition to St Pete's jazz scene is the fun and friendly Red Fox Jazz Café, a subterranean space that showcases jazz in the old-fashioned sense: big band, bebop, ragtime and swing music. Sunday changes it up with a jam session, featuring anybody who wants to participate. The menu is extensive and affordable.

SUNDUK Map p84

☎ 272 3100; wwww.cafesunduk.ru; Furshtatskaya 42; cover R100; 🕑 10am-last customer; Ⓜ Chernyshevskaya

This café promises 'art' and it delivers: live music fills up this tiny space every night from 8.30pm to 11pm. It's mostly blues and jazz, with the occasional chanteuse singing more poppy tunes. If this is not arty enough for you, check out the bathrooms. See p168 for a full restaurant review.

THE ARTS

top picks

The classical performing arts are one of the biggest draws to St Petersburg. Highly acclaimed professional artists stage productions in elegant theatres around the city, most of which have been recently revamped and look marvellous. Seeing a Russian opera or ballet in a magnificent baroque theatre makes for a magical night out, and Russian symphonic music is among the world's most moving.

While such shows remain an incredible bargain in other parts of the country, performing arts in St Petersburg is big business. The most popular theatres charge 'foreigners' prices', which are significantly more expensive than the price that locals pay. Generally speaking, even the foreigners' prices are still less than you would normally pay in the West for a similar performance, and rest assured that the cheapest tickets in the 'nosebleed' section are dirt cheap, no matter what your passport says.

Nearly all the drama is in Russian, which makes it more difficult for non-Russian-speakers to appreciate. However, the incredible 19th-century interiors and the sense of occasion surrounding the performances mean that seeing a play is an interesting night out, even if you only stay for the first half (and tickets are generally cheap enough to make this perfectly feasible).

The standard way to buy tickets is from a *teatralnaya kassa* (theatre kiosk) which are scattered about the city, from stores like Titanik (p156) or from the individual theatre box offices.

Listings and reviews appear in the *St Petersburg Times* and *In Your Pocket* (see p246).

BALLET & OPERA

Nobody has ever complained about a shortage of Russian classics at the ballet and opera. Take your pick from Tchaikovsky, Prokofiev, Rimsky-Korsakov or one of the other great Russian composers, and you are guaranteed to find him on the playbill at one of the theatres listed here. Choreography and staging of these classics is usually pretty traditional (some might even say uninventive), but then again, that's why they're classics.

Critics complain that the Russian renditions of well-known Western works often seem naive and overly stylised, so steer clear of Mozart. If you tire of Russian classics, keep your eye out for more modern productions and premieres, which are also staged at the Mariinsky and Mussorgsky-Mikhailovsky Theatres.

HERMITAGE THEATRE Map pp68–9

☎ 710 9030; www.hermitagemuseum.org; Dvortsovaya nab 34; Ⓜ Nevsky Pr

This austere neoclassical theatre – once the private theatre of the imperial family – stands on the site of the original Winter Palace of Peter I (p67). At the behest of Catherine the Great, Giacomo Quarenghi designed the theatre to resemble an amphitheatre, with statues of Apollo and the Muses occupying the niches. During the Soviet period, this hall was used more often for lectures and such, but it reopened as a theatre in the 1980s. Appropriate for the setting, performances range from Tchaikovsky to Tchaikovsky. Some of the musical festivals (see p16) also use this venue for performances.

MARIINSKY THEATRE Map p102

☎ 326 4141; www.mariinsky.ru; Teatralnaya pl 1; tickets R300-2000; ⏲ box office 11am-7pm, performances 7pm; Ⓜ Sennaya Pl

The most celebrated and most spectacular venue for ballet and opera in St Petersburg, the Mariinsky Theatre is an attraction in its own right, whether or not you manage to get tickets to see a performance. Known as the Kirov Ballet during the Soviet era, the dance company confusingly still tours the world under this name, as its Soviet-era association with Nureyev, Baryshnikov et al brings more ticket sales!

Despite this odd tie to the past, the current general and artistic director Valery Gergiev has led the venue bravely into the modern world. In 2004, plans were finally signed off to build a new theatre, known as Mariinsky II (see p57), behind the current building, attracting praise and derision from the usual quarters. The new venue is expected to be completed by 2009, although the original theatre will continue to function throughout the construction period. Recent artistic successes include the staging of Dmitry Shostakovich's first opera, *The Nose*.

MUSSORGSKY-MIKHAILOVSKY THEATRE Map pp68–9

☎ 545 4284; www.mikhailovsky.ru; pl Iskusstv 1; Ⓜ Nevsky Pr

While not quite as grand as the Mariinsky, this stage still delivers the Russian ballet or operatic experience, complete with multi-tiered theatre, frescoed ceiling and elaborate concerts. The inspiring pl Iskusstv (Arts Sq; p74) is a lovely setting for this respected venue, which is home to the State Academic Opera & Ballet Company. It's generally easier and cheaper to get tickets to the performances staged here than those at the Mariinsky.

YUSUPOV PALACE THEATRE Map p102

☎ 314 9883; www.yusupov-palace.ru; nab reki Moyki 94; Ⓜ Sadovaya

Housed inside the outrageously ornate Yusupov Palace (p102), this elaborate yet intimate venue was the home entertainment centre for one of the city's foremost aristocratic families. While you can visit the theatre when you tour the palace, seeing a performance here is a treat, as you can imagine yourself the personal guest of crazy Prince Felix himself. The shows are a mixed bag – usually a 'Gala Evening' that features fragments of various Russian classics.

CLASSICAL MUSIC

It's not unusual to see highly talented musicians working the crowds inside the metro stations, violinists single-handedly performing Vivaldi's *Four Seasons* and flautists whistling away at Mozart or Bach. That such talented musicians are busking in the streets (or under the streets, as the case may be) is testament to the incredible talent and training of Russian music students – and to the lack of resources of their cultural institutions. While it's possible to hear a good show in the metro station, a visit to one of the local orchestra halls is highly recommended. Besides the venues listed here, small-scale concerts are often hosted at the Vorontsov Palace (p75) and the Beloselsky-Belozersky Palace (p94).

GLINKA CAPELLA HOUSE Map pp68–9

☎ 314 1058; nab Reki Moyki 20; Ⓜ Nevsky Pr

This historic hall was constructed for the city's oldest professional choir, the Emperor Court Choir Capella, which was founded in 1473. Originally based in Moscow, it was transferred to St Petersburg upon the order of Peter the Great in 1703. These days, performances focus on choral and organ music.

GRAND CONCERT HALL Map p84

Bolshoy Kontsertny Zal (BKZ); ☎ 275 1300; www.bkz.spb.ru; Ligovsky pr 6; Ⓜ Pl Vosstaniya

This massive complex near pl Vosstaniya still often goes by its former name, Oktyabrsky. Seating almost 4000 people, this is the venue for Russian 'stars' with a national following, whether they are pop singers or ballet dancers.

MARIINSKY CONCERT HALL Map p102

☎ 326 4141; www.mariinsky.ru; ul Pisareva 20; Ⓜ Sadovaya/Sennaya Pl

In April 2007, Mariinsky director Valery Gergiev and the Mariinsky Theatre Symphony Orchestra opened the new Mariinsky Concert Hall – just in time for the annual Stars of White Nights Festival. The new building is a magnificent multifaceted creation. It preserves the historic brick façade of the set and scenery warehouse that previously stood on this spot facing ul Pisareva, but the modern main entrance, facing ul Dekabristov, is all tinted glass and angular lines, hardly hinting at the beautiful old building behind. The state-of-the-art facility was financed primarily by private investors, including Moscow Mayor Yury Luzhkov.

RIMSKY-KORSAKOV CONSERVATORY Map p102

☎ 571 0506; www.conservatory.ru; Teatralnaya pl 3; Ⓜ Sadovaya/Sennaya Pl

This illustrious music school – opposite the Mariinsky – was the first public music school in Russia. Founded in 1862, it counts Pyotr Tchaikovsky amongst its alumni and Nikolai Rimsky-Korsakov among its former faculty. Dmitry Shostakovich and Sergei Prokofiev are graduates of this institution, as are countless contemporary artistic figures, such as Mariinsky director Valery Gergiev. The Bolshoy Zal (Big Hall) on the 3rd floor is an excellent place to see the performances by up-and-coming musicians, which take place throughout the academic year.

SHOSTAKOVICH PHILHARMONIA Map pp68–9

www.philharmonia.spb.ru; Ⓜ Nevsky Pr

Under the artistic direction of world-famous conductor Yury Temirkanov, the St Petersburg Philharmonic Orchestra represents

EARLY MUSIC FESTIVAL

Marc de Mauny is a violinist with a strong interest in baroque and jazz music. In the 1990s, he was working for the British Council on cultural programmes in St Petersburg. Andrey Reshetin was a rock violinist who had been playing in the group Akvarium. Reshetin's creative development followed a path from rock to baroque, and he later founded the city's first baroque ensemble. When the two musicians discovered their overlap in interest, they came up with the idea to develop a festival celebrating baroque, medieval and other early music, now known as Early Music Festival (p19). We spoke to Marc about the development of the festival and early music in St Petersburg.

Why did you want to make a festival focusing on baroque and medieval music?
In Russia there is a strong musical focus on 19th and 20th century composition – and especially Russian composers. Our objective was to introduce the music of previous centuries and take advantage of its immense, rich musical legacy.

Why is St Petersburg fertile ground for such a project?
This city was born in the 18th century. It did not develop organically like Moscow. Peter the Great was determined to build this city according to a precise plan. It was built from scratch over the course of a few years and organised around 18th-century ideas. This space – the urban space – was crying out for more music from the same period.

Was the festival well received?
From day one. We have always attracted top names – the most talented individuals playing this kind of music. In 2007, we celebrated our 10-year anniversary. And now there are simultaneous festivals in Moscow, Nizhny Novgorod and all around the country.

What is the best way for visitors to St Petersburg to hear baroque and medieval music?
They should come in September and attend the events of the festival! At other times, there is much less early music being played in St Petersburg. But as a cultural form, early music has taken root. There is a strong following in the city and I am certain it will continue to develop. Now even Gergiev at the Mariinsky – and other directors at established institutions – are occasionally incorporating it into their repertoires.

the finest in orchestral music. The **Bolshoy Zal** (Grand Hall; ☎ 710 4257; Mikhailovskaya ul 2) on pl Iskusstv is the venue for a full program of symphonic performances, while the nearby **Maly Zal** (Small Hall; ☎ 571 8333; Nevsky pr 30) hosts smaller ensembles. Both venues are used for numerous music festivals, including the superb **Early Music Festival** (p19). The philharmonic is closed in July and August.

SMOLNY CATHEDRAL Map p84

☎ 271 9182; www.cathedral.ru; pl Rastrelli 3/1; Ⓜ Chernyshevskaya

Although the Smolny Cathedral (p83) was closed for renovation at the time of research, it is usually a venue for musical concerts. While not as attractive as some of the other concert halls in the city (and certainly not as ornate as its gorgeous exterior), it is still an atmospheric place to hear music.

THEATRE

Due to the language barrier, drama and comedy are less alluring prospects than music and dance. Nonetheless, St Petersburg has a long tradition in theatre, which remains vibrant today. Dozens of venues host local, national and international acting troupes. Performances are almost exclusively in Russian, but the repertoire is vast, from William Shakespeare to Anton Chekhov to Neil Simon and everything in between.

AKIMOVA COMEDY THEATRE

Map pp68–9

☎ 312 4555; www.komedia.spb.ru; Nevsky pr 56; Ⓜ Gostiny Dvor

Housed inside the incredible **Eliseevsky** (p152) building, this is a great place to see contemporary and classic comedies, including works by Neil Simon, Oscar Wilde and Mikhail Bulgakov.

ALEXANDRINSKY THEATRE

Map pp68–9

☎ 710 4103; www.alexandrinsky.ru; pl Ostrovskogo 2; Ⓜ Gostiny Dvor

Formerly the Pushkin State Drama Theatre, this magnificent venue is just one part of an immaculate architectural ensemble designed by Carlo Rossi (see pl Ostrovskogo, p75). The theatre's interior oozes 19th-century elegance and style, and it's worth taking a peek even if you don't see a production here. This is where Anton Chekhov premiered *The Seagull,* which was pretty much universally hated by the public and critics alike. These days, the company has a huge repertoire, ranging from Russian folktales to Shakespearean tragedies.

BALTIC HOUSE Map pp114–15

Baltiisky Dom; ☎ 232 9380; www.baltichouse.spb.ru; Alexandrovsky Park 4; Ⓜ Gorkovskaya
Known under the Soviets as Lenin Konsomol Theatre, this large venue has long hosted an annual festival of plays from the Baltic countries. Renamed in 1991, Baltic House also stages Russian and European plays, as well as a new and growing repertoire of experimental theatre.

BOLSHOY DRAMA THEATRE
Map pp68–9

BDT; ☎ 310 0401; www.bdt.spb.ru; nab reki Fontanki 65; Ⓜ Sennaya Pl
Named for acting pioneer Georgi Tovstonogov, the BDT became the city's most innovative and exciting theatre under his direction between the 1960s and the 1980s. His 1957 staging of Fyodor Dostoevsky's *The Idiot* is still remembered as one of the peaks of Soviet theatre. Unfortunately, when Tovstonogov died in 1989, a suitable replacement was not found. As such, the theatre company has not really progressed since that time. Nonetheless, the theatre is one of the city's grandest, and its location on the Fontanka River is delightful.

KOMISSARZHEVSKAYA THEATRE
Map pp68–9

☎ 571 0849; www.teatrvfk.ru; Italiyanskaya ul 19; Ⓜ Gostiny Dvor
Now buried in Tikhvin Cemetery (p90), Vera Fedorovna Kommisarzhevskaya was a great St Petersburg actress who gained her reputation as leading lady in Vsevolod Meyerhold performances. In the early years of the 20th century, Kommisarzhevskaya founded an acting troupe that performed in the Passage concert hall, staging plays by all of the famous playwrights of the day, including Mikhail Gorky and Anton Chekhov. Revived in the midst of the Siege, the theatre was renamed in honour of the great actress. These days, headed by artistic director Victor Novikov, it is known for its modern treatment of classic plays.

LENSOVET THEATRE Map p92

☎ 713 2191; Vladimirsky pr 12; Ⓜ Mayakovskaya
The LenSovet is among the more versatile theatre companies in town, staging performances of classical favourites as well as bold new experiments. Director Vladislav Pazi has received excellent reviews for his renditions of – among others – *A King, a Queen and a Jack,* based on the novel by Vladimir Nabokov, and *Lovely Sunday for a Picnic* by Tennessee Williams. Equally celebrated are some of the plays performed under guest directorship, including Samuel Beckett's *Waiting for Godot* (V Ozhidaniy Godo) and Harold Pinter's *The Lover* (Lyubovnik).

MALY DRAMA THEATRE Map p92

☎ 713 2028; www.mdt-dodin.ru; ul Rubinshteyna 18; Ⓜ Vladimirskaya
Also called the Theatre of Europe, the Maly is St Petersburg's most internationally celebrated theatre. Its director Lev Dodin is famed for his long version of Fyodor Dostoevsky's *The Devils,* which toured the world to great acclaim. He also got rave reviews for his version of Anton Chekhov's *Play Without a Name,* a superb *mise en scène* production that is sometimes subtitled in English for visitors during summer.

PRIYUT KOMEDIANTA THEATRE
Map pp68–9

☎ 310 3314; Sadovaya ul 27/9; Ⓜ Sennaya Pl
This delightful theatre's name means 'the actor's shelter' and it does a pretty good job of fulfilling its role, providing refuge for some of the city's best up-and-coming directors and producers. It was founded by actor Yury Tomashevsky in the late 1980s, when the city turned over a defunct cinema that the group still uses. Recent successes have included Peter Shereshevsky's adaptation of Fyodor Dostoevsky's *The Eternal Husband* and Georgy Vasiliev's ambitious staging of Viktor Yerofeyev's *Moscow Stations,* a sort of Russian *Trainspotting*. The theatre is slated for renovation in 2009.

MUSICAL THEATRE

While Russia does not have a musical theatre tradition in the 'Broadway' sense of the genre, there are a few theatres in St Petersburg that host folk shows and other musical variety acts.

FEEL YOURSELF RUSSIAN Map p102

☎ 312 5500; www.folkshow.ru; Nikolaevsky Palace, ul Truda 4; tickets R1280; show 6.30pm; Ⓜ Nevsky Pr

Terrible title, but not a bad show of traditional Russian folk dancing and music. The two-hour show features four different folk groups, complete with accordion, balalaika and Cossack dancers. It is worth attending to get a look inside the spectacular Nikolaevsky Palace, if nothing else.

MUSICAL COMEDY THEATRE
Map pp68–9

☎ 313 4316; Italiyanskaya ul 13; Ⓜ Nevsky Pr

Formerly the Palace Theatre, this neoclassical beauty on pl Iskusstv (Arts Sq; p74) was built in 1801 as a palace. Only in the 20th century was it redesigned, and it opened as a theatre in 1912. It is famous as one of the few theatres that stayed open throughout the blockade. Recently renovated, the place still retains the opulent atmosphere of a palace, with a gorgeous gala staircase and a famous 'grotto buffet'. These days it hosts a wide variety of musical and theatrical performances, including crowd-pleasing classical ballets and operas.

CIRCUSES & PUPPET SHOWS

To entertain your kids the good old-fashioned Russian way, take them to the circus or to one of the many impressive puppet theatres in town.

BOLSHOY PUPPET THEATRE
Map p84

☎ 272 8215; ul Nekrasova 10; tickets R50-60; Ⓜ Chernyshevskaya

This 'big' puppet theatre is indeed the biggest in the city, and has been active since 1931. The repertoire includes a wide range of shows for children and adults. Don't forget: you can get free tickets if you are staying next door in the Puppet Hostel (p208).

CIRCUS IN AVTOVO Map p65

☎ 783 1501; Avtovskaya ul 1A; tickets R100-400; Ⓜ Avtovo

This place is on the far southern outskirts of the city and it may take quite a journey to get here. But how far are you willing to go to see no-rules wrestling (only in Russia…)? Avtovo also hosts children's circus clubs and an annual international festival of circus schools. What a way to inspire your children to become tightrope walkers and lion tamers!

DEMMENI MARIONETTE THEATRE
Map pp68–9

☎ 571 2156; Nevsky pr 52; tickets R50-60; Ⓜ Gostiny Dvor

Since 1917, this venue under the arches on central Nevsky is the city's oldest professional puppet theatre. Mainly for children, the shows are well produced and professionally performed.

ST PETERSBURG STATE CIRCUS
Map pp68–9

☎ 314 8478; www.circus.spb.ru; nab reki Fontanki 3; tickets R100-600; Ⓜ Gostiny Dvor

The oldest and best established circus in the city, dating to 1827, occupies an ornate building on the Fontanka River. The performances, running about 2½ hours, usually tell a story based on a fairy tale or folklore. This venue also hosts circus troupes from other cities and countries.

CINEMA

While Hollywood blockbusters seem to be wildly popular, films are rarely shown in English: they are usually dubbed in Russian, and poorly at that. That said, subtitled films are occasionally shown; check the *St Petersburg Times* for current listings. Also, there are several foreign film festivals run by cultural centres such as the Alliance Française, Goethe Institute and British Council, with films often shown in the original language. See p50 for information about larger film festivals in St Petersburg.

AVRORA Map pp68–9

☎ 315 5254; www.avrora.spb.ru; Nevsky pr 60; Ⓜ Gostiny Dvor

Opening in 1913 as the Piccadilly Picture House, this was the city's most fashionable cinema in the early years of Russian film, and it has retained its position pretty consistently ever since. Renamed the more Soviet-sounding Avrora in 1932, it was here that a young Dmitry Shostakovich played piano accompaniment to silent movies. Today it's one of the best cinemas in town, and most premieres (to which you can nearly always buy tickets) take place here.

DOM KINO Map pp68–9

House of Cinema; ☎ 314 0638; www.domkino.spb.ru; Karavannaya ul 12; Ⓜ Gostiny Dvor

This cinema shows arty Russian and foreign films, as well as some higher brow Hollywood productions. It is also where the British Council holds its British Film Festival. Under renovation at the time of research, the whole place remains remarkably Soviet in a charming way.

JAM HALL ON PETROGRADSKY Map pp114–15

☎ 703 7414; www.jamhall.ru; Kamennoostrovsky pr 42; Ⓜ Petrogradskaya

Now this is the kind of place that could never have existed in 20th-century Russia. An old palace of culture has been transformed into a luxury cinema-going experience. With plush sofa-style seating, tables for your drinks and a well-stocked bar on site, this is the future – and we like it. Pity it mainly shows Hollywood blockbusters dubbed into Russian. There is another **Jam Hall on Leninsky** (off Map pp146–7; ☎ 703 7404; Leninsky pr 160; Ⓜ Moskovskaya).

MIRAGE UNIVER-CITY Map pp114–15

☎ 498 0758; www.mirage.ru; Bolshoy pr 35; Ⓜ Chkalovskaya; 💻

All the entertainment you ever need – under one roof. Come here to watch a film, eat sushi, play pool, hear live music (Thursday and Friday night) or surf the web (see p244). The films are generally the latest from Hollywood, but you are unlikely to see anything in English.

SPORTS & ACTIVITIES

top picks

- **Sunday-morning bike tour with Skat Prokat** (p199)
- **Zenith football match at Petrovsky Stadium** (p200)
- **Banya at Circle Baths** (p197)
- **Ice skating on Yelagin Island** (p198)
- **Splashing around at Waterville Aquapark** (p197)

SPORTS & ACTIVITIES

Traditionally, physical fitness is not exactly a priority in Russia, which is a kind of antithesis to Wellville. Exercise was always reserved for sportsmen and soldiers, while somebody running on the street was invariably trying to catch a bus. As in all areas of life, however, times are changing in this workout underworld. Russians – some of them, at least – are discovering the joys of health and wellness, not to mention the fun of an active lifestyle.

HEALTH & FITNESS

The number of gyms and fitness centres in St Petersburg is growing, but these private clubs are generally out of the price range of everyday middle-class Russians. Whether for reasons financial or cultural, attendance at such facilities is much lower than in the West. The same is not true of the Russian *banya* (bathhouse), which is still a popular way for Russians to relax and socialise. It is a uniquely Russian activity that all visitors should experience.

GYMS & POOLS

Most public swimming pools require bathers to obtain a health certificate prior to going in the water. There is usually an on-site doctor who can provide the necessary paperwork for a small fee (and sometimes without any sort of examination), as long as you look healthy.

FITNESS HOUSE Map pp108–9

☎ 715 8715; www.fitnesshouse.spb.ru; nab Makarova 2; one-time entry R1000, one-month membership R5000; 🕑 7am-11pm Mon-Fri, 9am-10pm Sat & Sun; Ⓜ Nevsky Pr

In a prominent place opposite the Strelka, this upscale gym offers a slew of fitness classes, from yoga to pilates to body sculpting. The huge complex has a dedicated room for every kind of equipment, including stationary bikes, cardio equipment and free weights. A sauna and spa are also on site, as is the lively Greenwich Pub.

PLANET FITNESS – PETROGRAD SIDE

Map pp114–15

☎ 332 0000; www.fitness.ru; Petrogradskaya nab 18; one-time entry R930-1240; 🕑 24hr; Ⓜ Petrogradskaya

The city's biggest Planet Fitness outlet is on the Petrograd Side in the prestigious City Centre business centre. Its facilities include a big swimming pool, tennis courts and the requisite machines. Classes include standards such as yoga and spinning, as well as more exotic fare like kickboxing and karate. For relaxation, finish up with a massage or a visit to the sauna. Rates are cheaper before 5pm.

PLANET FITNESS – SENNAYA

Map p97

☎ 315 6220; www.fitness.ru; Kazanskaya ul 37; 🕑 7am-11pm Mon-Fri, 9am-9pm Sat & Sun; Ⓜ Sadovaya

While rates and facilities differ dramatically between Planet Fitness locations, the outlet near Isaakievskaya pl (St Isaac's Sq) is among the most central and least costly. Facilities include weights and cardio equipment, as well as a steamy sauna.

PLANET FITNESS – SMOLNY

Map p84

☎ 275 1384; www.fitness.ru; nab Robespiera 12; 🕑 7am-11pm Mon-Fri, 9am-9pm Sat & Sun; Ⓜ Chernyshevskaya

St Petersburg's first and largest chain of fitness centres now has 11 locations around the city, but the first was in Smolny. Classes include aerobics and yoga, while weights machines and cardio equipment are also available. The cardio room overlooks the Neva River, offering a lovely view as you cycle or run. Afterwards, enjoy the sauna and hot tub, or a fresh fruit drink from the juice bar.

SPORTS COMPLEX Map pp114–15

☎ 232 8377; Kronverksky pr 9A; entry R300, medical exam R200; 🕑 6.30am-11pm; Ⓜ Gorkovskaya

While the new chains of private fitness centres cater to New Russians and other people with fancy pants, most people with athletic tendencies spend time at someplace similar to this sports complex, which is the Russian version of the YMCA. It's not as shiny and new as the private clubs, but the 25m swimming pool under a glass roof is heavenly.

Other facilities include weights, aerobics classes and clubs for every sport imaginable.

VMF POOL Map pp108–9

☎ 322 4505; Sredny pr 87; entry R350; 7am-9pm; M Vasileostrovskaya

Another old-school facility that is out of the way on Vasilevsky Island. Nonetheless, the huge pool was renovated in 2007 and now offers an excellent place to swim laps or cool down.

WATERVILLE AQUAPARK Map pp108–9

☎ 324 4700; www.waterville.ru; ul Korablestroiteley 14; adult/child Mon-Fri R500/350, Sat & Sun R700/530; 9am-11pm; M Primorskaya

Calling all kids! This huge complex at the Park Inn – Pribaltiyskaya (p211) features miles of water slides and rides, waterfalls, jet streams and wave pools. There is something for everyone here, as special pools for younger children have shallow waters and warmer temperatures, while a two-lane 25m pool is dedicated to water aerobics and lap-swimming (aka 'adult swim'). Also on site: an international 'sweating complex' featuring Russian *banya*, Finnish sauna, Turkish *hammam* and Indian sauna. Prices quoted are for four hours of fun, but all-day admission is also available.

BANYA

Nothing beats St Petersburg winter like the *banya* (bathhouse). Less hot but more humid than a sauna, the Russian bath sweats out all impurity, cleansing body and soul.

Enter the *parilka* (steam room) stark naked (yes, the *banya* is normally segregated by gender). Bathers can control the temperature – or at least increase it – by ladling water onto the hot rocks. You might add a few drops of eucalyptus to infuse the steam with scent. Then sit back and watch the mercury rise. To eliminate toxins and improve circulation, bathers beat each other with a bundle of birch branches, known as *veniki*. When you can't take the heat, retreat. A public *banya* allows access to a plunge pool, usually filled with ice-cold water. The contrast in temperature is invigorating, energising and purifying.

The *banya* has always been essential for surviving the coldest Russian months. (Apparently, in the early days, Peter the Great was often sighted running naked from the bathhouse to jump in the Neva.)

A *banya* is not complete without a table spread with snacks, or at least a thermos of tea. And just when you think you have recovered, it's time to repeat the process. As they say in Russia, '*S lyokum parom*': Easy steaming!

A few old-fashioned *bani* are recommended following. See also Gyms & Pools (opposite) and Spas (p198) for facilities that may have a sauna or *banya* on site.

CIRCLE BATHS Map pp122–3

Kruglye Bani; ☎ communal 550 0985, private 297 6409; ul Karbysheva 29a; communal per person R25, lux per person R320, private R800; 8am-10pm Fri-Tue; M Pl Muzhestva

Among the city's classiest communal bathhouses, the Circle Baths has a heated circular open-air pool. The 'lux' *banya* is an upgraded communal option, segregated by gender with certain days designated for men or women, so call in advance to find out the schedule. Otherwise, you can reserve a private *parilka* for up to four people, open around the clock

KAZACHIE BANI Map p97

☎ 712 5079; Bolshoy Kazachy per 11; per hour R1000; 24hr; M Pushkinskaya

Following a trend that is occurring throughout the city, the communal *banya* is no longer open, but the private 'lux'

EASY STEAMING

The dos and don'ts of the *banya* (bathhouse):

- Do take advantage of the plunge pool (or at least the cold shower, if there is no pool on site). It's important to bring your body temperature back down after being in the *banya*.
- Don't bother with a bathing suit. Most public *bani* are segregated by gender, in which case bathers steam naked. In mixed company, it is customary to wrap yourself in a sheet (provided at the *banya*).
- Do rehydrate in between steams. While it is customary to drink tea, or even beer, it is also important to drink water or juice.
- Don't stop at one! Most bathers will return to the *parilka* (steam room) anywhere from three to eight times over the course of an hour or two.

banya is an excellent option for a group of up to 10 people.

MYTNINSKAYA BANYA Map p84
☎ 274 4229; Mytninskaya ul 17-19; per hour R850; 24hr by reservation; M Pl Vosstaniya
Unique in the city, Mytninskaya Banya is heated by a wood furnace, just like the log-cabin bathhouses that are still found in the Russian countryside. In addition to *parilka* and plunge pool, the private 'lux' *banya* includes a swanky lounge area with leather furniture and a pool table.

SECOND COURTYARD Map pp108–9
Vtoroy Dvor; ☎ 321 6441; www.dvor.boom.ru in Russian; nab Leytenanta Shmidta 29; public per person R300, private per hr R1100; public 10am-4pm, private bookings 4pm-10am; M Vasileostrovskaya
The name of this place refers to its location, tucked into the second courtyard behind an apartment block on the Vasilevsky Island embankment. The small but sparkling facility includes a Finnish sauna and Russian steam room, as well as a small plunge pool. It's a public *banya* by day, but in the evening you can book the whole place out for your private party (up to eight people). A small on-site kitchen provides catering services, so you don't have to bring your own snacks.

SPAS

An upscale spa might have a Russian *banya* on site, however, a visit to such a facility is a completely different experience – with all of the delicious decadence of indulgence, but none of the democratic charm of the traditional *banya*.

BEAUTY FORMULA Map pp122–3
Formula Krasoty; ☎ 295 0436; www.salon-spa.spb.ru; Novolitovskaya ul 15a; by appointment; M Lesnaya
Indulge yourself at this amazing, all-in-one day spa. Whether you need a massage, a facial or a new tattoo, you can get it at this upmarket facility in the Akvilon business centre. In addition to the extensive menu of treatments, there is a Turkish bath, a Finnish sauna and a Russian *banya*.

THAI MASSAGE Map pp146–7
☎ 710 1451; www.e-med.spb.ru; Podolskaya ul 40; by appointment; M Tekhnologichesky Institut
Thai massage is a body treatment that is carried out by massage and medical therapists to give greater immunity to illness and better health. Similar to acupuncturists, massagists concentrate their efforts on a localised part of the body in order to activate trigger points and stimulate blood flow to the specific site. Advocates claim that the benefits are immediate. A visit to this clinic is not your typical relaxing massage session, but it may remedy what ails you.

ACTIVITIES

Ice skating, sledding and skiing are forms of entertainment that date back to St Petersburg's earliest days, as the aristocrats found plenty of fun to entertain themselves during the cold winter.

St Petersburg is still a great place to engage in such traditional activities, especially if you are here in winter. The younger generation has also discovered the appeals of other more Western activities, such as cycling and in-line skating. They are perhaps not as widespread as in European and American cities, but it is not unusual to see active types speeding along St Petersburg's sidewalks and streets.

ICE SKATING, SKIING & SLEDDING

There's no shortage of winter in St Petersburg, so take advantage of it. Several indoor and outdoor venues offer the opportunity to rent ice skates and see where all those great Russian figure skaters come from. Or if you prefer a softer landing, St Petersburg's parks offer miles of snowy slopes for skiing and sledding.

ICE PALACE Map p65
Ledoviy Dvorets; ☎ 718 6620; www.newarena.spb.ru; pr Pyatiletok 1; weekdays/weekends R270/300; M Pr Bolshevikov
This fancy arena was built for the World Ice Hockey Championships which took place here in 2000. The home arena for the local hockey team SKA (see p200), it also has a public skating rink. Hours are irregular, so call or check the website. Rental of ice skates is included in the price.

YELAGIN ISLAND Map pp114–15
☎ 430 0911; www.elaginpark.spb.ru in Russian; ice skating per hr R100-150; ice skating 11am-9pm; M Krestovsky Ostrov
This car-free island becomes a winter wonderland in colder temperatures, with

sledding, cross-country skiing and ice skating. Skis and skates are both available for hire. In summer months, it's a great place to rent in-line skates as there is no traffic to contend with. See p120 for more information on the island.

SWIMMING & SUNBATHING

Don't forget that St Petersburg – despite the northern clime – is surrounded by water. Of its 40-some islands, several have coastlines facing the Gulf of Finland. For swimming, sunbathing and otherwise escaping the city heat, the best beach is near Sestroretsk. Take an *elektrichka* (suburban train) from Finland Station to this village, from where it is a 10-minute walk through the forest to a long, sprawling beach facing the gulf. Alternatively, Ozerki, a series of small lakes in the northern part of the city have a pleasant coastline and warmer waters. Take the metro to Ⓜ Ozerki and walk west to the lakeshore. See p196 for information on indoor swimming pools.

If you just want to sunbathe, join the crowds on the southern side of Zayachy Island in front of the wall of the Peter & Paul Fortress. Swimming in the Neva River is not advisable, although many people do it and don't appear to die.

CYCLING

Pancake-flat St Petersburg is a great city for cycling (just make sure you avoid the major traffic-choked roads). For good information on cycling events in the city, see the website of the local cycling group VeloPiter (www.velopiter.spb.ru in Russian). A weekly group ride takes place at 11pm on Friday nights in summer, departing from Dvortsovaya pl and traversing the city.

Rent bikes at the shops listed following. Remember to bring your passport and a sizeable chunk of roubles (R3000 to R5000) for a deposit. See p246 for information on bike tours.

SKAT PROKAT Map p92

☎ 717 6838; www.skatprokat.ru; Goncharnaya ul 7; per hr/day R100/400; ⏰ 11am-10pm Sun-Thu, 24hr Fri & Sat; Ⓜ Pl Vosstaniya

This tight-run outfit offers excellent Sunday-morning bike tours of the city (see p246). Rental bicycles are brand new mountain bikes by the Russian company Stark. Weekend or weekly rates are also available. Or, if you are in town for a while, this place also sells second-hand bikes.

VELOCITY Map pp68–9

☎ 922 6383; www.velocity-spb.ru; Nevsky pr 3; per hr/day R100/400; ⏰ 10am-10pm; Ⓜ Nevsky Pr

The price of bike rental includes use of an mp3-player and a route map, so bikers can take a self-guided tour. Other offers include an all-night ride (summer only), two-for-one discounts at designated times and used bikes for sale. Enter through the courtyard.

BOWLING & BILLIARDS

Bowling has become a popular entertainment option in St Petersburg, with vast complexes offering bowling and billiards, as well as bars, video games and – in some cases – dancing.

BOWLING CITY Map p97

☎ 380 3005; www.bowlingcity.ru; ul Yefimova 3; per hr R360-960; ⏰ 24hr; Ⓜ Sadovaya/Sennaya Pl

This is the most central outlet of a network of bowling clubs, which provides countless entertainment options including bowling and billiards. Besides the 36 bowling lanes, there is karaoke, a sports bar and pool tables. Rates vary according to time, meaning that it's more expensive to play in the evenings and on weekends. The website is also a vast repository for information about bowling in Russia.

SPECTATOR SPORT

Russia's international reputation in sport is well founded, with athletes earning international fame and glory for their success in hockey, gymnastics and figure skating. In 2007, all of Russia was reeling from the announcement that the 2014 Winter Olympics would take place in Sochi, in southern Russia. St Petersburg governor Valentina Matvienko responded almost immediately, declaring that St Petersburg would propose itself as a candidate for the 2020 Summer Games (a second attempt after an unsuccessful bid in 2004).

Anna Kournikova attracted world attention to Russian tennis, but she was known more for her photogenic legs than her ripping backhand. Wimbledon champion Maria Sharapova leads a cohort of young Russians who dominate the women's game. The local favourite is Grand Slam–winner Svetlana Kuznetsova, also known as 'Kuzzi', who was born in Leningrad. Although she lost in the final round of the US Open in 2007, she rose in the rankings to her career-high No 2 in the world.

The St Petersburg Open is an international men's tennis tournament held in St Petersburg every year (see p19). This is where Marat Safin grabbed the attention of the tennis world, when he won in 2000 and 2001, before going on to win four Grand Slam titles.

The most popular spectator sport in Russia is football; the most popular St Petersburg team is **Zenith** (Zenit; www.fc-zenit.ru), which plays in Russia's *vyshaya liga* (premier league). Although Zenith is consistently ranked second behind the Moscow team Spartak, the St Petersburg team has a fan base that's loyal to the point of extremism, which makes for a fun and rowdy crowd at the games. In 2003 Zenith was triumphant, winning the Premier League Cup, but Spartak has won every other year since 1996, so the rivalry is intense. Despite the excellent matchups between the premier league's 15 teams, the most famous Russian football club these days is 'Chel-sky', billionaire Roman Abramovich's entry in the English premier league.

Despite (or maybe because of) the sport's popularity, running a football club in Russia has become a risky business – in the post Soviet-era, seven football officials have been the victims of assassination attempts. Corruption is believed to be rife in the clubs, with match fixing a particular problem.

Popular winter sports include ice hockey and basketball. Both of these sports lose many of their best players to the American professional leagues. The top local team is **Spartak** (www.bcspartak.ru in Russian), though it has not fared very well in Russia's *basketbolnaya super liga* (basketball super league).

In 2005, the National Hockey League (in North America) cancelled its season when players and management were unable to resolve a labour dispute. As a result, 72 players (many of them Russian) came to play in Russia's *super liga* – a windfall of the world's best hockey players. The St Petersburg ice hockey team is **SKA** (Army Sports Club; www.ska.spb.ru).

ICE PALACE Map pp122–3

Ledoviy Dvorets; ☎ 718 6620; www.newarena.spb.ru; pr Pyatiletok 1; weekdays/weekends R270/300; Ⓜ Pr Bolshevikov

The St Petersburg ice hockey team SKA play in this new stadium from September to June. Built for the World Ice Hockey Championships in 2000, this 12,000-seat stadium is a swanky state-of-the-art facility compared to other sports arenas in town. Tickets are available at the box office.

JUBILEE SPORTS PALACE

Map pp114–15

Yubileyny Dvorets Sporta; ☎ 323 9322; pr Dobrolyubova 18; Ⓜ Sportivnaya

This 7000-seat stadium is home to the local basketball team, Spartak, who play here from October to April. Buy tickets at the stadium box office or at a *teatralnaya kassa* (theatre kiosk scattered around the city).

PETROVSKY STADIUM Map pp114–15

☎ 328 8901; www.petrovsky.spb.ru; Petrovsky ostrov 2; tickets R100-500; Ⓜ Sportivnaya

Zenith, St Petersburg's top football team, normally plays at this huge stadium on Petrovsky Island (a small island on the Petrograd Side). The stadium was closed for renovation at the time of research, but is expected to reopen in time for the 2008 season. Tickets can usually be purchased at designated ticket outlets or at the stadium – check the website for the schedule or look for posters plastered around town.

SCC PETERBURGSKY STADIUM

Map p65

☎ 264 8958; pr Gagarina 8; Ⓜ Park Pobedy

This huge facility seats up to 25,000 fans. As such, it is often used for major concerts and sporting events, including the annual St Petersburg Open tennis tournament.

SLEEPING

top picks

- **Alexander House** (p210)
- **Andrey & Sasha's Homestay** (p210)
- **Anichkov Pension** (p205)
- **Hotel Astoria** (p203)
- **Casa Leto** (p203)
- **Nevsky Forum** (p208)
- **Pio on Griboedov** (p206)
- **Rachmaninov Antique Hotel** (p205)

SLEEPING

When choosing a place to lay your head, it is wise to remember two factors: proximity to historic sights, restaurants and bars is always a plus, but so too is easy access to transport. While the Historic Heart is packed with places that cater to all price levels, there are only the two linked metro stations on Nevsky pr, which are a vigorous 20-minute walk from the far corners of the neighbourhood.

Bordering the Historic Heart, Sennaya and Vladimirskaya and Vosstaniya are lively neighbourhoods that are better served by public transport. Liteyny and Smolny and Mariinsky are quaint but quiet neighbourhoods that are a bit further afield, though they each have their charms.

ACCOMMODATION STYLES

The most visible type of accommodation in St Petersburg is that of palatial four- and five-star hotels that have proliferated in the past few years. Priced for the business market, they may be prohibitively expensive for some travellers (although many offer far better deals through travel agents and hotel websites). At the other end of the spectrum, the city has a rather depressing collection of post-Intourist Soviet hotels, which are now slowly adapting to the needs of the modern traveller.

As St Petersburg started to be a popular backpacker destination in the 1990s, hostels began to spring up. This is not Prague, of course, but St Pete now offers a good choice of centrally located and well-run hostels.

Unique to St Petersburg but ubiquitous in the city, mini-hotels are a concept that gained currency in the run-up to the tercentennial celebrations in 2003, when it became abundantly clear that there were insufficient beds in the city for the influx of revellers. Ever-resourceful Russian entrepreneurs started opening up small, family-run hotels, many of which are in renovated apartments in unlikely locations. Today, these mini-hotels are some of the best-value and most atmospheric accommodation options in the city.

LONGER-TERM RENTALS

Anyone spending more than a few days in St Petersburg should consider renting a short-term apartment for the duration of their stay. As well as being financially beneficial (especially if you are travelling in a group), this is a great chance to live life more like the locals, rather than cloistered away in a hotel.

The following agencies and individuals can help you find a flat:

Apartment Reservation Network (☎ in Moscow 495-225 5012; www.apartmentres.com)

City Realty (Map p84; ☎ 570 6342; www.cityrealty.ru; Muchnoy per 2; Ⓜ Nevsky Pr)

Bed & Breakfast (☎ 315 5635; www.bednbreakfast.sp.ru)

Flatmates (www.flatmates.ru) A website for travellers looking for somebody to share short- or long-term accommodation.

HOFA (www.hofa.ru) A time-tested, reliable agency that organises homestays and rental of private flats.

Nevsky Hotels (☎ 703 3860; www.hon.ru)

Zimmer Frei (☎ 973 3757, 273 0867; www.zimmer.ru)

RESERVATIONS

It's wise to reserve a bed in advance, and essential during the summer months when St Petersburg is awash with travellers. It usually suffices to call ahead or send an email, but increasingly hotels will ask for credit card details to guarantee a room. Reservations will sometimes be tied up with visa support (see p249), in which case you may be charged for one night's accommodation in advance in any case.

ROOM RATES

Accommodation listings in this chapter are ordered by neighbourhood, then by budget (from most expensive to least). Prices quoted are high-season rack rates, which are usually in effect from May to September. Prices tend to be at least 20% cheaper from October to April (although prices may also vary within these periods). By using travel agents and hotel booking websites you can usually obtain lower prices at top-end hotels, so it's worth looking into these options for substantial discounts. Prices quoted also include the 18% VAT tax, which is chargeable on hotel rooms in Russia.

Accommodation prices in St Petersburg are often quoted in euros, but payment is usually

PRICE GUIDE

$$$	over €150 (R5250) per night
$$	€50-150 (R1750-5250) per night
$	under €50 (R1750) per night

in roubles. In this guide, we have quoted prices in whatever currency the hotel uses – in some cases euros and in others roubles. Breakfast is included in the price and all rooms have private bathrooms unless otherwise mentioned.

HISTORIC HEART

Many first-time visitors to St Petersburg will spend days without leaving the Historic Heart, with its endless array of museums, churches and canals. There's a huge range of accommodation here, including most of the city's very best hotels, a few excellent budget options and an ever-growing number of idiosyncratic mini-hotels that have opened to cater for the huge demand to stay in the neighbourhood.

WITHIN THE MOYKA

The blocks between the Moyka and the Neva Rivers are crowded with grandiose high-class hotels and modest mini-hotels.

TALEON IMPERIAL HOTEL

Map pp68–9 Boutique Hotel $$$

☎ 324 9911; www.eliseevpalacehotel.com; nab reki Moyki 59; r R10,000-15,000; Ⓜ Nevsky Pr;

In the pre-revolutionary home of the wealthy Yeliseyev family, this hotel (formerly the Eliseev Palace) is a grand, gaudy affair where every tap is gold-plated, every towel monogrammed and every room decorated with real and reproduction antiques. Enjoy the exclusivity of a hotel where all rooms have king-size beds, hydromassage baths and state-of-the-art entertainment systems; some have lovely views across the Moyka River.

HOTEL ASTORIA

Map pp68–9 International Hotel $$$

☎ 313 5757; www.roccofortehotels.com; Bolshaya Morskaya ul 39; s/d €490/550, ste €700-1550; Ⓜ Nevsky Pr;

What the Hotel Astoria has lost of its original Style Moderne décor, it more than compensates for in contemporary style and top-notch service. Little wonder it's beloved by visiting VIPs, from George W Bush to Mick Jagger. The hotel is now part of the Rocco Forte Hotels group and the rooms marry the hotel's heritage character with a more modern design. The best of the suites are sprinkled with antiques and period furniture and have spectacular views onto St Isaac's Cathedral. The same views – at a slightly lower price – are also available next door at the Angleterre Hotel. Breakfast is not included.

CASA LETO Map pp68–9 Mini-Hotel $$$

☎ 314 6622; www.casaleto.com; Bolshaya Morskaya ul 34; r €190-260; Ⓜ Sennaya Pl;

A dramatically lit stone stairwell sets the scene for this discreet and stylish boutique hotel. The Anglo-Italian owners have named the five guest rooms after famous St Petersburg architects (who also happen to have been Italian). With soft pastel shades and plenty of antiques, the spacious, high-ceilinged quarters are deserving of such namesakes. Enjoy plenty of five-star perks, such as king-size beds and heated floors, not to mention free international phone calls.

MOYKA 5 Map pp68–9 Mini-Hotel $$$

☎ 601 0636; www.hon.ru; nab reki Moyki 5; s/d R5950/6650; Ⓜ Nevsky Pr;

The newest property in the chain of Nevsky Hotels is on the Moyka River, behind the Church of the Saviour on Spilled Blood. It's a pretty slick location for a fairly simple hotel, with 24 rooms that provide all the necessary comforts.

COMFORT HOTEL

Map pp68–9 Mini-Hotel $$

☎ 570 6700; www.comfort-hotel.spb.ru; Bolshaya Morskaya ul 25; r from R3920; Ⓜ Nevsky Pr;

This aptly named hotel is indeed comfortable, with 14 cosy rooms, all decorated

top picks

CHEAP SLEEPS

- **Nord Hostel** (p204)
- **St Petersburg International Hostel** (p208)
- **Nils Bed & Breakfast** (p207)
- **Andrey & Sasha's Homestay** (p210)

in a simple, subdued style. The location is excellent – midway between St Isaac's Cathedral, Dvortsovaya pl and Nevsky pr. Alternatively, Herzen Hotel (☎ 315 5550; www.herzen-hotel.ru; r R3600-4600;) is a slightly larger facility of similar standards that is in the same building.

HOTEL SONATA Map pp68–9 Mini-Hotel $$

☎ 315 5112; www.hotel-sonata.com; Gorokhovaya ul 3; r R3500-4200; Ⓜ Nevsky Pr;

Sonata has mini-hotels in several locations around the city, but this one in the Historic Heart is by far the best. The location – just across from the Admiralty and one block from Dvortsovaya pl – is unbeatable. And the 19th-century building retains its historic feel, its high ceilings decorated with ceiling medallions and its floors covered in parquetry. In the same building, the Solo Hotel (☎ 315 9300; www.solo-hotel.ru; Gorokhovaya ul 3; s/d standard R3800/4200, comfort R4100/4600;) offers similar facilities and slightly higher prices.

PRESTIGE HOTEL ON GOROKHOVAYA Map pp68–9 Mini-Hotel $$

☎ 312 0405; www.prestige-hotels.com; Gorokhovaya ul 5; s/d from R2900/4320; Ⓜ Nevsky Pr;

The spire of the Admiralty is an apt logo for this little hotel, as that landmark is just a few steps away. This place provides excellent service and satisfactory accommodation. It lacks a coherent sense of style, however, and the unusual design seems to mix Zen-inspired minimalism with bargain-basement space age.

NEVSKY PROSPEKT B&B Map pp68–9 Mini-Hotel $$

☎ 325 9398; www.bnbrussia.com; Nevsky pr 11, apt 8; s/d with shared bathroom €80/100; Ⓜ Nevsky Pr;

Superbly located and delightfully decorated, this five-room facility is among the city's most charming, with tiled stoves, antique furnishings and the oldest functioning radio and TV you're likely to see anywhere. The English-speaking staff will make you feel right at home, serving breakfast and afternoon tea every day. The only downside is the shared bathroom facilities, which means the rooms are a bit overpriced. Airport transfers are included in the price, but visa support is additional.

NEVSKY INN Map pp68–9 Mini-Hotel $$

☎ 970 4029; www.nevskyinn.ru; Kirpichny per 2, flat 19; s/d Nevsky-1 €75/85, Nevsky-2 €85/95; Ⓜ Nevsky Pr;

Run by joint British-Russian management, this little inn is one of the best bargains in the city. It has two locations that are just around the corner from each other – both in the midst of the hustle and bustle of the city's historic heart. Eleven simple rooms enjoy a straightforward décor and plenty of natural light. All guests have access to kitchen facilities.

NORD HOSTEL Map pp68–9 Hostel $

☎ 571 0342; www.nordhostel.com; Bolshaya Morskaya ul 10; dm/d €24/65; Ⓜ Nevsky Pr;

The ideal location of this discreetly marked hostel – just under the archway from Dvortsovaya pl – is almost too good to be true. An impressive stairwell leads to the friendly 1st-floor hostel, which offers six- or 10-bed dorms, as well as a private double room. All of the rooms have high ceilings, Ikea-style furniture and plenty of natural light, making for a pleasant enough atmosphere. Other facilities include lockers, kitchen, laundry and – should you feel a tune coming on – an upright piano.

HOTEL NAUKA Map pp68–9 Hostel $

☎ 315 3368; Millionnaya ul 27; s €20-30, d €25-40, tr/q €20/26; Ⓜ Nevsky Pr

Soviet-era accommodation is an acquired taste, but if your budget is small and you're willing to forego bourgeois luxury, this good-value, no-frills hostel fits the bill. Advance booking is advised as it can fill up with impecunious academics who, no doubt, feel very much at home in its university dorm-style rooms. Bathrooms are shared and – depending on your room – showers may cost extra. Nobody really speaks English but that may also be part of the fun. Breakfast is not included.

BETWEEN THE MOYKA & THE FONTANKA

The streets between the Moyka and the Fontanka Rivers are at the centre of the action: surrounded by restaurants, bars and shops, and convenient to the Historic Heart's metro stations.

GRAND HOTEL EUROPE

Map pp68–9 International Hotel $$$

☎ 329 6000; www.grandhoteleurope.com; Mikhailovskaya ul 1/7; r from €556, ste from €910; Ⓜ Gostiny Dvor;

One of the world's iconic hotels, the Grand Hotel Europe lives up to its name. Since 1830, when Carlo Rossi united three adjacent buildings with the grandiose façade we see today, little has been allowed to change in this heritage building. No two rooms are the same, but most are spacious and elegant in design. The junior suites are particularly lovely with original patterned parquet floors and smatterings of antiques. Regular guests quite rightly swear by the terrace rooms which afford spectacular views across the city's rooftops.

KEMPINSKI HOTEL MOYKA 22

Map pp68–9 International Hotel $$$

☎ 335 9111; www.kempinski.com; nab reki Moyki 22; r/ste from €415/715; Ⓜ Nevsky Pr;

Kempinski's newest property is a fine addition to St Petersburg's portfolio of luxury hotels. The location on the Moyka River – and practically on the doorstep of the Hermitage – is marvellous. Rooms have a stylish marine theme, with cherry-wood furniture and a handsome navy blue and gold colour scheme. During the day, tour buses crowd the views of Dvortsovaya pl from the better rooms. However, the 360-degree panorama from the rooftop Belle View restaurant and bar is unbeatable (although you'll pay extra for your breakfast).

NEVSKY HOTELS

Map pp68–9 Mini-Hotel $$$

☎ 703 3860; www.hon.ru; Ⓜ Nevsky Pr

This excellent chain of mini-hotels is rapidly expanding to locations all over the centre. These three outlets are all clustered along Bolshaya Konyushennaya ul, a pleasant avenue that runs from Nevsky pr to the Moyka River. The most innovative (and the most expensive) is the Deluxe: taking full advantage of the building's high ceilings, each of the seven rooms has a mezzanine level which serves as the bedroom. The Aster is the cheapest and the largest of the bunch, though it lacks some amenities. In all cases, rooms are comfortable and modern, if a bit plain:

Nevsky Deluxe Hotel (☎ 312 3131; Nevsky 22-24; ste R7350;)

Nevsky Grand Hotel (☎ 312 1206; Bolshaya Konyushennaya ul 10; R5950/6650;)

Nevsky Hotel Aster (☎ 336 6585; Bolshaya Konyushennaya ul 25; s/d R5250/5950)

KORONA Map pp68–9 Mini-Hotel $$

☎ 571 0086; www.korona-spb.com; Malaya Konyushennaya ul 7; s/d from R4700/6100; Ⓜ Nevsky Pr;

With its funny combination of faux marble and citrus colours, some might dismiss the decorative choices at this place as lurid. But there's no faulting the size, location and service at this cut-above-the-average mini-hotel. Unlike some other hotels in this class, the Korona's 11 rooms have plenty of space to spread out.

ANICHKOV PENSION

Map pp68–9 Mini-Hotel $$

☎ 314 7059; www.anichkov.com; Nevsky pr 64, apt 4; s/d from R4680/5860; Ⓜ Gostiny Dvor

In the best tradition of exclusive European pensions, the unsignposted Anichkov is a place for those in the know. On the 3rd floor of a handsome apartment building with an antique lift, this self-styled pension has just six rooms. All are decorated in soft shades of beige and cream with walnut veneer furniture and antique-themed wallpaper. The delightful lounge offers balcony views of the bridge from which the pension takes its name.

PUSHKA INN

Map pp68–9 Boutique Hotel $$

☎ 312 0913; www.pushkainn.ru; nab reki Moyki 14; s/d R3600/6200, apt R8200-10,000; Ⓜ Nevsky Pr;

On a particularly picturesque stretch of the Moyka River, this charming inn is housed in a historic 18th-century building, just next door to the Pushkin Flat-Museum (p72). The rooms are decorated in dusky pinks and caramel tones, with wide floorboards and – if you're willing to pay more – lovely views of the Moyka. Multi-bedroom family-style apartments are also available.

RACHMANINOV ANTIQUE HOTEL

Map pp68–9 Mini-Hotel $$

☎ 327 7466; www.hotelrachmaninov.com; Kazanskaya ul 5; s/d R3600/4100; Ⓜ Nevsky Pr

Perfectly located and beautifully designed, the Rachmaninov Antique is as romantic

SLEEP LIKE A TSAR

Perhaps you have always wanted to sleep in a summer palace. Here is your chance. Peter the Great built his summer palace at Strelna, a town about 24km from St Petersburg (see p219), and now it is Putin's presidential palace. Putin houses his guests on the grounds at the **Baltic Star Hotel** (☎ 438 5700; www.balticstar-hotel.ru; Beriozovaya al 3; s & d €180-390, ste €375-1000, cottage €4200). If it's not otherwise occupied, you could stay here too.

The hotel opened in 2003, when a group of European leaders were in town for a Russia-EU summit. These days it is open to the public.

Besides the 100 well-appointed rooms in the main hotel, there are 18 VIP cottages on the shore of the Gulf of Finland. The cottages, named for different Russian cities, are decorated with original artwork appropriate to the region. Each is equipped with a private dining room, study, sauna, swimming pool and, of course, staff quarters for your entourage.

as the music of its namesake composer. Stuffed full of antiques, the understated rooms nonetheless enjoy a modern feel, with hardwood floors, exposed brick walls and otherwise minimalist décor. The premises are adorned with photography and paintings adorn the premises, which sometimes host gatherings of artists and musicians who are staying in the city.

BELVEDER NEVSKY

Map pp68–9 Mini-Hotel $$

☎ 571 2333; www.belveder-nevsky.spb.ru; Bolshaya Konyushennaya ul 29; s/d R3750/4500; Ⓜ Nevsky Pr; 💻

A little bit different from the cookie-cutter mini-hotels, this Finnish-managed business hotel takes things to the next level. Automatic doors open onto corridors covered with golden, diamond-patterned wallpaper. The effect is dazzling, matched by the efficiency of the English-speaking receptionist. The decoration of the large rooms also veers towards the opulent with gold-striped wallpaper, flowing window drapes and richly patterned bedspreads.

POLIKOFF HOTEL

Map pp68–9 Mini-Hotel $$

☎ 314 7925; www.polikoff.ru; Nevsky pr 64/11; r R3960-4680; Ⓜ Gostiny Dvor

A quiet haven of contemporary cool just steps away from Nevsky pr, the Polikoff Hotel can be hard to find. Enter through the brown door at Karavannaya ul 11 and dial 26. You will find a soothing décor that features subdued lighting, blond-wood veneer and the soft brown and cream tones beloved of modern-design hotels. A few smaller rooms are available at reduced rates – a great find for all those style gurus on a budget.

PIO ON GRIBOEDOV

Map pp68–9 Mini-Hotel $$

☎ 571 9476; www.hotelpio.ru; nab kanala Griboedova 35, apt 5; s/d/tr/q R2800/3100/4200/5000; Ⓜ Nevsky Pr; 💻

A hidden gem overlooking the Griboedov Canal, this pensionlike lodging has only six rooms, each painted in jewel tones and decorated with the utmost simplicity. Big windows look out onto the canal or onto an inner courtyard, allowing plenty of light into the spacious bedrooms, which share access to sparkling new toilets and showers. If Pio is booked out, you can try the less expensive but less appealing **Hotel Grifon** (☎ 315 4916; www.grifonhotel.ru; nab kanala Griboedova 35; s/d from R2390/2590) in the same building.

CUBA HOSTEL Map pp68–9 Hostel $

☎ 921 7115; www.cubahostel.ru; Kazanskaya ul 5; dm R500-650; Ⓜ Nevsky Pr; 💻

This fun and funky hostel has a super location behind the Kazan Cathedral, just next door to **Tinkoff** (p166). Rainbow-coloured paint covers the walls in dorm rooms that are equipped with metal bunk beds and private lockers. Rooms sleep four to 10 people and prices vary accordingly. Shared bathrooms are very cramped, but usually very clean. Staff members are young and eager to please, if sometimes a little overwhelmed. Breakfast is not included, but there is a kitchen available for guests. Visa support costs extra.

LITEYNY & SMOLNY

The area around Liteyny and Smolny is quieter than the other central districts of St Petersburg. It's a good choice for art-lovers, jazz connoisseurs and cost-conscious travellers, but the options for eating and nightlife are limited.

ARBAT NORD HOTEL

Map p84 Boutique Hotel $$$

☎ 703 1899; www.arbat-nord.ru; Artilleriyskaya ul 4; d R6610; Ⓜ Chernyshevskaya;

Facing the unsightly Hotel Rus, the sleek and modern Arbat Nord seems to be showing its neighbour how to run a good establishment. The modern rooms are decorated in gold and green hues, with wood furniture and plenty of space. Efficient English-speaking staff are on hand. An excellent Russian-European restaurant is also on site, which is a good thing, as there is not much else in the vicinity.

AUSTRIAN YARD HOTEL

Map p84 Mini-Hotel $$

☎ 579 8235; www.austrianyard.com; Furshtatskaya ul 45; s/d from R3750/3900; Ⓜ Chernyshevskaya

You must book ahead to stay in the super-secluded place located next to the Austrian consulate. It has four rooms – one on each floor – and they're all good ones. Each is stylishly designed with bright modern furnishings and kitchenettes. Breakfast is a do-it-yourself deal, with plentiful ingredients left in your room so you can eat at any time.

HOTEL VERA

Map p84 Boutique Hotel $$

☎ 702 7206; www.hotelvera.ru; Suvorovsky pr 25/16; economy s €82, classic s/d €119/149; Ⓜ Pl Vosstaniya;

Housed in a fabulous building from 1903, this sweet spot has slanted ceilings, stained glass windows, ceramic tile stoves and ornate mouldings that remember its Art Deco origins. With about 40 rooms, it's an excellent option for travellers who are turned off by the close quarters of a mini-hotel.

ART HOTEL

Map p84 Boutique Hotel $$

☎ 740 7585; www.art-hotel.ru; Mokhovaya ul 27/29; s/d €80/110; Ⓜ Chernyshevskaya;

An ornate wrought-iron gate guards the courtyard of this pre-revolutionary apartment building, now displaying a sort of dilapidated grandeur. Follow the signs to this hidden gem of a hotel, which retains a classical elegance in its 14 rooms. The mood is bourgeois-on-a-budget, with heavy pleated drapes framing the windows, crystal chandeliers and mouldings decorating the ceilings, and a ceramic tile stove in the corridor. In this quiet residential neighbourhood, you are a short walk from the picturesque banks of the Fontanka River and the leafy Summer Garden (p70).

HOTEL SUVEROV

Map p84 Mini-Hotel $$

☎ 271 0859; www.suvorovhotel.spb.ru; 5-ya Sovetskaya ul 3/13; s/d/apt R2850/3350/3400; Ⓜ Pl Vosstaniya;

On a quiet street and behind the enormous Oktyabrsky Concert Hall, this small but welcoming hotel offers excellent value. Housed on the ground floor of an attractive classical building, 20 comfortable rooms offer all the amenities you need, in a modern (albeit bland) setting. Fully renovated apartments (located nearby) are an interesting alternative for families and groups.

NILS BED & BREAKFAST

Map p84 Home-Stay $$

☎ 923 0575; www.rentroom.org; 5-ya Sovetskaya ul 21; s/d/tr from €65/80/95; Ⓜ Pl Vosstaniya;

Nils' new B&B is an excellent option at a great price. Four spacious rooms share two modern bathrooms, as well as a beautiful light-filled common area and kitchen. Nils renovated this place himself, taking great care to preserve the mouldings, wood floors and other architectural elements. He now exhibits the same consideration in taking care of his guests, who enjoy personal and hospitable treatment.

PIO ON MOKHOVAYA

Map p84 Mini-Hotel $$

☎ 273 3585; www.hotelpio.ru; Mokhovaya ul 39, apt 10 & 12; s/d/tr/q R2200/2800/3200/3600; Ⓜ Mayakovskaya;

This lovely lodging is the sister property to the Pio on Griboedov (opposite). While this place lacks the canal views, the two apartments are midway between the Fontanka River and the Cathedral of the Transfiguration of Our Saviour. Prices are slightly higher here because each of the 11 rooms has a bathroom. Bonus: there is also a Finnish sauna on site.

HOTEL NEVA

Map p84 Soviet Hotel $

☎ 578 0504; www.nevahotel.spb.ru; ul Chaykovskogo 17; s/d/tr/q with shared bathroom R960/1440/1800/2400, R2100/2700/3300/4400; Ⓜ Chernyshevskaya;

One of the city's oldest functioning hotels, the Neva opened its doors in 1913 and has a spectacular central staircase to show for it. Unfortunately the rooms are not quite as grand – in fact they retain a sort of Soviet scruffiness. But they are all comfortable and clean, offering a decent budget alternative with a bit of historic flare. On the premises is an old-fashioned Russian *banya* (bathhouse), an excellent option for a steam.

ST PETERSBURG INTERNATIONAL HOSTEL Map p84 Hostel $

☎ 329 8018; www.ryh.ru; 3-ya Sovetskaya ul 28; dm/d €20/48; M Pl Vosstaniya;

Russia's oldest hostel, this stalwart has been catering to budget travellers for over a decade, so you can be sure they know what they are doing. Large clean dorm rooms have three to five beds, and bathroom and kitchen facilities are modern and clean. There is no shortage of things to do: movies are shown every night and a walking tour departs from here every morning. The hostel is a 10-minute walk from the metro, Moscow Station and Nevsky pr.

ZIMMER FREI Map p84 Hostel $

☎ 973 3757, 273 0867; www.zimmer.ru; Liteyny pr 46, apt 23; dm €20; M Mayakovskaya;

More like an apartment than a hotel, this little place is accessed from the unmarked door on Liteyny pr (not through the courtyard). Rates (not including breakfast) are cheap for this highly convenient part of town although, as ever, you get what you pay for. The rooms, furnished with wooden floors and single beds, have benefited from a rudimentary renovation. Guests have access to lockers, as well as shared bathroom and kitchen facilities. The charming concierge speaks excellent English.

SLEEP CHEAP Map p84 Hostel $

☎ 715 1304; www.sleepcheap.spb.ru; Mokhovaya ul 18, apt 32; dm R700; M Chernyshevskaya

St Petersburg has scores of new mini-hotels so why not a mini-hostel? This place is tucked into an apartment in the courtyard on a residential street – you would never know it's here if you were not looking. Two dorm rooms (eight beds each) are spotlessly clean, featuring single and double beds so you can sleep with your mate if you have one. Friendly management will arrange for airport/railway pick-ups and visa registration for an extra charge.

PUPPET HOSTEL Map p84 Hostel $

☎ 272 5401; www.hostel-puppet.ru; ul Nekrasova 12; dm/d R670/840; M Mayakovskaya

This HI-affiliated place once offered accommodation for itinerant puppeteers, so it is not recommended for pupaphobes. Other budget-minded travellers, however, might appreciate the free tickets to the next-door Bolshoy Puppet Theatre (p192) – a fringe benefit for guests. The hostel also offers clean, basic rooms with two to five beds, standard Soviet décor and shared bathroom and kitchen facilities. The staff are friendly, though not always in English. Visa support is not included.

VLADIMIRSKAYA & VOSSTANIYA

Taking in the busy hub of pl Vosstaniya (Uprising Sq) and the quieter end of Nevsky pr, this is still very much the city centre. Furthermore, it is a short walk or even shorter metro ride away from the Historic Heart. Again, accommodation stretches from five-star to no-star.

HELVETIA HOTEL & SUITES
Map p92 International Hotel $$$

☎ 571 9597; www.helvetia-ste.ru; ul Marata 11; s/d €270/310; M Mayakovskaya;

Pass through Helvetia's wrought-iron gates into a wonderfully private and professionally run oasis of calm and class. Next door to the Swiss consulate and just a shopping-bag swing away from Nevsky pr, Helvetia occupies a mansion designed by Swiss architect Augusto Lange in 1828. The courtyard is a delightful place to escape from the city's bustle. Guest rooms are less atmospheric, but make up for it in comfort. The on-site Marius Pub is also useful to know about, as it serves tasty pub grub at all hours (in addition to a mean breakfast buffet).

NEVSKY FORUM Map p92 Boutique Hotel $$$

☎ 333 0222; www.forumhotel.ru; Nevsky pr 69; s/d from R6900/7500, designer room R7800-8400; M Mayakovskaya;

Nevsky's newest addition offers the expected amenities and sleek urban style of St Petersburg's most sophisticated hotels, but compared to the other luxury properties in town, it caters to a more cost-conscious traveller. All 20 rooms are spacious and comfortable, with king-size beds, big double-paned windows and environmentally friendly cork flooring. Trendsetters should look to the 'designer' rooms individually decorated with a keen eye toward hip and modern.

HOTEL DOSTOEVSKY

Map p92 International Hotel $$$

☎ 331 3200; www.dostoevsky-hotel.ru; Vladimirsky pr 19; s/d €191/216; Ⓜ Vladimirskaya;

Located above Vladimirsky Passage (p156), the Dostoevsky is a deceptively enormous place, with 200-plus modern rooms, many of which have views of Vladimirsky Cathedral across the road. The 7th-floor Raskolnikov lounge is a delightful place for a drink, offering a magnificent panorama of the square. Breakfast is not included in the price, so head to Baltic Bread (p171).

NEVSKY HOTELS Map p92 Mini-Hotel $$$

☎ 703 3860; www.hon.ru; Nevsky pr; Ⓜ Mayakovskaya/Pl Vosstaniya

Vosstaniya is home to two more outlets of this rapidly expanding mini-hotel chain. Although prices are slightly cheaper than the branches in the Historic Heart, the hotels are still very much in the thick of things. Pleasant rooms overlook quiet courtyards, which is important on this noisy (and often traffic-jammed) part of Nevsky pr:

Nevsky Central Hotel (☎ 273 7314; Nevsky pr 90-92; s/d/ste R5250/5950/8400; Ⓜ Mayakovskaya;)

Nevsky Express Hotel (☎ 277 1888; Nevsky pr 91; s/d R5250/5950; Ⓜ Pl Vosstaniya;)

FIFTH CORNER Map p92 Mini-Hotel $$

Pyatiy Ugol; ☎ 380 8181; www.5ugol.ru; Zagorodny pr 13; s/d from R5050/5750; Ⓜ Vladimirskaya;

Named after the junction of streets that it overlooks, this business hotel is a curious hybrid. The public areas are rather garish, standing in stark contrast to the warmer toned, streamlined rooms, which have received the nod of approval from style bible *Wallpaper**. The on-site restaurant Xren has an equally groovy design that makes it a great place for breakfast or a nightcap.

KRISTOFF HOTEL Map p92 Mini-Hotel $$

☎ 571 6643; www.kristoff.ru; Zagorodny pr 9; s/d from €140/160; Ⓜ Dostoevskaya;

It's hard to put your finger on exactly what sets this well-run mini-hotel apart from the pack. The rooms are smartly decorated, but not particularly memorable. The service from the English-speaking receptionist is friendly and efficient. There's also the popular and cosy restaurant downstairs (where breakfast is served) which, handily, is open round the clock. Add in the reasonable rates and it's hard to beat.

BROTHERS KARAMAZOV

Map p92 Boutique Hotel $$

☎ 335 1185; www.karamazovhotel.ru; Sotsialisticheskaya ul 11a; s/d from R4400/5180; Ⓜ Vladimirskaya;

Pack a copy of Fyodor Dostoevsky's final novel to read while staying at this appealing boutique hotel. It manages to mesh contemporary furnishings with late-19th-century elements that the great Russian writer would have found familiar, especially in the more expensive interior rooms, which are named for characters in his books. Incidentally, Dostoevsky penned *The Brothers-K* while living in the neighbourhood, so you'll want to visit the Dostoevsky Museum (p93) while you are here.

OKTOBER HOTEL Map p92 Soviet Hotel $$

Oktiabrskaya Gostinitsa; ☎ 277 6330; www.oktober-hotel.spb.ru; Ligovsky pr 10; s/d/ste R4200/5200/7200; Ⓜ Pl Vosstaniya;

Now fully privatised, this former bastion of Soviet-style hotel management is showing promising signs of revitalisation, with a professional, friendly approach to guests and improved room décor and amenities. The hotel is in two buildings and many visitors quite rightly prefer the smaller 'Filial' on the corner of Nevsky pr and Ligovsky pr – it has surprisingly spacious, not unpleasantly furnished rooms and a restaurant that harks back to the building's pre-revolutionary era.

SENNAYA

Directly south of the Historic Heart is the Sennaya neighbourhood, centred on Sennaya pl (the Haymarket of Dostoevsky's times). The district provides easy access to the city's main sights, especially if you stay on the north side of Sennaya pl. Two metro lines run through here, linking Sennaya to the rest of the city.

ARKADIA Map p97 Boutique Hotel $$

☎ 314 1900; www.arkadiahotel.ru; nab reki Moyki 58; s/d from R5440/5760; Ⓜ Sadovaya;

On the banks of the Moyka River, hidden away inside a flower-filled courtyard, this lovely little hotel provides a welcome respite from the city's crowds and chaos. Warm hues, wood floors and natural lighting characterise the guest rooms; the on-site sauna and swimming pool provide added luxury.

GOLDEN AGE RETRO HOTEL

Map p97 Mini-Hotel $$

Zolotaya Seredina; ☎ 710 8351; www.retrohotel.ru; Stolyarny per 10/12, code 44; s/d with shared bathroom R1600/1900, R2500/2800; Ⓜ Sadovaya; 💻

Tucked into a quiet courtyard in the narrow streets north of Sennaya pl, this friendly little hotel is one of St Pete's best bargains. These are the streets where roamed Fyodor Dostoevsky, the foremost writer of the Golden Age of Literature. A few antiques are scattered around the hotel premises to further justify its classification as a 'retro' hotel. Overall, the old-fashioned atmosphere is pleasant but not overbearing, as most furniture and facilities are quite modern.

ANDREY & SASHA'S HOMESTAY

Map p97 Home-Stay $

☎ 315 3330; asamatuga@mail.ru; nab kanala Griboedova 49; d €60; Ⓜ Sadovaya

Energetic owners Andrey and Sasha extend the warmest of welcomes to travellers who pass through St Petersburg. This is the biggest of three apartments they rent out (by the room or in their entirety) – all are centrally located and eclectically decorated. Andrey and Sasha have chipped back plaster to the brick walls, laid terracotta-tile floors (with underfloor heating) and installed iron candelabras. The bedrooms (two to four in each apartment) seem bigger than they actually are, thanks to the use of enormous mirrors. Bathrooms are shared, as are kitchen facilities. Socialising is definitely encouraged, and your hosts will likely invite you to join them sipping wine by the fire or drinking coffee on the rooftop.

HOSTEL ON SADOVAYA

Map p97 Hostel $

Hostel Na Sadovoy; ☎ 314 8357; www.budget-travel.spb.ru; Sadovaya ul 53; dm/s/d with shared bathroom €17/44/46, s/d €52/80; Ⓜ Sadovaya

Back in the day, Communist party apparatchiks used to stay here when they came to visit Leningrad. These days, budget travellers can enjoy the same Soviet service and style, as one portion of the cement block has been transformed into this friendly, funky hostel. Nobody speaks English downstairs, but the staff that run the hostel (on the 4th floor) know exactly what backpackers need.

MARIINSKY

Directly west of the Historic Heart, the neighbourhood around the Mariinsky Theatre is traversed by canals as the city tails off into the docklands. There are some charming accommodation options here, but be prepared to cab it or walk long distances, as there's no metro station in the entire area.

ALEXANDER HOUSE

Map p102 Boutique Hotel $$$

☎ 575 3877; www.a-house.ru; nab kanala Kryukova 27; s/d from €150/170; Ⓜ Sennaya Pl or Tekhnologichesky Institut; ❄ 💻

Owners Alexander and Natalya converted this historic building opposite Nikolsky Cathedral, styling each of the 14 spacious rooms after their favourite international cities. The themes are not laboured: a ceramic iguana clinging to the ceiling beam in the Barcelona suite; a tropical feel to Bali; Moorish touches in Marrakesh. And yes, a room named St Petersburg, with exposed brick walls and windows overlooking the canal. Lovely common areas include a fireplace-warmed lounge and a vine-laden courtyard.

MATISOV DOMIK

Map p102 Hotel $$

☎ 318 5464; www.matisov.spb.ru; nab reki Pryazhka 3/1; s/d standard R3000/4350, renovated R4050/5100; Ⓜ Sadovaya

About a 10-minute walk west of the Mariinsky Theatre, this small hotel is fronted by a charming garden with a gurgling fountain and pottery gnomes. Plain, monochromatic rooms have modern furniture, but few creature comforts. It's a secure, quiet and slightly off-beat place to stay, with very pleasant and helpful staff. It is, however, rather awkwardly located on tiny Madison Island. While it overlooks the Pryazhka River, it's a 20-minute walk from just about anything else.

GUESTHOUSE ON GALERNAYA

Map p102 Mini-Hotel $$

Gustavo Dom na Galernaya; ☎ 314 9936; galernaya@mail.ru; Galernaya ul 16; d R2500-2800, tr 2850-3200; Ⓜ Sadovaya; ❄

Putting the 'mini' in mini-hotel, this tiny guesthouse has only three rooms, which pretty much guarantees that guests receive attentive service. Rooms are small but bright, with stylish furniture and brand new bathrooms. The location is optimal – just walk under the archway from pl Dekabristov.

HOUSE IN KOLOMNA

Map p102 Mini-Hotel $

Domik v Kolomne; ☎ 710 8351; www.colomna.nm.ru; nab kanala Griboedova 174a; s/d/tr with shared bathroom €34/38/42, s/d €52/58; M Sadovaya;

Pushkin's family once rented rooms in this house, although the atmosphere evokes a Russian flat from the 1970s rather than anything antique. It may not be flash, but the friendly staff are eager to welcome foreign guests; they even have a Lonely Planet guidebook on hand for reference should you have forgotten yours. Meals (not included) are served in a small on-site café; otherwise it's a 15-minute walk to Sennaya pl.

VASILEVSKY ISLAND

Once planned to be the centre of Peter's city, Vasilevsky Island is a large and disparate place. Staying at the tip of the island around the Strelka (tongue of land) and university gives you a great base for exploring St Petersburg, but you probably don't want to go too far west.

PARK INN – PRIBALTIYSKAYA

Map pp108–9 Hotel $$$

☎ 329 2626; www.parkinn.com.ru; ul Korablestroiteley 14; s/d/ste R5250/5600/10,500; M Primorskaya;

If you – like Peter the Great – are only happy when you are near the sea, you might consider staying in the Park Inn – Pribaltiyskaya, the one hotel in the city with wonderful views over the Gulf of Finland. At the western end of Vasilevsky Island, it is miles from the city centre and not even that close to the metro, but it is like its own little city with 1200 rooms, two restaurants and a bowling alley on site. And the fun-filled Waterville Aquapark (p197) guarantees you'll go home waterlogged.

PRESTIGE HOTEL ON VASILEVSKY

Map pp108–9 Mini-Hotel $$

☎ 328 5338; www.prestige-hotels.com; 2-ya liniya i 3-ya liniya 52; s/d standard R2700/4200, renovated R3400/4800; M Vasileostrovskaya;

Slightly smaller – but no less spacey – than the Prestige Hotel on Gorokhovaya. See p204 for a full review.

SHELFORT HOTEL

Map pp108–9 Mini-Hotel $$

☎ 328 0555; www.shelfort.ru; 2-ya liniya i 3-ya liniya 26; s/d R2600/4200, ste R5400-5650; M Vasileostrovskaya;

In a convenient-but-quiet location close to the metro, this handsome building houses an excellent mini-hotel on its first two floors. Two sweet suites feature tiled furnaces that add an antique authenticity to an already classy place. For those not fortunate enough to score the spacious suites, the regular rooms are still pretty nice, sporting classically simple furnishings, high ceilings and plenty of space.

SPB VERGAZ HOTEL

Map pp108–9 Mini-Hotel $$

☎ 327 8883; 6-ya liniya i 7-ya liniya 70; s/d/apt €90/140/160, breakfast €6; M Vasileostrovskaya;

A place called 'Vergaz' doesn't sound like the most promising of prospects, but this classy property actually has a lot going for it. It's owned by a Franco-Russian gas piping company, so you get French- and English-speaking staff, and arty photos of St Petersburg and Paris hanging side by side in the lobby. There's a wide range of spacious, well-equipped rooms, some with splendid views across to the onion-domed church next door.

PETROGRAD SIDE

The Petrograd Side is appealing in that it offers its own neighbourhood attractions, restaurants and boutiques, so you need not be trekking into the centre all the time. When you do, however, two metro lines will take you across the river in a flash.

APART-HOTEL KRONVERK

Map pp114–15 Hotel $$

☎ 703 3663; www.kronverk.com; ul Blokhina 9; s/d R3680/3840, apt from R6400; M Sportivnaya;

If the baroque, rococo and Style Moderne architecture of St Petersburg leaves you hankering after something more contemporary, then here's a place for you. Occupying the upper floors of a slick new business centre, the Kronverk offers appealingly modern rooms with self-catering facilities. Frosted glass and streamlined black panelling create a crisp reception area where the English-speaking staff are efficient and professional.

HOTEL EURASIA

Map pp114–15 Mini-Hotel $$

☎ 230 4432; www.eurasia-hotel.ru; Gatchinskaya ul 5; s/d R2800/3100, s/d ste from R3450/3600; M Chkalovskaya

In an attractive 19th-century building, the Eurasia has 18 comfortable rooms that are modern, if not memorable (but frankly, when it comes to mini-hotels, that may be a good thing). White walls and plain furniture guarantee comfort, cleanliness and sound sleeping. This hotel group operates three other mini-hotels on the Petrograd Side, so if the Eurasia is full, staff should be able to point you in the direction of something similar.

HOTEL AURORA Map pp114–15 Mini-Hotel $

☎ 233 3641; www.hotel-aurora.ru; Malaya Posadskaya ul 15; s/d with shared bathroom R1575/2100, s/d R2275/2800; M Gorkovskaya

Tucked in behind the Peter & Paul Fortress, this is a spunky little mini-hotel offering affordable, friendly accommodation. Spacious rooms sport a charming, Soviet-style décor, with parquet floors, rickety beds and monochrome linens. Nonetheless, shiny new bathrooms and kitchen facilities make this an excellent deal.

VYBORG SIDE

There are not too many reasons to stay in the expanse of the Vyborg Side. But there is one option with easy access to the city centre.

HOTEL ST PETERSBURG

Map pp122–3 Soviet Hotel $$

%380 1919; www.hotel-spb.ru; Pirogovskaya nab 5/2; r standard R2300-3400, renovated R4000-4600; M Pl Lenina;

This is not the prettiest building in St Petersburg, but then again, you can't see it when you are inside. In fact, when you are inside, you will be admiring lovely views of the Peter & Paul Fortress or the Admiralteyskaya embankment across the Neva River. Rooms are perfectly comfortable, while the more expensive ones are downright classy. The place is huge so there are plenty of facilities on site.

SOUTHERN ST PETERSBURG

Southern St Petersburg doesn't have a lot to offer the independent traveller, unless you're looking for easy access to the airport (see below). Otherwise, a handful of huge post-Soviet monoliths usually cater to tourist groups.

AZIMUT Map pp146–7 Hotel $$

☎ 740 2640; www.azimuthotels.ru; Lermontovsky pr 43/1; s/d standard R2600/3100, renovated R3000/3900; M Tekhnologichesky Institut;

This former Intourist monolith finally changed its name from the long-standing Sovietskaya Hotel when it was bought by this fast-growing Russian chain. Of its many, many rooms, there are a slew of different categories, some of which have been nicely modernised. It still caters largely to tour groups who are indifferent to its hideous exterior, which mars the landscape along the otherwise lovely Fontanka River.

AIRPORT ACCOMMODATION

If you are looking for an easy-in, easy-out hotel from the airport, consider these options near Moskovskaya pl:

Park Inn – Pulkovskaya (Map p65; ☎ 740 3900; www.parkinn.com.ru; pl Pobedy 1; s/d/ste R5250/5600/10,500; M Moskovskaya;) This Soviet remake has a concrete exterior that fits right in with the architectural brutalism of the surrounding area, while inside an unintentional retro feeling of the 1960s prevails. Rooms are spacious and pleasantly furnished; some also afford splendid views of the Monument to the Heroic Defenders of Leningrad.

German Club (Nemetsky Klub; Map p65; ☎ 371 5104; www.hotelgermanclub.com; ul Gastello 20; s/d R2270/2700; M Moskovskaya;) Promising 'Russian hospitality and German order', this is a surprisingly convivial mini-hotel. The lobby is reminiscent of an Alpine chalet, while spacious rooms provide regular Russian comfort.

All Seasons Hostel (Map p65; ☎ 327 1070; www.hostel.ru; Yakovlevsky per 11, 4th fl; dm €10-12, s/d/tr €40/40/42; M Park Pobedy) The closest hostel to the airport. On the 4th floor of an early Soviet era apartment block, it looks and feels like a traditional Russian hostel. Rooms are the usual plain affairs with pine-framed single beds. No breakfast is served, but there is a spacious kitchen that doubles as a TV room.

EXCURSIONS

EXCURSIONS

As soon as you leave St Petersburg the fast-paced city fades from view, while the slowed-down, old-fashioned countryside unfolds around you. The subtly changing landscape is crossed by winding rivers and dotted with peasant villages – the classic provincial Russia immortalised by artists and writers over the centuries.

Before Russia was a cohesive nation, it was a collection of principalities – city-states that competed, traded and (sometimes) cooperated with each other. Ancient Rus – as this period is known – developed in the provincial towns around St Petersburg. The whitewashed walls of once-fortified cities still stand, in some cases. The golden spires and onion domes of the monasteries of these cities still mark the horizon, evoking medieval Rus. Bells ring out from towering belfries; robed holy men scurry through church doors; historic tales recall mysterious, magical times.

The St Petersburg elite has long escaped the heat and hustle of city life by retreating to the surrounding regions. Old aristocrats – including the imperial family – used provincial Russia as a venue for grand palaces, extensive gardens and extravagant art collections. Many of these retreats now house museums to inspire and amaze the rest of us.

IMPERIAL PALACES

In the wilderness of the sparsely inhabited Baltic Coast, Russia's aristocracy – and particularly the imperial family – outdid each other trying to create the ultimate summer palace. Throughout the 18th and 19th centuries the ruling class built fantastic façades, opulent interiors and glorious gardens, so that they might enjoy lavish lifestyles even when away from the capital. **Peterhof** (p216) boasts the most amazing grounds, with its world-famous cascades; while the interior of the **Catherine Palace** (p220) at Tsarskoe Selo is unparalleled, especially with its over-the-top amber room. **Konstantinovsky Palace** (p219) – only recently renovated and reopened by President Putin – is the latest addition to this list of palatial properties.

Other lesser-known estates – built by various Russian rulers over the years – are still enormously impressive and generally less crowded. In 1743 **Oranienbaum** (p223) became the summer residence of the future emperor Peter III. Its main buildings received a complete overhaul in 2007, so it is in fine form today. Later in the century, emperors Paul I and Alexander III spent their summers at **Gatchina** (p223), enjoying the setting amidst beautiful parkland and a lovely lake. Dating from the early 19th century, the estate at **Pavlovsk** (p221) was another favourite destination of Paul I. It is surrounded by 600 hectares of shady, wooded grounds. All of these imperial palaces are an easy day trip from the city, easily accessible by train, bus or boat.

MEDIEVAL RUS

Russia's earliest history was characterised by principalities, who competed and traded with each other, jostling for power and resources. **Veliky Novgorod** (p224) was one of the earliest and most influential cultural and religious centres. These days it still retains a magical, mystical air of history, which is reflected in the domes of its myriad churches and the arcs of its ancient trading arcades. You can see Novgorod in a day, although there are enough sights and activities to keep a traveller busy for two or more.

Dating back even further, **Staraya Ladoga** (p229) is generally considered to be Russia's oldest town. Its quaint streets contain a fascinating fortress, ruined churches and precious architectural relics from Russia's birth as a nation. Again, it's close enough for a day trip if you get an early start.

PROVINCIAL RUSSIA

For the 'real Russia', look no further than the country's pleasant provincial towns. Life here is decidedly languorous, and you'll see how the vast majority of the Russian population lives – a far cry from their cosmopolitan St Petersburg cousins.

The Finnish-Russian border town of **Vyborg** (p227) has a mixed history, having been passed between Russia and Finland constantly throughout its history. It's a run-down but charming town with cobblestone streets, a rich architectural heritage and a fascinating 13th-century Swedish fortress. While it's not

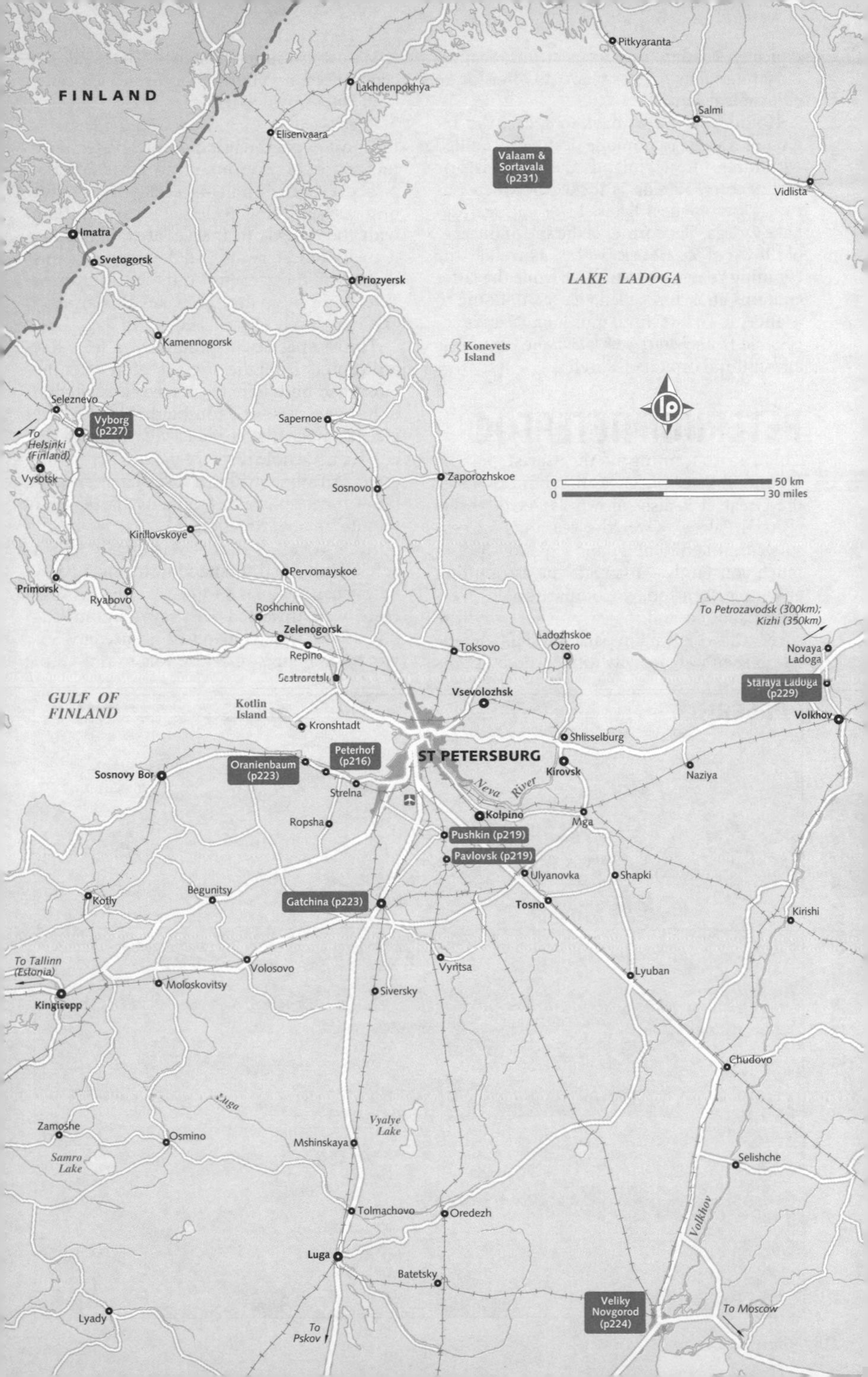
FINLAND
Pitkyaranta
Lakhdenpokhya
Salmi
Elisenvaara
Valaam & Sortavala (p231)
Vidlista
Imatra
Svetogorsk
Priozyersk
LAKE LADOGA
Kamennogorsk
Konevets Island
Seleznevo
Vyborg (p227)
To Helsinki (Finland)
Sapernoe
Vysotsk
Zaporozhskoe
Sosnovo
0
50 km
0
30 miles
Kirillovskoye
Pervomayskoe
Primorsk
Ryabovo
Roshchino
To Petrozavodsk (300km); Kizhi (350km)
Zelenogorsk
Ladozhskoe Ozero
Toksovo
Repino
Novaya Ladoga
Sestroretsk
Staraya Ladoga (p229)
GULF OF FINLAND
Kotlin Island
Vsevolozhsk
Volkhov
Kronshtadt
Shlisselburg
Peterhof (p216)
ST PETERSBURG
Oranienbaum (p223)
Sosnovy Bor
Kirovsk
Naziya
Strelna
Neva River
Kolpino
Mga
Ropsha
Pushkin (p219)
Pavlovsk (p219)
Ulyanovka
Shapki
Kotly
Begunitsy
Gatchina (p223)
Tosno
Kirishi
To Tallinn (Estonia)
Volosovo
Vyritsa
Lyuban
Moloskovitsy
Kingisepp
Siversky
Chudovo
Luga
Vyalye Lake
Zamoshe
Osmino
Mshinskaya
Samro Lake
Selishche
Tolmachovo
Oredezh
Volkhov
Luga
Batetsky
Veliky Novgorod (p224)
To Moscow
Lyady
To Pskov

typically Russian, due to its strong Scandinavian influence, it has plenty to offer for an enjoyable day trip.

If you have a few days to spare, the region of Karelia is a unique destination, filled with birch forests, inland lakes and historic architecture. Karelia is tucked between Europe's two biggest lakes, Lake Ladoga and Lake Onega. The former is the site of the age-old town of Staraya Ladoga (p229), as well as the stunning Valaam Monastery (p231); while the latter contains an island called Kizhi (p231), home to a fantastic architectural museum. Kizhi is accessible from Petrozavodsk (p230), the economic and cultural capital of Karelia.

PETERHOF ПЕТЕРГОФ

This most stunning of the tsarist palaces around St Petersburg was first built by Peter the Great; it is also known as Petrodvorets (Peter's Palace). Over the years his successors continued to build and expand – pretty much constantly – to create the astounding ensemble seen today. Comparisons to Versailles abound and it's easy to see why: the sheer scale of the main palace and its incredible garden were heavily influenced by Louis XIV's own summer residence. That said, the centrepiece at Peterhof, the Grand Cascade, is all Peter's own work.

Peterhof (☎ 420 0073; www.peterhof.ru in Russian) is the most popular day trip from St Petersburg for visitors. If you intend to go inside the palace, expect to wait, especially if you visit on a weekend. Nonetheless, it's worth jostling with the crowds to marvel at the amazing network of waterways and flowing fountains that adorn the gardens. And the trip from St Petersburg by hydrofoil makes this an easy and immensely enjoyable day trip.

The vast palace and grounds you see today are a far cry from the original cabin Peter the Great had built here to oversee construction of his naval base at Kronshtadt. He liked the place so much that he built a villa, Monplaisir, and then a whole series of palaces across the estate. All are set within a spectacular ensemble of gravity-powered fountains that are now the site's main attraction.

After WWII, Peterhof was largely left in ruins. Hitler had intended to throw a party here when his plans to occupy the Astoria Hotel were thwarted. He drew up pompous invitations, which obviously incensed his Soviet foes. Stalin's response was to pre-empt

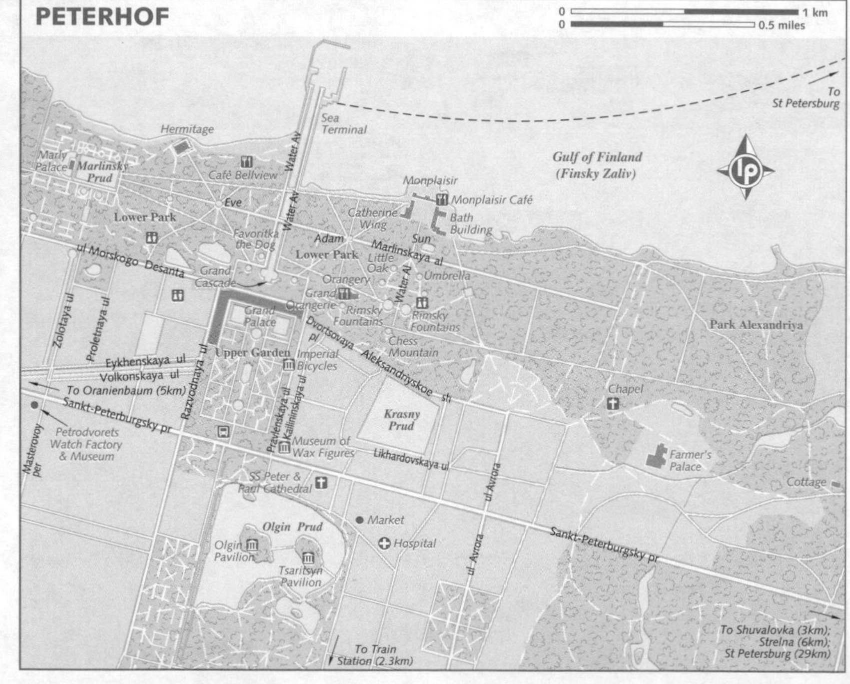

MAKE A WISH

Cast your kopek into any one of 150 fountains that adorn the grounds at Peterhof. Besides the Grand Cascade and Samson Fountain, here are some of our favourites.

Adam & Eve These two – prominently placed on either side of Water Ave – are the only outdoor sculptures remaining from the Petrine era.

Chess Mountain Flanked by a staircase, this black-and-white tiled chute is adorned with colourful dragons spitting water instead of fire.

Favoritka the Dog Often overlooked, this sweet fountain features four bronze ducks, swimming in circles, as they are chased by a silly-looking bulldog, seemingly shooting them with water.

Little Oak These gangly oak trees are rigged to spray when somebody approaches.

Rimsky Fountains Like two massive marble glasses bubbling over with champagne, these two beauties spray water 10m into the air, then into the pools below.

Sun Perched on a rotating axis, a disk radiates streams of water, creating the effect of sunrays.

Umbrella This circular bench looks like a pleasant shady spot. But anyone who sits down for a rest will discover that the umbrella drops a sheet of water from its edge, so you'll be shaded but soused.

Water Alley Most of the time, this looks like a regular shady path through the Lower Gardens. But at designated times, when hidden fountains are turned on, the walkway (and anybody walking there) gets wet!

any such celebration by bombing the estate himself, in the winter of 1941–1942. So it is ironic but true that most of the damage at Peterhof occurred at the hands of the Soviets. What you see today is largely a reconstruction; in fact, the main palace was completely gutted, as only a few of its walls were left standing.

Inexplicably, many museums within the estate have different closing days, although all the buildings are open from Friday to Sunday (and, with the exception of the Grand Palace, most buildings are open only on weekends between October and April). In any case, it's time-consuming and expensive to see all of the attractions from the inside, as they each charge separate hefty admission fees. You are better off focusing on a few museums, but spending the bulk of your time enjoying the grounds. All tours and posted information are in Russian, so it's worth investing in an information booklet, available at the kiosks near the entrances. Almost all of the buildings require an extra ticket to take photographs or videos.

Whether you arrive by water or by land, you will have to purchase a ticket to enter the **Lower Park** (Nizhny Park; adult/student R300/150; ⌚ 9am-7pm, fountains play 11am-5pm Mon-Fri, 11am-7pm Sat & Sun May-Sep), which is where you can wander to discover all the fabulous fountains. See the boxed text, above, for some suggestions.

Crisscrossed by bridges and bedecked by smaller sprays, **Water Avenue** is a canal leading from the ferry dock to the palace. It culminates in the magnificent **Grand Cascade**, a symphony of over 140 fountains engineered in part by Peter himself. The central statue of Samson tearing open a lion's jaws celebrates – as so many things in St Petersburg do – Peter's victory over the Swedes at Poltava. Shooting up 62m, it was unveiled by Rastrelli for the 25th anniversary of the battle in 1735.

Providing an amazing backdrop to the Grand Cascade, the **Grand Palace** (Bolshoy Dvorets; ☎ 450 6527; adult/student R500/250; ⌚ 10am-6pm Tue-Sun, closed last Tue of month) is an imposing edifice, although with 30-something rooms, it is not nearly as large as your typical tsarist palace. It is open to foreign tourists only at specific times during the day, so you are advised to come here immediately upon arrival if you are interested in going inside. Tickets are sold near the lobby where you pick up your *tapochki* (slippers to wear over your shoes to avoid damaging the wooden floors).

While Peter's palace was relatively modest, Rastrelli grossly enlarged the building for Empress Elizabeth. Later, Catherine the Great toned things down a little with a redecoration, although that's not really apparent from the glittering halls and art-filled galleries that are here today. All of the paintings, furniture and chandeliers are original, as everything was removed from the premises before the Germans arrived. The **Chesme Hall** is full of huge paintings of Russia's destruction of the Turkish fleet at Çesme in 1770. Other highlights include the

East and West Chinese Cabinets, Picture Hall and Peter's study.

The more humble, sea-facing villa Monplaisir (☎ 450 6129; adult/student R300/150; ⏲ 10.30am-5pm Tue & Thu-Sun May-Sep, Sat & Sun Oct-Apr) was always his favourite retreat. Snug and elegant, the wood-panelled cottage also provided the proximity to the sea that he craved.

To the west of Monplaisir is an annexe called the Catherine Building (Ekaterinsky korpus; ☎ 450 6129; adult/student R300/150; ⏲ 10.30am-5pm Tue-Sun May-Sep, Sat & Sun Oct-Apr), which was built by Rastrelli between 1747 and 1755. Its name derives from the fact that Catherine the Great was living here – rather conveniently – when her husband Peter III was overthrown. The interior contains the bedroom and study of Alexander I, as well as the huge Yellow Hall. On the right side is the magnificent Bath Building (Banniy korpus; ☎ 450 6129; adult/student R300/150; ⏲ 10.30am-4pm Thu-Tue May-Sep, Sat & Sun Oct-Apr), built by Quarenghi in 1800.

Along the shore to the west, the 1725 Hermitage (☎ 450 5325; adult/student R110/60; ⏲ 10.30am-5pm Wed-Mon, Sat & Sun Oct-Apr) is a two-storey pink-and-white box featuring the ultimate in private dining: special elevators hoist a fully-laid table into the imperial presence on the 2nd floor, thereby eliminating any hindrance by servants. The elevators are circular and directly in front of each diner, whose plate would be lowered, replenished and replaced. Further west is yet another palace, Marly (☎ 450 7729; adult/student R130/65; ⏲ 10.30am-5pm Tue-Sun), which was inspired by a French hunting lodge.

To the east of the Grand Palace, an old Orangery houses a restaurant. Outside, the Triton fountain shows off an 8m jet of water.

Even on summer weekends, the rambling, overgrown Park Alexandriya (admission free) is peaceful and practically empty. Built for Tsar Nicholas I (and named for his tsarina), these grounds offer a sweet retreat from the crowds. Originally named for Alexander Nevsky, the gothic chapel (☎ 450 6901; adult/student R110/60; ⏲ 10am-5pm Tue-Sun) was completed in 1834 as the private chapel of Nicholas I. Nearby is the cottage (☎ 450 6953; admission R150; ⏲ 10.30am-4pm Tue-Sun May-Sep, Sat & Sun Oct-Apr) that was built around the same time as his summer residence. Also part of this same ensemble, the Farmer's Palace is still undergoing renovations and is not open to the public.

In front of the Grand Palace, the Upper Garden is more manicured (and much drier), occupying the grounds between the palace and the town. A few small museums line the road out to town, including an exhibition on Imperial Bicycles (Imperatorskie Velosipedi; Pravlenskaya ul 11; adult/student R110/60; ⏲ 10.30am-6pm) and a Museum of Wax Figures (Pravlenskaya ul 12; ⏲ 11am-7pm).

In case you have not had enough, there is more to see in the centre of the town of Peterhof. In the midst of Kolonistsky Park, two islands sit side by side in the middle of a pond known as Olgin Prud (Olga's pond). The two islands house the Tsaritsyn & Olgin Pavilions (adult/student R450/250; ⏲ 10.30am-5pm). Nicholas I had these elaborate pavilions built for his wife (Alexandra Fedorovna) and daughter (Olga Nikolaevna) respectively. Only recently restored and reopened, they boast unique Mediterranean architectural styles reminiscent of Pompeii.

One bus stop west of the main palace entrance is the Petrodvorets watch factory & museum (☎ 420 50003; Sankt-Peterburgsky pr 60; admission €5; ⏲ boutique 10am-5pm Mon-Fri) with a little boutique selling *very* cool watches.

TRANSPORT: PETERHOF

Distance from St Petersburg 29km

Direction West

Travel Time About 45 minutes

Boat From May to September, a fine option is the *Meteor* hydrofoil (R350 one-way, 30 minutes) from the jetty in front of St Petersburg's Hermitage, which goes every 20 to 30 minutes from 9.30am to at least 7pm. Be aware that queues for the boat back to St Petersburg can get very long later in the day, so don't leave it too late to return.

Bus From Avtovo metro station you can take bus 424, or bus 103 from Leninsky Pr metro station. The trip takes about half an hour.

Train *Elektrichky* (suburban trains) leave St Petersburg's Baltic Station (Baltiysky vokzal) every 15 to 30 minutes throughout the day. You need to get off at the Novy Petrodvorets (not Stary Petrodvorets). From here you can either walk to the palace grounds (about 20 minutes) or take *marshrutka* 350, 351, 351A, 352, 353, 354 or 356, getting off at the fifth stop.

Eating

Café Bellview (meals R100-300; ⏲ 10am-6pm) A complex of restaurants overlooks the Gulf of Finland, just west of the boat dock, with several

DETOUR: STRELNA СТРЕЛЬНА

The small village of Strelna, about 6km east of Peterhof, is the site of another palace dreamed up by Peter I. Although construction began in the 18th century, current President Vladimir Putin deserves credit for completing this project.

Peter's original plan was to construct a small palace surrounded by water, for use as a summer home. He commissioned Jean Baptiste LeBlond to build the palace and park, but the famed French architect died before he made much progress on the project. Work came to a standstill when Peter turned his attention to Peterhof, as that site was better suited for his fountain fantasy. Years later, at the request of Empress Elizabeth, her favourite architect Rastrelli attempted to expand and elaborate on the existing palace at Strelna. But he too was distracted – this time by construction at Tsarskoe Selo – and never really finished. In 1797 Emperor Paul I presented this half-built palace to his son, Grand Duke Constantine Pavlovich. Construction of the Konstantinovsky Palace was finally completed several years later.

The estate fell into disrepair during the Soviet period, occupied by a children's camp and a secondary school. It was devastated by German occupation during WWII, and then left to languish for more than half a century.

In the lead-up to the tercentennial in 2003, President Putin decreed that the property would be rebuilt and converted to a presidential palace – in other words, the 'Palace of Putin'. Using LeBlond's original design, the **park** (admission R100) was landscaped with canals, bridges and fountains, as well as Peter's intended island chateau. Studded with sculpture, it makes a lovely place for a stroll or picnic.

Konstantinovsky Palace (☎ 438 5360; www.konstantinpalace.ru in Russian; Berezovaya al 3; adult/student R280/170; ⌚ 10am-5pm Thu-Tue) has also been fully restored. Excursions visit the fabulous 'parade rooms', including the Blue Room and the over-the-top ornate Marble Room, as well as the ceremonial guestrooms of the president and the first lady. Most impressively, visitors can take a peak into the wine cellar. Apparently, as far back as 1755 these premises were used to house the emperor's collection of Hungarian wine, when the Winter Palace was under construction. These days the *vinniy pogreb* contains a collection of more than 13,000 bottles from all over the world.

Also known as the Congress Palace, it is often used for official functions, hosting heads of state and other important delegations. For this reason, it's worth calling in advance to confirm that the grounds and palace will be open when you wish to visit. If you'd like to sleep like a tsar, consider staying at the Baltic Star Hotel, see the boxed text, p206.

different cafés, plenty of seating and (bonus) public toilets. Café Belleview offers the widest selection of dishes at lunchtime.

Grand Orangerie (☎ 450 6106; set menus R450-700; ⌚ 10am-6pm) If you want somebody to serve you lunch, you'll have to queue for a spot at this pleasant restaurant overlooking the pond.

Monplaisir Café (snacks R100-300; ⌚ 10am-6pm) For a quick sandwich or snack, head to this pleasant café next to Peter's favourite retreat. A few outdoor tables catch the breeze off the Gulf.

PUSHKIN & PAVLOVSK ПУШКИН И ПАВЛОВСК

The sumptuous palaces and sprawling parks at Pushkin and Pavlovsk are entrenched in Russian history and immortalised in literature: few places in Russia are more strongly associated with the country's history and culture. These two neighbouring complexes can be combined in a day's visit. If you are not in the mood to rush, however, there is plenty at either site to keep you entertained for an entire day.

The original estate at Tsarskoe Selo (Tsar's Village) was a gift from Peter I to his wife Catherine in 1710, and from around 1725 she started to spend more time here. It was under Empresses Elizabeth and Catherine the Great that the place began to take shape, as both the palace at Tsarskoe Selo and the estate of Pavlovsk were built, expanded and aggrandised.

The centrepiece is the vast 1752 to 1756 baroque **Catherine Palace** (Yekaterininsky Dvorets), designed by Rastrelli. It gradually became the favourite country estate of the royal family. In 1837 Russia's first railway line was built between St Petersburg and Tsarskoe Selo to shuttle the imperial family back and forth.

The town changed its name from Tsarskoe Selo to Pushkin in 1937 on the centenary of the poet's death. Pushkin studied here in the Lycée established by Alexander I. In the 1990s the name of the palace and grounds changed back to Tsarskoe Selo, although the town is technically still Pushkin. In reality, these two names are used nearly interchangeably.

Pavlovsk's park of woodland, rivers, lakes, statues and temples is one of the most exquisite in Russia, while its Great Palace is a classical contrast to the florid baroque Catherine Palace.

Catherine Palace

Most of the exterior and 20-odd rooms of the **Catherine Palace** (☎ 465 2024; www.tzar.ru; Sadovaya ul 7, Tsarskoe Selo; adult/student R520/250, private tour R7000; ⏲ 10am-5pm Wed-Mon, open for individuals noon-2pm & 4-5pm, closed last Mon of month) have been beautifully restored. As you tour the palace you can compare them to the photographs showing the devastation by the Germans. While the palace opens for individuals only at noon, it is usually necessary to queue up well in advance. All visitors are ushered into groups led by a tour guide; arrangements can be made for tours in English.

As at the Winter Palace, Catherine the Great had many of Rastrelli's interiors remodelled in classical style. Visits normally start with the **State Staircase**, an 1860 addition. South of here, two rooms by Rastrelli are open to tours: the **Gentlemen-in-Waiting's Dining Room** and the huge, frescoed **Great Hall**, all light and glitter from its mirrors and gilded woodcarvings. North of the State Staircase, you will pass through the **State Dining Room**, the **Crimson** and **Green Pilaster Rooms** and the **Picture Gallery**. The **reception room of Alexander I** holds portraits of his esteemed predecessors.

The highlight is Rastrelli's amazing **Amber Room**, completely covered with gilded woodcarvings, mirrors, agate and jasper mosaics. The exquisitely engraved amber panels were gifts from the King of Prussia to Peter the Great in 1716. But these treasures were plundered by the Nazis and went missing in Kaliningrad in 1945, becoming one of the art world's great mysteries. In 2004 the strange hoax was revealed – the Amber Room was

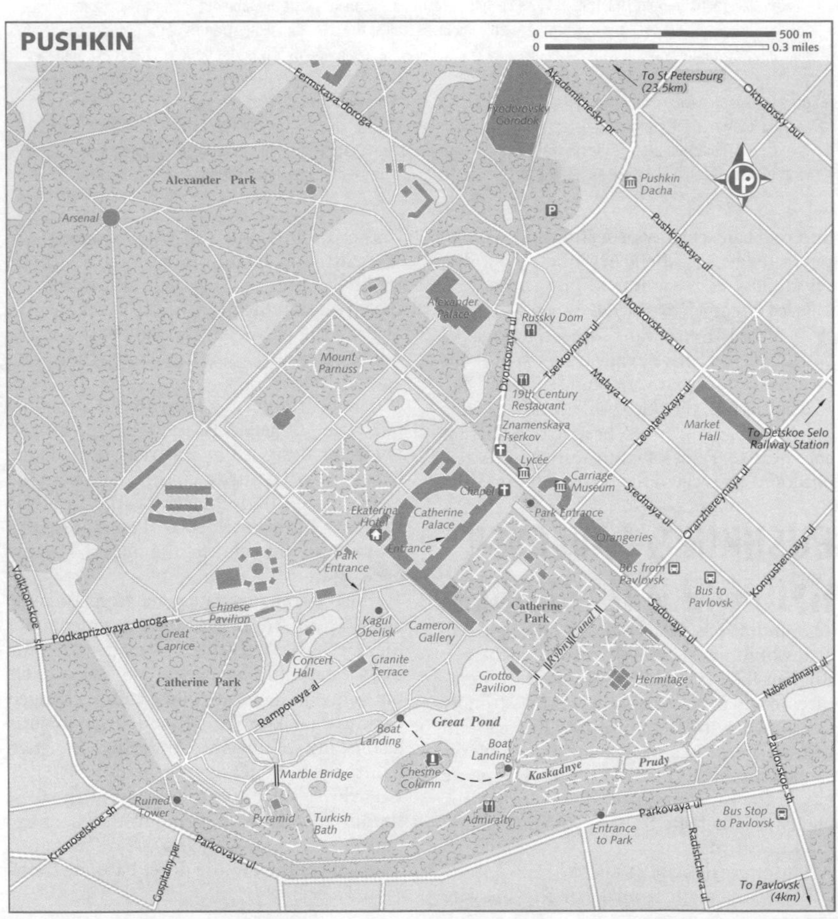

destroyed in a fire in Kaliningrad while under Red Army occupation. Those responsible for the loss were so terrified of Stalin's reaction that an elaborate myth was created of its disappearance – one that Soviet art historians spent years trying to solve. In 2004 President Putin and German Chancellor Gerhardt Schröder presided over the opening of a new Amber Room, restored largely with German funds. While this spectacular centrepiece is open to visitors, photography is forbidden.

Most of the north end is Charles Cameron's early classical work, including the perfectly proportioned Green Dining Room and the Pink Room with its inlaid wood floor.

Once you finish your tour, you can head to the southern Zubov Wing (Zubovsky korpus; adult/student R200/100; 10am-5pm Thu-Tue), which houses special exhibitions.

Tsarskoe Selo Parks

Around the Catherine Palace extends the lovely Catherine Park (Yekaterininsky Park; adult/student R160/80; 9am-6pm). The main entrance is on Sadovaya ul, next to the palace chapel. The Cameron Gallery (adult/student R200/100; 10am-5pm Thu-Tue) has rotating exhibitions. Between the gallery and the palace, notice the south-pointing ramp that Cameron added for the ageing empress to walk down into the park.

The park's outer section focuses on the Great Pond. In summer you can take a ferry (adult/child R300/150; noon-6pm May-Sep) to the little island to visit the Chesme Column. Beside the pond, the blue baroque Grotto Pavilion (adult/student R50/25; 10am-5pm Fri-Wed) houses temporary exhibitions in summer. A walk around the Great Pond will reveal other buildings that the royals built over the years, including the Turkish Bath, the Chinese Pavilion and a Concert Hall isolated on an island.

Alexander Palace & Park

A short distance north of the Catherine Palace, the classical Alexander Palace (466 6071; www.alexanderpalace.org; Dvortsovaya ul 2; adult/student R300/150; 10am-5pm Wed-Mon, closed last Wed of month) was built by Quarenghi between 1792 and 1796. It was built and named for the future Alexander I, but Nicholas II was its main tenant. Many tourists skip this spot, which has yet to be completely renovated, which means it is the least crowded and most intriguing of the palaces. The overgrown and empty Alexander Park (admission free) surrounds the palace.

TRANSPORT: PUSHKIN & PAVLOVSK

Distance from St Petersburg 25km (Pushkin) and 29km (Pavlovsk)

Direction South

Travel Time 45 minutes to one hour

Bus A large number of *marshrutky* (R25, 30 minutes) leave from outside Moskovskaya metro station in St Petersburg to Pushkin (aka Tsarskoe Selo). Take bus 286, 299 or 342. *Marshrutky* K299 and K545 connect Pushkin and Pavlovsk (R15, 10 minutes).

Train Suburban trains run from Vitebsk Station (Vitebsky vokzal) in St Petersburg, but they're infrequent except for weekends. For Tsarskoe Selo get off at Detskoe Selo Station (zone 3 ticket, 30 minutes) and for Pavlovsk (zone 4, 40 minutes) at Pavlovsk Station.

Pavlovsk Great Palace & Park

Between 1781 and 1786, on orders from Catherine the Great, architect Charles Cameron designed the Great Palace (452 2156; www.pavlovskart.spb.ru; ul Revolutsii, Pavlovsk; adult/student R370/180; 10am-6pm Sat-Thu, closed first Fri of month) in Pavlovsk. The palace was designated for Catherine's son Paul, and it was his second wife, Maria Fyodorovna, who orchestrated the design of the interiors. It served as a royal residence until 1917. Ironically, the original palace was burnt down two weeks after liberation in WWII by a careless Soviet soldier's cigarette which set off German mines (the Soviets blamed the Germans). As at Tsarskoe Selo, its restoration is remarkable.

The finest rooms are on the middle floor of the central block. Cameron designed the round Italian Hall beneath the dome and the Grecian Hall to its west, though the lovely green fluted columns were added by his assistant Vincenzo Brenna. Flanking these are two private suites designed mainly by Brenna – Paul's along the north side of the block and Maria Fyodorovna's on the south. The Hall of War of the insane, military-obsessed Paul contrasts with Maria's Hall of Peace, decorated with musical instruments and flowers.

On the middle floor of the south block are Paul's Throne Room and the Hall of the Maltese Knights of St John, of whom he was the Grand Master.

If you decide to skip the palace, you may wish to wander around the serene park grounds

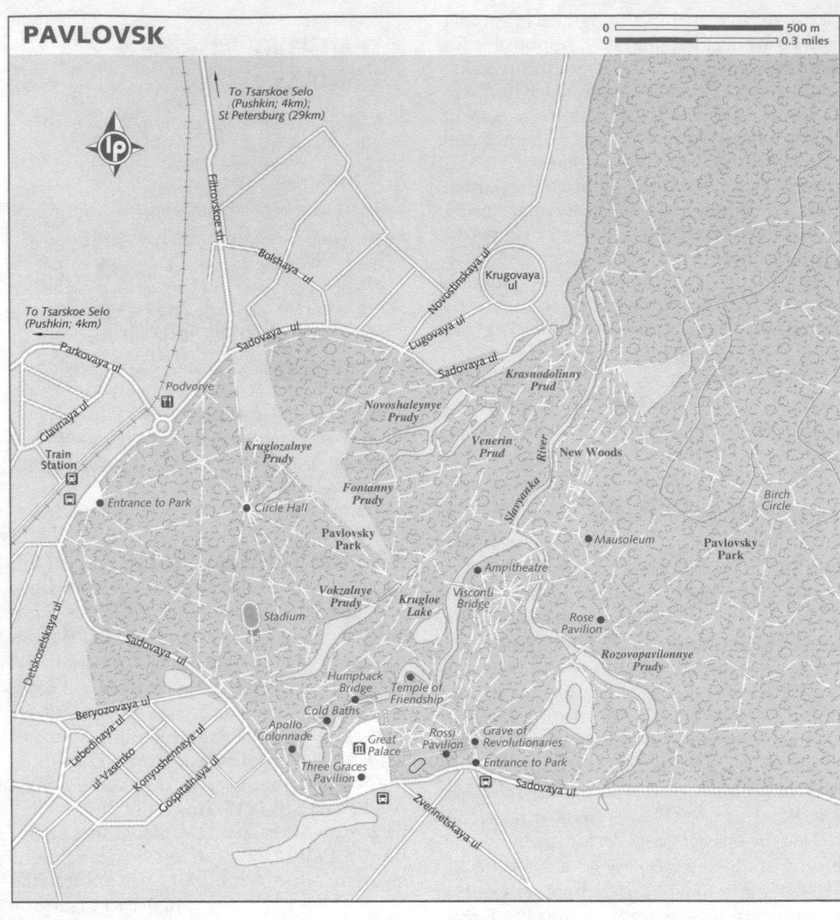

(adult/student R100/80; 10am-6pm) and see what you come across – or, do the same by **bicycle** (☎ 347 7743; per half-day R400; 11am-8pm). Filled with rivers and ponds, tree-lined avenues, classical statues and hidden temples, it's a delightful place to get lost.

Sleeping

Ekaterina Hotel (Map p220; ☎ 446 8042; www.hotelekaterina.ru; Sadovaya ul 5, Tsarskoe Selo; r €120;) Located inside the old servants' block at Catherine's Palace, this small, midrange hotel offers great views on the building's gilded façade. Rooms are modern and reasonably spacious. Best of all, perhaps, it is probably your best chance of being first in the queue to enter the palace. Room prices include continental breakfast.

Eating

The palaces at Tsarskoe Selo and Pavlovsk both have pretty mediocre and overpriced self-service cafeterias.

19th Century Restaurant (XIX Vek; Map p220; ☎ 465 2685; Srednaya ul 2, Pushkin; meals R400-600) Three different dining rooms each have an interesting interior décor, including the fairytale-like Lyceum Hall.

Admiralty (Admiralteystvo; Map p220; ☎ 465 3549; Catherine Park; meals R600-800; noon-11pm) Housed in the old brick Admiralty building overlooking the Great Pond in Catherine Park, this atmospheric restaurant serves traditional and tasty Russian food. The towerlike building does not have a lot of room, so reservations are recommended.

Podvorye (☎ 465 1399; Map p222; Filtrovskoye sh 16, Pavlovsk; meals R800-1200; noon-11pm) This traditional Russian log cabin is a short walk northeast of Pavlovsk station. Podvorye dishes up huge portions of delicious Russian food with a side-order of live Russian music and dancing. Apparently, President Putin is a regular here.

Russky Dom (Russian House; Map p220; ☎ 466 8888; Malaya ul 3, Pushkin; meals R800-1200; noon-midnight) Smartly decorated in a contemporary style with a lovely terrace, this popular spot serves lots of standard dishes including shashlyk, cooked on wood-fired braziers outside.

GATCHINA ГАТЧИНА

Originally owned by Peter's sister Natalya, the palace estate at Gatchina (☎ 81371-134-92; admission R350; 10am-6pm Tue-Sun, closed first Tue of month) is less refurbished, more overgrown, less touristy and more romantic than any of the other palaces. After Natalya died, the palace changed hands several times until Catherine bought it and gave it to her lover Grigory Orlov (a little gift for helping her get rid of her husband Peter III). The palace was later passed to Catherine's son Paul I, who spent most of his time drilling his troops on the parade ground here.

Although still impressive, today Gatchina is but a shadow of its former self. Shaped in a graceful curve around a central turret, the palace looks fine from the front, but is falling to pieces around the back. Inside, few of the rooms have been restored (work only began in 1985); the most interesting feature is a tunnel running from the palace to the ornamental lake.

The best reason to come to Gatchina is to wander around the leafy park, with its many winding paths through birch groves and across bridges to islands in the lake. Look out for the Birch House (Beriozoy Dom), with a façade made of birch logs, and the ruined Eagle Pavilion (Pavilion Orla).

In the nearby town there are a couple of interesting churches. At the end of the main shopping street, the baroque Pavlovsky Sobor (ul Gobornaya) has a grandly restored interior with a soaring central dome. A short walk west is the Pokrovsky Sobor, a red-brick building with bright blue domes. There are not too many places to eat; you are better off packing a picnic.

TRANSPORT: GATCHINA

Distance from St Petersburg 45km

Direction Southwest

Travel Time One hour

Bus From Moskovskaya metro station bus 431 (R40, one hour) runs often. In Gatchina it stops on pr 25 Oktyabrya: the park is immediately west.

Train Any suburban train bound for Kalishe or Oranienbaum from Baltic Station (Baltiysky vokzal) stops at Gatchina.

ORANIENBAUM ОРАНИЕНБАУМ

Anyone interested in Prince Menshikov – best friend of Peter the Great – will be fascinated by this testament to his growing vanity and general hubris. While Peter was building Monplaisir at Peterhof, Menshikov began his own palace at Oranienbaum (Orange Tree), 12km further down the coast. Peter was unfazed by the fact that his subordinate's palace in St Petersburg (Menshikov Palace, p110) was grander than his own; and likewise Menshikov outdid his master in creating this fabulous place. While not particularly opulent compared to the palaces that Elizabeth and Catherine the Great favoured, by Petrine standards Oranienbaum was off the scale. This grand enterprise would eventually bankrupt Menshikov.

Following Peter's death and Menshikov's exile, the estate served briefly as a hospital and then passed to Tsar Peter III. Of course, Peter III didn't much like ruling Russia, so he spent a lot of time here before he was dispatched in a coup led by his wife, Catherine the Great.

Spared Nazi occupation, after WWII Oranienbaum was renamed for the scientist-poet Mikhail Lomonosov. Now known as Oranienbaum again, it doubles as a museum and public park (adult/child R40/20; 11am-6pm Wed-Mon), with boat hire and fairground rides alongside the remaining buildings.

Menshikov's Grand Palace (☎ 423 1627; adult/student R380/190; 11am-5pm May-Oct) impresses the most with its size, though many of its rooms are still under renovation. The palace is accessible only by guided tour, which takes place every hour on the quarter-hour. Admission to the palace also includes the recently renovated Japanese Pavilion.

Beyond the pond, the Palace of Peter II (adult/student R280/140; 10am-5pm Wed-Mon May-Oct) – also called Peterstadt – is a boxy toy palace, with

TRANSPORT: ORANIENBAUM

Distance from St Petersburg 41km

Direction West

Travel Time 45 minutes to one hour

Bus *Marshrutky* to Oranienbaum depart from Ⓜ Avtovo.

Train The suburban train from St Petersburg's Baltic Station to Petrodvorets continues to Oranienbaum. Get off at Oranienbaum-I (not II) Station, an hour from St Petersburg. From the station it's a short walk south, then west at the Archangel Michael Cathedral (Sobor Arkhangela Mikhaila) along Dvortsovy pr until you reach the palace entrance.

rich interiors. Approach it through the monumental Gate of Honour, all that remains of a small-scale fortress where he amused himself drilling his soldiers.

Worth a peek also is Catherine's over-the-top Chinese Palace, designed by Antonio Rinaldi. It was closed for renovation at the time of research, so it's bound to be looking fabulous in the near future. Rococo on the inside and baroque on the outside, the private retreat features painted ceilings and fine inlaid-wood floors and walls.

Perhaps Oranienbaum's best feature is the several kilometres of quiet paths through pine woods and sombre gardens, with relatively small crowds; again it's a lovely place for a picnic. Otherwise, you can head across the street to Okhota (☎ 422 0659; Dvortsoviy pr 65a; meals R600-1000; ⌚ noon-midnight). If the name didn't give it away (*okhota* means 'hunt'), you'll get the message from the herd of stuffed animals hanging from the walls and ceilings: game is the order of the day.

VELIKY NOVGOROD ВЕЛИКИЙ НОВГОРОД

The name means 'new town' but Novgorod was here by the 9th century, and for 600 years this little town was Russia's most pioneering artistic and political centre.

In a sense, Russian history began here. This was the first permanent settlement of the Varangian Norsemen, who established the embryonic Russian state. By the 12th century the principality – known as 'Lord Novgorod the Great' – was the largest in medieval Rus. It was unique for its quasi-democratic form of governance, by which princes were hired and fired by a citizens' assembly. And, most enduringly, its strong, spare style of church architecture, icon painting and down-to-earth *byliny* (epic songs) were to become distinct cultural forms that would influence Russian art, architecture and music for centuries to come.

When other principalities were ravished by the Mongol Tatars, these warriors got bogged down in the marshes surrounding Novgorod, so the city was spared. Indeed, Novgorod suffered most at the hands of other Russians. Ivan III of Moscow attacked and annexed it in 1477; and Ivan the Terrible razed the city and slaughtered 60,000 people in a savage pogrom. When St Petersburg was founded, Novgorod slipped into obscurity as a trading centre.

Although the city was methodically trashed by the Nazis, it was a top priority for rebuilding by the Soviets – a sign of its historical importance. Today, some amazing architecture remains from the early days. Spires and steeples mark the skyline of this little city (population 240,000).

The ancient kremlin, the proliferation of churches and the still thriving artistic centre make Novgorod a fascinating place for medieval history buffs, art-lovers and anyone who wishes to relive the Russia of yesteryear.

Novgorod Kremlin

Part park, part museum, part archive, the kremlin (☎ 8162-773 608; www.novogorodmuseum.ru; admission free; ⌚ 6am-midnight) was referenced in chronicles as early as 1044. From here, Alexander Nevsky and his troops marched off to battle the Swedes; here the *vech* (Peoples' Assembly) met to elect the local leaders; and here stood the sacred St Sophia Cathedral. It was, in short, the heart and soul of ancient Novgorod. The kremlin walls standing today date from the 15th century. You can climb the highest of its nine towers, Kokuy Tower (⌚ 11am-7pm Apr-Sep), for a panorama of the Volkhov River and the town beyond.

Finished in 1052, the handsome Byzantine Cathedral of St Sophia (Sofiysky Sobor; ⌚ 8am-8pm) is one of the oldest buildings in Russia, built under the rule of Prince Vladimir of Kyiv. The simple, fortresslike exterior was designed to withstand attack or fire, especially since flames had taken out an earlier wooden church on the site. The

VELIKY NOVGOROD

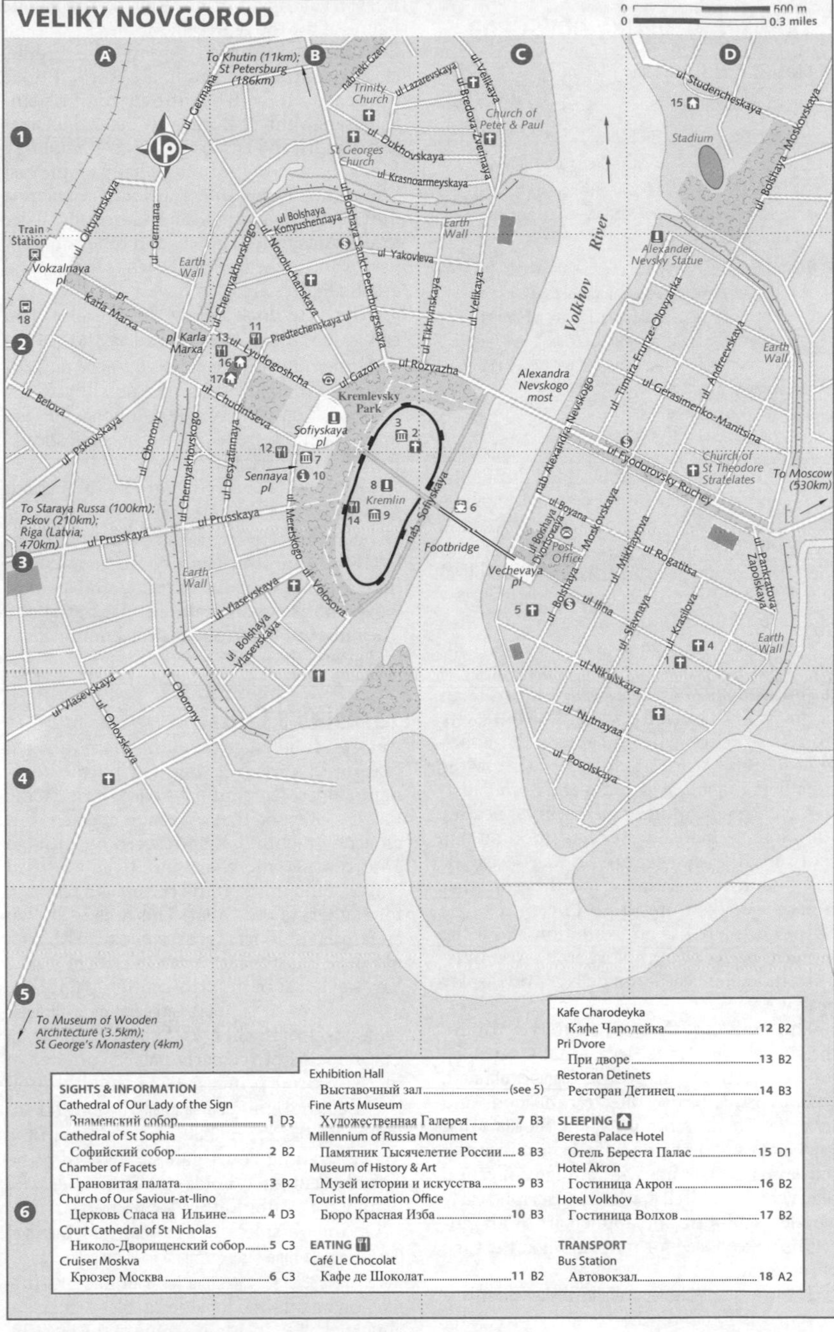

SIGHTS & INFORMATION

Cathedral of Our Lady of the Sign
Знаменский собор 1 D3
Cathedral of St Sophia
Софийский собор 2 B2
Chamber of Facets
Грановитая палата 3 B2
Church of Our Saviour-at-Ilino
Церковь Спаса на Ильине 4 D3
Court Cathedral of St Nicholas
Николо-Дворищенский собор 5 C3
Cruiser Moskva
Крюзер Москва 6 C3
Exhibition Hall
Выставочный зал .... (see 5)
Fine Arts Museum
Художественная Галерея 7 B3
Millennium of Russia Monument
Памятник Тысячелетие России 8 B3
Museum of History & Art
Музей истории и искусства 9 B3
Tourist Information Office
Бюро Красная Изба 10 B3

EATING

Café Le Chocolat
Кафе де Шоколат 11 B2
Kafe Charodeyka
Кафе Чаролейка 12 B2
Pri Dvore
При дворе 13 B2
Restoran Detinets
Ресторан Детинец 14 B3

SLEEPING

Beresta Palace Hotel
Отель Береста Палас 15 D1
Hotel Akron
Гостиница Акрон 16 B2
Hotel Volkhov
Гостиница Волхов 17 B2

TRANSPORT

Bus Station
Автовокзал 18 A2

TRANSPORT: VELIKY NOVGOROD

Distance from St Petersburg 186km

Direction Southeast

Travel Time Three to four hours

Bus From St Petersburg's Avtovokzal No 2 you can take buses to Novgorod (R250, 3½ hours, 14 daily), arriving at Novgorod's bus station, which is right next to the train station.

Train There is currently one evening train daily from St Petersburg's Moscow Station (Moskovsky vokzal) to Novgorod (R326, 3¼ hours, 5.15pm), returning to St Petersburg in the morning (8.05am). In effect, this means staying at least one – if not two – nights in Novgorod. Alternatively, you can take the bus in one direction or the other.

onion domes were probably added during the 14th century – even so, they are perhaps the earliest example of this most typically Russian architectural detail. The west doors, dating from the 12th century, have tiny cast-bronze biblical scenes and even portraits of the artists.

The interior is much more ornate, with fabulous frescoes from the 11th and 12th centuries. Of the icons, the most noteworthy is the miraculous *Znamenie Bozhey Materi* (Sign of the Mother of God), which saved the city from destruction when it came under attack in 1170. It is a working church, with services usually taking place at 10am and 6pm daily.

A picturesque whitewashed belfry is nearby. Although such a belltower has stood on this spot since the 15th century, it was destroyed and rebuilt several times: the structure that is here today is from the 17th century. The belfry normally has an exhibition about the 'Ancient Bells of Veliky Novgorod'. Appropriately, its ancient cast-iron bells are on display nearby.

The buildings that are scattered around the kremlin grounds occasionally open up for exhibitions. The gothic **Chamber of Facets**, built in 1433, has a collection of icons and other lavish church booty. The **Museum of History & Art** is said to be one of the best research museums of its kind, with a huge collection of early icons, birch-bark manuscripts, early wooden sculpture and applied art. Both museums were closed for renovation at the time of research.

The unique **Millennium of Russia Monument** was unveiled in 1862, on the 1000th anniversary of the founding of the city (marked by the arrival of Varangian Prince Rurik). The female figures at the top represent Mother Russia and the Orthodox Church. Around the middle, clockwise from the south, are Rurik, Prince Vladimir of Kyiv (who introduced Christianity), tsars Mikhail Romanov, Peter the Great and Ivan III, and Dmitry Donskoy trampling a Mongol Tatar. In the bottom band on the east side are nobles and rulers, including Catherine the Great with an armload of laurels for all her lovers; Alexander Nevsky and other military heroes are on the north side, while literary and artistic figures are on the west side.

From the dock below the kremlin, you can catch the **Cruiser Moskva** (☎ 8162-156 207; adult/student R200/100; ⏲ 12.30pm & 2pm May-Sep) for a one-hour float down the Volkhov River. On a good day, the surrounding marshes are lovely, with churches rising up majestically from the countryside.

The cool halls of Novgorod's the **Fine Arts Museum** (☎ 8162-73763; Sofiyskaya pl; adult/student R90/50; ⏲ 10am-6pm Tue-Sun) showcase paintings by 18th- and 19th-century Russian artists, including Andropov, Bryullov and Ivanov. Novgorod artists are featured on the 3rd floor. The museum is just outside the kremlin gates and across the square.

Yaroslav's Court

Across a footbridge from the kremlin is old Novgorod's market, marked by the remnants of a 17th-century **trading arcade** facing the river. Beyond that's the market gatehouse, an array of churches sponsored by 13th- to 16th-century merchant guilds and a 'road palace', built in the 18th century as a rest stop for Catherine the Great. This area is known as Yaroslav's Court (Yaroslavovo dvorishche), as legend has it that this was the site of Prince Yaroslav's elaborate 11th-century palace.

The Kyiv-style **Court Cathedral of St Nicholas** (Nikolo-Dvorishchensky Sobor; 1136) is all that remains of the early palace complex of the Novgorod princes. The cathedral itself is closed, but an **exhibition hall** (☎ 8162-233 465; adult/student R60/30; ⏲ 10am-4.30pm Wed-Sun) in the former trading court gate, across from the cathedral entrance, holds church artefacts and temporary exhibitions of local interest.

On the outside, the 14th-century **Church of Our Saviour-at-Ilino** (Tserkov Spasa-na-Iline; ul Ilina; adult/student R60/30; ⏲ 10am-5pm Tue-Sun) has graffiti-like ornaments and lopsided gables, which are almost playful. Inside are some of the few surviving frescoes by legendary Byzantine painter

Theophanes the Greek. Recent restoration has exposed as much of the frescoes as possible, though they are still faint. A small exhibition upstairs includes reproductions with explanations in Russian. Note Theophanes' signature use of white war-paint–style markings around the eyes and noses of his figures, and their soul-penetrating expressions. The church itself, east of Yaroslav's Court, is a prime example of Novgorod style (in contrast to the more complex 17th-century Moscow-style **Cathedral of Our Lady of the Sign** across the street).

St George's Monastery & Museum of Wooden Architecture

Set amid peaceful marshlands just outside of town, these two sights are worlds away from the city, making for a splendid outing if you are in Novgorod for more than a day. About 4km south of town along the Volkhov River, the 12th-century **St George's Monastery** (Yuriev Monastyr; 10am-8pm) still functions as a working Orthodox monastery. It features the heavily reconstructed Cathedral of St George and a clutch of 19th-century add-ons. Services are held in the Church of the Exaltation of the Cross (1761), which is attached to the monks' dorms. The monastery grounds are worth a visit, but what really warrants the trip out here is the windswept river setting, with gorgeous views out across the marshes.

Between Novgorod and the monastery is the beautiful **Vitoslavltsy Museum of Wooden Architecture** (adult/student R80/40; 10am-5pm), an open-air museum of peasant houses and beautiful intricate wooden churches from around the region. Take bus 7 from Novgorod to either place.

Information

Tourist Information Office (8162-773 074; www.visitnovgorod.ru; Sennaya pl 5; 10am-6pm) This little tourist information post is possibly unique in Russia for its helpful, English-speaking staff, assistance with hotel reservations and booking tours and plentiful free information.

Sleeping

A day trip to Novgorod is very rushed, so we recommend that you stay overnight at one of the following hotels.

Beresta Palace Hotel (8162-186 910; www.fclnovgorod.ru; Studencheskaya ul 2; s/d R3000/3500) The town's best hotel is on the east bank of the Volkhov, fully equipped with over 200 rooms, a fitness centre and a restaurant.

Hotel Volkhov (8162-335 505; www.novtour.ru; Predtechenskaya ul 24; s/d from R1500/2100) Next door to the Akron, the Volkhov is a large business hotel that is part of the NovTourInvest Hotel Group. Rooms are fine, though the place does not have much character.

Hotel Akron (8162-736 918; topol@mail.natm.ru; Predtechenskaya ul 24; s/d R1100/1620) This friendly hotel has received a complete overhaul, leaving the simple rooms in good shape with very modern bathrooms.

Eating

You'll eat decently in Novgorod, where a large number of traditional restaurants cater to both foreign and Russian tourists.

Kafe Charodeyka (8162-730 879; ul Volosova-Meretskogo 1/1; meals R300-400) Opposite the kremlin gate, this place has the ultimate a la carte menu, where you choose the ingredients of your meal and the chef cooks it according to your request.

Pri Dvore (8162-777 086; ul Lyudogoshcha 3; meals R150-200) Cheery little cafeteria with good prepared salads and hot dishes by the kilogram. A more formal sit-down restaurant is next door.

Restoran Detinets (8162-274 624; meals R400-800) Housed within the kremlin wall, this is an atmospheric and historic place serving Russian dishes. Enter the kremlin from the west bank, turn right and follow the wall beyond the WWII memorial and the first few buildings to the restaurant entrance.

Café Le Chocolat (8162-739 009; Lyudogoshcha 8; meals R300-600; 9am-11pm) Stop by this cute café for breakfast or for your daily fix of caffeine.

VYBORG ВЫБОРГ

Whether you are on your way to Helsinki or you want to get as close as you can to Finland without actually leaving Russia, the old Finnish town of Vyborg (population 81,000) is a fascinating and rewarding destination. Perched on the Finnish border, this ancient place has a melancholic, rather forgotten feel to it (the atmosphere of most Russian provincial towns in fact); but its quietly crumbling old architecture, winding cobblestone streets and magnificent fortress retain the magical atmosphere of a medieval town. Movie buffs may be interested to know that the critically acclaimed film *The Return* (Vozvrashcheniye) was filmed partly on location here in 2003, with the opening scene taking in the fortress as the young protagonists run through the town.

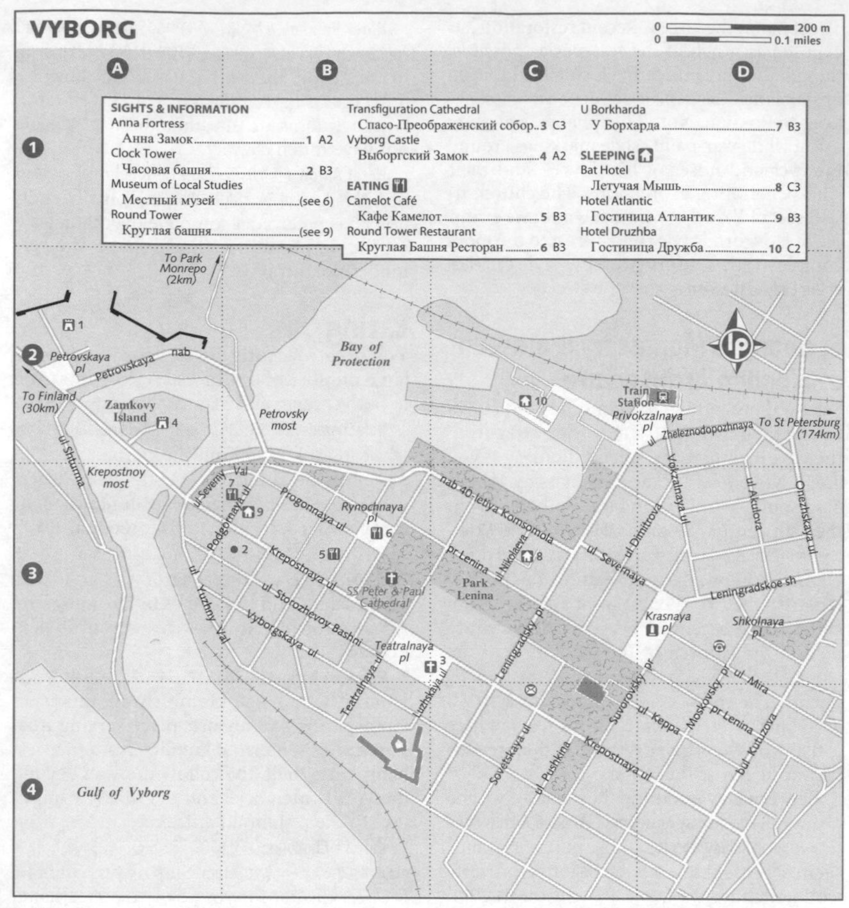

Vyborg (*vi*-berk) is built around the medieval, moated Vyborg Castle, built by the Swedes in 1293 when they first captured Karelia from Novgorod. Since then borders have jumped back and forth around Vyborg, giving the town its curiously mixed heritage and explaining the Finnish influence visible in everything from architecture to attitude.

Peter the Great took Vyborg for Russia in 1710. He had just recently established St Petersburg as his capital and he wanted to secure the region around it. A century later it fell within autonomous Finland and after the revolution it remained part of independent Finland (the Finns call it Viipuri). It changed hands several times during WWII, but finally ended up as Soviet territory, at which point all of the Finns fled west (or were deported, depending on whose side of the story you hear).

Today Vyborg looks like a Finnish town; and indeed, coach-loads of Finns arrive every weekend – many apparently coming just for the cheap alcohol. But the permanent residents are Russian fishers, timber-haulers and military men, as well as the service sector catering to the growing tourist industry.

The ancient and picturesque **Vyborg Castle** (☎ 81378-21515; admission R30; ⏲ 10am-7pm Tue-Sun), built on a rock in Vyborg Bay, is the city's oldest building, though most of it now consists of the 16th-century alterations. Inside, you can climb the tall **tower** (adult/child R70/50) and visit the small **museum of local studies** (adult/child R70/50), as well as a few other small exhibitions.

Across the bridge is the **Anna Fortress** (Anninskaya Krepost), built in the 18th century

TRANSPORT: VYBORG

Distance from St Petersburg 174km

Direction Northwest

Travel Time Around two to three hours

Bus Hourly buses (2½ hours, R120) run between St Petersburg and Vyborg from the bus stop to one side of Finland Station (Finlyandsky vokzal).

Train Suburban trains (three hours) run roughly every hour from Finland Station to Vyborg's train station. It's best to take the express services (R182, two hours, three times a day) or a Helsinki-bound train, all of which stop in Vyborg.

as protection against the Swedes and named after Empress Anna Ivanovna. It is not open to the public. Behind this is the Park Monrepo Reserve (☎ 81378-20539), a massive expanse of wooded and lake-dotted parkland. Laid out in a classical style, the wild forested park is packed with curved bridges, arbours and sculptures.

Vyborg is crossed by lovely streets and dotted with centuries-old churches, bell towers and cathedrals, especially along and off Krepostnaya ul. Look also for the many Style Moderne buildings that are in a similar state of disrepair. A short walk from the castle takes you to the crumbling 15th-century Clock Tower (Krepsotnaya ul 5; admission R30; Sat & Sun May-Sep). Climb to the top – if you dare – for fantastic views of the fortress and of the ruins of the nearby Transfiguration Cathedral (Spaso-Preobrazhensky Sobor, 1787). It is ruins – literally – but open around the clock if you want to climb around some crumbly walls.

Sleeping

Hotel Druzhba (☎ 81378-25744; booking@lens.spb.ru; ul Zheleznodorozhnaya 5; s/d R2400/3000) This old Soviet hotel is convenient to the train station, but otherwise does not have much to offer.

Bat Hotel (Letuchaya Mysh; ☎ 81378-34537; www.bathotel.ru; ul Nikolaeva 3, Vyborg; s R2280-2800, d R2740-3100; 💻) A very cosy option with newly renovated rooms on two floors and a cute café on the ground floor. Enter from the back.

Hotel Atlantic (☎ 81378-24778; atlantik.viborg@mail.ru; Podgornaya ul 9; s/d R1100/1500, s/d/tr/q with private bathroom R1500/1700/2000/2600, s/d upgraded from R1750/2000) On a quiet street near the castle, this pleasant place has decent rooms with fresh paint, clean white sheets and brand new bathrooms. The 'upgraded' rooms have been recently renovated and filled with new furniture, which explains the slightly higher prices.

Eating

U Borkharda (☎ 81378-34007; Podgornaya ul 10; meals R200-400) This place evokes old Vyborg in its décor, but the main feature of the menu is its beer list.

Round Tower Restaurant (Kruglaya bashnya; ☎ 81378-31729; Rynochnaya pl; meals R400-600; noon-11pm) On the main square, the old round tower has an excellent, atmospheric restaurant on its top floor.

Camelot Café (Krasnoarmeyskaya ul 14; meals R100-300) Choose between the arcaded interior or the covered outdoor 'summer garden'. Food is filling and affordable.

STARAYA LADOGA СТАРАЯ ЛАДОГА

You'd hardly guess it from the current state of this sleepy village, but Staraya (Old) Ladoga (population 3000) played a crucial role in the very birth of the Russian nation. Today there is little to see along its quiet streets other than an ancient fortress, several crumbling churches and some prettily painted wooden cottages. It's a pleasant place to wander for a few hours, particularly in summer when a swim in the river adds to the charm.

Dating from the 8th century, the town was known as Ladoga until 1704, when Peter the Great founded Novaya (New) Ladoga to the north as a transfer point for the materials arriving to build St Petersburg. Protected as a national reserve, the town's basic structure

TRANSPORT: STARAYA LADOGA

Distance from St Petersburg 125km

Direction East

Travel Time Around three hours

Train Take an *elektrichka* to Volkhov (Volkhovstroy I station) from Moscow Station in St Petersburg (R156, two hours, 8am). There was only one morning train at the time of research, so check the schedule in advance and get an early start. From Volkhov, take bus/minibus 23 (R20, 20 minutes) towards Novaya Ladoga.

RUSSIA'S ANCIENT CAPITAL

Just as the origins of ancient Rus are continually debated, so will Staraya Ladoga's status as 'Russia's first capital'. Nevertheless, its significance remains uncontested, as historians have given 753 AD as the village's birth date.

According to some ancient texts, when the Scandinavian Viking Rurik swept into ancient Russia in 862, along with his relatives Truvor and Sineus, they built a wooden fortress at present-day Staraya Ladoga and made this his base. You can see Rurik in a colourful mosaic on the side of the village school. Locals even claim the tumulus on the banks of the Volkhov River at the northern end of the village is the grave of Oleg, Rurik's successor.

Archaeological expeditions continue to uncover a wealth of information about the town's past. In 1997 a second 9th-century fortress was discovered 2km outside the village. The frescoes in the village's 12th-century churches exhibit Byzantine influences, indicating that the town was a cultural and commercial crossroads.

and street patterns have remained virtually unchanged since the 12th century, give or take a few ugly Soviet blocks.

The highlight is the **fortress** (Staroladozhskaya Krepost; 9am-6pm Tue-Sun Jun-Aug, 9am-4pm Tue-Sun Sep-May) at the southern end of the village, boasting wonderful views over the winding Volkhov River. The stone **St George's Church** (Tserkov Georgiya; admission R50) is open only during dry weather to protect the delicate 12th-century frescoes that are still visible on its walls. The wooden **Church of Dimitri Solun** is also contained within the partially ruined fortress walls. The main tower of the fortress is the **Historical-Architectural & Archaeological Museum** (☎ 81263-49331; admission R30; 9am-6pm Tue-Sun Jun-Aug, 9am-4pm Tue-Sun Sep-May) housing a retrospective of the area's history, including a scale model of the fortress in earlier times and items found on archaeological digs. Explanations are in English.

At one time, six monasteries worked in this small region. Now only the **Nikolsky Monastery** (9am-5pm) remains, 500m south of the fortress.

Atop the hill at the north end of the village, the striking blue, 17th-century **John the Baptist Church** (Ioanna-Predtechi Tserkov; 9am-6pm) is in much better repair, especially the frescoes and iconostasis inside. On this site was a 13th-century monastery. Nearby, beside the riverbanks, is an ancient burial mound and, beneath the church, caves where glass was once made.

Eating

Staraya Ladoga suffers from a shortage of eating options. The café above the general store on the main drag, Ladya, has decent food with an excellent ambiance.

Night Bird (Nochnaya Ptitsa; Volkhovsky pr; meals R100-200; 3pm-3am Mon-Thu & noon-3am Fri-Sun) A nicely decorated pub, about 100m north of the fortress.

PETROZAVODSK ПЕТРОЗАВОДСК

Nestled on the coast of vast Lake Onega, Petrozavodsk ('Peter's Factory') has a history directly linked to that of St Petersburg: it started as an iron foundry and armaments plant in 1703 – the same year as the northern capital. The capital of the autonomous republic of Karelia (the Russian region that borders neighbouring Finland), this is an exceptionally relaxed and pleasant Russian town (population 282,000), with countless green parks and pretty squares flanking its broad, tree-lined avenues.

The pretty crescents of neoclassical buildings on pl Lenina were built in 1775 as headquarters for Petrozavodsk armament plants. One of them houses the **Museum of Local Studies** (☎ 8142-780 240; pl Lenina 1; admission R100; 10am-5.30pm Tue-Sun), with nicely laid-out displays on the founding of the city and the history of Karelia. The best museum in town, however, is the **Fine Arts Museum** (☎ 8142-773 723; pr Marksa 8; admission R100; 10am-6pm Tue-Sun). It has

TRANSPORT: PETROZAVODSK

Distance from St Petersburg 420km

Direction Northeast

Travel Time Eight hours

Bus It's possible to take one of the daily buses (R200, nine hours) from St Petersburg's Avtovokzal No 2 but it's a hell of a journey.

Train The only enjoyable way to travel to Petrozavodsk is to take the overnight train (R950, eight hours, daily) from Ladoga Station (Ladozhsky vokzal), which gets you into Petrozavodsk in the early morning. Trains running between St Petersburg and Murmansk also stop in Petrozavodsk.

DETOUR: KIZHI КИЖИ

One of the most stunning sights in European Russia, the island of Kizhi on Lake Onega was once a centre of paganism, but it was invaded by Christianity in the 12th century. Over the centuries churches have come and gone, but the collection of churches you can visit today date from the 14th to 18th centuries and make for a fascinating half-day trip from Petrozavodsk.

The entire island of Kizhi comprises an open-air museum of history, architecture and ethnography (☎ in Petrozavodsk 8142-765 764; http://kizhi.karelia.ru; admission R500; 🕑 8am-8pm). The centrepiece is the 1714 fairytale Transfiguration Cathedral (Preobrazhensky Sobor), with its chorus of 22 domes, gables and ingenious decorations to keep water off the walls. It is a gem of Russian wooden architecture and not a single nail was used in its construction. Next door is the nine-domed Church of the Intercession (Pokrovskaya Tserkov), built in 1764.

The other buildings in the collection were brought from the region around Lake Onega. The 19th-century peasant houses, some more ornate than others, are nicely restored inside. The little Church of the Resurrection of Lazarus, from the 14th century, may be the oldest wooden building in Russia. The Chapel of the Archangel Michael, with an interesting tent-roofed belfry, has an exhibition on Christianity in Karelia and music students from Petrozavodsk play its bells in summer. There are numerous other houses, barns, windmills and buildings open to exploration.

While Kizhi is open year-round, it is only practical to visit between June and August, when the lake is open to navigation. Hydrofoils (return R1000, 1½ hours) make the trip a few times a day from the Petrozavodsk ferry terminal, allowing plenty of time for visitors on the island, and returning in the afternoon. Call the ferry terminal (☎ 8142-775 070) to confirm the schedule, which changes frequently.

In St Petersburg, you can also book two or three-day cruises that bypass Petrozavodsk, but stop at both Kizhi and Valaam. Contact Solnechniy Parus (☎ 332 9686; www.solpar.ru in Russian; return from R6700).

collections of 15th- to 17th-century Karelian icons, folk art and other art inspired by the *Kalevala*, Finland's national epic.

While Petrozavodsk is a pleasant place to spend a few hours, most people come here to visit the magnificent collection of old wooden buildings and churches on Kizhi, an island 66km northeast of the city in Lake Onega. See the boxed text, above, for details.

Information

Sampo.ru Internet Centre (☎ 8142-733 263; ul Anokhina 20; per hr R33; 🕑 9am-9pm) Internet access.

Tourist Information Centre (☎ 8142-764 835; www.ticrk.ru; ul Kuybisheva 5; 🕑 9am-5pm Mon-Sat Jun-Aug, Mon-Fri Sep-May) Provides helpful English-speaking staff and plenty of info.

Sleeping

Hotel Fregat (☎ 8142-764 162, 8142 764 163; pr Marksa 1a; s/d R2400/2650) Located on the lake side of the ferry-terminal building. You will pay a bit more for lake views.

Hotel Severnaya (☎ 8142-762 080; http://severnaja.onego.ru; pr Lenina 21; s/d R1980/2400, ste R3300-4300; 💻) Smack in the centre, this place is not flashy, but it's clean and comfortable.

Hotel Prionezhsky (☎ 8142-765 271; www.nikolaevskie-oteli.ru; ul Fedosovoy 46; s/d from R2900/4000; ❄ 💻) Petro's classiest hotel, on the lakeside 700m northwest of the ferry terminal, has just a dozen bright, modern rooms.

Eating

As well as the venues listed here, there are also restaurants in the hotels.

Karelskaya Gornitsa (☎ 8142-785 300; ul Engelsa 13; meals R300-500) Claiming to be the first restaurant serving Karelian cuisine, this excellent place offers plenty of fresh fish and game.

Fregat Restaurant (☎ 8142-764 162; pr Marksa 1a; meals R300-400) Attached to a small lakeside hotel, this airy restaurant has high ceilings, big windows and a wide terrace with a wonderful view.

VALAAM & SORTAVALA ВАЛААМ И СОРТАВАЛА

The delightful Valaam Archipelago, which consists of Valaam Island and some 50 smaller ones, sits in northwestern Lake Ladoga. The main attractions here are the 14th-century **Valaam Transfiguration Monastery** (Spaso-Preobrazhensky Valaamsky Monastyr; www.valaam.ru; ☎ 81430-38233) and the tree-covered island on which it stands. The island can be reached by boat or hydrofoil between mid-May and mid-October.

TRANSPORT: VALAAM & SORTAVALA

Distance from St Petersburg 240km

Direction Northeast

Travel Time Six to eight hours

Boat During the main tourist season, hydrofoils (45 minutes) and boats (up to three hours) to Valaam leave the dock in Sortavala. Otherwise, overnight cruisers depart from St Petersburg's River Passenger Terminal. Make arrangements through a tour agency such as Solnechniy Parus (☎ 332 9686; www.solpar.ru in Russian) for a one-day, two-night trip (return from R3300) to Valaam, or a longer cruise that visits both Valaam and Kizhi (return from R6700).

Train One slow train departs from Ladoga Station (Ladozhsky vokzal) bound for Sortavala (R510, six hours, every second day), continuing on to Petrozavodsk. The timing is very awkward and requires at least one overnight stay in Sortavala.

Most agree that the monastery was founded in the late 14th century as a fortress against Swedish invaders, who managed to destroy it completely in 1611. It was rebuilt and destroyed several times in the next few hundred years. When the Soviet Union took this region from Finland in WWII, many of the monks and much of the monastery's treasure were moved to Finland. Soviet authorities used the monastery as a home for war invalids.

Monks started returning to Valaam in 1989 and today it has a community of about 200 monks. The buildings are now protected architectural landmarks, but neglect has taken its toll and restoration work is ongoing. The centrepiece is the monastery's Transfiguration Cathedral with its five blue domes.

The usual access point for Valaam is the sleepy town of Sortavala, on the northern shore of Lake Ladoga. Stop by the Tourist Office (☎ 81430-24802; sortavala-info@onego.ru; Karelskaya ul 15, Sortavala) for more information.

SLEEPING & EATING

Hotel Zimnyaya (☎ 81430-38248; www.valaam.twell.ru; Tsentralnaya ul 4, Valaam; d R1900-2900) Bare rooms – most of which share bathroom facilities – occupy the 2nd floor of this old building near the monastery. There is a small café on site but it is not open during winter months.

Hotel Piypun Pikha (☎ 81430-23240; Promyshlennaya ul 44, Sortavala) This hotel is in a lovely lakeside location on the east edge of Sortavala and can arrange excursions to Valaam. Also on site are a restaurant and nightclub, which probably represent your best bet for dining and entertainment in town.

TRANSPORT

St Petersburg is the most accessible Russian city, thanks to its proximity to Europe. It is also relatively easy to navigate. Keep in mind that metro stops are quite spread out, so you'll likely spend a lot of time on your own two feet, unless you learn a few bus routes or spring for a taxi. Flights, tours and rail tickets can be booked online at www.lonelyplanet.com/travel_services.

Things Change...

The information in this chapter is particularly vulnerable to change. Check directly with the airline or a travel agent to make sure you understand how a fare (and ticket you may buy) works and be aware of the security requirements for international travel. Shop carefully. The details given in this chapter should be regarded as pointers and are not a substitute for your own careful, up-to-date research.

AIR

St Petersburg is Russia's second-largest air hub, although it lags far behind Moscow in terms of the number of long-haul connections. It's well-connected throughout Europe and the former Soviet Union, but from Asia, Australasia and the Americas you'll usually have to change planes in either Moscow or another European hub to fly into St Petersburg.

Airlines

Any airlines flying to and from St Petersburg not listed below will likely have an office at Pulkovo Airport (see p234):

Aeroflot (SU; Map p92; ☎ 438 5583, 718 5555; www.aeroflot.ru; ul Rubinshteyna 1/43; Ⓜ Dostoevskaya)

Air France (AF; Map pp68–9; ☎ 336 2900; www.airfrance.com; Malaya Morskaya ul 23; Ⓜ Sadovaya)

Alitalia (AZ; Map pp68–9; ☎ 334 4451; www.alitalia.com; Nevsky pr 30; Ⓜ Nevsky Pr)

Austrian Airlines (OS; Map pp68–9; ☎ 331 2005; www.aua.com; Nevsky pr 32; Ⓜ Nevsky Pr)

British Airways (BA; Map pp68–9; ☎ 380 0626; www.britishairways.com; Malaya Konyushennaya ul 1/3a, office 23b; Ⓜ Nevsky Pr)

CSA Czech Airlines (OK; Map pp68–9; ☎ 315 5259; www.czechairlines.com; Bolshaya Morskaya ul 32; Ⓜ Sadovaya)

Delta Airlines (DL; Map pp68–9; ☎ 571 5820; www.delta.com; Bolshaya Morskaya ul 36; Ⓜ Sadovaya)

Finnair (AY; Map pp68–9; ☎ 303 9898; www.finnair.com; Malaya Konyushennaya ul 1/3, office 33b; Ⓜ Nevsky Pr)

CLIMATE CHANGE & TRAVEL

Climate change is a serious threat to the ecosystems that humans rely upon, and air travel is the fastest-growing contributor to the problem. Lonely Planet regards travel, overall, as a global benefit, but believes we all have a responsibility to limit our personal impact on global warming.

Flying & Climate Change

Pretty much every form of motor transport generates CO_2 (the main cause of human-induced climate change) but planes are far and away the worst offenders, not just because of the sheer distances they allow us to travel, but because they release greenhouse gases high into the atmosphere. The statistics are frightening: two people taking a return flight between Europe and the US will contribute as much to climate change as an average household's gas and electricity consumption over a whole year.

Carbon Offset Schemes

Climatecare.org and other websites use 'carbon calculators' that allow travellers to offset the greenhouse gases they are responsible for with contributions to energy-saving projects and other climate-friendly initiatives in the developing world – including projects in India, Honduras, Kazakhstan and Uganda.

Lonely Planet, together with Rough Guides and other concerned partners in the travel industry, supports the carbon offset scheme run by climatecare.org. Lonely Planet offsets all of its staff and author travel.

For more information check out our website: www.lonelyplanet.com.

DOMESTIC FLIGHTS FROM ST PETERSBURG

Destination	One-way fare (R)	Duration (hr)	Frequency
Archangelsk	4200-4600	1½	daily
Chelyabinsk	5000-6100	2½	4 weekly
Ekaterinburg	4100-5000	2½	daily
Kaliningrad	2800-3400	1½	1-2 daily
Murmansk	4000	2	daily
Moscow	800-1300	1	8 daily
Norilsk	8000-9300	10	4 weekly
Novosibirsk	6000-6300	4	3 weekly
Samara	3800-4800	2½	3 weekly

All flights are from Pulkovo-1.

KLM Royal Dutch Airlines (KL; Map pp68–9; ☎ 346 6868; www.klm.com; Malaya Morskaya ul 23; Ⓜ Sadovaya)

LOT Polish Airlines (LO; Map pp68–9; ☎ 273 5721; www.lot.com; Karavannaya ul 1; Ⓜ Gostiny Dvor)

Lufthansa (LH; Map pp68–9; ☎ 320 1000; www.lufthansa.com; Nevsky pr 32; Ⓜ Nevsky Pr)

Rossiya Airlines (FV; Map p92; ☎ 333 2222; www.pulkovo.ru; Nevsky pr 61; Ⓜ Mayakovskaya)

SAS Scandinavian Airlines (SK; Map pp68–9; ☎ 326 2600; www.scandinavian.net; Nevsky pr 25; Ⓜ Nevsky Pr)

Transaero (Map p84; ☎ 579 6463; www.transaero.ru; Liteyny pr 48; Ⓜ Mayakovskaya)

Airport

St Petersburg has two terminals at its Pulkovo Airport, 17km south of the city (see Map p65). **Pulkovo-1** (☎ 704 3822; www.pulkovo.ru) handles domestic flights, as well as flights to some non-Russian cities within the former Soviet Union. The international terminal is **Pulkovo-2** (☎ 704 3444), a small, well-run airport that was given a decent face-lift for the tercentennial in 2003. There are plans to build a third terminal here because of increased demand.

There are ATMs in both terminal buildings, but make sure you have euros or US dollars to change just in case they are not working.

GETTING INTO TOWN

The airport is about 17km south of the city centre. The **Airport Express** (☎ 388 0055; www.airportexpress.ru; Moskovskaya/Pushkinskaya/roundtrip R50/70/130) runs between both airport terminals and Pushkinskaya metro station, stopping at Moskovskaya metro station along the way. Buses run every 20 minutes between 9am and 10pm. They are less frequent at other times, but they do run all night. Don't bother taking a taxi unless you have booked in advance, as the sharks waiting out the front will charge as much as R1500. Many hotels will book a taxi for you, in which case a reasonable fare is R400-600. All of the major car hire companies have offices at Pulkovo Airport, so you can pick up your rental car at the airport if you intend to drive into town.

BICYCLE

Bicycles are becoming more common on the streets of St Petersburg, but cycling is still difficult: pothole-riddled roads and lunatic drivers unaccustomed to cyclists make it a dangerous proposition. That said, the city's relatively compact size means that it is easy to get around by bike – and often much quicker than public transport. Many adventurers swear by their bikes as the ideal form of transport in St Petersburg (at least from May to October).

Especially when you are unfamiliar with traffic patterns, it is advised to stay off the busiest, traffic-clogged roads. Stick to the back streets and sidewalks. Both sides of the Neva River have wide sidewalks (with few pedestrians) that are perfect for pedalling. Car-free Yelagin Island (p120) is another excellent place for cycling, although bikes are not allowed on weekends and holidays.

Adventurous riders can cycle all the way to Tsarskoe Selo (p219) by heading due south on Moskovsky pr. It's a nightmare getting down there, but once you are south of the airport you are surrounded by lovely countryside. Look for the statue of Pushkin and appropriate signs that mark the turn-off to Tsarskoe Selo, which is about 25km south of the city. It's a long ride, but you can take your bike on the *elektrichka* (suburban train) to return to St Petersburg.

For bicycle hire, see p199. Note that bikes are prime targets for thieves, so be sure to lock up your bike with a serious bike lock, which is normally provided by the rental shop. Helmets, on the other hand, are not normally provided (nor will you see anyone wearing one).

BOAT

Around St Petersburg

For new perspectives on St Petersburg neighbourhoods, fine views of the Peter & Paul Fortress, or just good old-fashioned transportation, a boat ride along the Neva River and around the canals is one of the city's highlights. See p246 for boat tour companies.

To/From St Petersburg

Between April and September, international passenger ferries leave from the **sea station** (morskoy vokzal; Map pp108–9; ☎ 322 6052; pl Morskoy Slavy 1; Ⓜ Primorskaya). It's a long way from the metro, so it's actually easier to take either bus 7 or trolley bus 10 from outside the Hermitage.

At the time of research, however, there were no regular ferry services from St Petersburg to the Baltic or Scandinavian countries. Once a week, **Trans Russia Express** (☎ 703 5410; www.tre.de) operates a combined passenger-cargo vessel between St Petersburg and Lubeck (Germany), offering the experience of 'the real life of seamen'. Other companies have operated services to Tallinn (Estonia), Helsinki (Finland), Kaliningrad (Russia) and other destinations, so it's worth checking with a travel agency such as the **Ferry Centre** (Paromny Tsentr; Map p84; ☎ 327 3377; www.paromy.ru in Russian; ul Vosstaniya 19; Ⓜ Pl Vosstaniya) or **Baltic Tours** (Map pp68–9; ☎ 330 6663; www.baltictours.ru; per Sergeya Tyulenina 4/13; Ⓜ Nevsky Pr) for an updated schedule. These companies also sell tickets for one- and two-week cruises that depart from St Petersburg and sail around Scandinavia and the Baltics.

From June to August, regular river cruises depart from the **River Passenger Terminal** (off Map pp146–7; ☎ 262 0239, 262 6321; Obukhovskoy Oborony pr 195; Ⓜ Proletarskaya) and float along the Neva to inland Russia, including cruises to Valaam, Kizhi and Moscow. Prices and schedules vary, so book through a travel agency such as **Solnechniy Parus** (Map p92; ☎ 332 9686; www.solpar.ru in Russian; ul Vosstaniya 55; Ⓜ Pl Vosstaniya) or **Cruise Russia** (Map p92; ☎ 764 6947; www.cruise-ru.com; Ligovsky pr 87; Ⓜ Ligovsky Pr).

BUS

Around St Petersburg

Bus, tram and trolleybus stops are all marked by roadside signs, many of which also indicate the route number. Most transport runs from 6am to 1am. Buy your tickets (R14) from the attendants on the vehicle.

The following are some of the useful routes around the city:

Nevsky pr, from Dvortsovaya pl to pl Vosstaniya Buses 7 and 22; trolleybuses 1, 5, 7, 10 and 22. Trolleybuses 1 and 22 continue out to pl Alexandra Nevskogo. Trolleybuses 5 and 7 continue to Smolny.

Sadovaya ul, south of Nevsky pr Trams 3, 13 and 14. Tram 3 continues north of Nevsky pr and then crosses the Troitsky most to the Petrograd Side.

From Dvortsovaya pl to Vasilevsky Island Bus 7 and trolleybus 10.

To the Kirovsky Islands Tram 34 from Baltic Station (Baltiysky vokzal) or Liteyny pr goes along Kamennoostrovsky pr and ends up on Krestovsky Island. Bus 10 from the corner of Nevsky pr and Bolshaya Morskaya ul will also get you there.

To the Petrograd Side Bus 128 runs from Primorskaya metro station along both Bolshoy prospekts to the Botanical Gardens.

To/From St Petersburg

The city's main bus station is **Avtovokzal No 2** (Map pp146–7; ☎ 766 5777; www.avtovokzal.ru; nab Obvodnogo kanala 36; Ⓜ Ligovsky Pr), a recently remodelled building a little out of the city centre. (There is no No 1, in case you were wondering.) Domestic and international services leave from here. Note that buses to Moscow are all en route to somewhere else, which means you will be dropped off in the northern Moscow suburb of Khimki. It is far more convenient to take the train. In any case, it is recommended to buy bus tickets in advance, especially for

BUSES FROM ST PETERSBURG

Destination	Price (R)	Duration (hr)	Frequency (daily)
Helsinki	1700	8	2
Moscow	520	12	1
Novgorod	210	3½	14
Petrozavodsk	320	9	1
Pskov	345	5½	2
Riga	850	11	1
Tallinn	850	7½	7

long-distance journeys. For information on left-luggage facilities, see p239.

A few private companies operate international bus routes to Helsinki and the Baltics:

Ecolines (Map pp146–7; ☎ 314 2550; www.ecolines.ru; Podezdny per 3; Ⓜ Pushkinskaya) Daily overnight bus from Vitebsk Station to Rīga (R855, 9½ hours). Other buses run to Minsk, Kiev and Odessa.

Eurolines (Map pp146–7; ☎ 438 2839, 441 3757; www.eurolines.ee; Admiral Business Centre, Mitrofanievskoe sh 2; 9am-9pm; Ⓜ Baltiyskaya) Runs five daily buses from Baltic Station to Tallinn (R700-770, seven hours), including one express (R850, 5½ hours). Daily buses go from Baltic Station to Rīga (R850, 11 hours) and from Park Inn – Pulkovskaya (p212) to Turku (€45, 11 hours) via Helsinki (€33, eight hours).

Sovavto (off Map pp146–7; ☎ 740 3985; www.sovavto.ru; Park Inn – Pulkovskaya, pl Pobedy 1; Ⓜ Moskovskaya) One daily train departs from the Park Inn – Pulkovskaya to Helsinki (eight hours) and Turku (11 hours). Buses are timed to arrivals and departures of the Silja Line and Viking Line ferries from Turku to Stockholm.

CAR & MOTORCYCLE

Bearing in mind the frequently dire quality of roads, lack of adequate signposting and keen-eyed highway police, driving in Russia may not be for everybody. To legally drive your own or a rented car or motorcycle in Russia, you will need to be 18 years or older and have a full driving licence. Technically, you also need an International Driving Permit with a Russian translation of your licence, or a certified Russian translation of your full licence. Rental agencies are not likely to ask for such documentation, but the traffic police are.

Driving

Russians drive on the right and traffic coming from the right generally (but not always) has the right of way. Speed limits are generally 60km/h in town, but usually there are no signs to say so. Limits are between 80km/h and 110km/h on highways. Children under the age of 12 may not ride in the front seat, and seat belt use is mandatory.

Technically, the maximum legal blood alcohol content is 0.04%, but in practice it is illegal to drive after consuming any alcohol at all. This is a rule that is strictly enforced.

Left turns are illegal except where posted; you'll have to make three rights or a short U-turn (this is safer?). Street signs, except in the centre, are woefully inadequate and Russian drivers make Italian drivers seem downright courteous! Watch out for drivers overtaking on the inside; this seems to be the national sport. Potholes and jagged crevices are everywhere.

The State Automobile Inspectorate (Gosudarstvennaya Avtomobilnaya Inspektsia; GAI) skulks about on the roadsides, waiting for speeding, headlightless or other miscreant vehicles. Officers are authorised to stop you, issue on-the-spot fines and shoot at your vehicle if you refuse to pull over.

The GAI also hosts the occasional speed trap: the St Petersburg–Vyborg road has this reputation. By law, GAI officers are not allowed to take any money at all; fines should be paid via Sberbank. In reality, Russian drivers normally pay the GAI officer approximately half the official fine, thus saving money and the time consumed by Russian bureaucracy.

St Petersburg has no shortage of petrol stations that sell all grades of petrol. The private company **Neste** (www.neste.ru) currently operates over 40 full-service petrol stations in and around St Petersburg. Prices for petrol at these stations may be slightly higher, but service is faster and major credit cards are accepted. See the *St Petersburg Visitors' Guide Yellow Pages* for listings of parts, service and repair specialists.

BRIDGE TIMETABLE

From May until November all major bridges rise at the following times nightly to allow ships to pass through, meaning you cannot cross the river during these times. Call ☎ 326 9696 for more information. All times are am.

Bridge	Up	Down	Up	Down
Alexandra Nevskogo	2.20	5.10		
Birzhevoy	2.00	4.55		
Bolsheokhtinsky	2.00	5.00		
Dvortsovy (Palace)	1.25	4.55		
Finlyandsky	2.20	5.30		
Grenadersky	2.45	3.45	4.20	4.50
Kantemirovsky	2.45	3.45	4.20	4.50
Leytenanta Shmidta	1.25	2.45	3.10	5.00
Liteyny	1.40	4.45		
Sampsonievsky	2.10	2.45	3.20	4.25
Troitsky	1.40	4.45		
Tuchkov	2.00	2.55	3.35	4.55
Volodarsky	2.00	3.45	4.15	5.45

Hire

Expect to pay about €50 per day to rent an economy-class car in St Petersburg. The rental process is fairly straightforward, but driving is another matter. Unless you are going out of town, it is often easier, and around the same price, to hire a car and driver. The major international rental agencies have offices in the centre (listed here), as well as at Pulkovo-2 airport terminal:

Astoria Service (Map p92; ☎ 712 1583, 164 9622; www.astoriaservice.ru; Borovaya ul 11/13, office 65; per hr R270-460; Ⓜ Ligovsky Pr)

Avis (Map p92; ☎ 600 1213; www.avis-rentacar.ru; pl Alexandra Nevskogo 2; Ⓜ Pl Alexandra Nevskogo)

Europcar (☎ 703 5104; www.europcar.ru; Pulkovo-2 Airport)

Hertz (Map pp68–9; ☎ 326 4505, 324 3242; www.hertz.ru; Malaya Morskaya ul 23; Ⓜ Nevsky Pr)

Parking

In the town's centre uniformed parking attendants charge R30 to R50 to watch your car for you. There are guarded parking lots outside many hotels now. Never leave anything of value, including sunglasses, CDs and cigarettes, in a car. Street parking is pretty much legal wherever it seems to be, but it's illegal anywhere on Nevsky pr. Use common sense – avoid parking in dark side streets and isolated areas.

MARSHRUTKA

The *marshrutka* (a Russian diminutive form of *marshrutnoye taxi*) is a crucial form of transport in St Petersburg. These minibuses function like buses, only passengers are free to request a stop anywhere along the route and because of their size they zip through the traffic far faster than normal city buses.

The sheer number of routes is staggering – they connect the city to the suburbs, and far-flung residential neighbourhoods to metro stations, and are often the only public transport serving some parts of the centre (particularly the Mariinsky and Smolny neighbourhoods, where metro stations are almost nonexistent). A *marshrutka* is almost always the fastest and cheapest way to get from one end of Nevsky to the other.

Hold out your arm to flag down the *marshrutka* you want. If in doubt state your destination to the driver to confirm the *marshrutka* is headed there. The fare – payable to the driver – is displayed inside the bus and varies depending on the route, although it's usually R20 or R25.

When you reach your destination, you need to call out to the driver to stop. The standard phrase is '*ostanavityes pozhalsta!*' ('stop please!'). Although if you don't dare shout this out, 'stop please' in English is likely to suffice, as long as it's loud enough.

METRO

The St Petersburg **metro** (www.metro.spb.ru; 🕑 6am-midnight) is a very efficient four-lined system. The network of some 58 stations is most usefully employed for travelling long distances, especially connecting the suburbs to the city centre.

Look for signs with a big blue 'M' signifying the entrance to the metro. The flat fare for a trip is R14; you will have to buy an additional ticket if you are carrying a significant amount of baggage. If you wish to buy a single journey, ask for '*odin proyezd*' and you will be given a *zheton* (token) to put in the machine.

If you are staying more than a day or two, however, it's worth buying a 'smart card', which is good for multiple journeys to be used over the course of a fixed time period. Smart cards are plastic cards that the machine reads when you touch the circular light. The prices of smart cards at the time of research were as follows:

10 trips/7 days R115

20 trips/15 days R220

40 trips/30 days R432

Getting around on the metro can be a bit of an adventure if you do not read Cyrillic. Metro maps in English are available in the tourist publications that are distributed around town, but they are not posted at metro stations. Furthermore, even if you do read Cyrillic, the signs in the stations are difficult to read from the trains.

Listen out for the announcements: just before a departing train's doors close, a recorded voice announces '*Ostorozhno! Dveri zakryvayutsya. Sleduyushchaya stantsia* (name of next station)'. This means 'Caution! The doors are closing. The next station is (name of next station)'. Just before the train stops at the next station, its name is announced.

A confusing aspect of the St Petersburg metro is that where two lines cross and there is a *perekhod* (transfer), the two stations will

CATCHING A CAR

Stand on practically any street and stick out your arm: you can be assured that sooner rather than later a car will stop for you. Usually it's a well-worn little Lada or Zhiguli, but it can be anything – a snazzier car, an off-duty city bus, an army Jeep with driver in camouflage. The drivers may be on their way somewhere, or they may just be trying to supplement their income. These unofficial taxis are the cheapest way to cover distances in the city centre.

So, you've stuck your arm out and a car has stopped. This is where the fun starts. You state your destination, say, *'ulitsa Marata!'* The driver looks away for a second and shouts back *'skolko?'* ('how much?'). You bark back a price. If he's happy with that amount, he'll say, *'sadites!'* ('sit down!'), at which point you get in and drive off. If he's not happy with that price, a period of negotiation might ensue.

If you feel that the driver is trying to rip you off because of your accent, shut the door. If there's more than one person in the car, don't get in. And if the driver seems creepy, let him drive on. There'll be another car coming in a flash. At any time, you are welcome to give a gruff *'nyet!'* and slam the door

Alternatively, the driver might not ask you for a price and just tell you to get in or not depending on whether he wants to go your way. If that's the case, at the end of the ride you pay him what you think the fare was worth. If your ride is less than 10 minutes long, R100 to R150 is acceptable. For a greater distance reckon on paying R200. The airport from the city centre should be between R400 and R600.

As a bonus, often these drivers are very interesting characters you wouldn't ordinarily meet on your trip, and chatting with them about the potholes, how much better things were under the Soviets, their days in the army, how much you earn, Putin, Bush and Blair can be great fun.

have different names. For example, Nevsky Pr and Gostiny Dvor are joint stations: to all intents and purposes they are one and the same (you don't need to go outside to change), but each has a different name because it's on a different line.

TAXI

One of the most enduring Soviet traditions is that of 'catching a car'. The shadow economy is thriving and numerous people drive the city streets specifically looking to give people paid lifts in their 1970s Zhigulis and Ladas. See the boxed text (above) for more information about the cultural norms associated with this form of transport.

Nearly all official taxis are unmetered, so if you do flag one you'll have to go through a similar process of negotiation to that involved in catching a car, only the driver will want more money for being 'official'.

If you know in advance that you'll need a taxi, it's easiest to order one direct from your hotel. The operator will tell you the price, which will usually be considerably lower than what an official taxi will quote you on the street. Some recommended private taxi companies are listed following (all of these work 24 hours):

Peterburgskoye Taxi (☎ 068, 324 7777; www.taxi068.spb.ru in Russian)

Taxi-4 (☎ 633 3333; www.taxi-4.ru in Russian)

Taxi Blues (☎ 321 8888; www.taxiblues.ru in Russian)

Taxi Million (☎ 700 0000)

TRAIN

St Petersburg is well connected to cities throughout Eastern Europe, the Baltics, Finland and European Russia. Sample fares and schedules are listed in the boxed texts; unless otherwise noted, prices are for a *kupe* (2nd-class in a four-seat couchette) ticket on a *skory* (fast) train. A lux ticket is generally twice as much. Keep in mind that the whole Russian rail network runs on Moscow time. St Petersburg is on Moscow time anyway, but even in other time zones the timetables and station clocks are usually running Moscow time. Also be aware that trains to Warsaw and Berlin traverse Belarus, which requires purchasing a transit visa.

Stations

St Petersburg is served by five train stations:

Baltic Station (Baltiysky vokzal; Map pp146–7; ☎ 768 2859; nab Obvodnogo kanala 120; Ⓜ Baltiyskaya) *Elektrichky* (suburban trains) to Gatchina, Oranienbaum and Peterhof.

Finland Station (Finlyandsky vokzal; Map pp122–3; ☎ 768 7687; pl Lenina 6; Ⓜ Pl Lenina) Suburban trains to Vyborg and other towns in the north of the Leningradsky Oblast; the main Helsinki trains also depart from here.

Ladoga Station (Ladozhsky vokzal; Map p65; ☎ 768 5304; Zanevsky pr 73; Ⓜ Ladozhskaya) For trains to Karelia and Arctic Russia, including the overnight train to Petrozavodsk and the express services to Murmansk and Arkhangelsk. It is located on the Vyborg Side, across the river and east from pl Alexandra Nevskogo.

Moscow Station (Moskovsky vokzal; Map p92; ☎ 768 4597; Nevsky pr 85; Ⓜ Pl Vosstaniya) For trains to Moscow and Novgorod.

Vitebsk Station (Vitebsky vokzal; Map pp146–7; ☎ 768 5807; Zagorodny pr 52; Ⓜ Pushkinskaya) Trains to Rïga, Vilnius, Kaliningrad, Kyiv, Minsk, Berlin, Prague and Budapest. Local trains also leave here throughout the day to Detskoe Selo, the station for Tsarskoe Selo.

LEFT LUGGAGE

You can check your bags at most hotels and train and bus stations. Look for the signs Камера Хранения (*kamera khranenia;* left-luggage counter) or Автоматические Камеры Хранения (*avtomaticheskie kamery khranenia;* left-luggage lockers). Both options are usually secure, but make sure you note the opening and closing hours. To utilise the left-luggage lockers:

1 Buy two tokens *(zhetony)* from the attendant.

2 Find an empty locker and put your stuff in.

3 Decide on a combination of one Russian letter and three numbers and write it down.

4 Set the combination on the inside of the locker door.

5 Put one token in the slot.

6 Close the locker.

7 To open the locker, set your combination on the outside of the door. After you've set your combination, put a token in the slot, wait a second or two for the electrical humming sound, and pull open the locker.

Tickets

For long-distance trains, it's best to buy tickets in advance. Tickets can be purchased directly at the train stations, but in some cases it may be more convenient to buy tickets at the Central Train Ticket Office (Map pp68–9; ☎ 762 3344; nab kanala Griboedova 24; 🕒 8am-8pm Mon-Sat, 8am-4pm Sun; Ⓜ Nevsky Pr) or the Central Airline Ticket Office (Map pp68–9; ☎ 315 0072; www.cavs.ru; Nevsky pr 7; 🕒 8am-8pm Mon-Fri, 8am-6pm Sat & Sun; Ⓜ Nevsky Pr). It is also possible to buy train tickets from local travel agencies, although they charge a small fee for issuing the ticket. Always take your passport when buying a train ticket. For general information about timetables, contact Russian Railways (☎ 055; www.rzd.ru).

TRAINS TO MOSCOW

Train no & name	Departure (pm)	Fare	Duration (hr)
1 Krasnaya Strela	11.55	R1870	8
3 Express	11.59	R1704	8
5 Nikolaevsky Express	11.30	R1745	8
23 Yunost	1.05	sid R620, kupe R1660	8
53 Grand Express	11.40	lux R3700-4000	8
63 Nevsky Express	11.15	R1370-1660	4½
159 Avrora	4.00	sid R2000-2300, kupe R2430	5½
165 ER200	6.30	R2680-3000	4½

Trains depart from Moscow Station.

Types of Class

On long-distance trains, your ticket will normally give the numbers of your carriage *(vagon)* and seat *(mesto)*. For a detailed look

DOMESTIC TRAINS FROM ST PETERSBURG

Destination	Train no	Station	Departure	Fare	Duration (hr)
Arkhangelsk	390A	LS	10.03am Mon, Tue, Thu & Fri	R1403-1965	25
Ekaterinburg	072	LS	5.04pm	R3950	37½
Kazan	103	MS	6.49pm odd days	R2300-2700	26
Murmansk	022	LS	5.20pm	R1700-2072	28½
Novgorod	81	MS	5.18pm	sid R326	3
Petrozavodsk	658	LS	10.13pm	R600-946	8½
Pskov	677	VS	5.20pm	R510	5
Vologda	688	LS	8.40pm	R1200-1500	12½

LS = Ladoga Station (Ladozhsky vokzal)
MS = Moscow Station (Moskovsky vokzal)
VS = Vitebsk Station (Vitebsky vokzal)

INTERNATIONAL TRAINS FROM ST PETERSBURG

Destination	Train no	Station	Departure	Fare	Duration (hr)
Berlin	19	VS	11.40pm Tue, Wed, Thu & Sat*	R5140	35½
Brest	49	VS	3pm	R1662	19
Budapest	49	VS	3pm Tue	R5870	45
Helsinki	33 Repin	FS	7.27am	sid R1960	6
Helsinki	35 Sibelius	FS	3.40pm	sid R1960	6
Kaliningrad	079	VS	6.16pm	R1625-1970	26
Kyiv	053	VS	9.20pm	R1592	24
Minsk	051	VS	7.08pm	R2286	15
Odessa	19	VS	11.40pm except Thu	R1721	35
Prague	49	VS	3pm Wed, Thu	R4170	40
Riga	037	VS	10.08pm	R2573	12½
Vilnius	079	VS	6.16pm	R2070-2400	19½
Warsaw	19	VS	11.40pm Tue, Wed, Thu & Sat*	R2465	27

FS = Finland Station (Finlyandsky vokzal)
VS = Vitebsk Station (Vitebsky vokzal)
*more often in summer

at travelling on Russian trains, see Lonely Planet's *Russia & Belarus* or *Trans-Siberian Railway*.

Compartments in a 1st-class carriage, also called soft class *(myagkiy)* or sleeping car *(spalnyy vagon, SV* or *lux)*, have upholstered seats and convert to comfortable sleeping compartments for two people. Not all trains have a 1st-class carriage. Compartments in a 2nd-class carriage, usually called 'compartmentalised' *(kupeynyy* or *kupe)*, are four-person couchettes. Trains that are not running overnight may also offer 'seated' places (*sidyashchiy* or *sid*), which are basically seats in an open carriage.

Reserved-place *(platskartnyy)*, sometimes also called hard class or 3rd-class, has open bunk accommodation. Groups of hard bunks are partitioned, but not closed off, from each other. This class is low on comfort, privacy and security.

Types of Train

The regular long-distance service is a fast train *(skory poezd)*. It stops more often than the typical intercity train in the West and rarely gets up enough speed to merit the 'fast' label. Foreigners booking rail tickets through agencies are usually put on a *skory* train.

Generally, the best *skory* trains *(firmenny)* have cleaner cars, more polite attendants and much more convenient arrival/departure hours; they sometimes also have fewer stops, more 1st-class accommodation or functioning restaurants.

A passenger train *(passazhirskiy poezd)* is an intercity-stopping train, found mostly on routes of 1000km or less. These can take an awfully long time as they clank and lurch from one small town to the next.

When taking trains from St Petersburg, note the difference between long-distance and 'suburban' trains. Long-distance trains run to places at least three or four hours out of the city, with limited stops and a range of accommodation classes. Suburban trains, known as *prigorodnye poezda* or *elektrichky*, run to within just 100km or 200km of the city, stop almost everywhere, and have a single class of hard bench seats. You simply buy your ticket before the train leaves, and there's no capacity limit – so you may have to stand part of the way.

Most stations have a separate ticket hall for suburban trains, usually called the Prigorodny Zal and often tucked away at the side or back of the station building. Suburban trains are usually listed on separate timetables, and may depart from a separate group of platforms.

DIRECTORY

BUSINESS HOURS

The consumer culture is developing rapidly in Russia, and one place it is evident is hours of operation. Most shops are open daily, often from 10am to 8pm. Smaller shops might close on Sunday. Department stores and food shops are also usually open every day from 8am to 8pm. These days, many larger food shops stay open *kruglosutochno* (24 hours).

Restaurants typically open from noon to midnight, although – again – it is not unusual for restaurants to stay open 24 hours a day.

That said, while many businesses claim to open *kruglosutochno,* beware the highly contradictory *tekhnichesky pereryv* (technical break). So a '24-hour' exchange office might shut for a technical break for anywhere from 15 minutes to four hours.

Museum hours vary widely, as do their weekly days off. Most museums shut entrance doors 30 minutes or an hour before closing time. Many close for a *sanitarny den* (literally 'sanitary day'), a day of cleaning during the last week of every month.

Government offices open from 9am or 10am to 5pm or 6pm weekdays. Hours of banks and other services vary widely. Large branches in busy commercial areas are usually open from 9am to 5pm weekdays, with shorter hours on Saturdays. Smaller branches have shorter hours and often close for a one-hour *pereryv* (break) in the middle of the day.

Throughout this book, opening hours are cited only when they deviate from the following 'standard' opening hours:

Banks 9am-5pm Mon-Fri, some also open Sat

Businesses 9am-6pm Mon-Fri, some also open 9am-6pm Sat

Restaurants noon-midnight

Shops & supermarkets 10am-8pm

CHILDREN

You will know that Russia has made its transition to capitalism when you see the supermarkets well stocked with nappies, formulas and every other product your children might need.

St Petersburg does not present any particular hazards to your kids, save the ornery babushkas. (Although even they seem to have a soft spot for children.) Filled with museums, churches and theatres, St Pete may not seem like the most appealing destination, but it is surprisingly well equipped for youngsters. See p117 for a list of kid-friendly sights. In addition to these suggestions, circuses and puppet theatres are two carry-overs from the Soviet period that continue to thrive in St Petersburg (see p192). The concept of babysitting services has not yet developed in St Petersburg, although some upscale hotels offer this service. Lonely Planet's *Travel with Children* contains useful advice on how to cope with kids on the road and what to bring to make things go more smoothly.

CLIMATE

St Petersburg's climate is maritime and much milder than its northern latitude would suggest. January temperatures average -8°C; a really cold day will get down to -15°C. It's a windy city, especially in some areas exposed to the Gulf of Finland.

Summer is cool and takes a while to get going: snow in late April is not uncommon as temperatures suddenly drop when the melting ice blocks from Lake Ladoga come floating through the city's main waterways. Warm weather doesn't really start until June to August, when temperatures usually surpass 20°C. On the rare hot days of highs up to 30°C, residents flee to the beaches on the north bank of the Gulf of Finland or to their *dachas* (country cottages) in cool but mosquito-infested forests.

The city's northern latitude means long summer days and long winter nights. During White Nights, around the time of the summer solstice, night is reduced to a brief dimming of the lights

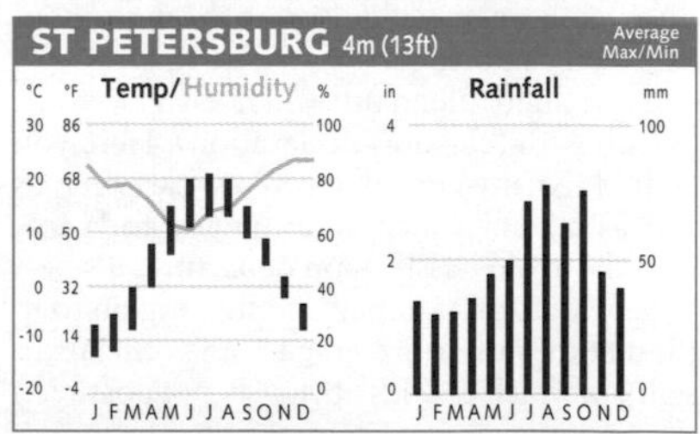

about 1am, only to turn to dawn a couple of hours later. In winter the city seems to be in constant dusk. See p16 for more information.

COURSES

A bonus of joining one of these courses is that the hosting organisation usually provides housing (or at least assistance finding it) and issues an invitation for a student visa (allowing you to pay Russian prices for museum admission and theatre tickets).

Language

Inspire your inner Russian-speaker:

Essex Russia Services (☎ in UK 01366-501445; www.russianlanguage.org.uk) Arranges for private lessons through the Benedict School or group classes at Herzen State Pedagogical University.

Extra Class Language Centre (☎ 315 2720; www.learnrussian.ru) Individual and group courses include entertainment activities as well as weekly lectures on Russian culture and history. Accommodation is with a local Russian family.

Herzen State Pedagogical University (☎ 314 7859; www.herzen.spb.ru) Caters mostly to students, offering semester-long courses and dormitory lodging.

Liden & Denz (☎ 334 0788; www.lidenz.ru) More expensive courses service the business and diplomatic community with less-intensive evening courses.

Writing

Inspire your inner Dostoevsky. The **Summer Literary Seminar** (☎ in USA 888-882 0949; www.sumlitsem.org) has two- and four-week courses hosted by Herzen University. Award-winning faculty from all over the world offer seminars in fiction, poetry, creative nonfiction, screenwriting, travel writing, arts criticism and translation.

CUSTOMS REGULATIONS

Customs controls in Russia are relatively relaxed these days. Searches beyond the perfunctory are quite rare. Apart from the usual restrictions, you are limited by the amount of cash you can bring in.

Your flight attendants will likely give you a *deklaratsiya* (customs declaration). Here you should list any currency you are carrying, as well as valuables such as computers and cameras. To avoid hassle upon departure, it's best to get this form stamped and to hang on to it. (Sometimes there are no customs officials in sight, in which case it's obviously not possible.) If you are carrying more than US$3000 – or valuables worth that much – you must declare it and proceed through the red channel.

Otherwise, on entering Russia, you can pick up your luggage and go through the green channel, meaning 'nothing to declare'.

If you intend to take home anything vaguely 'arty' (manuscripts, instruments, coins, jewellery) it must be assessed by the **Cultural Security Department** (Map pp68–9; ☎ 311 5196; Malaya Morskaya ul 17; 11am-5pm Mon-Fri; M Nevsky Pr). Take along your passport, a sales receipt and the item in question. The 'experts' will issue a receipt for tax paid and a certificate stating that the item is not an antique. It is illegal to export anything over 100 years old.

DISCOUNT CARDS

There are no discount cards currently operating on a citywide basis. Student cards have a high rate of hit and miss. Many kindly old ladies at museums will give you the benefit of the doubt if you claim to be a student and look relatively young, others will look at your ISIC card as if it were a document from Mars and throw it back at you with a demand for the full price. The Hermitage is the blissful exception where anyone with a student card from any country gets in for free. Senior citizens (usually anyone over the age of 60) are also eligible for discounts.

ELECTRICITY

St Petersburg, like the whole of Russia and most of Europe, uses the Continental plug with two round pins. Electricity is 220 volts, 50Hz AC and supply is very reliable. American and Japanese appliances need a 220V to 110V/100V converter. For more information, see www.kropla.com.

EMBASSIES & CONSULATES

If your country is not listed below, contact your embassy in Moscow in an emergency.

Australia (Map pp68–9; ☎ /fax 325 7333; www.australianembassy.ru; Italiyanskaya ul 1; M Nevsky Pr)

Austria (Map p84; ☎ 275 0502; fax 275 1170; Furshtatskaya ul 43; M Chernyshevskaya)

Belarus (Map p84; ☎ 274 7212; Bonch-Bruevicha ul 3A; M Chernyshevskaya)

China (Map p102; ☎ 714 7670; http://stpetersburg.chineseconsulate.org; nab kanala Griboedova 134; M Nevsky Pr)

Denmark (Map pp114–15; ☎ 703 3900; www.gksktpetersborg.um.dk; Bolshaya al 13, Kamenny Island; Ⓜ Chyornaya Rechka)

Estonia (Map pp114–15; ☎ 702 0920; www.peterburg.estemb.ru; Bolshaya Monetnaya ul 14; Ⓜ Gorkovskaya)

Finland (Map p84; ☎ 331 7600; www.finland.org.ru; Preobrazhenskaya pl 4; Ⓜ Chernyshevskaya)

France (Map pp68–9; ☎ 332 2270; www.francespb.org; nab reki Moyki 15; Ⓜ Nevsky Pr)

Germany (Map p84; ☎ 327 2400; www.sankt-petersburg.diplo.de; Furshtatskaya ul 39; Ⓜ Chernyshevskaya)

Latvia (Map pp108–9; ☎ 327 6054; www.am.gov.lv/stpetersburg; 10-ya i 11-ya liniya; Ⓜ Vasileostrovskaya)

Lithuania (Map p84; ☎ 327 3167; fax 327 2615; ul Ryleeva 37; Ⓜ Chernyshevskaya)

The Netherlands (Map pp68–9; ☎ 334 0200; www.nlcg.spb.ru; nab reki Moyki 11; Ⓜ Nevsky Pr)

UK (Map p84; ☎ 320 3200; www.britemb.msk.ru; pl Proletarskoy Diktatury 5; Ⓜ Chernyshevskaya)

Ukraine (Map p84; ☎ 271 2123; Bonch-Bruevicha ul 1; Ⓜ Chernyshevskaya)

USA (Map p84; ☎ 331 2600; http://stpetersburg.usconsulate.gov; Furshtatskaya ul 15; Ⓜ Chernyshevskaya)

EMERGENCY

Ambulance (☎ 03)

Fire department (☎ 01)

Police (☎ 02)

Police hotline for foreigners (☎ 702 2177)

GAY & LESBIAN TRAVELLERS

St Petersburg's proximity to Europe means that the city is not quite as conservative as other parts of Russia; the active gay and lesbian scene reflects this attitude. The *St Petersburg Times* features articles about gay and lesbian issues, as well as listings of gay and lesbian clubs. The newest publication of note is the glossy lesbian magazine *Pinx*, which now accompanies its gay counterpart *Queer* (Квир). Published in Moscow, both offer up articles and artwork aimed at, well, queers.

Most recently, gay activists announced plans for the city's first Pride parade in 2007 and a LGBT (Lesbian, Gay, Bisexual and Transgender) film festival to be held at Dom Kino in 2008. At the time of research, however, neither event was confirmed. Nonetheless, there are a few clubs aimed specifically at gay and lesbian patrons (see p181). Some other useful resources:

www.discovergaypetersburg.ru This gay tour agency promises, among other things, tours of the homoerotic art of the Hermitage.

www.gay.ru/english The English version of this site includes club listings and tour guides, plus information on gay history and culture in Russia.

www.krilija.sp.ru Krilija (Wings) is Russia's oldest officially registered gay and lesbian group, a human rights organisation aimed at uniting the community by hosting roundtable discussions and other activities.

www.lesbi.ru An active site for lesbian issues; Russian only.

www.xs.gay.ru Gay and lesbian news from St Pete, Moscow and around Russia. The links to the English version of the site do not actually work, so it's only useful if you read Russian.

HEALTH

St Petersburg does not pose any particular threats to your health, although you should be aware of the risks associated with drinking the tap water (see the boxed text, below). Also be aware that the city was built on a swamp,

TO DRINK OR NOT TO DRINK

Reports about the harmful effects of drinking tap water in St Petersburg have been widely publicised and greatly exaggerated. The city's water supplier, Vodokanal, insists that the water is safe to drink, as do many local residents. Nonetheless, the pipes are antiquated, so the water may contain some metal pollutants. Furthermore, traces of *Giardia lamblia* have been found on a very small scale. GI is a nasty parasite that causes unpleasant stomach cramps, nausea, bloated stomach, diarrhoea and frequent gas. There is no preventative drug, and it is worth taking precautions against contracting it.

To be absolutely safe, only drink water that has been boiled for 10 minutes or filtered through an antimicrobial water filter (PUR brand makes a good portable one). It's probably safe to accept tea or coffee at someone's house, and most restaurants and hotels likely have filtration systems. Bathing, showering and shaving should cause no problems at all.

If you develop diarrhoea, be sure to drink plenty of fluids, preferably including an oral rehydration solution. Imodium is to be taken only in an emergency; otherwise it's best to let the diarrhoea run its course and eliminate the parasite from the body. Metronidazole (brand name Flagyl) or Tinidazole (known as Fasigyn) are the recommended treatments for *Giardia lamblia*.

which means the mosquitoes are nasty in the summer months. Be sure to bring plenty of insect repellent. Also advised: aspirin, as you may need something to nurse your hangovers.

HOLIDAYS

During the major holiday periods – the first week in January (between New Year's Day and Orthodox Christmas) and the first week or two of May (around May Day and Victory Day) – St Petersburg empties out as many residents retreat from the city for much-needed vacations. Transport is often difficult to book around these periods, but accommodation is usually not a problem. Although many residents leave, the city is a festive place over New Year's and during the May holidays, usually hosting parades, concerts and other events in honour of the holidays. The downside is that many museums and other institutions have shortened hours or are closed altogether during these holiday periods.

By contrast, the Stars of White Nights Festival was designed with tourists in mind: theatres, museums and other institutions often host special events between late May and early July to appeal to the massive influx of visitors during this period. If you are visiting St Petersburg at this time, book your travel and accommodation in advance and expect to pay top rates. In August there are still plenty of tourists around, but residents tend to retreat from the city to recover. Many theatres close for the month of August, as do some of the smaller museums and galleries.

See p16 for an extensive list of special events in the city.

Public Holidays

New Year's Day 1 January

Russian Orthodox Christmas Day 7 January

Defenders of the Motherland Day 23 February

International Women's Day 8 March

Easter Monday April/May (varies)

International Labour Day/Spring Festival 1 & 2 May

Victory Day 9 May

Russian Independence Day 12 June

Day of Reconciliation and Accord (the rebranded Revolution Day) 7 November

Constitution Day 12 December

INTERNET ACCESS

If you are travelling without a computer, here are some good old-fashioned internet cafés:

abooks internet centre (Map pp108–9; ☎ 974 3919; 6-ya i 7-ya liniya 27; per hr R100; 9am-10pm; M Vasileostrovskaya)

Café Max (Map p92; ☎ 273 6655; www.cafemax.ru; Nevsky pr 90/92; per hr R40-70; 24hr; M Mayakovskaya) A big fancy place with 150 computers, a game zone and a comfy café and beer bar.

FM Club (Map p92; ☎ 764 3674; ul Dostoevskogo 6a; per hr R60; 24hr; M Vladimirskaya)

Kofe In (Map p92; ☎ 717 5793; Nevsky pr 148; per hr R60; 24hr; M Pl Vosstaniya)

Mirage Univer-City (Map pp114–15; ☎ 498 0758; www.mirage.ru; Bolshoy pr 35; per hr R120; 8am-2am; M Chkalovskaya)

Northwest Telecom (Severo-Zapadny Telekom; Map pp68–9; ☎ 069; cnr Bolshaya Morskaya ul & Gorokhovaya ul; per hr R60; 10am-10pm; M Nevsky Pr)

Players' Internet Club (Map p97; cnr Gorokhovaya & Kazanskaya ul; per hr R60; 24hr; M Sadovaya/Sennaya Pl)

Quo Vadis (Map p92; ☎ 333 0708; www.quovadis.ru; Nevsky pr 76; per hr R100; 24hr; M Mayakovskaya) Enter from Liteyny pr.

Vosstaniya-1 (Map p92; ☎ 579 5770; www.v1.spb.ru; pl Vosstaniya 1; per hr R120; 10am-9pm Mon-Sat, 10am-8pm Sun; M Pl Vosstaniya)

WI-FI ACCESS

Besides the plethora of internet cafés, wireless access is also becoming more common around St Petersburg. There is wi-fi access at most hotels and mini-hotels, as well as at a handful of cafés and pubs around the city. Unfortunately, it is usually not free; you might pay a daily access rate at a hotel, while cafés will usually sell you an access card for about R100 for an hour. You can log in at the following venues:

- Che (p170)
- The Idiot (p172)
- Red Club (p185)
- Stolle (p173)
- Zerno Istiny (p181)
- Zoom Café (p166)

For a list of places around town that offer free wireless access, see http://wifi.yandex.ru.

LEGAL MATTERS

It's not unusual to see *militsioners* (police officers) randomly stopping people on the street to check their documents. In recent years, this checking tends to focus on anyone remotely Caucasian-looking and other people with darkish skin, but the police have the right to stop anyone. Unfortunately, readers have complained about police pocketing their passports and demanding bribes. The best way to avoid such unpleasantness is to carry a photocopy of your passport, visa and registration, and present that when a police officer demands to see your *dokumenty*. A photocopy is sufficient for such inquiries, despite what the officer may argue. Threatening to phone your consulate usually clears up any such misunderstandings.

For legal purposes, Russians come of age at 18, when they are legally allowed to drink, drive and vote (but not simultaneously). Both heterosexual and homosexual sex is legal at 16.

MAPS

Maps in English and Cyrillic are widely available in bookstores – both overseas and in St Petersburg itself. Dom Knigi (p151) has an excellent selection, with maps of transport routes – including *marshrutka* (minibus) routes – and the excellent *Atlas Sankt Peterburg s kazhdym domom*, an invaluable A4 booklet covering the whole city and marking the location of every street number.

MEDICAL SERVICES

Emergency medical care is available at hospitals around town, but many international visitors might be put off by the sad state of public hospitals. The private clinics listed below have facilities that meet international standards. Services are pricey, but they generally accept major international insurance policies, including direct billing. In any case, it is worth checking with your health insurance provider to confirm that you are covered in Russia – and investing in travel insurance if you are not.

Clinics

In case of more serious health issues:

American Medical Clinic (Map p102; ☎ 740 2090; www.amclinic.ru; nab reki Moyki 78; Ⓜ Sadovaya)

Euromed (Map p84; ☎ 327 0301; www.euromed.ru; Suvorovsky pr 60; Ⓜ Chernyshevskaya)

Medem International Clinic & Hospital (Map p92; ☎ 336 3333; www.medem.ru; ul Marata 6; Ⓜ Mayakovskaya)

MedPalace (Map p84; ☎ 380 7979; www.medpalace.ru; ul Chaykovskogo 6; Ⓜ Chernyshevskaya)

Pharmacies

Look for the sign аптека *(apteka)* or the usual green cross to find a pharmacy. **36.6 Pharmacy** (http://spb.366.ru) is a chain of 24-hour pharmacies with many branches around the city:

Historic Heart (Map pp68–9; Gorokhovaya ul 16; Ⓜ Sadovaya)

Smolny (Map p84; Liteyny pr 41; Ⓜ Mayakovskaya)

Vosstaniya (Map p92; Zagorodny pr 6/8; Ⓜ Vladimirskaya)

MONEY

Russian currency is the rouble, written as рубль or abbreviated as руб. There are 100 kopecks (копеек or коп) in the rouble, and these come in small coins that are worth one, 10 and 50 kopecks. Roubles are issued in coins in amounts of one, two and five roubles. Banknotes come in values of 10, 50, 100, 500 and 1000 roubles. Small stores, kiosks and many other vendors have difficulty changing large notes, so save those scrappy little ones.

The rouble has been relatively stable since it was revalued in 1998. For details of costs in St Petersburg, see p19. For exchange rates, see the inside front cover.

ATMs

ATMs linked to international networks such as AmEx, Cirrus, Eurocard, MasterCard and Visa are now common throughout St Petersburg. Look for the sign Банкомат *(bankomat)*. Using a credit or debit card, you can always obtain roubles. The following outlets also give the option to withdraw US dollars or euros:

Alfabank (Map pp68–9; ☎ 329 8050; www.alfabank.ru; nab kanala Griboedova 6/2; Ⓜ Nevsky Pr)

Citibank Nevsky (Map p92; Nevsky pr 45/2; Ⓜ Mayakovskaya)

Citibank Petrograd Side (Map pp114–15; Bolshoy pr 18; Ⓜ Sportivnaya)

Citibank Sennaya (Map p97; Moskovsky pr 7; Ⓜ Sadovaya)

Citibank Smolny (Map p84; pr Chernyshevskogo 18; (M) Chernyshevskaya)

Citibank Vasilevsky Island (Map pp108–9; Sredny pr 27; (M) Vasileostrovskaya)

Changing Money

US dollars and euros are easy to change around St Petersburg, but other currencies will undoubtedly cause more hassle than they are worth. Whatever currency you bring should be in pristine condition. Banks and exchanges do not accept old, tatty bills with rips or tears. For US dollars make certain they are of the new design, which has the large offset portrait. When you visit the exchange office, be prepared to show your passport.

Credit Cards

Credit cards, especially Visa and MasterCard, are becoming more widely accepted beyond upmarket hotels, restaurants and stores. You can also use your credit card to get a cash advance at most major banks in St Petersburg.

Travellers Cheques

Travellers cheques are still relatively difficult to use in St Petersburg. The process can be lengthy, involving trips to numerous cashiers in the bank, each responsible for a different part of the transaction. Expect to pay 1% to 2% commission. Not all travellers cheques are treated as equal by Russian establishments willing to handle them. You'll have little or no luck with any brands other than AmEx, Thomas Cook and Visa.

NEWSPAPERS & MAGAZINES

All of the following English-language publications can be found at hotels, restaurants and cafés around town. For information on Russian-language media, see p58.

In Your Pocket (www.inyourpocket.com) This free monthly handout targets tourists and expats with club and restaurant listings, as well as more timely information.

St Petersburg Times (www.sptimes.ru) The long-running biweekly sister paper to the daily *Moscow Times* is a great resource for visitors. The Friday edition has theatre, club, cinema and concert listings, as well as Sergei Chernov's column, 'Chernov's Choice', which sets the weekend agenda.

Visitor's Guide Yellow Pages (www.yell.ru) An invaluable bilingual phone book.

ORGANISED TOURS

We would never recommend seeing St Petersburg from a seat on a bus, but the following options for organised tours offer interesting alternatives for seeing the city – by bike or by boat; from the air or from the water; or by the power of your own two feet.

Bike Tours

St Petersburg is relatively compact, which makes cycling an ideal way to see the sights. For more information about cycling in St Petersburg, see p234 and p199.

A joint project of Peter's Walking Tours (opposite) and Skat Prokat (p199), the **Sunday Morning Bike Tour** (Map p92; ☎ 717 6838; www.biketour.spb.ru; Skat Prokat, Goncharnaya ul 7; per person R800; 10.30am Sun May-Sep; (M) Pl Vosstaniya) is a great introduction to St Petersburg's various neighbourhoods and sights, from the banks of the Neva to the back alleys and courtyards of the city. The price of the tour includes bike rental for 24 hours.

Boat Tours

The most romantic way to see St Petersburg is from the water. Tour boats ply the canals and rivers all summer long. Indeed, it's hard to walk down Nevsky pr without being assaulted by megaphoned voices recruiting passengers. It's possible to chat up the owners of the smaller boats to arrange private excursions (particularly recommended at night). Expect to pay from R1500 to R2000 to hire the boat for a group of up to six people. Otherwise, there is little to differentiate between the boats, with the following exceptions.

Anglotourism (Map p92; ☎ 7-921-989 4722; anglotourismo@yahoo.com; nab reki Fontanki 64, most Lomonosova; adult R400-450, student R300-350; noon, 8.30pm & 12.30am May-Sep; (M) Dostoevskaya) This is the only regularly scheduled boat tour with English-speaking guides. (Surprisingly, it is not significantly more expensive than the Russian-speaking trips.) The daytime and evening trips tour the canals, while the more expensive night excursion goes out to the Neva to watch the raising of the drawbridges.

Driver (Map pp68–9; ☎ 716 5886; www.driver-river.ru; tours R300-350) Driver's boats stop at three different docks: hop on board in front of the Peter & Paul Fortress (Map pp114–15; Petrogradskaya nab 32; (M) Gorkov-skaya), in front of Kunstkamera (Map pp108–9; Universitetskaya nab 3; (M) Vasileostrovskaya) or in front of the Admiralty (Map pp68–9; Admiralteyskaya nab 2; (M) Nevsky Pr).

Three different routes circle around the Neva, while the longest one (1½ hours) loops around the Fontanka and the Griboedov Canal.

Helicopter Tours

See St Petersburg from the air. On weekends and holidays **Baltic Airlines** (Map pp68–9; ☎ 704 1676; www.balticairlines.ru; Nevsky pr 7/9; helicopter R1000, tandem parachute US$200; Ⓜ Nevsky Pr) offers copter flights over the Neva, taking a 15-minute orbit around the Admiralty and Smolny Cathedral. Baltic flies to Peterhof (p216) for the same price. Thrill-seekers can arrange a tandem parachute jump with the same company.

Walking Tours

Both of the following companies can also arrange guided visits (in English) to Kresty Prison (p122). For a series of self-guided walking tours around St Petersburg's neighbourhoods, see the Neighbourhoods chapter.

Peter's Walking Tours (www.peterswalk.com; per person R430; 10.30am) Peter Kozyrev is famous for his 'Original Walking Tour'. With no fixed itinerary, Peter (or one of the other fantastic English-speaking guides) is open to suggestions regarding route or theme. As a result, no two tours are the same. The four-hour walk departs daily from St Petersburg International Hostel (p208). Peter also organises a Friday-night pub crawl and a Saturday-morning excursion about the Siege of Leningrad. The schedule is posted on the website: no reservations required.

VB Excursions (☎ 928 0739; www.vb-excursions.com; per person €14-22) This new outfit offers specialised walking tours on subjects ranging from Revolutionary St Petersburg to *Crime and Punishment*. English-speaking tour guides promise to 'walk at your pace' and 'see things which regular tourists do not see'.

PHOTOGRAPHY

St Petersburg is nothing if not photogenic. The only possible complaint is that nearly all museums, churches and other sights will charge you extra to photograph the interior – usually R100 for photography and R300 for video. Fortunately, you can't put a price on the canals crisscrossed by bridges and golden domes rising above the river. Beware of one Soviet holdover: it's still forbidden to take photographs inside the metro, and those nasty babushkas are sure not going to let you get away with it! For more strategies on taking pictures refer to Lonely Planet's *Travel Photography*.

It's easy to purchase photographic equipment throughout the city. To transfer digital images onto CD, stop by one of the internet cafés (see p244).

If you are feeling nostalgic for old times, visit the **Second-hand Shop** (Map pp68–9; ☎ 571 2816; Nevsky pr 54; 10am-9pm; Ⓜ Gostiny Dvor), which carries an incredible selection of old-school Soviet-made cameras.

POST

Although service has improved dramatically in recent years, the usual warnings about delays and disappearances of incoming and outgoing mail apply to St Petersburg. Airmail letters take two to three weeks to the UK, and three to four weeks to the USA or Australasia.

To send parcels home, head to the elegant **main post office** (Map p102; ☎ 312 7460; Pochtamtskaya ul 9; Ⓜ Sennaya Pl). Smaller post offices may refuse to send parcels internationally; most importantly, your package is more likely to reach its destination if you send it from the main post office. Bring your item unwrapped: it will be wrapped and sealed with wax for you. You must provide an address in St Petersburg.

RADIO

Most of St Petersburg's popular stations play a mix of trashy Euro pop and its even more over-the-top Russian variant. Still, their play-lists can be unexpectedly eclectic. Some of the more popular FM stations include Eldoradio (101.4 MHz), Radio Modern (104 MHz), the grating Europa Plus (100.5 MHz) and the more diversified Radio Nostalgie (105.3 MHz). More Russian content can be heard on Kanal Melodia (91.1 MHz), Russky Shanson (100.9 MHz) and Russkoe Radio (104.4 MHz). Two stations focus on St Petersburg-related news, music and features: Eko Peterburga (91.5 MHz) and Severnaya Stolitsa (105.9 MHz).

SAFETY

You can disregard the horror stories you hear about the mafia in New Russia. While there has been a problem with crime and corruption since the early 1990s, the criminal elements have no interest in tourists.

A far bigger threat is petty theft, especially the notorious pickpocketing in the city centre. Take care among the crowds on Nevsky pr and in the metro: crowded quarters make for rich pickings for the criminally inclined. Be cautious about taking taxis late at night, especially near bars and clubs that are in isolated areas.

Never get into a car that already has two or more people in it.

One far darker problem is the rise of the skinhead and neo-Nazi movement in St Petersburg. You are unlikely to encounter these thugs, but you will undoubtedly read about some disgusting acts of violence that have been committed against Asian, Caucasian and other darker-skinned or foreign-looking residents of the city.

TELEPHONE

Russia's international code is ☎ 7. The international access code from landline phones in Russia is ☎ 8 followed by 10 after the second tone, then the country code and number. From mobile phones, however, just dial +[country code] to place an international call.

Mobile Phones

The mobile phone revolution in St Petersburg that has taken place in the past few years means that nearly everyone in the city has a phone. There are several large networks, most of which operate on the pay-as-you-go system.

Mobile phone numbers start with the country code (☎ 7), plus three digits that change according to the service provider (often ☎ 921), followed by a seven-digit number. To call a mobile phone from a landline, the line must be enabled to make paid calls (all local numbers are free from a landline anywhere in Russia). To find out if this is the case, dial ☎ 8, and then if you hear a second tone you can dial the mobile number in full. If you hear nothing, hang up – you can't call anywhere but local landlines from here.

Main mobile providers include Beeline GSM, Megafon, MTS-GSM and Skylink. You can buy a local SIM card at any mobile phone shop, which you can slot into your home handset during your stay. SIM cards cost as little as €15, after which you only pay to make (and to a lesser extent, to receive) calls, although prices are very low.

Phonecards & Call Centres

At kiosks and in metro stations you can buy a *taksfon karta* (phonecard) to make local, national and international calls from phone booths around the city. Cards are sold in units of 25, 50 or 100. The only trick is to remember to press the 'Talk' button (marked by a speaker) when the other party answers the phone.

Better value for international calls is using a call centre, where you give the clerk the number you want to call, pay a deposit and then go to the booth you are assigned to make the call. Afterwards you either pay the difference or collect your change. There are large numbers of call centres around the city – look for the sign *Mezhdunarodny Telefon*. The most central is the state-run **Telephone Centre** (Map p92; Nevsky pr 88; Ⓜ Mayakovskaya).

TIME

St Petersburg is GMT +3 hours, the same as Moscow time. Therefore, when it is midday in St Petersburg, it is 10am in Berlin, 9am in London and 4am in New York. Russia employs daylight savings along with much of the rest of the world.

TOILETS

Around nearly all metro stations and tourist attractions there's at least one disgusting blue Portakabin-type toilet manned by an attendant who will charge around R10 for the honour. There are also pay toilets in all mainline train stations and free ones in museums. As a general rule, it's far better to stop for a drink in a café or duck into a fancy hotel and use their cleaner facilities.

TOURIST INFORMATION

You may encounter friendly young people along Nevsky pr wearing T-shirts that ask 'Can I help?' These English-speaking youth are employed by the city and they are usually very helpful in answering questions and pointing you in the right direction. The half-hearted **City Tourist Information Centre** (☎ 310 8262; www.saintpetersburgvisit.ru) has two outlets, both with English-speaking staff and a variety of leaflets:

Dvortsovaya pl (Map pp68–9; Dvortsovaya pl; 🕑 10am-7pm Mon-Sat, 10am-4pm Sun; Ⓜ Nevsky Pr)

Sadovaya ul (Map pp68–9; Sadovaya ul 14; 🕑 10am-7pm Mon-Sat; Ⓜ Gostiny Dvor)

TRAVELLERS WITH DISABILITIES

Inaccessible transport, lack of ramps and lifts, and no centralised policy for people with physical limitations make Russia a challenging destination for wheelchair-bound visitors.

More mobile travellers will have a relatively easier time, but keep in mind that there are obstacles along the way. Toilets are frequently accessed from stairs in restaurants and museums; distances are great; public transport is extremely crowded; and many footpaths are in a poor condition and hazardous even for the mobile.

This situation is changing (albeit very slowly), as buildings undergo renovations and become more accessible. Most upscale hotels (especially Western chains) offer accessible rooms, and the Hermitage is also now fully accessible.

VISAS

All foreigners visiting Russia need visas. The visa lists entry/exit dates, your passport number, any children travelling with you, and visa type. The primary types of visas are tourist visas (for one entry, 30-day stay) or business visas (one-entry, two-entry or multi-entry, for 30- to 90-day stays). To obtain a student visa you must be enrolled in a Russian educational institute. You can also get a 'private' visa if you have a personal friend who is inviting you to Russia, but be aware that he or she will undergo some serious hassle to get you an invitation. For all visas you'll need the following:

1 A passport valid for at least a month beyond your return date.

2 Two passport-size (4cm by 4.5cm), full-face photos, not more than one year old.

3 A completed application form, including entry/exit dates (note that American citizens must fill out a special application form).

4 The handling fee, usually in the form of a money order. The handling fee varies depending on your citizenship: US citizens pay the most in retaliation for high fees for American visas.

5 A visa-support letter or letter of invitation issued by a tourist operator or some other Russian organisation.

Except for a private visa, you will also need a standard tourist confirmation or an invitation from a tourist company that is registered with the Ministry of Foreign Affairs. Your hotel may be able to provide this service. Some other companies offering visa support include the following:

City Realty (Map pp68–9; ☎ 570 6342; www.cityrealty.ru; Muchnoy per 2; tourist visas from US$25; Ⓜ Nevsky Pr) Registration is free if you stay in one of City Realty's rental units; otherwise, it's an additional €30. If you are short of time, the 'full visa service' is efficient and cost-effective.

Infinity (Map pp68–9; ☎ 494 5085; www.infinity.ru; Angleterre Hotel, Bolshaya Morskaya ul 39; Ⓜ Nevsky Pr) The St Petersburg branch of this efficient travel agency can help with visas, invites and registration. Staff speak English and can also book you train and air tickets.

Ost-West Kontaktservice (Map p92; ☎ 327 3416; www.ostwest.com; Nevsky pr 105; Ⓜ Pl Vosstaniya) A reliable outfit charging €30 to register visas for those not staying in hotels.

Application

Apply as soon as you have all the documents you need (but not more than two months ahead). Processing time ranges from 24 hours to two weeks, depending on how much you are willing to pay. Transit visas normally take seven working days, but may take as little as a few hours at the Russian embassy in Beijing.

It's possible to apply at your local Russian consulate by dropping off all the necessary documents with the appropriate payment or by mailing it all (along with a self-addressed, postage-paid envelope for the return). When you receive the visa, check it carefully – especially the expiry, entry and exit dates and any restrictions on entry or exit points.

Registration

When you arrive you will receive an immigration card, which you must fill out and keep with your passport for the duration of your stay. When you check in at a hotel, you surrender your passport and visa so the hotel can register you with OVIR (office of visas and registrations). You'll get your documents back the next morning, if not the same day. Alternatively, the tourist agency that issued your visa is responsible for your registration. All Russian visas must be registered within three business days of your arrival in town. The only exception is if you stay for less than three days. Sometimes you may have to pay a registration fee, especially if the registration is provided by an agency, not a hotel.

WOMEN TRAVELLERS

Although sexual harassment on the streets is rare, it is common in the workplace, in the home and in personal relations. Foreign women are likely to receive some attention, mostly in the form of genuine, friendly interest. An interested stranger may approach you out of the blue and ask: '*Mozhno poznakomitsa?*' (May we become acquainted?). The easiest answer is a gentle, but firm, '*Nyet*' (No). The conversation usually goes no further, although drunken men may be more persistent. The most efficient way to lose an unwelcome suitor is to enter an upmarket hotel or restaurant, where ample security will come to your aid. Women should certainly avoid taking private taxis alone at night.

Russian women dress up and wear lots of make-up on nights out. If you are wearing casual gear, you might feel uncomfortable in a restaurant, club or theatre.

WORK

Working in Russia can be an exciting, rewarding, enlightening, frustrating, insanity-inducing experience. There are still loads of Westerners employed by multinational and local companies. If you are interested in working in Russia, Jonathan Packer's *Live and Work in Russia and Eastern Europe* is a good reference. English-language publications such as the *St Petersburg Times* also have job listings. These groups can provide a wealth of information and important contacts for doing business in St Petersburg:

American Chamber of Commerce (☎ 326 4525; www.amcham.ru/spb)

Russian-British Chamber of Commerce (☎ 333 0718; www.rbcc.co.uk)

LANGUAGE

In prerevolutionary Russia, France was considered the epitome of high culture, an estimation reflected in cuisine, music and language. Indeed, among the well-educated upper classes, French was spoken more commonly than Russian.

All this changed in the 20th century, when the language of the people, solid, working-class Russian, became the language of the state. Western influences were generally frowned upon, in any case, and French in particular was derided for its classist pretences. In Russia, one spoke Russian. Indeed, in Ukraine, Belarus, Georgia etc, one spoke Russian. St Petersburgers could travel far and wide, but never leave the boundaries of their same-speaking country.

The legacy is that today everyone in St Petersburg speaks Russian. You can expect English to be spoken at most hotels and some restaurants, but the vast majority of Petersburgers speak only their native tongue. The city is becoming a bit more foreigner-friendly, with some signs in Latin letters and menus and maps in English at major tourist attractions, but at the very least you are advised to learn the Cyrillic alphabet and a few friendly phrases before setting out on your own.

To many people Russian language is as impenetrable and mysterious as Russia itself, because of the Cyrillic alphabet and its complex grammar. The alphabet is not difficult, but it has only five letters in common with the Latin alphabet. The grammar has six cases in which all nouns and adjectives potentially decline, and perfective and imperfective forms for every verb. If that sounds like gibberish to you, you'll understand why Russian is a linguist's dream, but everyone else's nightmare!

There is some good news: spelling closely reflects the way words are pronounced; you can determine a noun's gender by the way it ends; and there's only one irregular verb (*byt,* to be). Russian has fundamental similarities with English, being an Indo-European language, and learning a few basic phrases in Russian is no harder than learning them in French or German. Look for Lonely Planet's *Russian Phrasebook.*

THE CYRILLIC ALPHABET

Russian uses the Cyrillic alphabet, which is not as tricky as it looks. It's well worth the effort to familiarise yourself with it.

The list below shows the letters used in the Russian Cyrillic alphabet with their closest Roman-letter equivalents. If you follow the pronunciation guides included with the words and phrases below, you should have no trouble making yourself understood.

Cyrillic	Roman	Pronunciation
А а	a	as in 'father' when stressed; as in 'ago' when unstressed
Б б	b	as in 'but'
В в	v	as in 'van'
Г г	g	as in 'go'
Д д	d	as in 'dog'
Е е	ye	as in 'yet' when stressed; as in 'yeast' when unstressed
Ё ё	yo	as in 'yore'
Ж ж	zh	as the 's' in 'measure'
З з	z	as in 'zoo'
И и	i	as in 'police'
Й й	y	as in 'boy'
К к	k	as in 'kind'
Л л	l	as in 'lamp'
М м	m	as in 'mad'
Н н	n	as in 'net'
О о	o	as in 'more' when stressed; as the 'a' in 'ago' when unstressed
П п	p	as in 'pig'
Р р	r	as in 'rub', but rolled
С с	s	as in 'sing'
Т т	t	as in 'ten'
У у	u	as in 'rule'
Ф ф	f	as in 'fan'
Х х	kh	as the 'ch' in 'Bach'
Ц ц	ts	as in 'bits'
Ч ч	ch	as in 'chin'
Ш ш	sh	as in 'shop'
Щ щ	shch	as in 'fresh chips'

ъ		'hard' sign
Ы ы	y	as the 'i' in 'ill'
ь	-'	'soft' sign
Э э	e	as in 'end'
Ю ю	yu	as in 'Yukon'
Я я	ya	as in 'yard'

PRONUNCIATION

The sounds of а, о, е and я are 'weaker' when the stress in the word doesn't fall on them, eg in вода (*voda*, water) the stress falls on the second syllable, so it's pronounced 'va-*da*', with the unstressed pronunciation for о and the stressed pronunciation for а. Russians usually print ё without the dots, a source of confusion in pronunciation.

The 'voiced' consonants б, в, г, д, ж and з are not voiced at the end of words or before voiceless consonants. For example, хлеб (bread) is not pronounced 'khlyeb', as written, but 'khlyep'. The г in the common adjective endings -его and -ого is pronounced 'v'.

SOCIAL

Meeting People

Hello.
Здравствуйте. zdrastvuitye
Hi.
Привет. privyet
Goodbye.
До свидания. da svidaniya
Please.
Пожалуйста. pazhalsta
Thank you (very much).
(Большое) спасибо. (bal'shoye) spasiba
You're welcome. (ie don't mention it)
Не за что. nye za shta
Yes/No.
Да/Нет. da/nyet

Do you speak English?
Вы говорите по-английски?
vy gavarite pa angliyski?
Does anyone here speak English?
Кто-нибут говорит по-английски?
kto-nibud' gavarit pa-angliyski?
Do you understand?
Вы понимаете?
vy panimayete?
I (don't) understand.
Я (не) понимаю.
ya (nye) panimayu

Please repeat that.
Повторите, пожалуйста.
paftarite pazhalsta
Please speak more slowly.
Говорите помедленнее, пожалуйста.
gavarite pa-medleneye pazhalsta
Please write it down.
Запишите, пожалуйста.
zapishyte pazhalsta

Going Out

What's on ...?
Что происходит интересного ...?
Shto praiskhodit interyesnava ...?
locally
поблизости pablizasti
this weekend
на этих выходных na etikh vykhadnykh
today
сегодня syevodnya
tonight
вечером vyecheram

Where are the ...?
Где находятся ...?
gdye nakhodyatsa ...?
clubs
клубы, дискотеки kluby, diskoteki
gay venues
гей клубы gey kluby
places to eat
кафе или рестораны kafe ili restarany
pubs
бары bary (or irlandskii bary for 'Irish pubs')

Is there a local entertainment guide?
Есть обзор мест куда пойти в газете?
yest' abzor myest kuda paiti v gazete?

PRACTICAL

Question Words

Who?	Кто?	kto?
What?	Что?	shto?
When?	Когда?	kagda?
Where?	Где?	gdye?
How?	Как?	kak?

Numbers & Amounts

0	ноль	nol'
1	один	adin

2	два	dva
3	три	tri
4	четыре	chityri
5	пять	pyat'
6	шесть	shest'
7	семь	sem'
8	восемь	vosem'
9	девять	devyat'
10	десять	desyat'
11	одиннадцать	adinatsat'
12	двенадцать	dvenatsat'
13	тринадцать	trinatsat'
14	четырнадцать	chetirnatsat'
15	пятнадцать	petnatsat'
16	шестнадцать	shesnatsat'
17	семнадцать	semnatsat'
18	восемнадцать	vosemnatsat'
19	девятнадцать	devitnatsat'
20	двадцать	dvatsat'
21	двадцать один	dvatsat' adin
22	двадцать два	dvatsat' dva
30	тридцать	tritsat'
40	сорок	sorak
50	пятьдесят	pedesyat
60	шестьдесят	shesdesyat
70	семьдесят	semdesyat
80	восемьдесят	vosemdesyat
90	девяносто	devenosta
100	сто	sto
1000	тысяча	tysyacha
2000	две тысячи	dvye tysachi

Days

Monday	понедельник	panidel'nik
Tuesday	вторник	ftornik
Wednesday	среда	srida
Thursday	четверг	chetverk
Friday	пятница	pyatnitsa
Saturday	суббота	subota
Sunday	воскресенье	vaskrisen'e

Banking

I'd like to ...
Мне нужно ...
mne nuzhna ...
  cash a cheque
  обналичить чек
  abnalichit' chek
  change money
  обменять деньги
  abmenyat' den'gi
  change some travellers cheques
  обменять дорожные чеки
  abmenyat' darozhniye cheki

Where's the nearest ...?
Где ближайший ...?
gdye blizhayshiy ...?
  ATM
  банкомат
  bankamat
  foreign exchange office
  обменный пункт
  abmenniy punkt

Post

Where is the post office?
  Где почта? gdye pochta?

I want to send a ...
Хочу послать ...
khachu paslat' ...
  fax
  факс faks
  parcel
  посылку pasilku
  small parcel
  бандероль banderol'
  postcard
  открытку atkrytku

I want to buy ...
Хочу купить ...
khachu kupit' ...
  an envelope
  конверт kanvert
  a stamp
  марку marku

Phones & Mobiles

I want to buy a phonecard.
  Я хочу купить телефонную карточку.
  ya khachu kupit' telefonnuyu kartachku

I want to make a call (to ...)
Я хочу позвонить (в ...)
ya khachu pazvanit' (v ...)
  Europe/America/Australia
  европу/америку/австралию
  yevropu/ameriku/avstraliyu

Where can I find a/an ...?
Где я могу найти ...?
gdye ya mogu naiti ...?
I'd like a/an ...
Мне нужен ...
mnye nuzhen ...
  adaptor plug
  переходник для розетки
  peryehadnik dlya razetki

charger for my phone
зарядное устройство для телефона
zaryadnaye ustroistva dlya telefona
mobile phone for hire
мобильный телефон напрокат
mabil'niy telefon
SIM card for your network
сим-карта для местной сети
sim-karta dlya mestnoi seti

Internet

Where's the local internet café?
Где здесь интернет кафе?
Gde zdyes' internet kafe?

I want to ...
Я хочу ...
ya khachu ...
check my email
проверить мой имэйл
praverit moi imeil
get online
подсоединиться к интернету
padsayedinitsa k internetu

Transport

What time does the ... leave?
В котором часу прибывает ...?
f katoram chasu pribyvaet ...?
What time does the ... arrive?
В котором часу отправляется ...?
f katoram chasu atpravlyaetsa ...?

bus		
	автобус	aftobus
fixed-route minibus		
	маршрутное такси	marshrutnaye taksi
train		
	поезд	poyezt
tram		
	трамвай	tramvay
trolleybus		
	троллейбус	tralleybus

When is the ... bus?
Когда будет ... автобус?
kagda budet ... aftobus?

first		
	первый	pervy
last		
	последний	pasledniy
next		
	следующий	sleduyushchiy

Are you free? (taxi)
Свободен?
svaboden?
Please put the meter on.
Включите пожалуйста счетчик.
vklyuchite pazhalsta schetchik
How much is it to ...?
Сколько стоит доехать до ...?
skol'ka stoit daekhat' do ...?
Please take me to ...
Отвезите меня, пожалуйста в ...
atvezite menya pazhalsta v ...

EMERGENCIES

Help!
На помощь!/Помогите!
na pomashch'!/pamagite!
I'm lost.
Я заблудился/заблудилась.
ya zabludilsya/zabludilas' (m/f)
I'm sick.
Я болен/больна.
ya bolen/bal'na (m/f)
Where's the police station?
Где милиция?
gdye militsiya?

Call ...!
Позвоните ...!
pazvanite ...!

the police		
	в милицию	v militsiyu
a doctor		
	врача	vracha
an ambulance		
	в скорую помощь	v skoruyu pomosch'

HEALTH

Where's the nearest ...?
Где ближайшая ...?
gde blizhaishaya ...?

chemist (night)		
	аптека (дежурная)	apteka (dezhurnaya)
dentist		
	зубной врач	zubnoy vrach
doctor		
	врач	vrach
hospital		
	больница	bal'nitsa

I need a doctor (who speaks English).
Мне нужен врач (англоговорящий).
mne nuzhen vrach (anglagavaryaschii)

Symptoms

I have (a) ...
У меня ...
u menya ...

diarrhoea	
понос	panos
fever	
температура	temperatura
headache	
головная боль	galavnaya bol'
pain	
боль	bol'
stomachache	
болит желудок	balit zheludak

FOOD

breakfast	завтрак	zaftrak
lunch	обед	abed
dinner	ужин	uzhyn
snack	перекусить	peryekusit'
fast food	быстрая еда	bystraya yeda
eat	есть/съесть	est'/s'yest'
drink	пить/выпить	pit'/vypit'

Can you recommend a ...
Не могли бы вы порекомендовать ...
Nye mogli bi vi parekamendavat' ...

café	кафе	kafe
restaurant	ресторан	restaran

Is service/cover charge included in the bill?
Обслуживание включено в счет?
absluzhivanye vklucheno v schet?

For more detailed information on food and dining out, see p159-76.

Menu Decoder

Word stress falls on the syllables in italics.

BREAKFAST

блины (bli·*ny*) – pancakes/crepes; also eaten as an appetiser or dessert
блинчики (*blin*·chi·ki) – bliny rolled around meat or cheese and browned
каша (*ka*·sha) – Russian-style buckwheat porridge
кефир (ki·*feer*) – buttermilk, served as a drink
омлет (ahm·*lyet*) – omelette
творог (tva·*rok*) – cottage cheese
яйцо (yai·*tso*) – egg
яичница (ya·*ish*·ni·tsa) – fried egg

LUNCH & DINNER

вторые блюда (*fta*·ryye bl*yu*·da) – second courses or 'main' dishes
горячие блюда (gar·*ya*·chi·ye bl*yu*·da) – hot courses or 'main' dishes
закуски (za·*ku*·ski) – appetisers
первые блюда (*per*·vi·ye bl*yu*·da) – first courses (usually soups)
сладкие блюда (*slat*·ki·ye bl*yu*·da) – sweet courses/desserts

APPETISERS

икра (i·*kra*) – caviar
красная икра (*kras*·na·ya i·*kra*) – red (salmon) caviar
грибы в сметане (gri·*by* fsme·*ta*·ne) – mushrooms baked in sour cream; also called жульен из грибов (zhul·*yen* iz gri·*bov*)
салат (sa·*lat*) – salad
овощной салат (a·vash·*noy'* sa·*lat*) – 'vegetable salad'; salad of tomatoes and cucumbers
из помидоров (iz pa·mi·*dor*·ov) – tomato salad
чёрная икра (*chor*·na·ya i·*kra*) – black (sturgeon) caviar
столичный салат (sta·*lich*·ny sa·*lat*) – 'capital salad'; salad of vegetable, beef, potato and egg in sour cream and mayonnaise

SOUP

борщ (borsh) – beetroot soup with vegetables and sometimes meat, served hot or cold
лапша (lap·*sha*) – chicken noodle soup
окрошка (a·*krosh*·ka) – soup made from cucumbers, sour cream, potatoes, eggs, meat and kvas, served hot or cold
рассольник (ra·*ssol'*·nik) – cucumber and kidney soup
солянка (sal·*yan*·ka) – thick meat or fish soup
уха (u·*kha*) – fish soup with potatoes and vegetables
харчо (khar·*choh*) – traditional Georgian soup made of lamb and spices
щи (shi) – cabbage or sauerkraut soup

FISH

лосось/сёмга (*lo*·sos'/*syom*·ga) – salmon
осетрина (a·se·*tri*·na) – sturgeon
отварная (at·*var*·na·yah) – poached sturgeon
осетрина с грибами (a·se·*tri*·na zgri·*ba*·mi) – sturgeon with mushrooms
рыба (*ry*·ba) – fish
судак (su·*dak*) – pike perch
треска (tris·*ka*) – cod
форель (far·*yel'*) – trout
щука (*shu*·ka) – pike

POULTRY & MEAT DISHES

антрекот (an·tri·*kot*) – entrecote – boned sirloin steak
бефстроганов (bef·*stro*·ga·nov) – beef stroganov – beef slices in a rich sauce
бифштекс (bif·*shteks*) – 'steak', usually a glorified hamburger filling
говядина (gav·*ya*·di·na) – beef
голубцы (ga·lup·*tsy*) – cabbage rolls stuffed with meat

жаркое по домашнему (zhar·*koy*·e pa da·*mash*·ni·mu) – meat stewed in a clay pot 'home-style', with mushrooms, potatoes and vegetables
жаркое из птицы (zhar·*koy*·e iz *pti*·tsa) – poultry stewed in a clay pot
котлета (kat·*le*·ta) – usually a croquette of ground meat
котлета по киевски (kat·*le*·ta pa *ki*·ev·ski) – chicken Kiev; fried chicken breast stuffed with garlic butter
котлета по пожарски (kat·*le*·ta pa pa·*zhar*·ski) – croquette of minced chicken
мясные (*mya*·sni·ye) – meat
пельмени (pil'·*men*·i) – meat dumplings
плов (plov) – pilaf, rice with mutton bits
свинина (sfi·*ni*·na) – pork
шашлык (shash·*lihk*) – skewered and grilled meat

VEGETABLES

гарниры (gar·*ni*·ry) – any vegetable garnish
горох (ga·*rokh*) – peas
грибы (*gri*·by) – wild mushrooms
зелень (*zye*·lin') – greens
капуста (ka·*pus*·ta) – cabbage
картошка/картофель (kar·*tosh*·ka/kar·*to*·fil') – potato
морковь (mar·*kof'*) – carrots
овощи (*o*·va·shchi) – vegetables
огурец (a·gur·*yets*) – cucumber
помидор (pa·mi·*dor*) – tomato

FRUIT

абрикос (a·bri·*kos*) – apricot
апельсин (a·pel'·*sin*) – orange
банан (ba·*nan*) – banana
виноград (vi·na·*grad*) – grapes
вишня (*vish*·ni·ya) – cherry
груша (*gru*·sha) – pear
фрукты (*fruk*·ty) – fruits
яблоко (*ya*·bla·ko) – apple

STAPLES

масло (*mas*·la) – butter
перец (*pyer*·its) – pepper
рис (ris) – rice
сахар (*sa*·khar) – sugar
соль (sol') – salt
сыр (syr) – cheese
хлеб (khlep) – bread

DESSERTS

кисель (ki·*sel'*) – fruit jelly/jello
компот (kam·*pot*) – fruit in syrup
мороженое (ma·ro·zhi·ne·ya) – ice cream
пирожное (pi·*rozh*·na·ye) – pastries
торт (tort) – cake
шоколад (sha·ka·*lat*) – chocolate

GLOSSARY

aeroport – airport
alleya – alley
apteka – pharmacy
avtobus – bus
avtomaticheskie kamery khranenia – left-luggage lockers
avtovokzal – bus station
babushka – grandmother
bankomat – ATM
banya – bathhouse
basketbolnaya super liga – Russia's basketball super league
bolshaya – big, great, grand
bolshoy – big, great, grand
bulvar – boulevard
bylina – epic song
dacha – country cottage
datsan – temple
deklaratsiya – customs declaration
dom – house
duma – parliament
dvorets – palace
elektrichka – suburban train; also *prigorodnye poezd*
galereya – gallery
glasnost – openness; policy of public accountability developed under the leadership of Mikhail Gorbachev
gorod – city, town
kafe – café
kamera khranenia – left-luggage office or counter
kanal – canal
kladbische – cemetery
kolonnada – colonnade
kon – horse
korpus – building within a building
koryushki – freshwater smelt
kruglosutochno – open 24 hours
lavra – most senior grade of Russian Orthodox monastery
letny sad – summer garden
liteyny – foundry
malaya – small, little
maly – small, little
marshrutka – minibus that runs along a fixed route; diminutive form of *marshrutnoye taxi*
Maslenitsa – akin to Mardi Gras; fête that celebrates the end of winter and kicks off Lent
matryoshka – nesting doll; set of painted wooden dolls within dolls
mekh – fur
mesto – seat
militsioner – police officer
militsiya – police

morskoy vokzal – sea station
morzh – walrus
most – bridge
muzey – museum
naberezhnaya – embankment
novaya – new
novy – new
Novy God – New Year
ostrov – island
parilka – steam room (at a *banya*)
Paskha – Easter
passazhirskiy poezd – passenger train
perekhod – transfer
pereryv – break, recess
perestroika – reconstruction; policy of reconstructing the economy developed under the leadership of Mikhail Gorbachev
pereulok – lane, side street
pivnaya – beer bar
ploshchad – square
prigorodnye poezd – suburban train; also *elektrichka*
proezd – passage
prospekt – avenue
rechnoy vokzal – river station
reka – river
restoran – restaurant
Rozhdestvo – Christmas
rynok – market
ryumochnaya – equivalent of the local pub
samizdat – underground literary manuscript
sanitarny den – literally 'sanitary day'; a day during the last week of every month on which establishments such as museums shut down for cleaning
shosse – highway
skory poezd – fast train; regular long-distance service
smol – tar
sobor – cathedral
staraya – old
stary – old
stolovaya – cafeteria
taksfon karta – phonecard
tapochki – slippers
teatralnaya kassa – theatre kiosk; general theatre box office scattered about the city
tekhnichesky pereryv – technical break
troika – horse-drawn sleigh
tserkov – church
ulitsa – street
uslovie yedenitsiy – standard units, which is equivalent to euros; often abbreviated as y.e.
vagon – carriage (on a train)
veniki – bundle of birch branches used at a *banya* to beat bathers to eliminate toxins and improve circulation
vokzal – station
vyshaya liga – Russia's premier football league
zal – hall
zamok – castle
zheton – token (for metro etc)

BEHIND THE SCENES

THIS BOOK

This 5th edition of *St Petersburg* was researched and written by Mara Vorhees. The 4th edition was written by Tom Masters, the 3rd edition by Steve Kokker and the 1st and 2nd editions by Nick Selby. This guidebook was commissioned in Lonely Planet's London office, and produced by the following:

Commissioning Editors Amanda Canning, Janine Eberle, Will Gourlay

Coordinating Editors Maryanne Netto, Gabrielle Stefanos

Coordinating Cartographer Valentina Kremenchutskaya

Coordinating Layout Designer Katherine Marsh

Managing Editors Helen Christinis, Katie Lynch

Managing Cartographers Mark Griffiths, Andrew Smith

Managing Layout Designers Adam McCrow, Celia Wood

Assisting Editors Janice Bird, Jocelyn Harewood

Assisting Cartographers Fatima Basic, Wayne Murphy

Assisting Layout Designers Cara Smith

Cover Designer Nic Lehman

Project Managers Craig Kilburn, Fabrice Rocher

Language Content Coordinator Quentin Frayne

Thanks to Judith Bamber, Sasha Baskett, Katrina Browning, Lisa Knights, Susan Paterson, Naomi Stephens

Cover photographs Dancers with the Mariinsky Ballet, formerly the Kirov, wait in the wings during a performance of Giselle at the Mariinsky Theatre, St Petersburg, Steve Raymer/Corbis (top), The Hermitage museum, one of the world's richest, with 400 rooms and over 2.5 million works of art, St Petersburg, Antoine Gyori/Corbis (bottom)

Internal photographs p130, p135, p143, SIME/Giovanni Simeone/4Corners Images; p4 (#2), p8 (#1), SIME/Gräfenhain Günter/4Corners Images; p4 (#3), Hemis/Alamy; p7 (#4), Rolf Richardson/Alamy; p9 (#4), Dagmar Schwelle/Alamy; p10 (#1), Inga Leksina/Alamy; p12 (#1), Jeremy Nicholl/Alamy; p126, Choups/Alamy; p128 (bottom right), Culligan photo/Alamy; p128 (top left), DIOMEDIA/Alamy; p131 (top), Dagmar Schwelle/Alamy; p132, Larry Lilac/Alamy; p137, Peter Titmuss/Alamy; p139 (top), Jochem Wijnands/Picture Contact/Alamy; p138, Tibor Bognar/Alamy; p139 (bottom left), Rolf Richardson/Alamy; p141 (top right), Trevor Booth Photography/Alamy; p140, eMotionQuest/Alamy; p125, Glen Allison/Getty Images; p6 (#3), p7 (#5), p9 (#5), p12 (#3), p127 (bottom left and right), AFP/Getty Images; p131 (bottom left), Simon Watson/Getty Images; p134, Sisse Brimberg/Getty Images; p3, Demetrio Carrasco/Getty Images; p5 (#5), Erica Lansner/Getty Images; p6 (#2), Peter Essick/Getty Images; p11 (#3), Renaud Visage/Getty Images; p11 (#1), Richard Nowitz/Getty Images; p11 (#2), Simon Richmond. All other images by Lonely Planet Images: p129, Richard l'Anson; p141 (top left), Holger Leue; p2, p4 (#1), p5 (#4), p6 (#1), p7 (#6), p8 (#3), p10 (#4), p12 (#2), p144, Jonathan Smith; p8 (#2), p10 (#2), Holger Leue; p10 (#3), Roberto Gerometta.

THE LONELY PLANET STORY

Fresh from an epic journey across Europe, Asia and Australia in 1972, Tony and Maureen Wheeler sat at their kitchen table stapling together notes. The first Lonely Planet guidebook, *Across Asia on the Cheap*, was born.

Travellers snapped up the guides. Inspired by their success, the Wheelers began publishing books to Southeast Asia, India and beyond. Demand was prodigious, and the Wheelers expanded the business rapidly to keep up. Over the years, Lonely Planet extended its coverage to every country and into the virtual world via lonelyplanet.com and the Thorn Tree message board.

As Lonely Planet became a globally loved brand, Tony and Maureen received several offers for the company. But it wasn't until 2007 that they found a partner whom they trusted to remain true to the company's principles of travelling widely, treading lightly and giving sustainably. In October of that year, BBC Worldwide acquired a 75% share in the company, pledging to uphold Lonely Planet's commitment to independent travel, trustworthy advice and editorial independence.

Today, Lonely Planet has offices in Melbourne, London and Oakland, with over 500 staff members and 300 authors. Tony and Maureen are still actively involved with Lonely Planet. They're travelling more often than ever, and they're devoting their spare time to charitable projects. And the company is still driven by the philosophy of *Across Asia on the Cheap*: 'All you've got to do is decide to go and the hardest part is over. So go!'

THANKS

MARA VORHEES

No place to stay is as warm and welcoming as Sasha and Andrey's friendly flat on Gorokhovaya ul. There, I shared stories, insights and vodka shots with Peter and Natalya; Liza and Lyuba; and my various flat-mates from around the world. Lora, Evgeny, Sasha et al at Pushkinskaya 10 showed me the 'other' St Pete – and Daria ensured that I understood what was going on! I appreciate that Evgeny Tykotsky, Marc de Mauny and Yury Vosskresensky took the time to do interviews. Special thanks to Simon Richmond, who was not stingy with his St Petersburg expertise, and to the succession of commissioning editors – Will Gourlay, Janine Eberle and Amanda Canning – who have accompanied me on this project. And of course, to Jerry Easter, whose support and enthusiasm are as enduring and inspiring as the silhouette of the Bronze Horseman overlooking the Neva. Спасибо всем.

OUR READERS

Many thanks to the travellers who used the last edition and wrote to us with helpful hints, useful advice and interesting anecdotes:

Kaarina Aitamurto, Roger Andre, Lionel Billaud, Silvia Bogle, Niklas Borselius, Mark Bromfield, Fraser and Cath Brown, Tim Bryars, Oliver Buckley, Matt Carmody, Victoria De Atxer López, Stephanie Devine, Thea Edwards, Christine Ellis, Victoria Maria Formosa, Claire Frankel, Giorgio Frazzitta, Andreas Friedel, Julie Fu, Rosmarie Geissler, Janet Glensor, Günther Grychta, Arthur Thomas Hallett, Julia Henshaw, Filly Huang, Valeria Jacobs, Sian Jones, Carol Ann Khatri, Paul Korns, Olga Krupinska, Kimberly Lang, Andrew Lyons, Mike Lytton, Gian Carlo Marciano, Judy Moon, Chris Morey, David Morton, Sally Murphy, Anita Newcourt, M Ng, Marc Nicholson, Alan Nissel, Bob Otness, David Owens, James Pines, David Pollard, Marco Polo, Jacob Luning Prak, David Pratt, Sara Riedl, Bernadette Saglio, Caroline Sayre, Steen Sunesen, Sandra Tavenier, Alison and Mike Thirlwall, Sally Windsor.

SEND US YOUR FEEDBACK

We love to hear from travellers – your comments keep us on our toes and help make our books better. Our well-travelled team reads every word on what you loved or loathed about this book. Although we cannot reply individually to postal submissions, we always guarantee that your feedback goes straight to the appropriate authors, in time for the next edition. Each person who sends us information is thanked in the next edition – and the most useful submissions are rewarded with a free book.

To send us your updates – and find out about Lonely Planet events, newsletters and travel news – visit our award-winning website: www.lonelyplanet.com/contact.

Note: We may edit, reproduce and incorporate your comments in Lonely Planet products such as guidebooks, websites and digital products, so let us know if you don't want your comments reproduced or your name acknowledged. For a copy of our privacy policy visit www.lonelyplanet.com/privacy.

Notes

Notes

Notes

INDEX

See also separate indexes for:

000 map pages
000 photographs

INDEX

EATING

NIGHTLIFE

SHOPPING

000 map pages
000 photographs

PALACES & CASTLES

PARKS & GARDENS

PLANETARIUMS & OBSERVATORIES

STATUES & MONUMENTS

STREETS & SQUARES

UNIVERSITIES

SLEEPING

BOUTIQUE HOTELS

HOME-STAYS

HOSTELS

HOTELS

MINI-HOTELS

SOVIET HOTELS

SPORT & ACTIVITIES

BANYA

BOWLING

CYCLING

GYMS & POOLS

ICE SKATING, SKIING & SLEDDING

SPAS

SPORTS VENUES

TOP PICKS

000 map pages
000 photographs

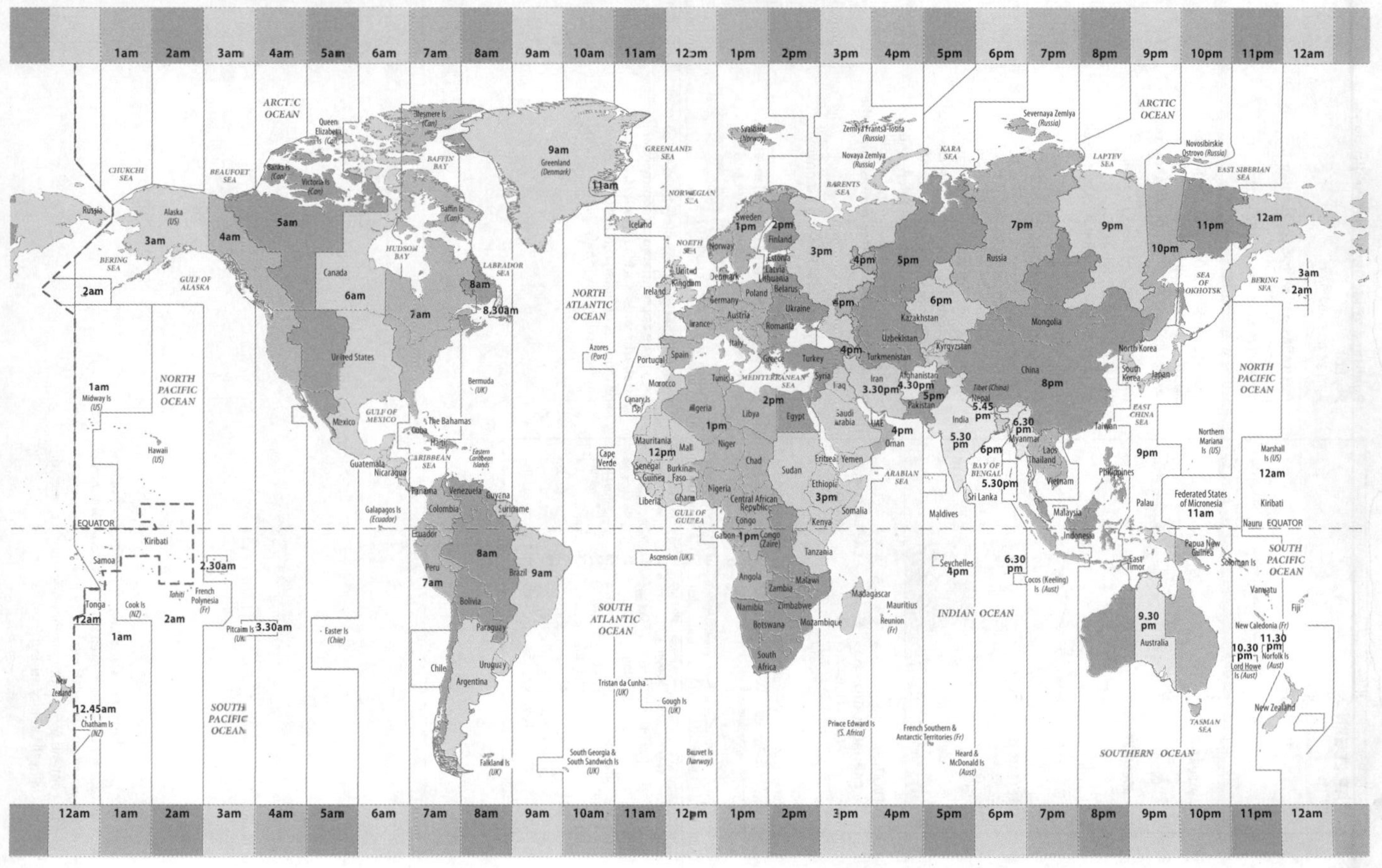
1am
2am
3am
4am
5am
6am
7am
8am
9am
10am
11am
12pm
1pm
2pm
3pm
4pm
5pm
6pm
7pm
8pm
9pm
10pm
11pm
12am
ARCTIC OCEAN
CHUKCHI SEA
BEAUFORT SEA
Queen Elizabeth Is (Can)
Ellesmere Is (Can)
Banks Is (Can)
Victoria Is (Can)
BAFFIN BAY
Baffin Is (Can)
Greenland (Denmark)
9am
11am
Russia
Alaska (US)
3am
4am
5am
BERING SEA
GULF OF ALASKA
2am
HUDSON BAY
Canada
6am
7am
LABRADOR SEA
8am
8.30am
United States
1am
Midway Is (US)
NORTH PACIFIC OCEAN
Hawaii (US)
Mexico
GULF OF MEXICO
The Bahamas
Cuba
Haiti
Bermuda (UK)
Eastern Caribbean Islands
CARIBBEAN SEA
Guatemala
Nicaragua
Panama
Venezuela
Guyana
Suriname
Colombia
Galapagos Is (Ecuador)
Ecuador
Peru
7am
8am
Brazil
9am
Bolivia
Paraguay
Chile
Uruguay
Argentina
Falkland Is (UK)
EQUATOR
Kiribati
Samoa
2.30am
Tahiti
French Polynesia (Fr)
Tonga
12am
Cook Is (NZ)
2am
1am
Pitcairn Is (UK)
3.30am
Easter Is (Chile)
New Zealand
12.45am
Chatham Is (NZ)
SOUTH PACIFIC OCEAN
GREENLAND SEA
NORWEGIAN SEA
Iceland
NORTH SEA
NORTH ATLANTIC OCEAN
Azores (Port)
Ireland
United Kingdom
Portugal
Spain
France
Morocco
Canary Is (Sp)
Cape Verde
Mauritania
12pm
Mali
Senegal
Guinea
Burkina Faso
Liberia
Ghana
GULF OF GUINEA
Ascension (UK)
SOUTH ATLANTIC OCEAN
Tristan da Cunha (UK)
Gough Is (UK)
South Georgia & South Sandwich Is (UK)
Bouvet Is (Norway)
Svalbard (Norway)
Sweden
1pm
2pm
Norway
Finland
Estonia
Latvia
Lithuania
Denmark
Poland
Belarus
Germany
Ukraine
Austria
Romania
Italy
Greece
Turkey
Tunisia
MEDITERRANEAN SEA
Syria
Algeria
Libya
2pm
Egypt
1pm
Niger
Chad
Nigeria
Central African Republic
Congo
Gabon
1pm
Congo (Zaire)
Sudan
Eritrea
Yemen
Ethiopia
3pm
Somalia
Kenya
Tanzania
Angola
Zambia
Malawi
Namibia
Zimbabwe
Botswana
Mozambique
South Africa
Madagascar
Mauritius
Reunion (Fr)
Prince Edward Is (S. Africa)
Zemlya Frantsa-Iosifa (Russia)
Novaya Zemlya (Russia)
BARENTS SEA
KARA SEA
3pm
4pm
5pm
4pm
Iraq
Saudi Arabia
Iran
3.30pm
UAE
4pm
Oman
ARABIAN SEA
Kazakhstan
6pm
Uzbekistan
Turkmenistan
Kyrgyzstan
Afghanistan
4.30pm
5pm
Pakistan
India
5.30pm
Nepal
5.45pm
Tibet (China)
6pm
BAY OF BENGAL
5.30pm
Sri Lanka
Maldives
Seychelles
4pm
6.30pm
Cocos (Keeling) Is (Aust)
INDIAN OCEAN
French Southern & Antarctic Territories (Fr)
Heard & McDonald Is (Aust)
Severnaya Zemlya (Russia)
Russia
7pm
9pm
LAPTEV SEA
ARCTIC OCEAN
Novosibirskie Ostrovo (Russia)
EAST SIBERIAN SEA
10pm
11pm
12am
Mongolia
China
8pm
6.30pm
Myanmar
Laos
Thailand
Vietnam
Malaysia
Indonesia
SEA OF OKHOTSK
BERING SEA
3am
2am
North Korea
South Korea
Japan
EAST CHINA SEA
Taiwan
Philippines
9pm
Palau
East Timor
Papua New Guinea
9.30pm
Australia
TASMAN SEA
SOUTHERN OCEAN
NORTH PACIFIC OCEAN
Northern Mariana Is (US)
Marshall Is (US)
12am
Federated States of Micronesia
11am
Kiribati
Nauru
EQUATOR
Solomon Is
SOUTH PACIFIC OCEAN
Vanuatu
Fiji
New Caledonia (Fr)
11.30pm
10.30pm
Norfolk Is (Aust)
Lord Howe Is (Aust)
New Zealand

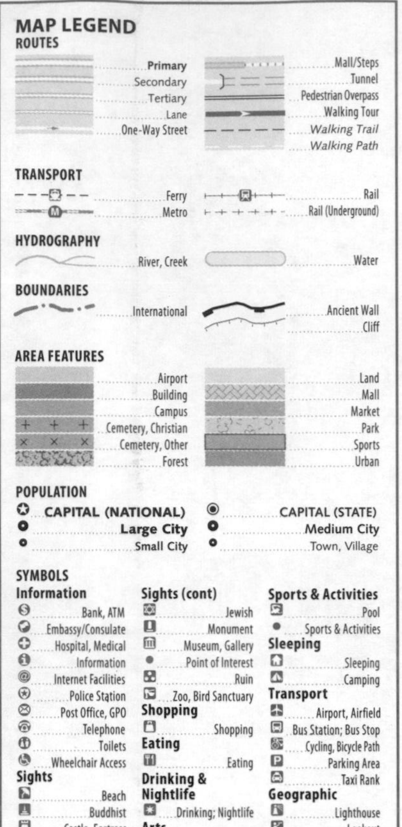

Published by Lonely Planet Publications Pty Ltd
ABN 36 005 607 983

Australia Head Office, Locked Bag 1, Footscray, Victoria 3011, ☎03 8379 8000, fax 03 8379 8111, talk2us@lonelyplanet.com.au

USA 150 Linden St, Oakland, CA 94607, ☎510 893 8555, toll free 800 275 8555, fax 510 893 8572, info@lonelyplanet.com

UK 2nd Floor, 186 City Road, London, ECV1 2NT, ☎020 7106 2100, fax 020 7106 2101, go@lonelyplanet.co.uk

Printed by Hang Tai Printing Company. Printed in China.